Building the International Criminal Court

The International Criminal Court (ICC) is the first and only standing international court capable of prosecuting humanity's worst crimes: genocide, war crimes, and crimes against humanity. It faces huge obstacles. It has no police force; it pursues investigations in areas of tremendous turmoil, conflict, and death; it is charged both with trying suspects and with aiding their victims; and it seeks to combine divergent legal traditions in an entirely new international legal mechanism.

International law advocates sought to establish a standing international criminal court for more than 150 years. Other temporary single-purpose criminal tribunals, truth commissions, and special courts have come and gone, but the ICC is the only permanent inheritor of the Nuremberg legacy.

In *Building the International Criminal Court*, Oberlin College Professor of Politics Benjamin N. Schiff analyzes the International Criminal Court, melding historical perspective, international relations theories, and observers' insights to explain the Court's origins, creation, innovations, dynamics, and operational challenges.

Benjamin N. Schiff received his Ph.D. in political science from the University of California, Berkeley. He has been teaching at Oberlin College since 1979 and has authored three major works on international politics, including *Refugees unto the Third Generation: U.N. Aid to Palestinians* (1995). In 2005–6, Schiff was a visiting professor at Leiden University's Grotius Centre for International Legal Studies in The Hague, and he has published journal articles, newspaper op-ed pieces, and book reviews on international relations, foreign policy, and military topics.

Building the International Criminal Court

BENJAMIN N. SCHIFF
Oberlin College

CAMBRIDGE
UNIVERSITY PRESS

CAMBRIDGE UNIVERSITY PRESS
Cambridge, New York, Melbourne, Madrid, Cape Town, Singapore, São Paulo, Delhi

Cambridge University Press
32 Avenue of the Americas, New York, NY 10013–2473, USA

www.cambridge.org
Information on this title: www.cambridge.org/9780521694728

First published 2008

Printed in the United States of America

A catalog record for this publication is available from the British Library.

Library of Congress Cataloging in Publication Data
Schiff, Benjamin N., 1952–
  Building the international criminal court / Benjamin N. Schiff.
    p.   cm.
  Includes bibliographical references and index.
  ISBN 978-0-521-87312-3 (hardback) – ISBN 978-0-521-69472-8 (pbk.)
    1. International Criminal Court.   2. International Criminal Courts.   3. International
  Tribunal for the Prosecution of Persons Responsible for Serious Violations of
  International Humanitarian Law Committed in the Territory of the Former
  Yugoslavia since 1991.   4. International Tribunal for Rwanda.   I. Title.
  KZ6310.S35 2008
  345′.01–dc22   2007033930

ISBN 978-0-521-87312-3 hardback
ISBN 978-0-521-69472-8 paperback

For June Goodwin, who taught me about truth;
and Naomi Schiff, a tireless fighter for justice;

and in memory of Hendrik (H. W.) van der Merwe,
for his selfless, iron-willed pursuit of justice and peace.

Contents

Preface

I spent a year in The Netherlands conducting the research upon which this book is based. I commuted frequently from my home in Leiden to The Hague to interview officials of the International Criminal Court and the International Criminal Tribunal for the Former Yugoslavia, nongovernmental organization personnel, embassy officials, journalists, and academics.

I was honored and much assisted by an appointment as visiting professor at Leiden University's Grotius Centre for International Legal Studies and by the hospitality of the T. M. C. Asser Institute, both in The Hague. At the Grotius Centre, I especially thank John Dugard, Roelof Haveman, Machteld Boot, and Christine Tremblay. At the Asser Institute, I am grateful to Olivier Ribbelink, Avril McDonald, and Paula Kersbergen. For his general enthusiasm, help in making various arrangements, and for his wonderful family's kind hospitality, I thank Sam Muller. Susan Somers warmly included me and my family into her circle of friends, for which we are very grateful.

Isebill V. Gruhn of the University of California, Santa Cruz, provided me with invaluable comments while I was writing this book. Mistakes of fact or judgment herein, I'm sorry to say, are entirely my own.

In The Hague at the International Criminal Court, in embassies, and while visiting nongovernmental organizations, journalists, and academics, I was very fortunate to receive candid commentary on the monumental tasks facing the Court. With very few exceptions, because of the sensitivity of their comments and/or positions, my interlocutors did not want to be quoted or cited. I don't want to outweigh their views by citing the few people willing to go on record, so I do not cite my interviewees directly; and to preserve their anonymity, I cannot thank them here. But I deeply appreciate their willingness to speak with me.

I am most grateful for the sabbatical leave and support I received from Oberlin College that made this project possible. I appreciate as well the kind encouragement I've received from my colleagues in the Department of Politics, particularly Ron Kahn's reading of the manuscript underway.

I believe that important human endeavors – such as the pursuit of international justice – deserve serious evaluation and analysis, not to demonstrate their futility, but to better understand their challenges and to assist in achieving their objectives. I hope that this book will help explain the International Criminal Court and bring wider support to it, and that my comments will be taken as those of a constructive ally in the fight against impunity.

Ben Schiff

Oberlin, Ohio
June 29, 2007

Acronyms

ACABQ	(UN) Advisory Committee on Administrative and Budgetary Questions
AI	Amnesty International
ASF	Advocats sans Frontìers
ASP	(ICC) Assembly of States Parties
ASPA	American Servicemen's Protection Act or American Service Members Protection Act
BIA	bilateral immunity agreement
CAR	Central African Republic
CBF	(ICC ASP) Committee on Budget and Finance
CIA	U.S. Central Intelligence Agency
CICC	NGO Coalition for the International Criminal Court
Coco	coordinating committee
CPA	Comprehensive Peace Agreement (Sudan)
DRC	Democratic Republic of the Congo
ECOSOC	(UN) Economic and Social Council
EU	European Union
FIDH	International Federation of Human Rights Leagues
FPLC	Patriotic Front for the Liberation of the Congo
FRPI	Force de Résistance Patriotique en Ituri
GA	(UN) General Assembly
HRW	Human Rights Watch
HSM	Holy Spirit Movement (Uganda)
ICB	International Criminal Bar
ICC	International Criminal Court
ICJ	International Court of Justice

ICL   International Criminal Law
ICRC   International Committees of the Red Cross
ICTJ   International Center for Transitional Justice
ICTR   International Criminal Tribunal for Rwanda
ICTY   International Criminal Tribunal for the Former
               Yugoslavia
IDP   internally displaced persons
IFOR   International Force (in the Former Yugoslavia)
IHL   International Humanitarian Law
ILC   International Law Commission
IMET   (U.S.) International Military Education and Training
IMT   International Military Tribunal (Nuremberg)
JCCD   (ICC OTP) Jurisdiction, Complementarity, and
               Cooperation Division
JEM   Justice and Equality Movement (Sudan)
LMS   like-minded states
LRA   Lord's Resistance Army (Uganda)
MERCOSUR   South American Common Market
MINURCA   UN Mission in the Central African Republic
MLC   Movement for the Liberation of the Congo
MONUC   UN Mission in the Democratic Republic of the Congo
NATO   North Atlantic Treaty Organization
NGO   non-governmental organization
NPWJ   No Peace Without Justice
NRM/A   National Resistance Movement/Army (Uganda)
OIOS   (UN) Office of Internal Oversight Services
ONUB   UN Operation in Burundi
OTP   Office of the Prosecutor
PIU   Public Information Unit
PrepCom   Preparatory Committee
PTC   (ICC) Pre-Trial Chamber
RENAMO   Mozambique National Resistance
RPE   Rules of Procedure and Evidence
RPF   Rwandan Patriotic Front
SATRC   South Africa's Truth and Reconciliation Commission
SFOR   Stabilization Force (in the Former Yugoslavia)
SLM/A   Sudan Liberation Movement/Army
SOAT   Sudan Organization Against Torture
SPLA   Sudan People's Liberation Army
SWGCA   Special Working Group on the Crime of Aggression

U.K.	United Kingdom
U.S.	United States
UDHR	Universal Declaration of Human Rights
UN	United Nations
UNESCO	United Nations Educational, Scientific, and Cultural Organization
UNHCHR	United Nations High Commissioner for Human Rights
UNSC	United Nations Security Council
UPC	Union of Congolese Patriots
UPDF	Ugandan People's Defense Forces
VPRS	(ICC Registry) Victims Participation and Reparations Section
VTF	(ICC) Victims' Trust Fund
VWU	(ICC Registry) Victims and Witnesses Unit
WFM	World Federalists Movement

Building the International Criminal Court

Introduction

The International Criminal Court (ICC) soars with the loftiest of ideals as it grapples with the basest of human acts. This first and only permanent international criminal court intends to counter impunity by prosecuting perpetrators of genocide, crimes against humanity, and war crimes. It seeks to deter depredations against citizens in violent conflicts and to contribute to justice, peace, political transition, and reconstruction.

Ideally, domestic societies use legitimate political processes to devise and promulgate their laws. Then the laws are fairly implemented by legal systems that remove the politics from justice. This ideal is often compromised by extralegal influences, by biased legal structures, and by maladministration; nonetheless, the ideal is a widely accepted model of an objective, dispassionate, truth-based mechanism for upholding society's rules.

If this model represents a goal toward which societies strive with only partial success, international law is even more tenuous. International law is based on an ephemeral society that lacks a legislative structure, and it seeks to constrain sovereign states that recognize no consolidated authority for enforcement. International organizations operate at the sufferance of states, subject to their desires, dependent upon their generosity, and victims of their ploys. Moreover, international organizations are subject to the same weaknesses as domestic ones – outside influences, bias, and maladministration. Nonetheless, since the beginnings of the modern state system, advocates of law have tried to extend to the international level the logic and structures familiar in the domestic context. International law has proliferated. This quest for the "legalization" of international politics has added arbitration and judicial decision making to diplomacy and the naked exercise of power as means of settling conflict between sovereign states.[1] Legalization has arrived as well at the doorstep of individual responsibility.

Since all human action is in the end individual, crimes committed on behalf of states have perpetrators just as do domestic crimes. For approximately 150 years, from at least the origins of the International Red Cross movement in the mid-nineteenth century, international lawyers, diplomats, and advocates contemplated the creation of an international criminal court to hold individuals responsible for criminal acts carried out in the name of the state. Finally, in Rome in July 1998, the Statute for the International Criminal Court opened for signature and ratification. The Court emerged on July 1, 2002, much sooner than most observers had believed possible.

The Court began with a five-member transition team in 2002, and mushroomed past 700 employees in 2007. It is built upon a range of national legal systems and incorporates structural elements common to other international organizations. Its structure, rules, and operations reflect experiences of the ad hoc international criminal tribunals for Yugoslavia and Rwanda but differ significantly from them. The ICC's objectives include the prosecution of transgressors and rehabilitation of victims, its mechanisms combine traditions of civil law with common-law precepts, and it seeks to incorporate lessons from the tribunals in order to improve the effectiveness and efficiency of international criminal trials.

The Court's most profound effects may be invisible and tangential to the cases it pursues directly. If it deters criminality or leads states to tighten their domestic laws and enforce international humanitarian norms, it could be considered successful. On the other hand, it may be deemed irrelevant if potential perpetrators don't recognize it as a threat, if its efforts are thwarted by noncooperation or lack of resources, or if victims regard it as useless in their search for justice. The Court could become an unprecedented, sterling achievement, or it may be a great idea whose time has not arrived. This book is intended to explain where the Court comes from and what it's for, what its challenges are, and how it is managing them in its first years of operation.

---

[1] Goldstein et al., "Introduction: Legalization and World Politics" (2000), evaluate the degree of legalization implemented in interstate arrangements along three dimensions: the nature of the *obligation* that states accept, from nonlegal at one end of a spectrum to binding rules of behavior at the other; the *precision* of the rules under adjudication, from vague principles to highly elaborated rules; and the degree of *delegation* of decision-making authority to the forum, from an arena of discussion or diplomacy to a definitive judicial process and/or incorporation into domestic law.

THE COURT

The Court consists of three "organs" – the Presidency and Chambers (the judges),[2] the Office of the Prosecutor, and the Registry. The Rome Statute details the legal framework for Court operations, empowering the Court to investigate cases, issue warrants, take custody of arrested suspects, and carry out trials, and enjoins it to protect witnesses and victims involved with its proceedings and to aid the victims of the crimes under its jurisdiction.

The Statute establishes the Assembly of States Parties (ASP) to the Treaty as the legislative organ responsible to elect (and remove) ICC judges and chief and deputy prosecutors, approve and allocate the organization's budget, approve official cooperative arrangements with other organizations (such as the United Nations), and adopt the Court's Rules of Procedure and Evidence, its Elements of Crimes, and the rules of the separate organs. The ASP can also create subsidiary bodies and establish their rules for implementing the Statute (for instance, the Trust Fund for Victims), and it can amend the Statute.

The ICC and especially its founding document, the Rome Statute, are the subjects of an enormous literature. A relentlessly expanding list of books and a torrent of legal journal articles examine the sources, structure, intricacies, ambiguities, and implications of the Statute. The Court itself has so far been rather less analyzed because it has only recently begun operating, but there are useful introductions to its structure and law, and some books illuminate particular aspects of its founding, implications, early operation and possible effects.

The Court is a work-in-progress, an amalgam of normative commitments,[3] legal understandings, political interests, diplomatic bargains, and organization dynamics. It embodies idealistic, largely legalistic conceptions of international norms that were pursued doggedly by international legal experts from the end of World War II onward, shaped by diplomatic bargains and pushed by nongovernmental organizations. Embarked on a course fraught with contradictions stemming from its broad set of objectives, the

---

[2] Sometimes the Presidency and the Chambers are cited in Court documents as separate "organs," so that the ICC is said to be composed of four organs; sometimes it is described as tripartite. The President and Vice Presidents are elected from among the judges, which appears to make the combination of Presidency and Chambers a reasonable classification. However, the Presidency has administrative duties disconnected from its members' roles as judges, so in that sense they are two separate organs that share some personnel.

[3] By "normative commitment," I mean dedication to behavior bounded by a conception of appropriate behavior based on some nonmaterial value, such as the value of human dignity or fairness.

Court faces the requirements of all organizations – leadership, internal coordination, resource acquisition and deployment, efficiency, seeking to demonstrate success and relevance to major interlocutors. The decisions it makes in its early years about its role, focus, and operations will be crucial to how it survives, thrives, or withers.

THEORETICAL PERSPECTIVE

My choice of topics and the language I use come from the study of inter-national organizations, international relations, and theories about both. This is not primarily a theoretical book; however, international relations and international organization theories help elucidate my topic and so I think it is useful here to present the general theoretical context in which I am working.

Especially since the end of the Cold War, international relations texts and journals have been contrasting the analytical perspectives of realists, neo-liberal institutionalists, and constructivists. Rather than apply these as fully deployed theories or complete rivals, I use them to explain different aspects of an extremely complicated world.[4] Their alternative emphases sometimes place them and their enthusiasts at odds with one another, but I am by nature a synthesizer, so I prefer to use them together, the best to explain what I seek to understand. I introduce the three kinds of theory here in the order that they developed in post–World War II American political science.[5]

Realist Theorists
Realist theorists assume that humans are self-seeking, rational beings. Sovereign states are the international system's primary actors. Because there is no global government, realists assert that *anarchy* is the condition (or structure) of the existing international system.[6] Real sovereignty – the state's

---

[4] For an explanation of the virtues of analytical eclecticism, see Sil, "Problems Chasing Methods or Methods Chasing Problems? Research Communities, Constrained Pluralism, and the Role of Eclecticism" (2004), and Sil, "Analytic Eclecticism and Research Traditions in International Relations" (2007).

[5] There are many and interesting variations of the three general theoretical approaches amongst which vigorous debates continue. I present and apply here the general thrust of the three viewpoints without delving into these variations.

[6] I use the idea of *system* simply as a mechanistic or organic metaphor to denote the collectivity of states as they interact with each other. Kenneth Waltz, in *Theory of International Politics* (1979), is the foremost expositor of (mechanistic) realist system theory. For Waltz, states act according to rules prescribed by the condition of anarchy. Hedley Bull, in *The Anarchical Society*, 3rd ed. (2003), distinguishes between the idea of a mechanistic international system and a value-imbued *society* of states (both under anarchy), and I use his distinction further in Chapter 1.

capacity to maintain domestic order and to protect itself from other states – resides in its military and economic capabilities. Formal sovereignty – the state's right to a monopoly on the domestic use of force to maintain order and its freedom to use force externally to protect itself – is an institution[7] of the (post-1648, European) international system. States affect each other by using, or threatening to use, coercive power defined in material (military and economic) terms. The *relative* power of any state as against others is the key measure of its capacities for action, and thus independence. Balances of power emerge from confrontations among states, and realist theorists generally regard the balance of power as the primary ordering institution of the anarchic system.

For realists, two kinds of change are possible. Change *in* the international system means that the relative power of particular states, or the power hierarchy, varies due to war, differential economic growth, technological innovation, and so on; however, anarchy persists, and the institutions of sovereignty and balance survive. Change *of* the system, on the other hand, would mean transforming the conditions under which international politics takes place. If some international authority were to arise and terminate international anarchy, if new actors of a different sort appeared that could powerfully constrain states, or if states were to base their actions on some principle other than self-help, then the system would be transformed and the balance of power would give way to other institutions.

For realists, international organizations fit into the system as tools of states in their competition with each other, but they are not instruments of an escape from anarchy. It would make little sense for states to sacrifice sovereignty to enforce international laws against genocide, crimes against humanity, and war crimes, unless to do so would confer some relative advantage or to oppose it would entail some relative costs. Realists might

---

[7] *Institutions:* The term "institution" appears in the international relations literature in at least four different ways. For some, an institution is an *organization*. For others, it is a *routinized pattern of behavior* (such as free trade, democracy, or domestic legal processes) that can be characterized by principles (antiprotectionism, majoritarianism, rule of law) and decision-making routines (global negotiations, voting, trials) that may or may not necessitate organizations. The term is also used to denote *an important general characteristic*; for example, sovereignty is considered by many to be an institution of the post–Westphalian international system and states within it. Lastly, an institution can be *a common, expected dynamic* within the system, such as war or the balance of power. When referring to a concrete organization – with a headquarters, officials, mandate, functions, and the like – I use the word "organization." When referring to the broader idea of an accepted pattern of behavior, accepted characteristic (such as sovereignty), or common dynamic, I use "institution."

thus explain why states would seek to limit the Court's powers (to retain their own freedoms) or go along with it once it was created by others, but they have no explanation for its creation in the first place. This is where additional theoretical perspectives can help.

Neoliberal Institutionalist Theorists

The theories of the neoliberal institutionalists overlap with the realists' vision of international relations but differ in important ways. Liberals too believe in rationality. Classical liberals believed as well in the idea of progress, human goodwill, and the (rational) perfectibility of mankind through collective institutions.[8] Neoliberal institutionalists combine liberalism with realism. They grant the realist premise that states are the primary international actors but argue that states can experience incentives to cooperate for improvements in their own welfare, seeking *absolute* gain, rather than exclusively *relative* gain.[9] When states seeking absolute gains cooperate to reduce international transaction costs, to create new collective goods, and to prevent collective bads, they may establish organizations to implement these objectives.[10] To the extent that these organizations' mere existence and/or requirements of membership entail changes in domestic legislation and international behavior, organization participation may alter and constrain states' behavior. A pervasive enough web of interdependence could create areas of international interaction in which behavior is limited by law or other orderly institutions, and in such areas anarchy could recede. The international system could thus incrementally change as states become increasingly enmeshed in a web of institutionalized interdependencies.[11] Liberal institutionalists also accept that actors other than states – such as international organizations, nongovernmental (or civil society) organizations, transnational movements, and multinational corporations – can affect

---

[8] Mingst, *Essentials of International Relations*, 3rd ed. (2004), 63–4, explains that liberalism assumes that human nature is basically good, societal progress is possible, and behavior is malleable and perfectible through institutions, based on the Greek idea that individuals can understand universal laws of nature and society through rationality. Immanuel Kant is an example of a classical liberal. Liberals believe in cooperation driven by rational individualism.

[9] Mingst, ibid., describes neoliberal institutionalists, such as Robert Axelrod and Robert Keohane, as reviving liberalism (and rescuing it from utopianism) by finding in iterative international interactions principles of cooperation, even in an anarchic environment, that can lead to the creation of international institutions.

[10] Abbott and Snidal, "Why States Act through Formal Organizations" (1998), 3–32.

[11] Jacobson, *Networks of Interdependence: International Organizations and the Global Political System* (1979).

states, and that states' objectives are defined, at least in part, by internal political dynamics such as interest groups and political parties, and not just deduced by realist calculations flowing from a structurally determined national interest.

Seeking to explain how organizations can affect states, and vice versa, neoliberal institutionalists argue that states will support cooperation if it produces absolute or relative gains. If they see cooperation damaging their interests, they will oppose, constrain, or defect from it. Thus, if the ICC assists in implementing states' normative objective of countering impunity, it should receive continued or increasing support.

For liberal institutionalists, the more the Court can serve states' interests, the greater its autonomy and legitimacy. Its ability to convince states that it is operating to enhance their objectives depends largely on what it does, compared to what it was designed to do, and how efficient it is in achieving these ends. Neoliberal institutionalism thus helps explain aspects of the organization's form, operations, survival, momentum, and growth, but it doesn't explain why the antiimpunity norm and international criminal law grew in the first place. For that purpose, a constructivist perspective is very useful.

Social Constructivists

Social constructivists observe that all visions of how the world works are based on ideas that people develop within a social, historical context. For constructivists, both realism and institutionalism assume that human motivation is primarily materialist, and that states' actions are primarily dictated by anarchy.[12] Constructivists argue, however, that not all motives are materialist and the vision of a world based in anarchy is a particular mental construction. Other motives and visions are possible. Non-materialist motives can include normative objectives.

Because the assumption of anarchy leads to certain conclusions (the importance of relative power, for instance), a different set of assumptions

---

[12] As Ruggie, "Introduction," *Constructing the World Polity: Essays on International Institutionalization* (1998), 3, put it, realism and institutionalism "share a view of the world of international relations in utilitarian terms: an atomistic universe of self-regarding units whose identity is assumed given and fixed, and who are responsive largely if not solely to material interests that are stipulated by assumption. The two bodies of theory do differ on the extent to which they believe institutions (and by extension institutionalization) play a significant role in international relations. ... But they are alike in depicting institutions in strictly instrumental terms, useful (or not) in the pursuit of individual and typically material interests." For a much more detailed discussion of social constructivism and international relations theory, refer to Wendt, *Social Theory of International Politics* (1999).

could lead to different conclusions. For example, under anarchy, relative material advantage is vital for self-preservation. Were people to conceptualize the world not as an anarchic, state-centric environment but as an ecologically and ethically shaped, human-centered environment, perhaps relative material advantage (power and money) would be less compelling to foreign policy decision makers than environmental preservation or uplifting human dignity. Constructivism expands the realm of apparent free will, as against realism's determinism and neoliberal institutionalism's tepid optimism. However, constructivism's vulnerability lies in the difficulty of changing people's conceptions of themselves (identities) on a scale massive enough to move away from the standard framework and the lack of any logic that would indicate what (if any) evolution in consciousness is most likely. Identity shifts can, after all, move in humane or inhumane directions.

Constructivists argue that international institutions embody normative commitments that denote personal, national, and global identities.[13] Identities are malleable; thus, changing identities could be a source of system change (that is, *of* the system as well as *within* the system). In one historical example, people in many countries decided that basing a government on formal racial discrimination was inhumane and uncivilized. Their leaders found it either politically advantageous or morally compelling (or both) to adopt this stand domestically and in their foreign policies (although there was no apparent material advantage in doing so). The resulting global anti-apartheid movement ultimately helped force the minority South African government to negotiate transition to majority rule.[14]

Similarly, as government leaders became convinced in the late 1980s and during the 1990s that passivity in the face of genocide, crimes against humanity, and war crimes was incompatible with their identities (perhaps as compelled by civil society groups, international lawyers, and public pressures arising from ongoing conflicts), they sought action (or at least the appearance of action) against those crimes. The United Nations Security Council established the International Criminal Tribunals for the Former Yugoslavia and Rwanda (ICTY, ICTR), and a few years later negotiators considering a Statute for the ICC agreed on an organizational form for the institutionalized criminalization of these core international crimes. For constructivists, creation of the ICC could demonstrate a change *of* the

---

[13] Identity includes the conception of what it is to be human or to be civilized. Ruggie, op cit., 4, says constructivism "attributes to ideational factors, including culture, norms, and ideas, social efficacy over and above any functional utility they may have, including a role in shaping the way in which actors define their identity and interests in the first place."

[14] Klotz, *Norms in International Relations: The Struggle against Apartheid* (1995).

system in the sense that collectively, without clear relative advantage and for apparently nonmaterial reasons, states committed themselves to cooperate within an international organization established to prosecute collectively proscribed acts whose prosecution had previously been considered (if at all) on an ad hoc, war-by-war basis. Although historically realism came first, then neoliberal institutionalism, and last, constructivism, they are useful in explaining the ICC in a different order. The constructivists explain development of the consensus on which the Court is based; the realists explain states' compulsions to protect sovereignty and to seek relative advantage; the liberal institutionalists explore how the ICC embodies states' cooperative efforts to improve absolute welfare. In the balance of the book, the theories will appear in this logical, rather than historical, order.

CONUNDRUMS

The ICC faces a set of challenges that flow from its nature as an international treaty-based judicial organization with a broad membership and wide mandate. These challenges were built into it in the process of negotiating its creation; they create dilemmas that its officials must manage.

Judicial–Political Dilemma

The ICC was created as a judicial institution to prosecute individuals accused of heinous international crimes. But these are crimes that occur in contexts of violent international and internal conflicts in which the political stakes drive people to extreme behavior. Thus, the ICC is a judicial organization operating in the most political of environments. Court officials insist that, as a judicial institution, the Court cannot gear its actions according to what will win it political favor (although they are happy for nongovernmental organizations to advocate it as a cause or for members of the ASP to encourage other countries to join), and they must make decisions on purely judicial grounds. The Court's actions, however, have political ramifications for states and for actors within states, and will inevitably be interpreted politically,[15] and the distinction between judicial and political grounds is not always clear. The Court seeks to build legitimacy, hence support, by acting transparently and on purely judicial grounds. However,

---

[15] I use "political" here to refer to choices that are made according to calculations of advantage in the allocation of power or resources by self-seeking actors, as opposed to strictly "judicial-legal" choices made according to principles of law. It can be argued that legal decisions too are political in nature – having power effects and being based on principles capable of being interpreted according to decision makers' subjective preferences.

much of its activity is necessarily confidential, and as in any organization, some amount of its decision making will be the product of negotiation and bureaucratic conflict. Given the charged environment in which the ICC operates, the limits of openness, the vague boundary between political and legal judgment, and the compulsions of organization behavior, it cannot be purely judicial, and it will be interpreted politically even as it strives so to appear.

Structural–Administrative Dilemma

The ICC's organizational structure seeks to replicate in one organization the independent responsibilities and powers usually allocated to separate legislatures, ministries, and courts in domestic systems. An architecture designed to create judicial neutrality and prosecutorial independence, however, is not an optimal design for administrative efficiency and coordination. The Court's objectives of administrative efficiency cut against its objectives of judicial insularity and prosectorial independence.

The Broad Mandate Dilemma: Retributive and Restorative Justice

The Statute creates mechanisms of traditional (retributive) and newer (restorative) justice,[16] but the emphasis between the two remains in flux, and the mechanisms for the second are particularly sketchy. There is strong pressure on the Court to embrace the broadest range of both retributive and restorative justice activities, but the more broadly the mandate is pursued, the more difficult it will be to fulfill. The very innovative qualities that made the Statute achievable and attractive also constitute threats to the organization's welfare.

Civil- and Common-Law Heritage

The Statute and rules combine common-law and civil-law traditions.[17] The Court's Prosecutor is patterned on a common-law model, following from

---

[16] "Retributive justice" refers to arrest, trial, and sentencing of suspects; "restorative justice" refers to bringing victims back into society as full members and reconciling parties in conflict. This is explained further in Chapter 1.

[17] *Common law, civil law:* Two major patterns of judicial structure have developed in the Western legal tradition. In *common-law* systems, identified with Anglo-American procedure, prosecutors assemble cases against defendants and present evidence in court before a jury of nonexperts. The defendant is usually represented by a defense counsel who responds to the prosecutor's case in court with cross-examination of prosecution witnesses, presentation of defense witnesses, and challenges to evidence and procedure. The judge serves as an impartial referee between the prosecution and defense, instructing the jury on

the precedent of the tribunals for the former Yugoslavia and for Rwanda. In contrast to the tribunals' structures, however, and in part as a consequence of their experiences, the ICC Statute negotiators tilted the Court back to a more even balance between the two traditions. In practice, a common-law-oriented Office of the Prosecutor is contending with civil-law-oriented Pre-Trial Chamber judges to establish operational and legal precedents for the Court's operations. The structure of the situation, the orientation of the personnel involved, and the many areas in which precedents can be established only by operating the machinery are causing clashes between the judges and prosecution.

Peace versus Justice

Because the Statute gives the Court jurisdiction over specified crimes from the inception of the Court, the ICC can pursue investigations and trials of

the admissibility of evidence and explaining the standards of guilt and innocence for the jury. Evidence must generally be presented in court orally. Exhibits must be identified and explained to the jury in court.

Rules of evidence in common-law systems are explicit and binding, and the decisions of prior court cases serve as precedent for the interpretation of laws and procedure that counsel and judges may use to justify their own arguments.

In common-law systems, with the exception sometimes of sentencing procedures, victims are involved in cases as witnesses only, subject to cross-examination. Once convicted, criminals generally "pay their debt to society" in the form of incarceration or fines, not in direct response to victims or their needs.

In *civil-law* systems, identified with Roman law, continental European systems, and the legal systems of their former colonial possessions, cases are initiated by magistrates or judges who assign to prosecutors the task of assembling information about the crime and suspect. The prosecutor is expected to develop exculpatory as well as inculpatory information. The information is assembled in consultation with an accused's counsel, into a "dossier," a complete case file, that is forwarded to a judge. The judge then decides whether the case should go forward to trial. The judge may instruct the prosecutor to collect more information of a specified nature. Trial consists of consideration of the dossier and additional material from the prosecutor and defense counsel before a separate judge or judicial panel. Because the judge or judicial panel is considered expert in the evaluation of evidence, the rules of evidence are less stringent than in common-law systems. Under civil-law systems, the trial judges may take into account hearsay, document and summary written statements, and evidence not exposed in court to direct cross-examination or testimony.

In civil-law systems, particularly the French system from the 1990s onward, victims are more closely involved in the justice process than are victims in common-law systems. Victims may demand initiation of procedures against an accused, they may present to the trial judge their views on the nature of the crime and appropriate punishment, and the Court may respond to their demands with orders of compensation or other action by a convicted criminal.

Generally, precedent plays a much smaller role in civil law than in common law, the civil code exhaustively recording the relevant rules.

suspects involved in crimes that are part of ongoing conflicts, internal or international. This sets up a potential conflict of objectives, between bringing criminal perpetrators to justice and achieving peace between warring parties.

Chapters

The following chapters describe these dilemmas and dissect the Court's internal dynamics, international significance, and likely future, from constructivist, realist, and neoliberal institutionalist perspectives. Chapter 1 argues that the ICC is the product of a gathering stream of norms that extend from divine law to post–Cold War revulsion against individual responsibilities for mass civilian killings.

Chapter 2 explains how the genesis, commitments, and precedents of the Yugoslavia and Rwanda tribunals contributed to construction of the ICC's Statute and argues that although some of their lessons were incorporated into the Court's founding documents, other insights were recognized too late to be initially built into the Court. Court personnel must still incorporate conclusions from the tribunals' later experience into their operations.

Chapter 3 asserts that the ICC Statute represents the outer limits – as of 1998 – of an incomplete but very significant international consensus over international criminal justice and procedural norms. As a negotiated treaty, it incorporates a broad range of elements that are not fully compatible with each other, and hence build frictions into the Court's operations.

Chapter 4 contains considerable detail about the operations of the Court in its early years. It is a long chapter because I think these details are important evidence of the Court's main internal problems, how difficult, contentious, and complicated the start-up of this organization has been, and how Court personnel are working to resolve their challenges.

Chapter 5 focuses on the role of nongovernmental organizations (NGOs) in influencing the establishment and operation of the ICC. It argues that NGOs have been crucial to the Court, but that their influences represent organizational headaches as well as important support for it.

Chapter 6 similarly analyzes ICC relations with its member states, dwelling in particular on the still somewhat underdeveloped role of the Assembly of States Parties.

Chapter 7 describes the Court's role in the situations in the Democratic Republic of the Congo, Uganda, Sudan, and the Central African Republic (CAR), the first to move beyond preliminary investigation stages. In each situation, controversy has emerged – over the charges (in the Congo), over peace versus justice (in Uganda), in confrontation with an uncooperative government (Sudan), and over what some observers felt was too delayed an initiation of a formal investigation (in the CAR) – illustrating pitfalls and dilemmas facing the Court.

The Court is being shaped by challenges at international, organizational, and personal levels. As constructivists would argue, the ICC is the product of international normative shifts toward individual accountability and restorative justice. Realists would point out that, normative convergence notwithstanding, sovereignty and self-help still dominate states' actions: States seek to use the Court for their own purposes, and alternative priorities mean that even its supporters' attention wanders. Liberal institutionalist analysis shows that the unprecedented nature of the Court's activities, its broad mandate, tripartite structure, hybrid legal foundation, lack of enforcement capacity, officials' and interlocutors' differences of view over priorities within the mandate, and a lack of direction from states thwart easy establishment of organizational independence and momentum. Moreover, the Court's early operations have been made ever more complicated by its simultaneous construction and operation. Nonetheless, from its small beginning in 2002, the Court is rapidly growing, developing operational routines, learning to manage internal chaos and external challenges, elaborating plans, and working toward stability. Its trajectory is promising but uncertain.

I

River of Justice

The International Criminal Court exists to implement a treaty, the Rome Statute of 1998, which contains objectives, principles, and mechanisms over which there was long debate, dispute, compromise, and finally both elation and disappointment. The Statute should be thought of more as a negotiated cognitive and political map than an architectural plan because even though it charts the territory and encompasses crucial compromises, there is no guarantee that it is a coherent design for an organization. The Statute's negotiators – diplomats, nongovernmental organization activists, lawyers, and scholars from diverse countries – shared many of the same ideas coming into the negotiation. They came to agree on the general legal territory upon which the Court would operate and on many of its features; however, details of the organization's structure and its overall trajectory remained to be charted in further negotiation and in practice.

Like maps drawn through the ages on the basis of explorers' reports, rumors, imagination, and creative draftsmanship, the Statute is a snapshot of perceptions and compromises at a particular historical moment. A long history precedes it, and developments in which it is a milestone continue. To better understand the Statute and Court, metaphors even more dynamic than "map" might serve. The map reflects a moment, but the moment is only a slice from a stream of events.

Constructivist international relations theorists Martha Finnemore and Kathryn Sikkink discuss how new ideas develop at the international level[1] and use the term "norm cascade" to describe the moment at which they become irresistible. A cascade is an area of turbulence and transition in a longer

---

[1] Finnemore and Sikkink, "International Norms and Political Change" (1998).

14

riparian metaphor. Such a stage seems to have been reached in the area of international justice in the 1990s. The river has had normative tributaries, eddies, currents, and dams, as well as a cascade or two already, and it is reasonable to imagine that more of these will be reached.

The river metaphor has its limits, too. Tributaries flowing into a river aren't self-conscious. They merely arise at higher altitudes, flow downhill following paths of least resistance, and merge into the mainstream. In contrast, international legal currents were shaped at least partly by conscious efforts of legal practitioners, scholars, politicians, decision makers, and civil society advocates. Intention and self-consciousness need to be added to gravity to explain the flow and direction of the river of justice because many of the normative changes and legal innovations reflected in the Statute were thought out by people with purposes in mind. The international justice river arose in the mists of time from divine and natural law sources.[2] As it grew and its current accelerated, legal engineers shaped its flow, and advocates broadened its appeal. The Statute Conference was a moment of grand engineering, bringing various streams together; the norm cascade was tamed, channeling a wide range of objectives into an international organization. The broad range of objectives submerged in the Statute, and the political challenges that lie in the path of orderly implementation may yet divert the flow of justice or swamp efforts to keep its course.

This chapter describes the confluence of justice norms, historical conditions, and activists' efforts that led to the Statute. It argues that the norms and compromises embedded in the Statute create huge demands on the Court, potentially unresolvable dilemmas for it, and grounds for internal conflict within it.

LAW: DIVINE, NATURAL, AND POSITIVE

The headwaters of the international justice river lie obscured in the distant past, gradually gathering force from philosophies of divine and natural law. International humanitarian law, that is, law related to the conduct of war,

---

[2] Brague, *The Law of God: The Philosophical History of an Idea* (2007), distinguishes between law that is divine because of its own qualities (as viewed by classical Greek philosophy) as contrasted with law that is divine because of its godly origin (as found in Jewish and Christian traditions) or its equation with religion itself. Hart, *The Concept of Law* (1961), 182, defines theories of natural law as those asserting "that there are certain principles of human conduct, awaiting discovery by human reason, with which manmade law must conform if it is to be valid."

has ancient roots.[3] Traces of limits to what armies and soldiers are permitted to do (justice in war, *jus in bello*) surface in the Old Testament and in a wide variety of works from ancient cultures. Greek and Roman philosophers considered when war itself could be justified (justice of war, *jus ad bello*). A theory of "just war" is generally attributed to theologian St. Augustine in the fifth century A.D., who argued that if war is a lesser evil than the evil against which it is fought, it can be justified. The distinction between legitimate and illegitimate kinds of force can already be seen in the chivalric codes of the Middle Ages,[4] based on the relationship of divinely ordained nobles to their more earth-bound vassals.

A more recent sign that norms of behavior have long existed even in the context of violent conquest is the trial and conviction in 1474 of Peter von Hagenbach by an ad hoc tribunal of local notables for crimes he committed against civilians during his occupation of Breisach, Alsace, on behalf of Charles, Duke of Burgundy.[5] There is thus evidence that by the late fifteenth century, both justice of war and justice in war attracted thought and even led to action demonstrating commitment to norms of behavior in the context of conflict.

Western medieval legal scholarship attributed to religion and God the sources of law, with the Ten Commandments being a prime example. With the turn to Enlightenment at the end of the fifteenth century, natural-law theorists proposed that laws are genuine when they are common to all civilized humans, deducible from the nature of human existence.[6] Debate followed over the content of natural law and, by the mid-seventeenth century, whether states, as opposed to individuals, could themselves be subject to law.

Dutch philosopher and lawyer Hugo Grotius, often described as the "father" of international law, argued in 1605 that states have no property rights to the open sea, but that they do share a common right for innocent maritime passage. The important point for our purposes is that Grotius asserted that states had rights. He said that, as a variety of natural law, international law could be derived from the application of reason. His later works justified war to protect a state's inherent natural rights of survival and property but contended that violence was justified only for defense. In his 1625 work, *De jure belli ac pacis libri tres* (*The Law of War and Peace*

---

[3] Green, *Essays on the Modern Law of War*, 2nd ed. (1999).
[4] Walzer, *Just and Unjust Wars: A Moral Argument with Historical Illustrations*, 3rd ed. (2000), 34.
[5] Schwarzenberger, *International Law as Applied by Courts and Tribunals* (1968), 462–6.
[6] Clark, "A Methodology for Determining an International Legal Rule" (2003), 24.

in Three Books), he argued, as Benjamin Ferencz paraphrased him, "that those who made war for gain or other wrongful intent deserved conviction; those who commenced a war unlawfully were responsible for the foreseeable consequences of their aggression; and even generals and soldiers who could have prevented the harm would be held to account."[7]

The problem with natural law was that it left open to interpretation the imperatives of the law, and was thus subject to abuse. In the eighteenth century, utilitarian philosophers, contractarians that they were, responded by proposing that law had to be enacted – it wasn't something handed down, discovered, or deduced but could be discovered with reference to existing state practice. Such discovery required an inductive method.[8] According to their views, this positively enacted law – positive law – was real law; divine and natural law had no solid basis in society. Laws would be truly legitimate only when enacted by legitimate authority. This created a problem for international law because if legal positivism proposed that law was created by legitimate authority, and states were sovereign, where was the legitimate authority that could create international law, a law above the states? International law required an analogue to domestic legislative authority. Because states could be bound only voluntarily by their own acts, international law would be limited to obligations that states explicitly accepted. Treaties (conventional law) became the strongest basis, for the positivists, for international law. States could exercise their sovereignty by withdrawing from treaties, so the law they created might be only temporarily binding. Though a tenuous form of law, it was law nonetheless in the sense that acts of states delimited permissible and impermissible behavior and could attach sanctions to violations. The river of justice widened.

Even without a formal legislative authority, from the mid-eighteenth century, institutions of international organization and law accumulated around a coalescing concept of Europe as a community of states with a common (Christian) heritage.[9] A community or a society could perhaps have laws, even if it lacked formal legislative processes. Philosophers, parliamentarians, and legal experts proposed the creation of international laws and representative institutions to implement them in the peace plans of

---

[7] Ferencz, "International Crimes Against the Peace" (undated). Ferencz was a prosecutor at the Nuremberg trials and has been a tireless advocate since then for the outlawing of aggression and creation of an international criminal court.

[8] Clark, op cit.

[9] Hinsley, *Power and the Pursuit of Peace: Theory and Practice in the History of Relations Between States* (1963), Part I.

the time.[10] In the nineteenth century, legal experts proposed codification of various aspects of international law, including laws of war. Rather than being purely philosophical exercises or the description of actions already undertaken, these proposals were motivated by combinations of nationalist and altruist purposes and aimed at instituting international law.

The ideas about international law that developed in the mid-nineteenth century were fundamentally different from those of Grotius and his immediate successors. Martti Koskenniemi[11] describes publicists of international law in the nineteenth century as a group of legal reformists who came together across national boundaries to launch a society and a journal advocating the scientific development of international law, just as domestic law had long been elaborated by professional exegesis and analysis. The reformists sought in their journals and through legislation to build international law based on what they believed to be scientific, deductive principles and motivated by what they considered the worst threats to order in their day. Harking back to natural law, the legislative urge was to transform natural precepts into legitimate, accepted institutions, a positivist project. Koskenniemi argues that these European international legal theorists imagined an international law independent of sovereign bias, but proposed schemes that conformed to their home states' interests. German theorists identified international law with the firm construction of sovereignty, which would help solidify the new German state. French theorists focused on a more internationalist vision of international society, which would disseminate values already consolidated in the French nation. But the proposals nonetheless demonstrated that, for international lawyers, the way forward was to translate precepts drawn from whatever sources (national interest, natural law) into positive law, with organizations to implement regulation of states' behavior, creating alternatives to war. By the turn of the twentieth century, new legal streams and organizational channels were shaping a swelling flow, leading to creation of the Permanent Court of Arbitration (1899) and the Permanent Court of International Justice (1922), headquartered in The Hague at the Peace Palace constructed for the purpose by the Carnegie Endowment, and intended as organizations that could resolve conflict among states judicially, without recourse to violence.

---

[10] For example, Hinsley describes the peace and European Parliament proposals in the seventeenth through nineteenth centuries of William Penn, John Bellers, Charles François, Irénée Castel de Saint-Pierre, and the nineteenth-century proposals of Rousseau and Kant. Ibid., 33–80.

[11] Koskenniemi, *The Gentle Civilizer of Nations: The Rise and Fall of International Law 1870–1960* (2001).

INTERNATIONAL HUMANITARIAN AND CRIMINAL LAW

Even as legal commentators sought to create organizations that would reduce states' resort to violence, the carnage of contemporary conflict bred efforts to constrain behavior during wars. Today's humanitarian law, humanitarian organizations, and arms control treaties can be traced to mid-nineteenth-century lawyers' and legal scholars' responses to wars' devastation.

The first modern military code and both international rules of war and their main organizational manifestation developed in the second half of the nineteenth century. At U.S. President Abraham Lincoln's request, Columbia University international law professor Francis Lieber wrote the first modern rules of war, the 1863 "Instructions for the Government of Armies of the United States in the Field," a code for the Union Army's treatment of prisoners, wounded soldiers, and civilians under occupation.[12] Lieber was a former Prussian army officer and jurist who had immigrated to the United States and pursued a distinguished career as a professor and philosopher of law, first in South Carolina and then in New York.

At about the same time that Lieber was working on the code, Swiss lawyer Gustave Moynier, businessman Henri Dunant, and three colleagues founded the organizational predecessor to the International Committee of the Red Cross. In 1859, Moynier, a lawyer with a doctorate in law, became chairman of the Geneva Society for Public Welfare. That year, Henri Dunant, fortuitously present at the battle of Solferino, a bloody engagement of Napoleon III's army, was horrified especially by the dead and dying soldiers who lay in the mud in large numbers after the battle, bereft of assistance. In 1862, Moynier received Dunant's book, *A Memory of Solferino*, that described the 1859 battle and its appalling aftermath and proposed creating neutral relief societies to care for combatants on all sides in time of war.

In 1863, Dunant and Moynier cofounded the International Committee for Relief to the Wounded (which became the International Committee of the Red Cross in 1876). They successfully pressed the Swiss government to convene international negotiations that led to the Geneva Convention of 1864. Negotiators created rules to protect conflict victims and agreed that care should be provided for wounded and sick soldiers without discrimination and that medical personnel, vehicles, and equipment bearing an agreed upon

---

[12] U.S. Army, "Instructions for the Government of Armies of the United States in the Field" (Lieber Code).

common emblem (the red cross on a white background that transposed the colors of the Swiss flag) should be respected. The norm that injured or ill soldiers out of combat should be treated humanely had thus been established.

Moynier sought to push law further into the affairs of states, proposing in 1872 that international criminal courts be created by combatants as soon as a conflict broke out, to deter and, if necessary, adjudicate violations of the 1864 Geneva Convention. The proposed judicial panels would mix nationals of the combatants with neutrals. Respecting sovereignty, they would pass sentences that the states would carry out.[13]

At the turn of the century, the Hague Conventions (1899, 1907) expanded and integrated the earlier Geneva Convention with extensive rules drawn from the Lieber Code, forming the mainstream of subsequent international humanitarian law (IHL), also called the laws of war, or war crimes law.

While the sources of humanitarian law still flowed from our understanding of divine, natural, or rational law, international lawyers codified the humanitarian agenda, seeking its transformation into positive law. The natural-law impulse is still recognizable in debates over precedent – what constitutes compelling (*jus cogens*) law internationally based on apparent norms of behavior even when not inscribed in treaties.[14] But even while asserting precedent, lawyer-advocates have sought to make such debates moot by establishing treaty-defined limits to states' freedom. Treaty writing accelerated after both of the twentieth century's world wars and after the end of Cold War rivalry between the U.S. and Soviet blocs. In each period, states' sovereign interests constrained implementation, but as normative agreement expanded, the river of justice broadened.

World War I and International Criminal Law

From World War I through the interwar period, concepts of crimes against humanity, the crime of aggression, and potential individual responsibility converged with the 1907 Hague proscriptions against mistreatment of noncombatants.

Crimes against Humanity

On May 24, 1915, World War I allies France, Great Britain, and Russia notified the enemy Ottoman authorities in Constantinople (via a message

---

[13] Glasius, *The International Criminal Court: A Global Civil Society Achievement* (2005), 6.
[14] Bassiouni, "Accountability for Violations of International Humanitarian Law and Other Serious Violations of Human Rights" (2002), 14–26.

delivered by the still-neutral United States) that the Ottomans would be held responsible for Turkish massacres of the Armenian population. Having enumerated locations of large-scale murders and accused the Ottoman government of ill treatment of its "inoffensive Armenian population," the telegram warned that "[i]n view of those new crimes of Turkey against humanity and civilization, the Allied governments announce ... that they will hold personally responsible [for] these crimes all members of the Ottoman government and those of their agents who are implicated in such massacres."[15] "Crimes against humanity" flowed into the stream, and, at least momentarily, individual culpability was claimed to override the prerogatives of states.

In 1920, the Treaty of Sevres proposed to carry out the prosecution of Turks that the Allies had threatened in 1915 for crimes against the Armenians. When the unratified Sevres was superseded by the Treaty of Lausanne in 1923, amnesties were extended, and no proceedings took place,[16] but the proposal was an important conceptual extension beyond established (Hague) international humanitarian law. IHL dealt with crimes of one state's military or occupation forces against the soldiers or civilians of another state. Up to that point, international law hadn't dealt with crimes carried out by a government against its own citizens or international crimes outside the context of international war.[17] The new concept of crimes against humanity denoted crimes as international in nature not because they crossed national boundaries but because the violation was offensive to the international community. For such crimes, in addition to war crimes, the term "international criminal law" (ICL) subsequently came into use. ICL could include crimes that crossed borders (such as aggression or war crimes) or not (such as the crimes against humanity that Turks were suspected of perpetrating against their Armenian conationals). Long-standing international crimes – such as piracy and slavery – also came to be included in the ICL concept. Additional crimes (such as torture and hijacking) were defined and added much later.

Precursors of Genocide
Interested in Turkish crimes against Armenians during World War I and massacres of Arameans in Iraq in the 1930s, Polish prosecutor Rafael

---

[15] France, Great Britain and Russia Joint Declaration (May 24, 1915).
[16] Schabas, *An Introduction to the International Criminal Court*, 2nd ed. (2004), 3–4.
[17] By the late 1800s, piracy and slavery had been outlawed, and it was accepted that states were justified in acting unilaterally on the high seas against pirates and slave traders. These were international (nonterritorial) crimes, but enforcement was up to states. There was no international jurisdiction.

Lemkin proposed to a League of Nations conference in 1933 a definition of a "crime of barbarity" for international prosecution. Lemkin continued to develop and advocate international law responses to war and war crimes as a Polish diplomat and then in exile in the United States during and after World War II.[18] His 1944 book, *Axis Rule in Occupied Europe*, included a definition and explanation of his neologism, "genocide."[19] Through Lemkin's tireless efforts and the compelling qualities of the concept, genocide entered the mainstream of international criminal law after World War II, finally being inscribed in treaty terms in 1948.

Aggression

In the 1919 Versailles Treaty ending World War I, Germany was punished for its role in World War I by territorial losses, assessment of reparations, demilitarization, and limits on rearmament. The victors also proposed to establish a criminal tribunal to prosecute Kaiser Wilhelm II for starting the war, but their intentions were purely symbolic. The Kaiser avoided prosecution in pleasant refuge in The Netherlands, which refused to extradite him for trial. French and British policy makers, moreover, lacked enthusiasm for the prosecution as they realized that such a proceeding would likely rouse political ferment in Germany against the fragile Weimar Republic. Although the principle of individual culpability was not implemented against the Kaiser, Versailles also recognized the right of the Allies to set up military tribunals to try German soldiers accused of war crimes.[20] A few trials eventually were held in Germany. The courts languished but the principle ran deep.

Proposing a New Court

As part of the effort to avert future wars, the Versailles Treaty established the League of Nations. The 1920 Commission of Jurists that met in 1920 in The Hague to prepare a draft Statute of the Permanent Court of International Justice (which had been called for in the League Covenant) recommended creation of a separate High Court of International Justice "competent to try crimes constituting a breach of international public order or against the universal law of nations."[21] Discussions followed in

---

[18] Power, *"A Problem from Hell": America and the Age of Genocide*, 2nd ed. (2004), 42–3.
[19] Lemkin, *Axis Rule in Occupied Europe: Laws of Occupation, Analysis of Government, Proposals for Redress* (1944), Chapter IX.
[20] Maogoto, *War Crimes and Realpolitik: International Justice from World War One to the 21st Century* (2004), 62.
[21] Quoted in Hudson, "The Proposed International Criminal Court," *The American Journal of International Law* (1938), 550.

nonofficial venues. In 1922, the International Law Association issued an endorsement of the idea of creating an international criminal court, and a draft statute was discussed in 1924 and 1926.[22]

In 1925, the European Inter-Parliamentary Union, a nongovernmental organization, supported by the newly founded Association Internationale de Droit Penal (International Association of Penal Law), suggested that the existing Permanent Court of International Justice should extend its jurisdiction to include prosecutions of individuals and states for the crime of aggression.[23] Subsequently, the International Law Association and the International Association of Penal Law proposed that the League of Nations establish a criminal jurisdiction, and in 1937 the League adopted a treaty to establish an international criminal court. The treaty failed to attract enough ratifications to come into force, but the goal had been sighted.

Trying to Outlaw War

The quest to define crimes and create a court to prosecute individuals for violations of international criminal law was mirrored by international law advocates' continued effort to hold states accountable for aggression. In the Kellogg-Briand Pact of 1928, signatory states agreed to "condemn recourse to war for the solution of international controversies, and renounce it, as an instrument of national policy in their relations with one another,"[24] and to settle their differences only by "pacific means."[25] They sought to outlaw war, but they did not go so far as to proclaim aggression a crime that could be committed by an individual.

The Kellogg-Briand Pact perhaps demonstrated more explicitly than any other agreement before or since that codification does not guarantee compliance when the law runs so clearly counter to national interest. On the eve of World War II, E. H. Carr castigated the interwar diplomacy of the League of Nations in general, and the Kellogg-Briand Pact in particular, arguing that the coming war showed the terrible consequences of utopian approaches to international politics. After the war, for lasting peace, foreign policy would need to be built on a mixture of realism and utopianism.[26] Even utopianism had its practical virtues, however. After the war, the

---

[22] Ibid.
[23] Glasius, op cit., 7.
[24] Kellogg-Briand Pact (1928), Article I.
[25] Ibid., Article II.
[26] Carr, *The Twenty Years' Crisis 1919–1939* (1964).

Kellogg-Briand Pact served as a basis for building a legal case at Nuremberg against top Nazi leaders for the planning and conduct of aggressive war.

World War II and Nuremberg

World War II strengthened politicians', lawyers', and diplomats' desires to apply international law against the people who caused the war and those who committed war crimes in it. In the Moscow Declaration of October 30, 1943, Great Britain, France, the United States, and the Soviet Union declared that Germans who had committed war crimes would be sent for trial to the countries where they had committed their atrocities. The "major criminals whose offences have no particular geographical location" would be punished by the Allies.[27] Even though the post–World War I effort to prosecute the Kaiser had evaporated, the idea of prosecuting individual criminality in war was alive and well. The declaration reaffirmed both national and international jurisdiction over war crimes, and the United States, Britain, and Soviet Union indicated their intention to create some kind of postwar legal process for the Nazis responsible for initiating the war.

Following the Moscow Declaration, the allies established a United Nations Commission for the Investigation of War Crimes, which prepared a "Draft Convention for the Establishment of a United Nations War Crimes Court," conceptually basing its text largely on the (unratified) 1937 League of Nations treaty draft, and inspired by work carried out during the early years of the war by an unofficial body, the London International Assembly.[28]

After the war, at the London Conference in August 1945, Great Britain, France, the United States, and the Soviet Union laid the groundwork for the Nuremberg trials.[29] The Hague Conventions provided the basis for definition of war crimes; the Kellogg-Briand Pact, for crimes against peace. To enable prosecution of German crimes against German citizens, the category "crimes against humanity" that had emerged in connection with the Armenian massacres of World War I was included among the potential charges.[30] The four Nuremberg crimes were conspiracy to commit crimes

---

[27] Moscow Conference, "Joint Four-Nation Declaration, Statement on Atrocities" (October 1943).

[28] "Draft Convention for the Establishment of a United Nations War Crimes Court," U.N. War Crimes Commission, Doc. C.50(1) (30 September 1944), as cited in William Schabas, *An Introduction to the International Criminal Court* (2002), 5.

[29] London Agreement (August 8, 1945).

[30] Schabas, op cit., 6.

against peace; planning, initiating, and waging wars of aggression; war crimes; and crimes against humanity. The formula was similar for trials of Japanese war crimes suspects at the International Military Tribunal for the Far East, commonly known as the Tokyo Tribunal, which prosecuted crimes against peace, war crimes, and crimes against humanity.[31]

Institutionalization Interrupted and Restarted

In the few years between World War II and solidification of the Cold War, institutionalization of human rights and international law norms took giant steps. In the Convention against Genocide, states finally agreed to Raphael Lemkin's conviction that efforts to exterminate people on the basis of inherited characteristics and without regard to their individual actions should be outlawed. In the Universal Declaration of Human Rights, UN negotiators sought to establish general standards for individuals' rights against state prerogatives. In the Nuremberg Principles, formulated by the International Law Commission, common understandings of individual culpability were enunciated with general applicability (rather than being specific to German suspects).

Genocide Convention

In the wake of the Nuremberg trials, Rafael Lemkin's effort to outlaw the crime of genocide finally succeeded when on December 9, 1948, the UN General Assembly adopted the Convention on the Prevention and Punishment of the Crime of Genocide.[32] The Convention established genocide as an international crime and referred to possible machinery for its enforcement, but created no such capacity. An early UN Secretariat draft of the Convention included a model statute for a court, based on the League of Nations' 1937 draft treaty and the 1944 UN Commission Draft Convention, but the proposal was dropped in favor of a vaguer call for prosecution of the crime at either the national or international level, before "a competent tribunal of the State in the territory of which the act was committed, or by such international penal tribunal as may have jurisdiction with respect to those Contracting Parties which shall have accepted its jurisdiction."[33] Consideration of such machinery was taken up by the newly created International Law Commission.

---

[31] Charter of the International Military Tribunal for the Far East, Article V.
[32] UN General Assembly, Convention on the Prevention and Punishment of the Crime of Genocide, adopted December 9, 1948, entered into force January 12, 1951.
[33] Ibid., Article 6.

Universal Declaration of Human Rights

On the day following adoption of the Genocide Convention, the General Assembly passed and proclaimed the Universal Declaration on Human Rights (UDHR),[34] a nonbinding enumeration of civil rights possessed by all individuals (and later supplemented by covenants on civil and political rights,[35] and economic, social, and cultural rights[36]). Although the UDHR is not a treaty, it is regarded by many nongovernmental organizations, governments, and scholars as the foundational postwar statement of norms of individual rights and liberty, as the UDHR says in its preamble, "a common standard of achievement for all peoples and all nations." (The Soviet bloc, South Africa, and Saudi Arabia abstained from the vote adopting the declaration.)

International Law Commission and the Nuremberg Principles

The UN Charter gave to the General Assembly the responsibility, among other things, to initiate studies and make recommendations for "promoting international co-operation in the political field and encouraging the progressive development of international law and its codification."[37] To carry out the mandate, in 1947 the General Assembly created the International Law Commission.[38]

The ILC consists of thirty-four people chosen "as persons of recognized competence in international law" from "the main forms of civilization" and "the principal legal systems of the world." Elected for five-year terms by the General Assembly from candidates nominated by UN member states, they serve part-time and meet annually for about twelve weeks in the summers, usually in Geneva. The various topics under consideration are usually assigned to individual members, who then serve as special rapporteurs on

---

[34] UN General Assembly, "Universal Declaration of Human Rights," adopted and proclaimed by General Assembly December 10, 1948.

[35] UN General Assembly, "International Covenant on Civil and Political Rights," adopted and opened for signature December 16, 1966, entered into force March 23, 1976.

[36] UN General Assembly, "International Covenant on Economic, Social, and Cultural Rights," opened for signature December 16, 1966, entered into force January 3, 1976.

[37] UN Charter, Chapter IV, Article 13.1.a.

[38] Article 1 of the ILC's Statute provides that the "Commission shall have for its object the promotion of the progressive development of international law and its codification." Article 15 defines "progressive development" as the preparation of draft conventions on subjects that have not yet been regulated by international law, or in regard to which the law has not yet been sufficiently developed in the practice of states. It defines "codification" as the more precise formulation and systemization of rules of international law in fields where there already have been extensive state practice, precedent, and doctrines. Statute of the International Law Commission (1947).

the item concerned, carry out the necessary studies between sessions, and submit reports to the commission at its annual sessions.

Proposals for the areas in which the ILC is to work come from the General Assembly, UN member states, or other agencies, or from the ILC members themselves. Its efforts may result in the "progressive development" of law or "codification" of existing law. In either case, the ILC produces draft international conventions that can then be adopted by the UN General Assembly.

In 1950, the General Assembly asked the ILC to codify the Nuremberg principles,[39] to explore questions of international criminal jurisdiction in connection with the Genocide Convention (that is, where and how genocide could be prosecuted), and to consider the problem of defining the crime of aggression. In 1950, the ILC was asked to develop a draft code of offenses against the peace and security of mankind, and it submitted a draft to the UN General Assembly in the following year along with a proposal for an international criminal court. The General Assembly referred the report back to the ILC.[40] The ILC's projects to develop a criminal jurisdiction – to design a court and its procedures – and to develop a code of offenses – to define the laws that the court would enforce – flowed intermittently and in parallel, but with little interconnection, thereafter. The ILC submitted a draft international criminal court statute and a revised draft code of offenses in 1954, but the General Assembly then shifted its attention away from the statute and code, according to international law expert William Schabas, "ostensibly pending the sensitive task of defining the crime of aggression. In fact, political tensions associated with the Cold War had largely dammed progress on the war crimes agenda."[41]

Turbulent Late 1970s

Progress in the development of international criminal law drifted in the 1960s and early 1970s. Flowing from the commitments of the Universal Declaration on Human Rights, however, nongovernmental activity on

---

[39] The Nuremberg principles held that (I) an individual who commits a crime under international law is responsible for it and liable to punishment; (II) an individual's responsibility for upholding international law is not relieved by domestic law not containing penalties for the act; (III) being an official including the head of state of a government does not relieve responsibility under international law; (IV) acting under orders of a government or superior officer does not relieve a person of responsibility as long as choice was possible; (V) a person charged with a crime under international law has the right to a fair trial; (VI) the punishable crimes under international law are (a) crimes against peace, (b) war crimes, (c) crimes against humanity; (VII) complicity in the commission of the crimes under VI is also a crime. *Yearbook of the International Law Commission* (1950), Volume II, 191–5.
[40] Morton, *The International Law Commission of the United Nations* (2000), 38.
[41] Schabas, *An Introduction to the International Criminal Court* (2002), 9.

human rights grew, stimulated by the actions of oppressive communist and authoritarian governments. Amnesty International was founded in 1961 to assist "prisoners of conscience" worldwide, even while the Soviet and U.S. blocs used human rights as part of their ideological combat. The terms "war crimes" and "war criminals" were liberally applied by detractors of the United States in connection with Vietnam; "human rights travesties" and "human rights abusers," by critics of the Soviet Union for oppressing its citizens and those in the countries of its bloc.

The 1970s was a watershed decade in global strategic relations and activism on environmental and human rights fronts. While the East and West continued their military, ideological, and rhetorical confrontation, domestic civil society organizations were rapidly developing in the West in reaction to threats of nuclear war, threats to the environment, and threats to human rights. Much of this activism was led by international nongovernmental organizations. For example, in 1972, at the UN Conference on the Environment, the effects of the environmental movement that had begun in the United States reached the international stage.

Civil society organizations had come of age. In 1973, the General Assembly passed a resolution declaring apartheid, the racially discriminatory basis of government in South Africa, to be a crime against humanity.[42] Nongovernmental organizations and sympathetic governments sought economic sanctions against South Africa, but direct pursuit of apartheid criminals and the reconstitution of South African society remained objectives for a future generation of activists. In 1974, in an echo of the Kellogg-Briand Pact, the General Assembly adopted a definition of state aggression[43] but again did not define a crime of aggression for which an individual could be held responsible. Also in 1974, a much expanded Amnesty International declared torture, ill treatment, and capital punishment to be its main targets.

As part of U.S.–Soviet efforts to reduce the likelihood of war and normalize relations between the two sides in Europe, thirty-five countries pledged in the Helsinki Accords of 1975 to accept the post–World War II territorial settlements as final, to settle disputes peacefully, to respect human rights, to endorse equal rights and self-determination, and to fulfill obligations under international law.[44] The human rights aspects of the Accords led to creation of a nongovernmental organization called the Fund for Free

---

[42] UN General Assembly, "International Convention on the Suppression and Punishment of the Crime of Apartheid," adopted and opened for signature November 30, 1973, entered into force July 18, 1976.

[43] UN General Assembly, "Definition of Aggression" Resolution 3314(XXIX) (1974).

[44] Conference on Security and Cooperation in Europe, "Helsinki Final Act," August 1, 1975.

Expression. In 1978, the name was changed to Helsinki Watch, which established civilian human rights monitoring groups that sought to ameliorate human rights violations by monitoring and reporting them. In 1988, along with its affiliates Americas Watch, Asia Watch, and Prison Watch, it became Human Rights Watch. International nongovernmental organizations, prominently but not exclusively represented by Amnesty International and Human Rights Watch, agitated for states to respect individuals' rights through publicity campaigns and private diplomacy, drawing upon the 1948 Universal Declaration of Human Rights and subsequent human rights conventions as the fountainhead of their legitimacy.

Uprisings of school children in Soweto in the summer of 1976 reinvigorated international condemnation of the apartheid system in South Africa, and the required twenty ratifications of the 1973 resolution against apartheid brought it officially into force. U.S. President Jimmy Carter (1976–1980) embraced human rights as a major plank of his foreign policy, explicitly calling upon Latin American authoritarian governments especially to return to democracy and to cease the oppression of their populations.

In 1981, the General Assembly asked the ILC to restart its work on a draft code of crimes. The General Assembly adopted an international Convention Against Torture in 1985.[45] As the 1980s wore on, the Cold War system began to crack, and by 1991, it had disintegrated. The international lawyers who had been working to consolidate international human rights, humanitarianism, and criminal law under the shadow of the Cold War were about to enjoy a confluence of opportunities and crises that vastly accelerated the current.

SWELLING STREAMS OF JUSTICE

During the Cold War, international concern over human rights burgeoned, indicated especially by the flood of nongovernmental human rights organizations. At the interstate and interbloc level, human rights concerns suffered from politicization, as Western critics of East bloc violations could too easily be criticized for using the subject as a political tool rather than being genuinely concerned about victims of abuse, particularly given Westerners' acceptance of similar depredations by their authoritarian allies. With the end of the Cold War, that politicization receded in significance. Meanwhile, the development of globalized international communications and the

[45] UN General Assembly, "Convention Against Torture and Other Cruel, Inhuman or Degrading Treatment or Punishment," adopted and opened for signature, ratification, and accession December 10, 1984, entered into force June 26, 1987.

increasing effectiveness of nongovernmental organizations in using these technologies to publicize violations the world over enhanced the salience of human rights issues.

Truth Commissions and "Lustration"

Declining East–West polarization in the 1980s, combined with erosion of corrupt authoritarian governments that had been propped up by the largesse of the United States and Soviet Union as they sought allies in their ideological conflict, led to a series of transitions toward more democratic governments in Latin America and Africa. From late in the decade through the mid-1990s, Argentina, Brazil, Chile, South Africa, Chad, Uganda, Guatemala, and El Salvador embarked on democratization adventures that, with varying amounts of international support, included efforts to deal with crimes of the old regimes. In somewhat different form, as the states of the old Soviet bloc created new, more democratic governments, they too dealt with old injustices, albeit much less broadly. In the East bloc, processes of "lustration," opening the files of the secret police and other government bureaucracies, gingerly informed the public of the pervasiveness of the old Cold War secret police penetrations of society, the high degree to which all institutions of the state and society had been corrupted by political operations, and, at its most destructive, the extent to which trust in society, neighbors, and friends had often been misplaced.[46] In the African and Latin American cases, more formal efforts, generally falling under the rubric "truth commissions," were undertaken to separate the innocent from the guilty, to expose the crimes, to find and rehabilitate the victims. This stream, called transitional justice, flowed in parallel with, and in some respects in contrast to, mainstream international legal traditions, but the two shared a watershed, and norms from each flowed into the other.

Criminal Tribunals

While domestic transitions in many states included experiments with transitional justice mechanisms, major conflict enveloped another Cold War relic, Yugoslavia. Progressively disintegrating since the death of Marshall Josip

---

[46] "Lustration" was the term given to a variety of measures that shared the characteristic of opening to public view at least some of the Eastern European states' secret activities aimed at monitoring and subverting political activities and popular movements. Rosenberg, *The Haunted Land: Facing Europe's Ghosts After Communism* (1995).

Broz Tito in 1981, Yugoslavia no longer interested the Western powers as an outpost of anti-Soviet socialism when the Cold War thawed. Without support from the West, without its old dictator, and in the midst of severe economic decline, the Yugoslav state could not maintain its unity.[47] With political leaders whipping up nationalist fervor, Yugoslavia descended into civil war. The same Western powers that had nonchalantly ignored Yugoslav economic and social dissolution failed to muster a political-military response to its political disintegration, and nationalist ethnic war raged. In 1993, the UN Security Council finally took what appeared to be a small and symbolic step, creating the International Criminal Tribunal for the Former Yugoslavia, mandated to prosecute Nuremberg-type crimes in the Yugoslav conflict. In 1994, when massive internal violence overtook Rwanda, the Security Council again responded with a criminal tribunal, adopting essentially the same structure and mandate as the ICTY, and sharing its prosecutor. What appeared in 1993–1994 to be minor gestures toward international criminal responsibility proved to be major steps in the intstitutionalization of international criminal law and important precedents for the ICC. In the 1990s, two streams of justice converged: transitional justice from the wave of democratizations and the Nuremberg-type justice in the ICTY and ICTR.

Both the truth commissions and the criminal tribunals sailed forth under the banner inscribed "an end to impunity." The ICTR and ICTY were founded upon the Nuremberg principles and sought to apprehend, try, and punish the perpetrators of war crimes, genocide, and crimes against humanity.[48] The tribunals changed the course of justice by expanding and clarifying the Nuremberg crime definitions, including raising to the highest level of concern gender crimes such as rape and sexual slavery. Instituted under the UN Charter's (International Peace and Security) Chapter VII, the tribunals asserted a connection between justice and peace.

In contrast, truth commissions were more experimental, more varied, and less traditional. Testing new mechanisms and pursuing what had been at best secondary objectives of standard judicial systems, they significantly broadened the channels of justice, seeking to focus on victims instead of perpetrators in efforts to restore justice in society and to promote reconciliation between perpetrators and victims of human rights violations.

---

[47] Woodward, *Balkan Tragedy: Chaos and Dissolution after the Cold War* (1995).

[48] Statute of the ICTY, UN Security Council Resolution 827 of May 25, 1993. The full name of the ICTY is the "International Tribunal for the Prosecution of Persons Responsible for Serious Violations of International Humanitarian Law Committed in the Territory of the Former Yugoslavia since 1991." The ICTR was established by UN Security Council Resolution 955 of November 8, 1994, and its Statute was appended to the Resolution.

Justice Paradigms

The Bible's "eye for an eye" injunction suggests a proportionate law of revenge. The common pattern of investigation, arrest, trial, and punishment focuses legal mechanisms upon finding and punishing transgressors, forcing them to "pay their debt to society." This kind of justice focuses on retribution against those who disturb the social order: Commentators have labeled it "retributive justice."

An alternative to retribution can be found in rituals that seek to mend harm that has been done to victims by gaining perpetrators' contrition, enabling transgressors to accept responsibility for their crimes and to reenter society by confessing guilt and paying penance. This "restorative justice" paradigm is an alternative to retribution.

In historical and anthropological senses, it is probably wrong to call one paradigm "old" and the other "new," but dominant forms of justice in the post–World War II period in developed countries are built around the retributive model. Drives for penal reform, expanded concern with victims first in civil-law and then in common-law jurisdictions, and then the challenges of transitional justice in the late 1980s and the 1990s brought restorative justice into the mainstream. These two justice paradigms, the retributive and the restorative, have converged into a set of demands and expectations that were incorporated into the Rome Statute. To make it easier to refer to them, I call these streams the "old" (retributive) and "new" (restorative) paradigms.

The Old (Retributive) Justice Paradigm

Retributive justice in its modern form implies a theory of society, law, and criminality. Retributive justice focuses on criminals and their crimes. Punishment constitutes the criminal's payment to society for infractions against the community. Once society is thus compensated, the (former) criminal's relationship with society comes back into equilibrium. The crime is a crime against order in society, a violation of law, not against victims per se. Moreover, if punishment is proportionate to the crime, which it should be, perpetrators lose whatever benefits they sought to gain from their acts. People who might otherwise consider embarking on crime should be deterred by the knowledge that the benefits didn't outweigh the costs. Enforcement and deterrence are coeval. In the criminal phase of judicial proceedings, the prosecutor presses charges on behalf of the state; the victims are objects but not subjects of proceedings.

The New (Restorative) Justice Paradigm

Critics of retribution argue that the model is flawed for normal society, but even more so for societies emerging from periods of oppression and large-scale illegality. Mending transitional societies requires much broader efforts than the perpetrator-focused retributive model attempts. Because criminal authoritarian regimes victimize large numbers of people, reestablishing justice should entail restoring victims to full membership in society, recognizing and compensating the wrongs done to them.[49] Because large numbers of people become perpetrators of crimes under such regimes – particularly members of security forces – transitional societies need a way to rehabilitate them too. Because part of what needs to be set right in a transitional process is the perversion of history that denied full personhood to victims and whitewashed the crimes of the state, a full, fair, and inclusive history of the old regime needs to be created. These elements – victim orientation, perpetrator rehabilitation, full exposure of history – became the core elements of the restorative justice movement.

The retributive–restorative dichotomy, in a conventional or a transitional context, can be illustrated with the following chart:[50]

Traditional Justice (Retributive and Rehabilitative)	Restorative Justice
Victims are peripheral to the process.	Victims are central to the process.
The focus is on punishing or on treating an offender.	The focus is on repairing the harm between an offender and victim, and perhaps also an offender and a wider community.
The community is represented by the state.	Community members or organizations take a more active role.
The process is characterized by adversarial relationships among the parties.	The process is characterized by dialogue and negotiation among the parties.

The old justice paradigm pursues as its primary objective holding criminals accountable for their acts. The objective of accountability is the opposite of permitting impunity – allowing criminals to get away with

---

[49] An indicator of the trend toward rethinking the role of victims in criminal proceedings was a UN General Assembly, "Declaration of Basic Principles of Justice for Victims of Crime and Abuse of Power," General Assembly Resolution 40/34 of November 29, 1985.

[50] Daly, "Revisiting the Relationship between Retributive and Restorative Justice" (2000).

their crimes. Even while transitional and restorative justice movements developed, human rights advocates, such as those found in the leading international nongovernmental organizations Amnesty International and Human Rights Watch, sought to "end impunity" for violations of international criminal law. Human rights organizations generally have been suspicious of justice mechanisms that diverge too far from the mainstream of retributive justice because, with nonjudicial proceedings, they may not uphold due process standards, they may contribute to impunity by leaving perpetrators unnamed or by amnestying or pardoning perpetrators, and, in their pursuits, they may taint evidence in ways that destroy its evidentiary value in court. In short, retributive justice advocates fear that restorative justice methods may contribute to impunity.

Transitional Justice Mechanisms

Some of the Nuremberg trials' aims included what would now be called transitional justice objectives. The Allies sought to demonstrate to the German population, as well as the rest of the world, that those most responsible for Nazi crimes could be separated from the general population and punished.

In the transitions from authoritarianism in the 1980s and 1990s, fledgling and restored governments implemented a range of justice mechanisms.[51] The Nuremberg model didn't easily fit the newer transitional contexts because Nuremberg was made possible by absolute military conquest. Negotiated transitions of power often left former leaders free, with parts of their establishments intact and in power in government bureaucracies. In some of the transitions, officials of the old regimes were granted amnesties, immunity from prosecution, or pardons. New rulers couldn't act without regard to the old power centers. In many cases, the police and judicial systems were inherited from the old system and remained largely under the control of people who had operated them before. They could not be expected to carry out judicial processes against their former superiors. In some of the transitional societies, judicial capacity was very limited, masses of victims and large numbers of perpetrators would conceivably have overwhelmed them.

Formal judicial processes might be the sine qua non of justice, but in transitional situations they were often impractical. In Argentina, investigations began, but the threat from the generals to the state was considered so serious that proceedings were suspended. In Chile, Augusto Pinochet left

---

[51] Hayner, *Unspeakable Truths: Confronting State Terror and Atrocity* (2002).

office having passed a full amnesty for himself and his cohorts. In Guatemala and Chile, investigative commissions reported on the crimes of the past, but they did not publicize the names of the criminals. In South Africa, the negotiated transition produced the Truth and Reconciliation Commission (SATRC). The SATRC could award amnesty to those who committed "grave violations" of human rights on the condition that they testified voluntarily and fully about their crimes, which had to have been politically motivated. The idea was that testimony by some would motivate (defensive) testimony by others, and thus a fuller record of the apartheid era could be obtained than would be possible through trials, especially since the justice system was compromised and inadequate.

Dilemmas of Transitional Justice

Peace versus Justice

Political pragmatists, particularly those engaged in seeking a cessation of violence within societies or between them, often argue that justice in the sense of a reckoning between perpetrators and victims can wait: What is needed in the short run is peace, and peace may require political accommodation. What sense is there in engaging justice mechanisms when violence and instability continue? Dictators and warlords need a way out – to condemn them to trial will rigidify their resistance to political settlement. Pardons and amnesties may be needed to gain peace.

Partisans of traditional justice accuse the pragmatists of opening the door to impunity, sacrificing justice and accountability. The common wisdom of transitional justice advocates is that some form of justice, by which they mean the exposure of the perpetrators and the rehabilitation of victims of oppression, is necessary for long-term peace within society, but they are often stuck between those pursuing peace and those pursuing traditional legal accountability. Transitional justice advocates generally seek a peaceful transition of power and social stabilization, but accept the idea that blanket amnesties or pardons amount to impunity, which perpetuates psychological damage to victims and leaves residues of hostility that may motivate future violence.

The examples of post-Franco Spain, in which a reckoning from the fascist period has still not taken place; Cambodia, where twenty years after the mass killings trial processes have yet to start; and Mozambique, where murderous RENAMO (Mozambican National Resistance) factions were ultimately amalgamated into coalition governments, are cited as cases demonstrating the practicality of awaiting peace before pursuing justice. The 1996 Dayton negotiations, in which Yugoslav President Slobodan Milosevic was a primary interlocutor, is another example of peace negotiations taking priority over indictment of a war crimes suspect.

On the other hand, had the perpetrators of the Cambodian atrocities, Mozambican depredations, or Yugoslav wars been certain of punishment before they set out on their courses of action, would they have perhaps demurred? Certainty of justice might promote peace – it's the creation of certainty that's the problem, and to create it requires major changes in the operation, if not the nature, of international society. Tensions between peace and justice remain.

Truth and Justice

Critics of traditional (retributive) justice mechanisms argue that courts produce only partial truth, focused on perpetrators and their crimes. This "micro-truth" misses broader, social truths that are likely to help heal societies.[52] Micro-truth is fact-oriented and perpetrator-focused and deals with witnesses and victims only to the extent necessitated to establish perpetrators' guilt. Restorative justice advocates argue that mechanisms such as truth commissions can produce historical records that help rehabilitate victims and enable perpetrators to reenter society. Such truth requires fuller contextualization, testimony by perpetrators and victims, and other information that is normally irrelevant to traditional prosecution. For transitional justice advocates, the establishment of a historical record may trump traditional retribution as an objective, opening the way for the use of amnesties if they can produce useful information as in South Africa's Truth and Reconciliation Commission.

In South Africa, 7,112 petitions resulted in only 849 amnesties, and advocates regarded it as a stringent process. However, although the legal alternative to being amnestied could have been prosecution in regular courts, very few prosecutions took place, and large areas of the apartheid regime's misdeeds remained obscured even after the end of the SATRC. In particular, while extensive exposure of policy activities followed from testimony for amnesty by senior police officials, South Africa Defense Force records were never revealed, and defense officials were not lured by the amnesty offer. The highest-level prosecution, of former Defense Minister General Magnus Malan, ended in acquittal in a trial viewed by critics as

---

[52] Sachs, Fourth D. T. Lakdawala Memorial Lecture (New Delhi, December 18, 1998), typescript text.

subverted by weak prosecution. Transitional justice in South Africa lauded but sacrificed full accountability.[53]

END OF THE COLD WAR AND RESURFACING
OF INTEREST IN AN ICC

The late-1980s convergence of West and East bloc rhetoric about human rights universality permitted restarting of ILC consideration of an international criminal court, stimulated by rising concerns about transnational crimes of all sorts – significantly including the international drug trade as experienced by Caribbean states. In 1989, Trinidad and Tobago Prime Minister Arthur Robinson (who was trained as a lawyer and during 1972–87 had been the executive director of an NGO called the Foundation for the Establishment of the International Criminal Court) proposed to the UN General Assembly the "establishment of an international criminal court with jurisdiction to prosecute and punish individuals and entities who engage in, inter alia, the illicit trafficking in narcotic drugs across national borders."[54]

Robinson drafted a motion for the General Assembly with the help of his friend and longtime ICC advocate Robert Woetzel, former Nuremberg prosecutor Benjamin Ferencz, and international criminal law expert Professor M. Cherif Bassiouni, proposing that the ICC idea be studied by the International Law Commission (ILC). On December 4, 1989, the General Assembly adopted the motion requesting the ILC, when considering at its next session the Draft Code of Offenses against the Peace and Security of Mankind, "to address the question of establishing an international criminal court or other international criminal trial mechanism with jurisdiction over persons alleged to have committed crimes which may be covered under such a code, including persons engaged in illicit trafficking in narcotic drugs across national frontiers."[55] The key phrasing was to ask the ILC to consider a court or other mechanism to try crimes *including*, but not limited

---

[53] The ideal of accountability may, however, simply not have been attainable. See Schiff, "Do Truth Commissions Promote Accountability or Impunity? The Case of the South African Truth and Reconciliation Commission" (2002), 325–44.

[54] Glasius, *The International Criminal Court: A Global Civil Society Achievement*, 11; *World Leader Magazine*, "Biography, Arthur N. R. Robinson" (1994).

[55] UN General Assembly, "International Criminal Responsibility of Individuals and Entities Engaged in Illicit Trafficking in Narcotic Drugs across National Frontiers and Other Transnational Criminal Activities: Establishment of an International Criminal Court with Jurisdiction over Such Crimes" (1989).

to, illicit drug trafficking. This allowed ICC advocates to develop a proposal much broader than one limited to drug crimes.

The outbreak of the post-Yugoslavia wars in 1991, followed by the paralysis of an international machinery for conflict resolution and peace enforcement, resounded through the international media in demands to the major powers to do something about the conflict, especially as evidence accumulated of large-scale attacks against civilian populations by army and militia forces under the command of nationalist leaders.

Professor Bassiouni, a leading advocate and codifier of international criminal law (and an author of the 1987 UN Convention Against Torture), proposed and eventually became the head of a UN Commission of Experts on the Situation in Yugoslavia.[56] The Commission's efforts, against great political and material obstruction, led ultimately to the Security Council's creation in 1993 of the ad hoc Criminal Tribunal for the Former Yugoslavia, the first international criminal tribunal since Nuremberg.

With subsequent creation in 1994 of the Rwanda tribunal, states overcame their inhibitions to prosecute individuals suspected of international crimes. The end of the Cold War permitted development of international judicial institutions that previously had been rejected because of the fear they would be used for political purposes by one ideological bloc against the other.

Meanwhile, in 1993, the ILC prepared a draft ICC statute under the direction of Special Rapporteur James Crawford.[57] Professor Bassiouni assembled an NGO Committee of Experts in Siracusa, Italy, to further develop the draft, and the General Assembly considered it in 1994.[58] With questions and comments from states (very prominently including the United States), the General Assembly sent it back for further consideration. The General Assembly also directed that a preparatory committee begin meeting to set the stage for a conference for final negotiation of a statute for the ICC in 1998, to be held in Rome.

As the drafts for an ICC Statute moved toward the Rome Conference, several streams of interrelated thought converged. After Nuremberg, individual culpability, command responsibility, rejection of a "superior orders" defense, and the idea of crimes against humanity and crimes against peace were mainstreamed. With the Declaration of Human Rights, activism of

---

[56] Hazan, *Justice in a Time of War: The True Story Behind the International Criminal Tribunal for the Former Yugoslavia* (2004), 46–7.
[57] Glasius, op cit., 9.
[58] Bassiouni, "Historical Survey 1919–1998" (1999), 20–31.

NGOs, and conventions against apartheid and torture, additional tributary crimes joined the flow.

NGO activists, lawyers, jurists, scholars, and other observers who had participated in or observed transitional justice mechanisms at work channeled their concerns for addition of victims' rights, reparation, and reconciliation into meetings that considered the objectives of the planned Court. Still other NGOs interested in gender rights, gender crimes, and child soldiers and their conscription contributed even more issues to the mixture.

In the initially becalmed post–Cold War diplomatic environment, new atrocities and growing international attention added momentum to what had been the project of a small group of international lawyers to convert conceptual agreement into generally accepted positive international criminal law. The many streams of IHL, ICL, retributive, restorative, and transitional justice poured into draft texts to be discussed and considered at formal and informal meetings leading up to the Rome Conference. To the surprise of many participants and observers, on July 17, 1998, the negotiators at Rome broke through the final blockages to agreement, and their efforts enabled the Rome Statute of the ICC to be opened for signature and ratification.

EXPLAINING THE GATHERING TIDE

Describing the gathering stream of ideas about international criminal law as the progress of a river enables the use of linked metaphors with some apt characteristics. Obstructions, for instance the Cold War, temporarily hindered the flow, but as time went on, the current was restored. Tributaries, such as restorative justice, added volume, but sometimes made it harder to confine the river within traditional banks – the "softer" law of truth commissions shares some objectives with traditional trial justice, but it isn't part of the old mainstream.

The metaphor helps illustrate but does not explain. For explanation, the discussion needs to examine the motives and characteristics of human action, individual and collective. Constructivist, realist, and neoliberal institutionalist viewpoints help. The paramount challenge is to explain how nonmaterial objectives without clear advantages for states as sovereign actors could motivate those states to create an international organization. A hard-edged national interest of powerful states cannot be shown to have dominated these developments, nor did weaker states coalesce to counteract the powerful. States were occasionally important, but what seems to have propelled the flow of international law to its convergence in Rome was a gathering tide of ideas.

Constructivists

For constructivists, the evolution of international law is evidence for the existence of an international society and growth of collective norms that redefine national interests and lead to creation of new international institutions. Martha Finnemore and Kathryn Sikkink[59] argue that norms emerge as a consequence of *norm entrepreneurs*, gather adherents as a consequence of *norm leadership* and, if they become generalized, move beyond a tipping point to become a *norm cascade*, which leads to the internalization of the norm as part of normal, expected behavior. International humanitarian law norms have followed this pattern. By the time the ICC Statute negotiations commenced, the norms were little in question; however, the range of the rules and the mechanism for implementing them remained highly controversial.

Realists

Realists generally view international law as an emanation of power, motivated by the quest for relative gain, not by altruism or social consciousness. A powerful state will push others to abide by laws that are to the advantage of the hegemon and will ignore or oppose laws' application to themselves; therefore, law has no compelling quality and is simply a tool of politics and power. Weak states will coalesce around laws designed to constrain the powerful, but will throw them over should circumstances change.

The American structural realist school, exemplified by Kenneth Waltz,[60] argues that states are part of a *system*, but a system is not a society. States are utility maximizers acting in an anarchic structure and thus will accede only to arrangements from which they benefit in relative terms. They will be willing at any moment to defect from a collective that no longer serves their purposes. International law will have no compelling quality.

British realism is more moderate. International relations theorist Hedley Bull, for example, argues there are three basic values all societies endorse – freedom from violence, the dependability of contract, and stability of property. Since all humans accept these norms, a form of human society – that is, a communal consciousness – exists, beyond mere mechanical interaction.[61]

---

[59] Finnemore and Sikkink, "International Norms and Political Change" (1998).
[60] Waltz, *Man, the State, and War: A Theoretical Analysis* (1959); Waltz, *Theory of International Politics* (1979).
[61] Bull, *The Anarchical Society*, 3rd ed. (2003).

Even though states answer to no higher authority (they exist in anarchy), they can constitute a society because, being human institutions, they inherently ascribe to these common human understandings, and within such a society, law is possible but very limited. The ICC Statute was negotiated, and the Court has come into existence. However, the Statute includes strong protections for state sovereignty, in the forms of limited Court jurisdiction, checks on the Court's independent power, and the necessity of states' cooperation for the ICC to succeed.

Neoliberal Institutionalists

Neoliberal institutionalists explain law as a tool to reduce the realm of disorder in international relations, making it a pragmatic step for states concerned not only with relative power, but even more with absolute well-being. Legal institutions arise as states seek to stabilize their relations by replacing power political conflict with orderly legal processes – labeled by some observers the process of "legalization."[62] Once state interests have been defined (a process described by the constructivists when norms, rather than material objectives, are the interests) and protected (as realists explain), the neoliberal institutionalist framework is most useful to explore the subsequent pattern of organization construction and the operational challenges and dynamics of the organizations thus created.

The River of Justice

The river of justice widened from the inflow of norms as people broadened their conceptions of what it is to be human and to be civilized. They shaped their identities around consensus over an expanding set of normative conceptions. The currents included people's rights as against sovereigns, the ethic of accountability, and the social responsibilities of both retributive and restorative justice, all while maintaining the institution of state sovereignty. Once the norms were established and institutionalization began, in the form of international negotiations, the problem was to craft a statute that would incorporate these streams and be capable of implementation by an international organization. Prototypes for a statute already existed in the ILC drafts, and in the statutes and rules of the two ad hoc criminal tribunals, which are the topics of Chapter 2.

---

[62] Abbott et al., "The Concept of Legalization" (2000), 401–19.

Learning from the Yugoslavia and Rwanda Tribunals

Reacting to murderous conflict and genocide in Yugoslavia and Rwanda, the Security Council created the first international criminal tribunals since Nuremberg and Tokyo. At the same time, the ICC Statute discussions continued to percolate in the International Law Commission, among legal experts, and within states and nongovernmental organizations. A community of lawyers, activists, and international organization officials interested in international criminal law congregated around the tribunals and sought to instill their expertise and experience into the construction of the ICC Statute. The leading lesson of the tribunals was that, in contrast to Cold War intransigence, Security Council members could agree to create international criminal tribunals, and then agree on the mechanisms needed to establish and operate them. With help from states, suspects could be apprehended and brought to court. A paramount negative lesson was that state cooperation, especially for providing financial support and for bringing suspects to court, was crucial but not easily obtained. The tribunals struggled to recruit, retain, and manage staff, lawyers, and judges and to meld the skills of people from differing legal and social backgrounds into effective organizations.

Once the tribunals began operating, many people in former Yugoslavia and Rwanda remained suspicious, believing the tribunals were illegitimate, politicized, and biased. Those interested in cooperating with the tribunals feared retribution, witness protection was problematic, and potential witnesses often refused to cooperate. Organizationally highly independent from the rest of the United Nations, the tribunals' management of finances, records, and personnel was chaotic and, in some cases, corrupt.

Although the tribunals operated during intense ICC Statute negotiations, not all their lessons were learned quickly or clearly enough to be incorporated in the Statute. Some of the tribunals' shortcomings were reproduced in the Court, but some flowed from the existential contradictions embedded in institutions of international justice and thus were perhaps unavoidable for both the tribunals and the ICC.

This chapter discusses the tribunals' mandates, organization and leadership, tribulations, and innovations. It focuses on the experiences of the tribunals most instructive to the ICC, those recognized early on and incorporated into the ICC, and those understood subsequently that affect the ICC's operations. In conclusion, I argue first that creation of the tribunals was motivated more by decision makers' identities (as constructivists would argue) than from materially defined national interest (that realists would expect). Second, I contend that, as neoliberal institutionalists would predict, the tribunals acquired a momentum of their own that affected states' decision making. Third, I maintain that political and organizational dynamics constitute limiting conditions for all organizations, including those pursuing nonmaterial objectives. The chapter ends with an overview of how the ICC Statute negotiators responded to the tribunals' perceived shortcomings.

THE TRIBUNALS' MANDATES

The UN Security Council created the International Criminal Tribunal for the Former Yugoslavia and the International Criminal Tribunal for Rwanda in response to specific events and for limited purposes. The ICTY was created in 1993 to pursue individuals suspected of committing war crimes, genocide, and crimes against humanity in the context of conflicts in former Yugoslavia from 1991 onward. Even while the ICTY began to operate, the wars rumbled on, and further crimes were being committed. Although the tribunal's proponents hoped that the ICTY would help to deter crimes by making potential perpetrators aware they might face international justice, detractors claimed the tribunal was just a fig leaf for major power inaction to stop the conflict.

The Security Council created the ICTR in 1994 in the wake of the genocide in Rwanda. The mass killings (of more than 800,000 people) were over by the time the Rwanda tribunal was set up, so unlike the ICTY, it was engaged in retrospective justice. Similar to its action in creating the ICTY, though, the Security Council's decision to establish the ICTR followed failures to take action that might have prevented the killings or reduced the magnitude of the carnage.

Both tribunals appeared to be motivated by leaders' guilt. The failures to act were not due to a paucity of options or to misunderstanding of what was transpiring – intelligence organizations and decision makers in major states had excellent information about events in both Yugoslavia and Rwanda before and during the events for which prosecutions were eventually instituted.[1] The problem was a lack of political will to intervene and a failure to be decisive. Realist calculations – insufficient interests at stake for countries capable of intervening in the conflicts – prevented the UN or other organizations from devoting significant political or material resources to intervention. The failure to act, however, was increasingly embarrassing to leaders as their publics became aware through media (especially television) reports about what was going on. Although national (system-level) interests were not engaged, domestic political concerns eventually drove states in the Security Council to establish the two tribunals. Even this measure (in the Yugoslavia case) was taken only after resistance to it was skirted through private initiatives (in support of M. Cherif Bassiouni's Experts Commission, described further later), and nongovernmental organizations' efforts explicitly to make inaction a political liability.[2]

Both tribunals were given the power to prosecute persons "responsible for serious violations of international humanitarian law."[3] The tribunals' statutes differed from each other slightly because the ICTY dealt with both international and internal conflict, while the Rwanda tribunal dealt only with crimes committed in a noninternational conflict. When the Security Council finally established the Yugoslavia tribunal,[4] the justification was that the criminality taking place in the region constituted "a threat to international peace and security," and that putting an end to such crimes would "contribute to the restoration and maintenance of peace." This justification enabled the tribunal to be created on the basis of UN Charter Chapter VII, International Peace and Security, and as a Security Council resolution, all UN member states were bound to cooperate.

Similarly for Rwanda, the Security Council resolved that a failure to punish the crimes of 1994 would be a threat to peace and security; however, the resolution included a new, restorative justice element:[5] "The prosecution

---

[1] See Williams and Scharf, *Peace with Justice* (2002), 48; Melvern, *Conspiracy to Murder* (2004), 128.

[2] See Human Rights Watch, *War Crimes in Bosnia-Hercegovina*, Volume I (1992), HRW Index No. 0839.

[3] Statute of the ICTY, Article 1; Statute of the ICTR, Article 1.

[4] UN Security Council Resolutions 808 and 827 of 1993.

[5] As noted in Chapter 1, retributive (old) justice refers to indicting, apprehending, charging, trying, and sentencing of criminals in order to punish and deter criminality. In retributive justice, victims can serve as witnesses but are not a primary focus of legal process. Restorative (new) justice is victim-centered, seeking to restore victims to society, including them in justice processes as participants, and mending the rent social fabric. See section entitled "Justice Paradigm" in this chapter.

of persons responsible for serious violations of international humanitarian law would ... contribute to the process of national reconciliation."[6] Both organizations' mandates created implementation problems.

The Security Council left to the tribunal judges development of the tribunals' rules of procedure and evidence. By 1998, critics of the tribunals argued that they were too independent of states' oversight, and the judges had too much latitude in their abilities to modify the rules under which they themselves, and the tribunals generally, proceeded. The negotiators of the ICC Statute spelled out Court procedures in much greater detail than did the tribunal statutes and shifted rule-making responsibility to the ICC's quasi-legislative organ, the Assembly of States Parties to the Treaty, rather than leaving it (as in the tribunals) to the judges. (Considerable discretion remained with the ICC judges, however, in their ability to interpret those rules.)

Because of uncertainties in Yugoslavia about the status and connections of various fighting groups to old and new political units, the distinction between crimes committed in a context of international conflict and those of internal conflicts eroded. In a different way, but with a similar result, the Security Council established an international interest in an internal conflict by creating the Rwanda tribunal. The ICC Statute explicitly deals with both kinds of conflict. The two tribunals broadened the scope of the crimes prosecuted in part in reaction to victims' advocacy groups that also pressed restorative justice principles. The ICC Statute adopted a new (restorative) justice logic, along with traditional (retributive) justice objectives, committing the Court to victim-centered justice.

Although major lessons from the tribunals were incorporated into the ICC Statute, important differences remain. Perhaps most significantly, even though the limited-purpose and temporary tribunals had formal jurisdictional primacy over state procedures (under Security Council authority), the standing ICC was to be complementary to (without primacy over) domestic jurisdictions. Established under its own Statute, rather than under UN Charter Chapter VII, ICC jurisdictional definitions are quite different from those of the two ad hoc tribunals and were highly controversial in negotiation.

ORGANIZATION AND LEADERSHIP

The international tribunals' structures imposed management problems that the ICC statute negotiators attempted to ameliorate, but they still plague the Court. The ICC thus learned from the tribunals, but the lessons include

---

[6] UN Security Council Resolution 955 of 1994.

some difficult truths. To expose these truths, this section first briefly describes the structure of the tribunals and the Court. It then explains how this differs from domestic court systems, the consequences of these differences, and the nature and outcome of efforts to solve the problem in the ICC.

Tribunal and Court Structure

The two ad hoc tribunals' statutes drew heavily on International Law Commission drafts being developed for the ICC.[7] The tribunals' statutes (like the 1994 ILC ICC draft) created tripartite organizations made up of Chambers (judges), the Office of the Prosecutor (headed by the Chief Prosecutor), and the Registry (headed by the Registrar).[8] For the tribunals, the judges are elected to four-year terms by the General Assembly from a list supplied by the Security Council. These individuals, who were nominated by the states, were to be persons of "high moral character, impartiality and integrity and who possess the qualifications required in their respective countries for appointment to the highest judicial offices."[9] The Security Council was supposed to consider judicial candidates' experiences in criminal and international law, including international humanitarian and human rights law, when nominating them for General Assembly election to the tribunals' chambers. The permanent judges elect a President (to once-renewable two-year terms) who would preside over the Appeals Chamber and would assign the other judges to Chambers.[10] The judges "shall adopt rules of procedure and evidence for the conduct of the pretrial phase of the proceedings, trials and appeals, the admission of evidence, the protection of victims and witnesses and other appropriate matters."[11]

The tribunals' statutes describe the Office of the Prosecutor and the Registries, the processes of investigation and indictment, trial proceedings, accused's rights, victim and witness protection, judgment, penalties, appellate proceedings, review proceedings, enforcement of sentences, and conditions for pardon or commutation of sentences. The Security Council resolution requires states to cooperate with the international tribunals in the investigation and prosecution of the accused, saying that states "shall comply without undue delay with any request for assistance or an order

---

[7] Schabas, *An Introduction to the International Criminal Court*, 2nd ed. (2004), 11.
[8] Statute of the ICTY, Article 11; Statute of the ICTR, Article 10.
[9] Statute of the ICTY, Article 12; Statute of the ICTR, Article 11.
[10] Statute of the ICTY, Article 14; Statute of the ICTR, Article 13.
[11] Statute of the ICTY, Article 15; Statute of the ICTR, Article 14.

issued by a Trial Chamber."[12] The tribunals' expenses "shall be borne by the regular budget of the United Nations in accordance with Article 17 of the Charter."[13] The mandatory language did not guarantee, however, that vigorous support would be forthcoming.

Like the tribunals' statutes, the ICC Statute creates judicial Chambers (and Presidency), the Office of the Prosecutor (and Chief Prosecutor), and the Registry (headed by the Registrar). Unlike the tribunals, the Registrar in the ICC is elected by the judges and serves under the authority of the President (a change explained in more detail later).

Tribunals without Context

The tribunals' and Court's lack of the kind of governmental framework within which domestic justice systems operate creates two sets of problems: an authority vacuum and management uncertainty.

Authority Vacuum

For the ICTY and ICTR, the Security Council served as a surrogate legislature, albeit a delinquent one. Especially in their early years of operation, the tribunals struggled to gain international support because the Security Council largely ignored them, and they suffered from underfunding and a lack of administrative oversight. The tribunals' statutes left to the judges the development of their own rules of evidence and procedure, thus mixing judicial and legislative functions. Because the judges were designing their own legal processes and executing them, critics could question the legitimacy and neutrality of their proceedings.[14]

For the ICC, founded under an international treaty, the Assembly of States Parties (ASP) serves the function of a legislative body. With the responsibility to establish rules of procedure and evidence and with the power of the purse, the authority vacuum experienced by the tribunals was not reproduced in the ICC treaty structure. Even though judges have some latitude in interpreting the rules, they do not invent their procedures as they go along, and the Court and the ASP are learning to coordinate the budgetary process. How the ASP will relate to the Court is still being worked out because the Court, like the tribunals, has a high degree of autonomy.

[12] Statute of the ICTY, Article 29; Statute of the ICTR, Article 28.
[13] Statute of the ICTY, Article 13; Statute of the ICTR, Article 30.
[14] Raab and Bevers, "The International Criminal Court and the Separation of Powers" (2006), 98–104.

States disagree over the amount of oversight they should exert over the ICC, and many of them are concerned about not intruding on the independence of its judicial processes. The situation appears to be more stable than that of the ad hoc tribunals, but some state representatives, observers, and even Court officials believe that a higher level of state engagement would benefit the organization (see Chapter 6).

Management Uncertainty

The lack of a governmental apparatus creates a tendency toward management chaos or paralysis. The tribunals and the Court, with their tripartite structure of Chambers, Prosecution, and Registry, seek to keep a firewall between the judges, who must maintain neutrality, and the prosecution, which needs to be independent. In domestic systems, law enforcement is separated organizationally from justice procedures – the courts and judges are organized under a separate ministry or department from the police and prosecutors, so judges maintain distance from enforcement, enhancing their neutrality, and investigators and prosecutors are organizationally independent, enhancing their ability to pursue transgressors. These tripartite organizations suffer from the tensions caused by efforts to operate a single organization efficiently, while retaining the necessary internal separation between their major organs.

Because the Presidents of the tribunals (and the Court) formally head the organizations, while the Prosecutors set the pace of action by bringing cases, presidential and prosecutorial policies may come into conflict, with no clear way for such conflicts to be resolved. Similarly, when Registrars clash with Presidents or Prosecutors, Problems arise in maintaining prosecutorial independence as well as judicial impartiality (toward cases that may come before the President as judge). The three organs of the tribunals and Court are locked in tight embrace, while simultaneously needing to delineate responsibilities clearly and attempt to run their organizations efficiently.

TRIBUNAL TRIBULATIONS

The ad hoc tribunals' rules were devised hurriedly primarily by experts from the United States and Great Britain.[15] As a consequence, apart from lacking juries, they are built on common-law blueprints of adversarial proceedings mediated by neutral, "referee" judges. The pattern of prosecutorial initiative in bringing and shaping cases in the tribunals reflects the dominance

[15] Williams and Scharf, *Peace with Justice* (2002), 106.

of common-law concepts in their creation. By the time they had been operating for a few years, and the ICC Statute was under intensive nego-tiation, civil-law advocates sought to tilt the balance of the new court back toward their tradition. In the ICC, a Pre-Trial Chamber of judges was interposed between the Prosecutor and the Trial Chambers, opening at least the possibility of greater judicial involvement in shaping cases.

Coordination between the tribunals' organs was poor. The ICTYs judges were empaneled in November 1993 and set to work on their rules of pro-cedure. Appointment of the Prosecutor turned out to be problematic. The United Kingdom opposed the obvious choice for the position, Professor M. Cherif Bassiouni, the head of the Experts Commission who had reported to the Secretary-General about crimes taking place in the former Yugoslavia. The British feared that Bassiouni would quickly move to indict Serbian officials who were then involved in the (ill-fated) Vance–Owen peace nego-tiations.[16] The first Prosecutor, South Africa's Richard Goldstone, took up his post in summer 1994, following appointment by the UN Secretary-General. Relieved that a prosecutor had finally been appointed, President Judge Antonio Cassese sought to speed judicial operations; Prosecutor Goldstone, however, was consumed with building external support for the tribunal.[17] Tensions between the Chambers and the Office of the Prosecutor (OTP) continued even after cases were under way. Goldstone pursued a "bottom-up" strategy of seeking lower-level suspects before ascending to major suspected criminals, frustrating the judges. Even after Louise Arbour replaced Goldstone on October 1, 1995, tensions between judges and Pros-ecutor continued. The common-law structure of the tribunals lent weight to the independent Prosecutor, but the ability of the judges to write new rules meant that they could swing the pendulum back in their own direction when they decided to do so.

In both tribunals, the Registry, which is the administrative bureau, came under the direct authority of the Secretary-General of the United Nations, as the top administrative officer of the international organization. Particularly at the ICTR, the Registrar interpreted his administrative and budgetary role as establishing him as the executive officer of the tribunal. All hiring, expenditures, and logistical management flowed through the Registrar. The ICTR suffered from mismanagement and a lack of oversight. A 1997 UN Office of Internal Oversight Services (OIOS) investigation showed that the

---

[16] Ibid.
[17] Hazan, *Justice in a Time of War: The True Story behind the International Criminal Tribunal for the Former Yugoslavia* (2004), Chapter 3.

Registrar, dominating all activities by virtue of budgetary control, had brought the tribunal to a halt and was engaged in conflict with both the President and the Prosecutor.[18] The Secretary-General accepted the resignations of Registrar Andronico Adede and Deputy Prosecutor Honore Rakotomanana.[19]

The second Registrar, Agwu Okali, who had previously been Director of the UN Centre for Human Settlements (Habitat), immediately came into conflict with the judges and Prosecutor, wielding the same authority as had his predecessor. A major struggle for power ultimately resulted in his departure, the Secretary-General having acted only because of stringent pressure from then–President Judge Navathenem Pillay of South Africa. The terms of the conflict were very similar to the prior difficulties, with the tribunal all but crippled by a failure of the administrative apparatus to support the judicial and investigative activities, leaving crucial positions vacant or staffed by incompetent individuals and failing to develop effective document management and other necessary support systems for investigations and trials.[20]

In November 1999, Judge Claude Jorda was elected President of the ICTY. Concerned about the slow pace of trials, he proposed to the Security Council in June 2000 measures to streamline pretrial case preparation and to add temporary (*ad litem*) judges to the trial chambers to increase the number of simultaneous proceedings. Jorda argued that the tribunal should focus on leading suspects and, connected with this, promote the creation and turning over of other suspects to national tribunals. He believed that these measures could reduce by half the time needed for cases, and thus finish trials of first instance (that is, not including appeals) by the end of 2007, instead of an estimated 2019.[21] The Security Council adopted Jorda's recommendations in December 2000, and the package became known as the ICTY's "completion strategy."[22] The completion strategies are discussed in more detail later, but it is important to note here that the President's introduction of the idea did not sit comfortably with the Prosecutor. Prosecutor Carla del Ponte indicated that the Court could not itself fully determine the pace of activity because cases depended upon the speed with which indicted suspects could be apprehended, additional evidence

---

[18] UN General Assembly, "Financing of the International Criminal Tribunal for Rwanda," A/51/789 (1997).
[19] Allison, "News from the International War Crimes Tribunals" (1997).
[20] Cruvillier, "ICTR: A Wind of Change" (2001).
[21] Raab, "Evaluating the ICTY and Its Completion Strategy" (2005), 84–5.
[22] Ibid., 85; UN Security Council Resolution 1329, 2000.

could bring new cases to light, and time needed for both prosecution and defense was to some extent in the hands of the judges as they heard cases.

With the new completion strategy, the OTP increased its use of plea bargaining arrangements, assisted in the establishment of a Bosnia special war crimes tribunal, and began procedures to turn cases over to that Court. The process required that the OTP petition the Chambers for approval to send cases down to the local court; some of these were approved, but others were retained at the ICTY by judicial decision. (There was disagreement in some cases within the OTP whether such petitions should be submitted.)

In December 2000, the ICTY judges responded to the frictions of interorgan coordination, creating a Coordination Council, made up of the President, Registrar, and Prosecutor,[23] and a management committee of judges, the Registrar, Deputy Registrar and the Chief of Administration to "assist the President ... concerning all Registry activities relating to the administrative and judicial support provided to the Chambers and to the Judges," including in the preparation and implementation of the tribunal's budget, with the exception of budgetary lines specific to the activities of the OTP.[24]

Nonetheless, according to the ICTY's former Registrar, writing in 2004, the tribunals became generally regarded as "unwieldy instruments, with a cumbersome bureaucratic structure."[25] The independence of the Chambers, OTP, and Registry "created a problem of accountability on two levels." Since each of the organs is largely independent, they aren't answerable to each other, and the nominal head of the tribunal, the President, reports to the Security Council but is subject to little oversight. "The decentralization of power and accountability, coupled with the need to respect judicial and prosecutorial independence, have been chronic problems for which no solution has been found."[26]

In response to the problems of the tribunals, and in particular the overwhelming role of their Registrars, under the ICC Statute, the Registrar is elected by the judges[27] and reports to the President of the Court. The ICC early instituted a coordinating committee, made up of the President, Prosecutor, and Registrar, to ameliorate the problems of the tripartite organizational structure. As explained further in Chapter 4, organizational problems persist.

---

[23] Rule 23*bis*, ICTY, Rules of Procedure and Evidence, IT/32/Rev.36 (2005), 18.
[24] Rule 23*ter*, ICTY, Rules of Procedure and Evidence, IT/32/Rev.36 (2005), 19.
[25] Zacklin, "The Failings of ad Hoc International Tribunals" (2004), 542.
[26] Ibid., 543.
[27] Statute Article 43.

Judging the Judges

The process of selecting permanent judges for both ICTR and ICTY is a largely diplomatic one, in which states nominate candidates, and the Security Council selects a candidate list from among the nominees and forwards this list for election by the General Assembly by absolute majority vote. Permanent judges are elected for four years and can be reelected. The process has been criticized by observers who charge that neither the ICTY nor the ICTR have consistently empaneled the most qualified or experienced judges. States' diplomatic representatives have apparently viewed success in nomination of judges to the tribunals and to the Court as adding to their state's prestige – and thus elections have become exercises in campaigning and logrolling rather than the determination of expertise.

ICC judges are elected by the Assembly of States Parties for nine-year, nonrenewable terms. Despite criticism about the quality and qualifications of tribunal judges, the ASP election process for ICC judges is no less political than the General Assembly campaign and elections for the tribunals (see Chapter 4).

Prosecutorial Confusion, Poor Information Management

Under pressure from ICTY judges and public critics to begin trying suspects, Prosecutor Richard Goldstone moved against a target of opportunity in 1995. Dusko Tadic had been a rather low-level functionary of the Serb military who was suspected of participating in the severe mistreatment of Muslim prisoners in Bosnia. He was living in Germany, where his actions during the conflict were well-known, and German authorities willingly transferred him to The Hague. Goldstone argued that he was pursuing a "build up from the bottom" prosecution strategy; however, the case exacerbated observers' concerns that the tribunal would be useful only for catching the "small fry." They were worried that the tribunal would leave major transgressors free, protected by their political connections and NATO's reluctance to add to its operational mandate the problem of apprehending suspected war criminals. However, the Tadic case became important for the legal precedents set by the judges in the course of the trial. Tadic's defense included an attack on the tribunal's legality, and the Appeals Chamber used the opportunity unequivocally to establish the Court's legitimacy.[28]

---

[28] ICTY, "Decision on the Defense Motion for Interlocutory Appeal on Jurisdiction" (October 2, 1995), para. 55.

When Louise Arbour took over as Chief Prosecutor of the two tribunals in 1996, she strengthened prosecutorial operations, used public demands and media appearances to build support for the Court, and pressured major countries to take responsibility for implementing the tribunals' mandates. Her implicit threat to shame Western countries into supporting the Court helped the tribunals establish themselves as serious factors in international criminal justice. To make the threat clear, Arbour reversed her predecessor's pattern of issuing public indictments and then decrying failures to arrest suspects. She issued secret indictments, informed the International Force and Stabilization Force (IFOR and SFOR) authorities, and indicated that if arrests were not forthcoming, the secret indictments would be publicized, indicating to the public that the international forces had not acted to support the law. Resistance and opposition gradually gave way to arrests in late 1997.[29]

But even with the improved process of bringing suspects to The Hague seat of the ICTY and Arusha courtrooms of the ICTR, internal problems slowed prosecutions. Trial attorneys at the ICTY complained that the lack of prosecutorial direction led to collection by investigators of huge amounts of information that was, unfortunately, not explicitly tied to legal charges or cases. Thus, much of the information was ultimately unusable, and assembling cases for presentation in Court was hindered by inaccessibility, poor cross-referencing, and an excess of disorganized materials that needed to be reviewed in order to find the information necessary to build the cases.

Judges found that prosecutors, following common-law practice, tended to charge suspects with all possible crimes for which they could be held to account, resulting in lengthy indictments (in *Blaskic*, for example, more than sixty separate charges). These then required enormous evidentiary proof for conviction. No mechanisms existed in the formal structure of the Court to limit prosecution aims. Gradually the judges exerted increasing control over the proceedings, infusing the otherwise common-law (adversarial, accusatory)-dominated process with some of the conventions of civil-law (inquisitorial) systems.

For example, successive amendments to ICTY Rule 65 show the increasing involvement of judges in the early stages of cases. The original rule (1994) dealt with the provisional release of suspects under the authority of the Trial Chamber. In July 1997, the judges amended the rules, adding Rule 65*bis* under which the Trial Chamber (or a single judge thereof) would convene a "status conference" within 120 days of the initial appearance of

---

[29] Hazan, *Justice in a Time of War* (2004), 94–8.

the accused (and on 120 intervals thereafter) to expedite preparations for the trial, review the status of the case, and permit the accused to raise issues. The intention was to keep the process moving on a schedule not established by the Prosecutor, but under the compulsion of the rules.

In July 1998, Rule 65*ter* was added, and then amended in 1999 and 2001 with increasingly detailed procedures giving responsibility for expediting and monitoring the pretrial activities of prosecution and defense to a "pretrial judge." The rule moreover calls for the pretrial judge to develop a "work plan" with obligations and deadlines for the parties to the trial. Not only did it require a senior legal officer to file reports regarding progress and difficulties as the prosecution and defense moved toward trial, but it also required the prosecution to file a pretrial brief with summaries of evidence and the form of accountability to be adduced for each count against the accused, along with a statement of agreed facts not under contention by the two parties and a list of witnesses with various details about how they will be used in the trial. When the ICC Pre-Trial Chambers set about pressing the Prosecutor for more information about what he was doing, it appeared that they were seeking to duplicate this structure without it having been created in the rules of the new court.

Even as the judges sought to expedite the trials, due-process standards, prosecution and defense maneuvers, and the accumulated problems of connecting investigation evidence to prosecution cases continued to drag on the process. Objectives for efficient trials, due process for defendants, adequate scope for prosecution, appeals, and other incidental circumstances such as the health of defendants clashed throughout the tribunals' histories, perhaps most infamously demonstrated by the four-year-long prosecution of former Yugoslav President Slobodan Milosevic that ended with his death and the inconclusive termination of the trial in March 2006.

The negotiators of the ICC Statute implemented formally what had evolved in the ICTY/ICTR rules by establishing Pre-Trial Chambers along with the Trial and Appeals Chambers in the new Court. According to Claude Jorda, former President of the ICTY and a judge of the ICC from France, the Pre-Trial Chamber of the ICC "is the embryo of a true Investigative Chamber,"[30] a primary structure of civil law (and the French legal system). Chapters 6 and 7 describe the dynamics of the ICC Pre-Trial Chambers' relations with the Office of the Prosecutor; Judge Jorda has played a major role.

---

[30] Jorda, "The Major Hurdles and Accomplishments of the ICTY: What the ICC Can Learn from Them" (2004), 578.

Cooperation with States and International Institutions

International cooperation with the two tribunals was mandated by their creation under Chapter VII of the UN Charter by the Security Council. Formal requirements of cooperation, of course, don't produce action unless those who are supposed to cooperate decide to do so. For the ICTY, cooperation was needed from the governments controlling areas in which suspects were to be found, from governments of countries where crimes took place (and hence where evidence should be available), and from organizations working in these areas, such as outsider military forces (NATO, United Nations) that could locate suspects and help apprehend them.

Lack of cooperation has been a major hindrance for both tribunals. Political leaders in the states in which suspects and evidence were to be found sometimes opposed the operations of the tribunals, protected suspects, and kept information and evidence secret. The most glaring examples are Serbia's failure to apprehend, arrest, and transfer to the ICTY Serbian General Ratko Mladic and Bosnian Serb leader Radovan Karadzic, both charged with responsibility for, among other crimes, the massacre of more than 7,000 Bosnian Muslims at Srebrenica. Despite the indictments issued in 1995 by Louise Arbour, pressure from the European Union and United States, and the assertion by Prosecutor Carla del Ponte that the Serb government knew the men's locations and was protecting them, neither had been turned over to The Hague tribunal eleven years later. Prime Minister Vojislav Kostunica of Serbia has generally rejected the legitimacy of The Hague tribunal, using the refusal of cooperation as proof of his nationalist credentials.

In addition, international actors have only opportunistically supported the tribunals. Arrest of war crimes suspects has taken second place to other political priorities for peacekeeping and intervention forces, which have been reluctant to arrest suspects due to fears that this would inflame local resentments, possibly leading to armed confrontations, and could reduce the perception that the intervention forces were neutral. The rule of law took second place to the quest for the peace for which the intervention and peacekeeping forces were mandated. Louise Arbour and later Carla del Ponte both criticized NATO forces for avoiding confrontations with suspects and their supporters, even apparently permitting free passage to known indictees through checkpoints and across borders. For NATO to become involved would require command decisions establishing arrest as an objective for soldiers on the ground. This finally began to happen under the media pressure created by Louise Arbour in highly publicized actions such as her visit to the Kosovo border seeking entry in 1998 to document violations there.[31]

Resource Problems

Because of the difficulties of gaining financial and political support for the tribunals especially in their early years, the Chief Prosecutors[32] spent enormous amounts of time away from the direct prosecutorial aspects of their jobs and were instead leading diplomatic efforts seeking financial support, striving to convince countries and alliances to help apprehend suspects, and pressing for governmental cooperation with investigations in the territories where crimes were committed. During its first several years, the ICTY operated on a shoestring. Its budget had to be approved through the Advisory Committee on Administrative and Budgetary Questions (ACABQ), whose procedures, mandated by the United States in the early 1990s, requires consensus to pass the UN budget. The United States originally insisted on the condition in order to exert greater control over the UN budget; however, a quarrel erupted in the committee over whether the Security Council, by mandating General Assembly appropriation of funds for the tribunals, had overstepped its authority. In its first year of operation, compared to the $32.6 million requested by the Secretary-General for the ICTY, the General Assembly, at the behest of the ACABQ, appropriated only about $11 million.[33] Prosecutor Goldstone spent his first months in office seeking to raise the awareness of the Secretary-General and the UN bureaucracy about the needs of the tribunal. In addition, he raised contributions of $8.3 million from thirteen countries and the promise of services of fifty-three countries, mostly the United States; personnel were donated to the tribunal free of charge.[34] Nonetheless the funding problems continued to be so serious that the OTP was initially unable to pursue vigorous investigations into the site of the Srebrenica massacre in the summer of 1995, and the Tadic case, slated to begin in November, had to be delayed until the subsequent May due to a shortage of funds for defense counsel and investigators.

---

[31] Hazan, op cit., 125-7.
[32] Richard Goldstone, 1994–1995; Louise Arbour, 1995–1999; Carla del Ponte, both ICTY and ICTR, 1999–2003; Carla del Ponte, ICTY only, 2003–current; Hassan Jallow, ICTR, 2003–current.
[33] Williams and Scharf, *Peace with Justice* (2002), 110.
[34] Ibid., 111.

In August 1995, the General Assembly decided to shift half of the tribunals' budgets to the peacekeeping budget, which circumvented the ACABQ. From then, the financial situation eased for both tribunals. The ICTY reached its peak size in 2003 with an annual budget of approximately $130 million and a staff complement of more than 1,060 official UN posts.[35] The Rwanda tribunal peaked in 2006 at an annual budget of approximately $130 million and 1,040 official UN posts.[36]

By 1999, Security Council members were becoming nervous about the expanding budgets and lengthening estimates of time necessary to fulfill the mandates of the two tribunals. The judges too were concerned about the slow pace of trials, and both tribunals set about developing plans for bringing their activities to a close. Their completion strategies and the discussions and innovations that followed filtered directly into thinking about the ICC as it began operations after 2002.

The principles behind the strategies are (a) to focus on high-level viola-tors, (b) to turn cases over to local tribunals when possible, especially those of lower-level functionaries, (c) to limit cases to the most important charges rather than saturating the cases with all possible charges that then need to be presented in court, and (d) to use judicial authority to expedite court presentations by limiting extraneous testimony, limiting cross-examination, encouraging defense and prosecution to submit agreed facts on paper, and requiring both sides to submit information to the judges about their planned courses in trial. The ICTY/ICTR strategies do not establish direction from above (the Security Council) or within (the judiciary) about case choice or charges. The principle of Prosecutor independence has been well main-tained, but within the constraints of a hiring freeze and increasing pressure to hold down the budgets.

In 2005, tribunal completion strategies that included "joining of cases with a similar crime base and the conduct of trials with multiple accused"[37] were reaffirmed to the General Assembly. For the Rwanda tribunal, new amendments to the rules of procedure and evidence allowed judges to streamline and accelerate pretrial and trial proceedings by various methods, including considering motions on written pleadings instead of holding hearings, taking judicial notice of adjudicated facts or documentary evidence from other proceedings before the tribunal, continuing with trial for

---

[35] ICTY, "Tenth Annual Report to the General Assembly" (2003).
[36] ICTR Web site, General Information.
[37] UN General Assembly, "Report on the Financing ..." of the ICTR and ICTY (December 15, 2005), para. II.4.a.

a limited time in the absence of a judge, and allowing parties to have "stand-in" witnesses to replace witnesses who are unable to testify.[38] Both tribunals pursued other measures to expedite translations, transcripts, and document sharing electronically and to reduce defense counsels' incentives to prolong the trials. By this time, administrative reforms in the tribunals were drawing upon the logistical innovations of the ICC Registry as it established its new methods, and the ICC Registry was in continual contact with the tribunals' Registrars to learn about what methods had helped them to streamline their processes – learning was taking place in both directions.

OPERATIONAL AND LEGAL INNOVATIONS

The ad hoc tribunals, for all their difficulties in getting under way, broke new ground in the development of international criminal law. Their primary accomplishment was simply to show that the United Nations could create machinery to counter the impunity of perpetrators of international crimes. Their creation led, in some observers' views, to "tribunal fatigue" in the Security Council, but that fatigue reinforced pressures to create a standing international criminal court.[39] The tribunals established milestone international criminal legal precedents important to the ICC and other international and mixed international–domestic courts. They contributed, both with their achievements and their shortcomings, to the accumulating wisdom of the international criminal justice practitioners' community.

While the theory behind the tribunals may have included elements of restorative justice, and a conviction on the part of their supporters that justice would contribute to peace, the operational mandates of the two tribunals called upon them to investigate, apprehend, and try perpetrators of the crimes. To do this, the statutes set up an independent and powerful Prosecutor, an independent set of judges' Chambers, and the Registry, to support the operations. What began, in one critic's terms, as "acts of political contrition, because of egregious failures to swiftly confront the situations in the former Yugoslavia and Rwanda,"[40] gradually evolved to include greater elements of civil law structures, to build coordination mechanisms to increase court efficiency, to improve prosecution focus to speed trials, and to implement "outreach" programs to seek to have some positive effect in the areas where crimes were originally committed.

---

[38] Ibid., para. II.4.b.
[39] Scheffer, "Challenges Confronting International Justice Issues" (1998), 1–6.
[40] Zacklin, "The Failings of ad Hoc International Tribunals" (2004), 542.

An Old (Retributive) Justice Paradigm

The ICTY Statute is purely an "old justice" document. Although the preambular paragraphs of the ICTR Statute pay some respect to "new justice" objectives (see following discussion), it does not set up any restorative (new) justice mechanisms.[41] The two tribunals' missions are fully articulated in their formal, long names found in UN documents: the "International Tribunal for the Prosecution of Persons Responsible for Serious Violations of International Humanitarian Law Committed in the Territory of the Former Yugoslavia since 1991" (ICTY) and the "International Criminal Tribunal for the Prosecution of Persons Responsible for Genocide and other Serious Violations of International Humanitarian Law Committed in the Territory of Rwanda and Rwandan Citizens Responsible for Genocide and Other Such Violations Committed in the Territory of Neighbouring States, between 1 January and 31 December 1994" (ICTR). In neither of the (practically identical) statutes is mention made of duties toward victims or witnesses, save that the judges, via their rules of procedure and evidence, will provide for the protection of victims and witnesses, including the conduct of *in camera* (closed) hearings and protection of victims' identities.[42]

In the hurry to establish the ICTY, tribunal President Antonio Cassese turned to U.S. proposals for the Rules of Procedure and Evidence.[43] The Rwanda tribunal adopted the ICTY rules. Coming from U.S. sources, the tribunals were constructed as primarily common-law, old-justice-paradigm institutions. Trials were adversarial, pitting prosecution against defense in front of a panel of judges that would serve as referees, occasional inquisitors, and determiners of guilt. There were some non-common-law aspects to the rules, in that hearsay evidence was acceptable, there was no jury (verdicts to be determined by the judges), and verdicts and sentences could be appealed by both the defendant and the prosecution. As outlined in the next section, a stream of amendments to the rules gradually increased the judges' roles in managing the tribunals and tilted in the direction of civil-law procedures.[44]

In their original form and actions, the two tribunals regarded victims and witnesses as important for providing evidence for prosecution and of concern to the extent that their participation in the operations of the tribunals

---

[41] ICTR Statute, preambular paragraphs, "Convinced" and "Stressing."
[42] ICTY Statute, Articles 15, 22; ICTR Statute, Article 14.
[43] Williams and Scharf, *op cit.*, 106.
[44] Knoops, *An Introduction to the Law of International Criminal Tribunals: A Comparative Study* (2003).

might be dangerous for them. Neither tribunal focused upon the effects of their actions upon the larger societies in which the witnesses and victims continued to live, or directly upon the lives of those people. Trials were to be held in locations remote from the crimes (The Hague and Arusha, Tanzania, respectively), and contact back to the areas in which the crimes took place was basically for collection of evidence. In the ICTY, the best that could be hoped for was that its mere existence would provide a measure of deterrence to potential perpetrators of additional crimes while the conflict over which it had jurisdiction continued.

Tribunals' Evolution: Toward Civil Law and New (Restorative) Justice

The ICTY and ICTR passed their tenth anniversaries as much larger organizations with somewhat different objectives than those with which they began. Pressures to improve efficiency, respond to victims, affect local populations, and contribute to development of legal systems in the conflict areas had led to changes in their operations and expansion of their tasks. Many of the activities eventually undertaken by the ad hoc tribunals, added by this evolutionary process, are now expected of the ICC and largely built into its Statute.

Victims

Neither the ICTY or ICTR Statute mentions victims. The term "victim" is defined in the 1994 Rules of Procedure and Evidence of the ICTY.[45] Rule 34 creates a Victims and Witnesses Unit under the Registrar to (i) recommend protective measures for victims and witnesses and (ii) provide counseling and support for them, in particular in cases of rape and sexual assault.[46] The rules give a judge or chamber the right to order measures for the privacy and protection of victims and witnesses, as long as these don't interfere with the rights of the accused. Such measures can include cloaking the identity or whereabouts of victims or witnesses or their relatives, removing names from the tribunal's public records, and not disclosing identifying records, testimony through image- or voice-altering devices, and assignment of pseudonyms.[47] The Registry's Victims and Witnesses Unit is to advise witnesses that their identity might be disclosed later and/or in

---

[45] Rule 2 Definitions. "Victim: A person against whom a crime over which the Tribunal has jurisdiction has allegedly been committed."

[46] Rule 34, February 1994. The rule was amended in 1999 (adding Part B) instructing the Registrar to give "due consideration" to the "employment of qualified women."

[47] Rule 75.

another case. The Court (judges) is to "control the manner of questioning to avoid any harassment or intimidation." Special rules apply in cases of sexual assault, stipulating that (i) no corroboration of the victim's testimony shall be required; (ii) consent shall not be allowed as a defense if the victim has been threatened or has reason to fear violence, duress, detention, or psychological oppression or had reason to fear that another would suffer these if the victim didn't comply; (iii) before a claim of victim consent can be admitted, the accused shall "satisfy the Trial Chamber in camera that the evidence is relevant and credible"; and (iv) prior sexual conduct of the victim shall not be admitted in evidence. In sum, articles dealing with witnesses and victims seek to enable testimony while minimizing trauma and retribution but go no further than the involvement of these people as part of the trial functions of the tribunal.[48]

Gender Crimes

The ICTY, under the leadership of U.S. Judge Gabrielle Kirk McDonald and Costa Rican Judge Elisabeth Odio-Benito, added Rule 96 to the tribunal's Rules of Procedure and Evidence to protect victims and witnesses who were involved in testifying about sexual crimes. Chief Prosecutor Judge Richard Goldstone responded to women's groups' suggestions by appointing a gender legal adviser to his office, and, responding to further briefs and suggestions from women's advocates, he gradually "mainstreamed" gender crimes into indictments. The Foca indictment of June 1996 was the first in which rape was charged as a form of torture, and enslavement and other forms of sexual violence such as forced nudity and sexual entertainment were charged as inhumane treatment.[49]

At the ICTR, Judge Navanethem Pillay, the only woman on the Trial Chamber hearing a genocide and crimes against humanity case against Jean-Paul Akayesu, insisted herself on questioning women who had been testifying about other alleged crimes. In a pivotal moment for international justice, Judge Pillay evoked from the women testimony that they had witnessed rape and had themselves been rape victims. A coalition of NGOs came together as the Monitoring Project on Gender-Related Crimes, and the ICTR sent "numerous critical letters"[50] to Chief Prosecutor Judge Louise Arbour. Briefs were filed, Rwandan women's groups organized protests, and the indictment

---

[48] Rule 96.

[49] Copelon, "Gender Crimes as War Crimes: Integrating Crimes Against Women into International Criminal Law" (2000), 230; ICTY, Prosecutor v. Gagovic et al., Indictment, Trial Chamber (June 26, 1996), Case No. IT-96-23/2.

[50] Copelon, op cit., 225.

was amended,[51] although ICTR officials claimed that this was due to the testimony, not the agitation. On September 2, 1998, the ICTR Trial Chamber convicted Akayesu of genocide and crimes against humanity, including rape as a crime against humanity and as an instrument of genocide.[52]

Outreach

In 1999, President Gabrielle Kirk-McDonald was dismayed to discover that Serbs did not care about the findings of the Tadic case, as far as could be determined, because they viewed the ICTY as a tool of the Muslims for propaganda against the Serbs.[53] After consultations with NGOs, the ICTY initiated its "outreach" program, although no regular budget funds were allocated to it. The program has been supported by the United States, United Kingdom, European Union, and Scandinavian countries, with some project funds contributed by private foundations.

Despite great suspicion about the tribunal in former Yugoslavia, an outreach coordinator was only first hired in the fall of 1999, a staff was assembled in 2000, and regional offices were set up in Zagreb (mid-2000) and in Belgrade, Sarajevo, and Pristina in 2001. The tribunal's Hague headquarters' Public Information Office did not include speakers of local languages until 2006, and only when the outreach program hired local language speakers after 1999 did the ICTY's communications in the area begin to connect with the local populations.[54] As an ICTY official put it in 2006, "We can't undo the damage" of losing six years between the startup of the tribunal and the beginnings of the outreach program in late 1999. When the outreach program finally began, the tribunal was in a deep public relations hole; political actors demonized it to establish their own nationalist credentials.

Seen locally as an exercise in victors' justice, critics charged that the tribunal was illegitimately created. Leaders in Serbia and the Serb areas of Bosnia-Herzegovina impeded investigators' access, intimidated potential witnesses, and actively prevented police and military personnel from speaking with investigators. Even victims see its failings more than its utility, according to outreach personnel. Since the tribunal has focused on major perpetrators and not local ones, the vast majority of victims don't see

---

[51] ICTR, Prosecutor v. Jean Paul Akayesu, Amended Indictment, ICTR Trial Chamber (June 1997), Case No. ICTR-96-4-1, Indictment Counts 1, 2, 13–15. Available at <http://www.ictr.org>.

[52] Askin, "Legal Precedents in Rwanda Court" (May 2001).

[53] Interview, ICTY outreach personnel, spring 2006.

[54] Interview, ICTY outreach personnel, spring 2006.

their own persecutors brought to book. Since prosecutions take place on multiple sides of the conflict, people from every group can point to prosecutions of their own heroes – and this grates more seriously than is compensated by prosecution of the enemy.

In 1999, during NATO's air war intended to drive Serbian forces out of Kosovo, NATO spokesperson Jamie Shea gave ammunition to the tribunal's critics when he made it sound as if the ICTY worked at NATO's behest. When asked whether NATO would fall under ICTY scrutiny following Serbian complaints about indiscriminate bombing, Shea said that the tribunal would investigate only if NATO permitted it to do so. Although Carla del Ponte did investigate the Serbian charges, when she decided there was no case to be pursued against NATO, it looked like a put-up job.[55]

Faced with local ignorance and misunderstanding, the tribunal sought to bring greater knowledge of its operations into the area primarily by bringing legal professionals to The Hague for seminars and information sessions and, gradually, by establishing the field offices and putting on local events to publicize the work, achievements, and nature of the tribunal.

The Security Council's rationale for creating the Rwanda tribunal explicitly cited some of the "new justice" objectives missing in the ICTY resolution. The council was convinced that "the prosecution of persons responsible for serious violations of international humanitarian law would ... contribute to the process of national reconciliation and to the restoration and maintenance of peace" and stressed "the need for international cooperation to strengthen the courts and judicial system of Rwanda, having regard in particular to the necessity for those courts to deal with large numbers of suspects."[56] The seat of the tribunal, in Arusha, Tanzania, guaranteed that contact with local populations would be a major problem, however, and tense relations with the Rwandan government also ensured

---

[55] NATO press briefing, Jamie Shea, spokesperson (May 16, 1999): "I think we have to distinguish between the theoretical and the practical. I believe that when Justice Arbour starts her investigation, she will because we will allow her to. It's not Milosevic that has allowed Justice Arbour her visa to go to Kosovo to carry out her investigations. If her court, as we want, is to be allowed access, it will be because of NATO so NATO is the friend of the Tribunal, NATO are the people who have been detaining indicted war criminals for the Tribunal in Bosnia. We have done it, 14 arrests so far by SFOR, and we will continue to do it. NATO countries are those that have provided the finance to set up the Tribunal, we are amongst the majority financiers, and of course to build a second chamber so that prosecutions can be speeded up so let me assure that we are all one on this, we want to see war criminals brought to justice and I am certain that when Justice Arbour goes to Kosovo and looks at the facts she will be indicting people of Yugoslav nationality and I don't anticipate any others at this stage."

[56] ICTR Statute, preambular paragraphs, op cit.

that a positive reputation for the tribunal in Rwanda would not easily be established. ICTR personnel recognized the need for some kind of outreach program, but like the ICTY, these efforts commenced in 1998, only several years after the tribunal began operating. Unlike the ICTY, no separate office was established to coordinate them. Outreach was added to existing press and public affairs responsibilities.[57]

The ICTR outreach program sought to "win the hearts and minds of a skeptical populace in two ways: (i) 'improve the image and gain support of local people through local information dissemination and (ii) communication and training of Rwandan media and legal professionals.'"[58] The ICTR set up an internship program for Rwandan students to serve in the tribunal and opened an information center in Kigali in the fall of 2000. Court judgments began to be translated into Kinyarwanda in 2000, but these materials are not regularly distributed to Rwandan courts, lawyers, or other interested people. The Web site contains all the judgments, but it is not available to the vast majority of citizens. Rwandans were not selected as judges or other high-level officials at the tribunal, so there is little knowledge transfer directly into the legal community. Only in 2005 was a Rwandan trial lawyer added to the Office of the Prosecutor to argue a case in Arusha.

Another problem for the ICTR's legitimacy in Rwanda is its tense relationship with the government. A dilemma confronts the tribunal. To promote reconciliation between the perpetrators and victims of the genocide in Rwanda, the tribunal may need to consider prosecuting Tutsi suspects for crimes against Hutus, in addition to the ongoing prosecution of Hutus. However, the tribunal also needs good relations with the government in order to carry out any operations in Rwanda, and prosecution of Tutsis is exactly what the Rwandan Patriotic Front (RPF) government has been resisting. Building credibility with the population and contributing to reconciliation, therefore, runs directly against building credibility with the government, which is needed in order to operate in the country at all.

Building on the lessons of the tribunals, the ICC Statute incorporates "new justice" objectives extensively in its treatment of victims and witnesses, as is discussed in the next chapter. Perhaps since the outreach failures of the tribunals were becoming clear only after the Rome Statute negotiations were completed, that document does not mention outreach or public information;

---

[57] Peskin, "Courting Rwanda: The Promises and Pitfalls of the ICTR Outreach Program" (2005).

[58] ICTR Web site, as quoted by Peskin, ibid., 952.

however, the public information and outreach functions of the ICC are a main area of concern to the new Court's Registry, Assembly of States Parties, and particularly the NGOs that monitor and seek to influence the Court.

CONSTRUCTIVISM, REALISM, NEOLIBERAL INSTITUTIONALISM

The tribunals' creation is commonly explained in two ways. One is that the Security Council created them so that it could claim *something* useful had been done, having abysmally failed to act when action could have helped avert the disasters to which the tribunals were legalistic responses. Second, the international community converged on the idea that impunity for the crimes committed in former Yugoslavia and Rwanda was unacceptable, and the tribunals were a collective response.

The tribunals' creation was thus a response to perceived domestic pressure. Public opinion on which perception was based depended upon people's conviction that mass crimes elsewhere in the world concern them, and thus should concern their governments. Regarding both former Yugoslavia and Rwanda, exposure of the scale of the crimes (through media coverage) and the dilatory and feeble reactions of the major powers led governments to perceive inaction as politically risky domestically. This is easily explained only in a constructivist framework, in which values may affect leaders' identities directly or are channeled by electoral systems (that is, they seek to be popular to get elected, and their constituents do identify with international justice values) into the calculations of foreign policy makers who would otherwise not include these nonmaterial commitments in their national interest definitions.

Neither of the explanations fits easily into a realist paradigm, although realism does explain states' reluctance to intervene forcefully. No powerful nation's vital interests were at stake in the Yugoslav conflicts of the early 1990s. The interested powerful actors such as European states, the United States, Great Britain, and Russia sought, moreover, to avoid clashing with each other. In the Rwanda case, there was no clear threat to major powers' international security or national interest at stake; therefore, there was no willingness to sacrifice resources or lives in reaction.

The form of the response, creation of ad hoc tribunals by the UN Security Council, can be explained with a neoliberal institutionalist view. The International Law Commission's spadework carried out by (constructivist-explained) international legal experts who were also advocates, first of a fact-finding mission in Yugoslavia and then of an ad hoc tribunal, provided an institutional answer to the question of what could be done through the Security Council in response to the political pressures explained earlier. The ILC draft work had created a path, and the hurried drafters of the ICTY Statute followed the path hewn by the ILC and mapped by the U.S. State Department's Office of the Ambassador at Large for War Crimes Issues to create an institution that then gradually took on an independent institutional existence.

By 2002, the ICTY and ICTR had developed significantly beyond what was envisioned in 1993. Surmounting some of the problems of their earlier years – even though they appeared to critics to be very expensive for what they were producing in terms of convictions – the two tribunals were successfully prosecuting high-level perpetrators of international crimes. The ICC Statute negotiators incorporated their understandings of lessons from and reactions to the tribunals, up to that time, into the final Statute of July 1998. Later tribunal lessons influenced some aspects of the Court's operations through its personnel after it came into existence in 2002. From a neoliberal institutionalist perspective, as explained in the next chapter, an epistemic community was growing up around the tribunals and influenced the drafting process of the ICC Statute.

Recognizing problems with judicial processes, the tribunals evolved an increasingly hybrid legal system combining civil- and common-law procedures, and the ICC Statute explicitly combines the two traditions. Discovering that their credibility and legitimacy were being undermined by strenuous efforts of their opponents locally in the areas where they were carrying out investigations, the tribunals (belatedly) developed outreach programs and geared up their public information efforts. By 2006, the ICC had generated a "strategic plan for outreach," responding to NGO and ASP pressure. The tribunals' isolation within the UN system early on resulted in substandard financial and administrative control especially in the ICTR, but the bureaucracy of the parent organization eventually asserted itself, and operations improved. For the ICC, the ASP was created to provide supervision and support for the organization. Funding would be provided by assessed contributions. The inherent weaknesses of the tribunals' tripartite structure moved the ICC negotiators to subordinate the Registry to the Presidency. The long trials, appeals, and evidentiary challenges produced by diffuse and multiple charges against suspects in the tribunals resulted in the ICC Statute limiting the grounds for appeals and led the Prosecutor to seek concise charges and better coordination between investigation and prosecution activities. The tribunals' demonstration of the indispensability of witness protection produced much greater attention in the ICC, giving all three organs of the Court some relevant responsibilities. New (restorative) justice objectives were institutionalized by the Statute's establishment of a trust fund for victims. Chapter 3 explains the development, major features, and theoretical implications of the ICC Statute.

3

The Statute – Justice versus Sovereignty

The Rome Statute of the ICC reflects states' agreement over how to institutionalize a broad range of international criminal justice norms while still protecting national sovereignty. In some areas, most prominently the issue of jurisdiction, the Statute's final provisions can be characterized as a lowest common denominator outcome, keeping on board all but the states most concerned about a potential erosion of sovereignty. On other topics, such as reparations and victims' rights, the Statute represents the cutting edge of normative development. From the Court's standpoint, the Statute is broadly permissive, even quite demanding, because of the range of objectives it outlines. But the Court faces the conundrum that while charged with an immense task, it must rely upon states to support and enforce its actions. As this chapter will show, the Court's leverage is weak.

A large literature skillfully describes the negotiations and the legal fine points of the Rome Statute process.[1] Starting with a brief chronology,

---

[1] Bassiouni, "Historical Survey: 1919–1998" (1999); Benedetti and Washburn, "Drafting the International Criminal Court Treaty: Two Years to Rome and an Afterword on the Rome Diplomatic Conference conference" (1999), 1–38; Cassese et al., *The Rome Statute of the International Criminal Court – A Commentary* (2002); Glasius, *The International Criminal Court: A Global Civil Society Achievement* (2005); Kaul, "Special Note: The Struggle for the International Criminal Court's Jurisdiction" (1998), 48–60; Kirsch and Holmes, "The Birth of the International Criminal Court: The 1998 Rome Conference" (2004), 3–39; Lee, *The International Criminal Court: The Making of the Rome Statute: Issues, Negotiations and Results* (1999); McGoldrick et al., *The Permanent International Criminal Court: Legal and Policy Issues* (2004); Politi and Nesi, *The Rome Statute of the International Criminal Court: A Challenge to Impunity* (2001); Sadat, *The International Criminal Court and the Transformation of International Law* (2002); Schabas, *An Introduction to the International Criminal Court*, 2nd ed. (2004); Triffterer, *Commentary*

then discussing the Statute's major features, this chapter uses theoretical standpoints of realist interests, the neoliberal institutionalist dynamic, and the constructivist logic to explain the outcome of the negotiations and states' attitudes toward the Court. Realist assumptions show why states might be reluctant to sign; institutionalism helps elucidate the structure of the Court and pinpoints major organizational challenges. Constructivism clarifies why states protective of their sovereignty nonetheless join the ICC.

The ICC teeters between values of sovereignty and internationalism. Mechanisms devised to maintain the balance shape the Court's operational dynamics. Under the principle of "complementarity," states established the ICC as a backup justice system in the event that national mechanisms fail. They gave the Court wide purview to look into three sets of crimes (genocide, crimes against humanity, war crimes) that were carefully defined to include some new areas of international concern; however, negotiators left out crimes that, had they been included in the Statute, would likely have driven important states out of the consensus. Since some states adamantly sought and others equally strongly resisted the inclusions of the crime of aggression in the Court's jurisdiction, the term was included in the Statute but the definitions and mechanisms necessary for the Court to exert such jurisdiction were left to future negotiations and amendment of the Statute.

To soothe worried states, the negotiators established hurdles that must be surmounted before the ICC can bring suspects before judges. For example, the Prosecutor has considerable discretion to launch preliminary investigations, but continuing the process requires judicial approval that the seriousness of the case justifies ICC involvement and that no appropriate domestic proceedings are under way. The Court's potential jurisdiction is broad, but its operations are tightly constrained by the sovereign independence of states.

BRIEF NEGOTIATING HISTORY

The International Law Commission's 1994 draft ICC Statute proposed jurisdiction over genocide, aggression, violations of laws and customs applicable in armed conflict (war crimes), crimes against humanity, and a set of crimes from previous conventions that were listed in an annex to the draft.[2] The report was

---

on the Rome Statute of the International Criminal Court: Observers' Notes Article by Article (1999).
[2] Namely, grave breaches of the Geneva Conventions, unlawful seizure of aircraft (Hague Convention, 1970), crimes against the safety of civil aviation (Montreal Convention, 1971), Apartheid (1973), Convention on the Prevention and Punishment of Crimes against

submitted to the General Assembly, which set up an ad hoc committee to discuss it in anticipation of a General Assembly discussion at its 1995 session.

In 1995, the General Assembly decided to convene a Preparatory Committee (PrepCom) to further develop the draft Statute, with the idea that there would follow a plenipotentiary conference.[3] The PrepCom met twice in 1996 and three times in 1997, with additional, unofficial "intercessional" meetings to help prepare the PrepCom meetings. The last intercessional meeting, in January 1998 in Zutphen, The Netherlands, was key in consolidating proposals for a draft that was considered at the final PrepCom meeting in April, whose product was then submitted to the Statute Conference.

From 1995 to 1998, the original 43-page 1994 ILC draft Statute expanded into a draft Statute of 173 pages replete with bracketed options, alternative phrasing, and footnotes for consideration at the Rome Conference.[4] According to participants, the preparatory process ended with elation over what had been accomplished and foreboding that the upcoming negotiators at Rome might not be able to complete the job.[5]

The Conference on the Statute convened on June 15, 1998, at the headquarters of the Food and Agriculture Organization. More than 160 states sent delegates. Hundreds of NGO representatives attended and participated directly and through the Coalition for the International Criminal Court (CICC), and a range of international organizations were represented too. Most delegates were enthusiastic, strongly hoping the conference would succeed in completing a statute.

A large group, called the "like-minded states" (LMS), dominated the structure of the Conference, supplying most of the chairs of the working groups and most of the members of the Bureau, the executive body that directed the daily agenda. LMS members generally sought a court highly independent of the United Nations and with broad jurisdiction. There were other influential groups: "Non-aligned movement" states joined together to

---

Internationally Protected Persons, including Diplomatic Agents (1973), International Convention against the Taking of Hostages (1979), Convention against Torture and Other Cruel, Inhuman or Degrading Treatment or Punishment (1984), crimes defined in the Convention for the Suppression of Unlawful Acts against the Safety of Maritime Navigation (1988) and against the Safety of Fixed Platforms Located on the Continental Shelf (1988), and crimes identified in the UN Convention against Illicit Traffic in Narcotic Drugs and Psychotropic Substances (1988).

3 That is, a conference of official delegates that would produce a final treaty available for signature by states.
4 Bassiouni, op cit., 26.
5 Schabas, op cit., 14–15; Benedetti and Washburn, op cit., 2.

urge that the crime of aggression be included within the Court's jurisdiction, the Southern African Development Community pressed for expanded human rights definitions, and a group of Arab and Islamic states sought to inscribe a prohibition of nuclear weapons and a death penalty provision in the Statute. Shortly before the conference, the Labour Party came to power in Britain, following which the United Kingdom broke from the UN Security Council members (the United States, Russia, and China) and others that sought a tightly constrained court under Security Council control. The United Kingdom joined with the LMS group that included France, Germany, and most European Union members.[6]

The United States, which eventually became the Court's most vigorous opponent, played an extremely important and in many ways constructive role throughout the negotiations. The delegation from the United States was the largest at the Conference. Its legal experts contributed key elements to the Statute and, subsequently, to the Court's Rules of Procedure and Evidence. Many of the compromises negotiated during the Conference were aimed at bringing the United States into the fold; however, in retrospect, it is doubtful that any statute that met the objectives of the LMS and other states that sought an independent court would have been acceptable to the United States.

During the June 15–July 18 Conference, the much-bracketed PrepCom draft was turned into a final statute for the ICC. Observers credit the chairman of the Committee of the Whole, Canadian Ambassador Philippe Kirsch, Drafting Committee Chair M. Cherif Bassiouni, working group chairs, and some individual state delegates with driving the negotiations to completion. NGOs provided an important avenue for information exchange throughout the Conference, urged the delegates on, and in some cases provided position statements and research and analysis used directly in the discussions.

Negotiations moved slowly on central issues because of the complicated interdependence of key provisions. Down to the last week of the Conference, it wasn't clear that a statute would be completed; however, Kirsch and his committee chairs managed to preserve momentum by constantly developing new drafts, avoiding stalemate by dropping unpopular proposals (even when strongly held), and pressing for compromise language. In general, the negotiations were most difficult when they sought to deal with the tension between the prerogatives of the Court and protection of state sovereignty. How would Court jurisdiction be established, when and how would its

---

[6] Schabas, op cit., 16–17.

action be triggered, and what (if any) role would the UN Security Council play in the process? Over what crimes and individuals would the Court have jurisdiction? How broad would the range of crimes be? Would crimes committed in the context of internal conflicts be treated the same as those in international conflicts? How independent would the Prosecutor be? Except for Part 2 of the Statute, which dealt with these most difficult issues, the document was largely settled by July 15, with a planned end of the Conference on July 17.[7] In the last two days, crucial breakthroughs accumulated, and a document emerged that commanded the support of the vast majority of participating states. An effort to delay final adoption was defeated with 120 votes against, 7 in favor, and 21 abstentions, two hours past midnight on July 17, and the Statute was adopted without a further vote. The United States, China, Israel, Iraq, Libya, Yemen, and Qatar had voted to delay.[8]

Advocates of an independent court with broad jurisdiction were disappointed by compromises that limited the Court to proceeding against individuals who were either citizens of a state that had joined the Statute or had committed crimes on the territory of a such a state. They criticized the Statute for giving the Security Council a potential role in both assigning cases to the Court and suspending its activities. Arms control advocates complained that it made little sense to include war crimes provisions against acts defined at The Hague in 1907 but not to criminalize the use of weapons of mass destruction. In contrast, defenders of state sovereignty argued that the Statute left too much independence to the Court and its Prosecutor, that jurisdiction should require approval by the state of a suspect's nationality in all cases, and that there was insufficient oversight and political control of the Court. Enthusiasts for the Court pointed to the long history of attempts to establish such an international jurisdiction, viewed the Statute as a major accomplishment, and awaited the actual operation of the Court to see whether the compromises were workable and the organization could acquire credibility through its actions.

THE PREAMBLE: SOVEREIGNTY, PERFECTIBILITY, AND IDENTITY

International organizations operate in an environment shaped both by state power and by the power of ideas. The preamble captures the idealism

---

[7] Bassiouni, op cit., 31.
[8] Human Rights Watch, "The United States and the International Criminal Court" (2006); Kaul, op cit., 57.

of the ICC project and mirrors the tensions between a universalistic image of humanity and a global society riven by national loyalties. The preamble (see Appendix 3A) asserts the universalistic idea that "all peoples are united by common bonds, their cultures pieced together in a shared heritage." Asserting that the cultures together constitute a collective heritage, it cautions that this "mosaic" of shared heritage is "delicate" and "can be shattered at any time." The violent history of the twentieth century shows the mosaic's vulnerability, including "unimaginable atrocities that deeply shock the conscience of humanity."

The portrayal of humanity in general as a global society, not a system of states, is compatible with religious or natural law, independent of positive law and antithetical to a narrowly based, national interest view of the world. The preamble adopts a social, normative, and universalistic outlook. The Court should be created, however, for practical reasons, too: An end to impunity would contribute to the prevention of atrocious crimes; therefore, the most serious crimes must "not go unpunished." And since "grave crimes threaten the peace, security and well-being of the world," action against these crimes should lead to a more peaceful, secure, and happy world. In calling for states to create an organization to improve the world, the preamble launches the Statute as a document of liberal, universalistic institutionalism. Humanity will pursue its perfectibility by creating this legal institution to step in when states fail to respond to threats against its fragile mosaic.

The preamble affirms state sovereignty, declaring that the ICC's jurisdiction will be complementary to that of national courts. If national courts don't prosecute when they should, the ICC will be enabled to do so, but national responsibility comes first. Thus, while the preamble asserts the existence of a collective human identity shocked by international crimes and endorses a neoliberal institutionalist project to create an organization to improve general welfare, it still pays respect to the power and formal independence of states, cornerstones of the realist vision and balance-of-power system. Paying further respect to sovereignty, the preamble adds the caveats that its objectives do not justify the use of force against states, interference in their internal affairs, or other acts inconsistent with the UN Charter.

The conception behind the ICC Statute, inherited ultimately from the Nuremberg precedents, is that the rule of law is violated by criminals acting individually when they carry out their most heinous crimes. No one can have an excuse for carrying out such a crime, and a system of laws cannot be complete without the capacity to prosecute such criminality. The

Statute negotiation was a neoliberal institutionalist moment in a post–Cold War environment motivated by cascading international (antiimpunity) norms and asserting a cause-and-effect relationship between the ability to adjudicate international crimes and the deterrence of those crimes.

THE CRIMES

The Statute limits ICC jurisdiction to the international crimes that nego-tiators agreed are the most heinous and massive that can be attributed to individuals – genocide, crimes against humanity, war crimes, and aggres-sion.[9] The first three of these are defined at length[10] in the Statute (see Appendix 3B). Security Council member states were extremely reluctant to include a crime of aggression[11] under the Court's jurisdiction, while many other (especially formerly colonized) states were equally adamant that it be included. Proponents of aggression's criminalization were assuaged by its inclusion as a crime under the Court's jurisdiction; opponents were satisfied by a provision indicating that jurisdiction could be exercised only after additional provisions defined the crime and the conditions under which it could be prosecuted.[12] The soonest this could take place would be at a review conference scheduled to take place seven years following the opening of the Court.[13]

Already in the ILC draft ICC Statute (1994) and Code of Crimes Against Peace and Security (1996), attention was focused on these four "core" crimes, with the broader list of separate international crimes, including those defined in international conventions, such as apartheid and torture, relegated to an annex (see footnote 2 in this chapter). In the final Statute, many of these "convention" crimes reappeared as subcategories of crimes against humanity and war crimes, but others that had been central to early negotiations (such as drug trafficking) did not.[14]

---

[9] Statute Article 5.1(a–d).
[10] Statute Articles 6, 7, 8.
[11] UN General Assembly Resolution 3314(XXIX) of 1974 defines aggression as a state act, but for ICC jurisdiction, the acts of an individual (probably including, for instance, planning or conspiring to cause a state to commit the state crime) that would constitute a crime of aggression will need to be specified.
[12] Statute Article 5.2.
[13] Statute Article 123.
[14] The "convention" crimes not included in the ICC's purview are unlawful seizure of aircraft, crimes against civil aviation, crimes against the safety of maritime navigation and the safety of fixed platforms located on the continental shelf, and crimes involving illicit traffic in narcotic drugs and psychotropic substances.

The Statute breaks new ground in defining international criminal acts. Although the ad hoc tribunals prosecuted crimes against humanity, and the concept was nearly 100 years old, no international treaty defined the crime's until the ICC Statute did so. Similarly, following from the ICTR's conviction of defendants for gender crimes (rape, sexual slavery, enforced prostitution, forced pregnancy, enforced sterilization, or any other form of sexual violence of comparable gravity), these crimes were included in the Statute as both crimes against humanity and war crimes.[15] Negotiations over the "gender crimes" were contentious because some states and religiously based NGOs feared that including them in the Statute would impinge on domestic laws about abortion and gender relations.[16] The problem was overcome by including provisions stating that the Statute doesn't supersede national laws "affecting pregnancy"[17] and that in the Statute "gender" means only male and female.[18] Another newly defined crime stemmed from human rights violations particularly in Latin America: NGOs and successor states' representatives led successful efforts to criminalize "enforced disappearance of persons."[19]

Unlike "crimes against humanity," war crimes were long inscribed in international law, going back at least to the Hague Conventions of 1899. The judges of the ICTY helped speed the convergence of the laws pertinent to internal and international conflict. The Statute's war crimes definitions[20] include three general categories: (a) grave breaches of the Geneva Conventions of 1949, (b) the list of "violations of the laws and customs *applicable in international armed conflict*," and (c) those that pertain "*in the case of an armed conflict not of an international character*." All of the part (c) crimes can be found in some form under parts (a) and (b), although the reverse is not the case.[21] Large areas of commonality in the Statute

---

[15] Statute Article 7(g), 8.2(b)(xxii), 8.2(e)(vi).
[16] Glasius, *The International Criminal Court* (2005).
[17] Statute Article 7.2(f).
[18] Statute Article 7.3
[19] Statute Article 7.2(i)
[20] Statute Article 8.
[21] Crimes enumerated in Statute Article 8, War Crimes, as applicable in international conflicts that do not show up explicitly in the noninternational context were precluded from the noninternational list of crimes because they refer to nationality, citizenship, or occupation or were established earlier as positive treaty law between states and refer to signature of specific international instruments. They are: "2b(ii). Intentionally directing attacks against civilian objects, that is, objects which are not military objectives;" "2b(iv). Intentionally launching an attack in the knowledge that such an attack will cause incidental loss of life or injury to civilians or damage to civilian objects or widespread, long-term and severe damage to the natural environment which would be clearly excessive in relation to the concrete and

between internal and international conflict show how the distinction is being abolished.

Negotiators updated the war crimes list by including recent treaty crimes such as the Environment Convention;[22] crimes committed against the personnel, installations, or equipment involved in humanitarian assistance or peacekeeping under UN authority;[23] crimes against cultural institutions;[24] the crime of conscripting children under the age of 15;[25] and the crime of using hostages to protect military forces or installations.[26]

Some NGOs and states urged that the Statute should add the use of nuclear or other weapons of mass destruction to existing weapons proscriptions from The Hague and other conventions. They argued that such weapons are inherently indiscriminate and their use would constitute humanitarian crimes at least as heinous as other defined war crimes and crimes against humanity. It was clear, however, that outlawing, for example, the use of nuclear weapons would be a deal breaker for the nuclear weapon states, and outlawing chemical and biological weapons (and not nuclear weapons) would be viewed as discriminatory by some nonnuclear states. Thus, including such measures would have jeopardized the Statute as a whole.[27] The problem was finessed by providing that if such crimes were defined in the future in separate international conventions, their terms could be annexed to the Statute under its amendment procedures.[28]

The Statute drew together what might be considered the "state of the art" international criminal law. This major step forward would provide an

---

direct overall military advantage anticipated;" "2b(viii). The transfer, directly or indirectly, by the Occupying Power of parts of its own civilian population into the territory it occupies . . . ;" "2b(xv). Compelling the nationals of the hostile party to take part in the operations of war directed against their own country, even if they were in the belligerent's service before the commencement of the war;" 2b(xvii)–(ix). The Hague and later proscriptions against (2b(xvii)) poisoned weapons, (2b(xviii)) asphyxiating poisonous or other gases, (2b(xix)) expanding bullets; 2b(xx). Weapons that cause "superfluous injury or unnecessary suffering or which are inherently indiscriminate in violation of the international law of armed conflict, provided that such weapons, projectiles and material and methods of warfare are the subject of a comprehensive prohibition and are included in an annex to this Statute, by an amendment in accordance with the relevant provisions set forth in articles 121 and 123."

[22] Statute Article 8.2(b)iv.
[23] Statute Article 8.2(b)iii.
[24] Statute Article 8.2(b)ix.
[25] Statute Article 8.2(b)xxvi.
[26] Statute Article 8.2.(b)xxiii.
[27] Burroughs and Cabasso, "Confronting the Nuclear-Armed States in International Negotiating Forums: Lessons for NGOs" (1999), 457–80.
[28] Statute Article 8.2.(b)xx.

international jurisdiction that could prosecute genocide, that for the first time codified in treaty form a definition of crimes against humanity, that would also incorporate important crimes (most prominently gender-related crimes) not before explicitly included in war crimes or crimes against humanity, and that make prosecutable transgressions such as apartheid, torture, disappearance, hostage taking, environmental warfare, and attacks against humanitarian and peacekeeping forces. The Statute does not push forward the legal frontiers – for more crimes could have been included – but does define the perimeter of consensus, with some respect paid to the crimes still just over the boundary. Moreover, because states that join the Statute are obligated to align their domestic legal codes with the stipulations of the Statute so that they can fully cooperate with the Court, the crime definitions in the Statute are relevant not only for their consolidation of precedent at the international level, but also for standardizing domestic law.

TAKING SOVEREIGNTY SERIOUSLY

The ad hoc tribunals didn't threaten most states' sovereignty because they were exclusively focused on crimes in defined territorial areas (former Yugoslavia and Rwanda) and for specific time periods (from 1991 onward and during 1994, respectively). For Yugoslavia and Rwanda, the tribunals had jurisdictional "primacy" – they could demand extraction of suspects for trial at The Hague even if prosecution was under way in domestic courts. A permanent court was different. States were willing to permit the Court to look widely into the possibility that crimes were taking place, but they interposed careful limits and tests between the Court identifying possible crimes and actually bringing suspects to The Hague for prosecution. No primacy for the ICC: complementarity is its watchword.

The preamble emphasizes "that the International Criminal Court established under this Statute shall be complementary to national criminal jurisdictions," and Article 1 repeats that the ICC "shall be complementary to national criminal jurisdictions," but the terms "complementary" and "complementarity" are nowhere explicitly defined. The general principle is that national prosecution of international crimes takes precedence over international prosecution, as long as the national process is legitimate. Should appropriate states fail to carry out their responsibilities, and the Court has jurisdiction, the Court can step in. The finer points of complementarity rest in the Court's range of jurisdiction, the criteria for cases' admissibility for trial, the scope of, and limits to, the Prosecutor's independence, the Court's relationship to the UN Security Council, and the range of states' obligations to the Court. How these are implemented determines how organizational autonomy will be limited by state dominance.[29]

Triggers

The referrals to, and investigations carried out by, the Prosecutor are of "situations," a term unique to the Statute that refers to conflict situations, rather than to specific cases. This somewhat oblique term was developed during the Statute negotiations to avoid prejudging the existence or nature of a conflict that might be taking place. Once a "situation" is under investigation, evidence of crimes may emerge that implicates particular suspects. That's where criminal charges come in. During the Rome negotiations, states agreed on three "trigger" mechanisms for the Court.[30] The UN Security Council can refer a (conflict) situation to the Court under Chapter VII of the UN Charter; a state that is party to the Statute can refer a situation to the Court's Prosecutor; or the Prosecutor can initiate an investigation into a conflict situation on his or her own authority (*proprio motu*). In all of these, the Prosecutor begins with an informal investigation to determine whether crimes under the Statute have taken place. If the Prosecutor determines that such crimes have taken place, under a Security Council referral he or she can proceed with a formal investigation and then request warrants for arrest from a Pre-Trial Chamber (of judges) if particular suspects have been identified. If the Prosecutor proceeds on the basis of a state referral or *prioprio motu*, a go-ahead must be obtained from a Pre-Trial Chamber to move from the informal stage to a formal investigation.

Jurisdiction

How would the Court determine when it could step in, beyond a preliminary investigation? Countries that approached the Statute negotiations primarily concerned with protecting their sovereignty (and these tended to be the permanent members of the Security Council) sought a limited Court under the control of the Security Council and from whose jurisdiction their own nationals could be exempt.[31] A UN Security Council referral would be

---

[29] El Zeidy, "The Principle of Complementarity: A New Machinery to Implement International Criminal Law" (2002), 869–975.
[30] Statute Article 13.
[31] Kaul, "Special Note," 50.

analogous to the ad hoc tribunals' founding Security Council resolutions. Such a resolution would indicate that a situation appeared to present a threat to values enshrined in the UN Charter and would bind all UN member states to cooperate with the Court. NGOs, the LMS group, and other states sought to maximize the Court's independence from the Security Council to prevent it from becoming another adjunct of the permanent five states' power. Negotiations to resolve the question of jurisdiction, when states referred cases or the Prosecutor proceeded independently, were the most highly contentious of the Rome Conference and were resolved only on its last day. These negotiations finally created a framework for implementing complementarity.

Agreement over the complementarity principle – that the Court would take cases only when domestic courts in an appropriate state failed genuinely to prosecute[32] – had emerged early in the development of the Statute as a key protection of state sovereignty. Implementing the doctrine required establishing a connection between a crime and a duty to prosecute in the first instance on the part of a state or states and, secondarily (if they didn't act), for the ICC. In theory, a state's duty to prosecute could be established by any one or a combination of four possible links to the crime and suspect: if the crime took place on the state's territory (territorial state principle); if the victims of the crime were nationals of the state (victim state principle); if the suspect (having committed the crime on the state's territory or elsewhere) was on the state's territory (custodial state principle); and/or if the suspect was a national of the state (suspect state principle). The negotiations and ultimate compromise showed that some states desired to create a court with as close to universal jurisdiction as possible and that others were reluctant to accept it.

The ILC draft of 1994 had proposed a voluntary jurisdiction regime that came to be called an opt-in/opt-out system. States would join the Statute and then accept or reject the competence of the Court on a case-by-case basis. Alternatively, a "state consent regime" based on a 1996 French proposal would have required acceptance of ICC involvement by all states concerned (territorial, victim, custodial, and suspect states) in every individual criminal proceeding against every individual suspect. The United States and some other states, concerned to limit ICC jurisdiction, argued that the only relevant criterion should be that the suspect state (state of nationality of the suspect) would have to both be a party to the Statute and agree to Court proceedings. Pursuing universal jurisdiction, in 1996

[32] Statute Article 17.

Germany proposed "automatic jurisdiction" under which states would automatically accept Court jurisdiction when they acceded to the Statute. At Rome, South Korea proposed as a compromise that if one or more of the concerned (territorial, custodial, victim, or suspect) states was a Party, then the ICC would have jurisdiction.[33]

The automatic jurisdiction proposal became the position of the LMS and was ultimately adopted in the form of Statute Article 12(1), which says that upon becoming a party to the Statute, a state "thereby accepts the jurisdiction of the Court."[34] However states' *acceptance* of jurisdiction is distinguished from the Court's ability to *exercise* jurisdiction, which it can do only if the territorial state or suspect state are parties to the Statute[35] or have agreed to the Court's jurisdiction by a declaration to the Registrar.

NGOs and many LMS viewed this compromise as much inferior to the South Korean proposal, which would have included the custodial and victim states as potential links to the Court. The controversy demonstrated the continuing importance of sovereignty claims in the context of institution building, even when the institution is being constructed on the basis of new international norms. Some states found even the compromise unacceptable. Most importantly, the United States objected that by making jurisdiction possible on the basis of the suspect *or* territory, the home state of a suspect might have no ability to claim prior jurisdiction over the Court (proceeding under territorial jurisdiction), and thus a United States citizen could be brought before the Court even though the United States had not joined the Statute. The United States claimed that this violated the principle that a state could not be bound by a treaty that it had not signed.

Admissibility

The jurisdictional compromise established criteria linking the Court to situations where crimes under its purview are suspected. Under complementarity, however, a case is inadmissible to the Court if a responsible state is investigating or prosecuting the case, has decided after investigation not to prosecute, or has tried the case already, unless such investigation or trial was carried out to shield the suspect.[36] This deferral to state authority

---

[33] Kaul, op cit., 53.

[34] Statute Article 12.1: "A State which becomes a Party to this Statute thereby accepts the jurisdiction of the Court with respect to the crimes referred to in article 5."

[35] Statute Article 12.2(a) and (b).

[36] Statute Article 17.1(a–d).

continues an old pattern, of both unsuccessful and successful attempts to create international jurisdictions, of subordinating international to state authority.[37]

The ICTY and ICTR are aberrations from the pattern of putting domestic jurisdiction first, international jurisdiction second (or, in ICC terminology, the pattern of complementarity). The two ad hoc tribunals were established with "concurrent jurisdiction," but "shall have primacy over national courts."[38] Primacy was confirmed by the ICTY Appeals Chamber in the Tadic case.[39]

Discussions in the ICC ad hoc committee and at the PrepCom meetings sought a formula that would enable the Court to act if no state-level prosecutions were taking place or if prosecutions that were undertaken were somehow fraudulent. Long negotiations produced an agreement that for the Court to take a case, it would have to be convinced that the state(s) that should be prosecuting were "unwilling or unable genuinely" to do so.

Unwillingness would be shown when proceedings were not being pursued or appeared to be intended to shield the person from responsibility,[40] were unjustifiably delayed,[41] were not conducted "independently or impartially" or were conducted in a manner "inconsistent with an intent to bring the person concerned to justice."[42] Inability considerations would include "whether, due to a total or substantial collapse or unavailability of its national judicial system, the State is unable to obtain the accused or the necessary evidence and testimony or otherwise unable to carry out its proceedings."[43] For a case to go to trial, the Prosecutor would need to

---

[37] El Zeidy, op cit., 870–4, argues that states' primary responsibility to punish international crimes is shown, for example, by the decision of the victorious allies of World War I to turn over prosecution of Germans suspected of committing war crimes to the German Supreme Court at Leipzig. They also proposed in the (unratified) 1920 Treaty of Sevres to grant themselves the right to try Turkish perpetrators of massacres against Armenians, but in the 1922 Treaty of Lausanne, deferred to Turkish sovereignty by dropping the idea.

Under the London Agreement after World War II, the International Military Tribunal (IMT) at Nuremberg tried only the select few Germans who were accused of being "the major criminals, whose offenses have no particular geographic localization," the rest of the suspects were to be tried in courts set up in the countries where they had committed their crimes.

The Genocide Convention's Article 5 conceived of an international tribunal but affirmed the responsibility of the state in which the crime has taken place to prosecute transgressors.

[38] ICTY Statute Article 9; ICTR Statute Article 8.
[39] ICTY, Prosecutor v. Dusko Tadic, appeals para. 55.
[40] Statute Article 17.2(a).
[41] Statute Article 17.2(b).
[42] Statute Article 17.2(c).
[43] Statute Article 17.2(d).

convince a Pre-Trial Chamber that the case was admissible. Thus, state jurisdiction is primary; the ICC is complementary: sovereignty is protected.

Prosecutor's Independence

Beyond jurisdiction and admissibility, a third major area in which concerns over sovereignty entered into the negotiations was the ICC Prosecutor's independence. Under the ILC draft, the Prosecutor could have initiated investigations after having received a complaint under the Genocide Convention from a state that was party to both the Convention and the Statute, or having received a complaint from a custodial or victim state about a crime having been committed for which the state had accepted jurisdiction of the Court, or by referral from the Security Council under Chapter VII of the UN Charter. But NGOs and some of the LMS pressed for a much more independent prosecutor, and the Statute reflects their victory. Under the Statute, the Prosecutor can initiate inquiries under his own authority (*proprio motu*) upon receipt of information from any source. The United States and some other states vigorously opposed this degree of prosecutorial independence, concerned that it could produce an out-of-control prosecutor lacking accountability to an appropriate judicial or legislative body.

In an effort to assuage concerns about the potential for a loose-cannon prosecutor, and taking a page from the civil-law tradition, the Statute negotiators agreed to establish a pretrial judicial chamber to which the Prosecutor would have to go to gain approval for pursuing *proprio motu* investigations, to issue arrest warrants, and to move toward trial with hearings on the confirmation of charges once a suspect was arrested. Under civil-law traditions, presentation of cases to Court by a prosecutor generally follows submission of information to a judge who decides whether there is reason to proceed with the case. Judges in this stage typically review entire case dossiers prepared by prosecutors (unlike common-law procedures wherein the trial judge comes to the trial without prior review of the case against the defendant).

Creation of the Pre-Trial Chamber was also a reaction by civil-law country representatives to what they perceived as the overly common-law-dominated structure of the ICTY and ICTR. Once the Court began operating, the Pre-Trial Chambers appeared to be seeking an expansion of their responsibilities to more closely approximate the judges of a civil-law proceeding, and the Office of the Prosecutor sought to restrain inroads upon prosecutorial independence (see Chapters 4 and 7).

The Security Council

The clash between states' sovereign prerogatives and the powers they confer upon multilateral organizations is not new. Depending upon how specific instruments are worded, at least on paper, primacy can be awarded to states or to an international organization; in practice, of course, states (at least ones with the military capabilities to make their positions stick) always have the last word.[44] So far, only the UN Security Council has routinely been accorded primacy in the area of security, and there the requirement of permanent member unanimity has reduced its scope for action under Chapter VII to subjects and moments when the victors of World War II can agree. For the two ad hoc tribunals, primacy was possible because they were established under Chapter VII.

Referral

The United States and the other permanent members of the UN Security Council sought an ICC Statute in which the Council would initiate ICC action by referring cases to it. While the United States pressed for Court jurisdiction to be triggered by a Security Council resolution (which would have made it more closely analogous to a standing version of the ad hoc tribunals), its negotiating interlocutors sought to find a compromise formula that would keep the United States in the Court, but establish greater independence. In the end, the Security Council could refer situations to the ICC Prosecutor under Chapter VII of the Charter,[45] but jurisdiction could also be exercised if a state party referred a situation to the Prosecutor[46] or if the prosecution initiated an investigation *proprio motu*.[47]

For the ICC, only in the event of a Security Council referral would it be able to claim primacy over national jurisdiction (under the rationale that it was operating under Chapter VII of the UN Charter, which requires all states to cooperate with the Security Council), but even there, the territorial state may resist intrusion upon sovereignty unless the Security Council decides to undertake enforcement action as well as refer the situation to the Court. This problem is shown by recent events in Sudan (see Chapter 7).

---

[44] See Krasner, *Sovereignty: Organized Hypocrisy* (1999), 221–38.
[45] Statute Article 13(b).
[46] Statute Article 13(a).
[47] Statute Article 13(c).

Suspension

The negotiations reversed the original proposal that the (UNSC) Security Council be the source of referrals to the Court. Under Statute Article 16, instead of UNSC agreement being required to trigger an investigation, the Security Council can act to suspend an ongoing investigation for 12 months (renewable) if the conflict situation is on the UNSC agenda and the Court's involvement is believed to threaten efforts to create peace. Even though the UNSC referral process makes possible a positive Security Council role in referrals, and the suspension provision makes it possible for the UNSC to stop an investigation, these powers are much weaker than would have been reliance on a Security Council trigger for Court involvement. The suspension provision responded to the objection that ICC activities could potentially impair peacemaking efforts under Chapter VII of the UN Charter that the Security Council might pursue, but preserved the Court's independence.

Cooperation, Information Sharing, and National Security

States that accede to the ICC Statute obligate themselves to cooperate with the Court[48] and to have procedures in place in their domestic laws for the cooperation specified in the Statute. Parties to the Statute are obligated to arrest and surrender persons sought by the Court, either as suspects or as witnesses, and to have laws and procedures in place to do so.[49] In addition, states pledge to provide various kinds of information to the Court when so requested; take evidence, testimony, and expert opinions for the Court; question people; serve documents; carry out forensic investigations; provide records; protect witnesses and victims; trace financial records and seize assets, among others. The Statute provisions that oblige states to cooperate broadly with the Court also, however, contain protections for states that were the subject of extensive negotiation at the Statute Conference. If a state would have to violate "an existing fundamental legal principle of general application" in order to comply with a Court request, the state and Court are supposed to consult, and if no solution can be found, the Court is to modify its request.

Perhaps more significantly, a state can withhold information or intervene at any stage in Court proceedings to prevent disclosure of information that it deems to be prejudicial to its national security.[50] The Statute sets out extensive procedures for consultation in such an event, but in the end it's the

---

[48] Statute Article 86.
[49] Statute Article 88.
[50] Statute Article 72.

state's decision. The most that the Court can do in response is report noncooperation to the Assembly of States Parties or, in the event that the case flows from a Security Council referral, to the Security Council.[51]

OLD AND NEW JUSTICE PARADIGMS IN THE STATUTE

The Statute emerged as a bargained document in which ICC enthusiasts' objectives for a highly independent court were toned down in exchange for the embrace of a broad range of objectives, including both old and new justice norms. The states most worried about sovereignty could rest assured that the new Court's powers would be limited (not only by statute but also by its need for states' cooperation), while embracing the broad range of norms or, in the most rejectionist cases, by embracing (or not) the norms but declining to join the Statute.

In Chapter 1, I argued that traditional retributive justice ideas converged with newer concepts of transitional reparative justice in the post–Cold War environment. They flowed together into the Statute. While the first and strongest impetus for positive implementation of international criminal law came from international lawyers, the new justice norms were championed by nongovernmental organizations and posttransition governments, such as South Africa's, that sought to emphasize victims' rights and reparative justice, along with civil-law states (such as France) that had, during the recent past, elevated victims' rights in their own systems' priorities.[52]

Old Justice and General Principles

The Statute calls for creation of a judicial institution to investigate, try, and punish perpetrators of international crimes. In this sense, it follows the old, retributive justice model. Negotiators included in the Statute the general principles of law that underpin traditional jurisprudence. Under the principle of legality, the ICC can prosecute only crimes defined in the Statute (*nullum crimen sine lege* – no crime without a law) that took place within the jurisdiction of the Court, and punish such crimes only in accord with the Statute (*nulla poena sine lege* – no punishment without a law).[53] The Court has no retroactive jurisdiction.[54] As a criminal court, only

---

[51] Statute Article 87.7.
[52] Interviews.
[53] Statute Articles 22, 23.
[54] Statute Article 24.

individual persons are culpable under the Statute. Persons can be culpable for committing a crime alone, with others, or through others or if they ordered, solicited, or induced commission of a crime (whether committed or only attempted). Persons can be prosecuted for aiding, abetting, or otherwise assisting or contributing to commission or attempted commission of the crime by a group of persons working with a common purpose. For the crime of genocide, incitement and initiating an attempt to carry out genocide can be considered a crime, even if the crime ultimately didn't take place.[55] A person is culpable only if the material elements of the crime are committed with intent and knowledge,[56] and persons cannot be tried more than once for a particular crime.[57]

Persons under 18 at the time of the crime are not under the Court's jurisdiction.[58] Following from the Nuremberg principles, the Statute applies to everyone regardless of official capacity or domestic or international rules of immunity.[59] Commanders have responsibility for the actions of their subordinates; subordinates are not excused from culpability by virtue of having been ordered to commit a crime.[60] Following the 1968 UN General Assembly Resolution, the Statute declares that there is no statute of limitations for prosecution of the crimes under ICC jurisdiction.[61]

Traditional rights are conferred upon the defendants: a presumption of innocence; a standard of guilt "beyond reasonable doubt";[62] the right to a public hearing, to be promptly informed of the charge, to have adequate time and facilities to prepare a defense and to communicate freely with defense counsel; a right of non-self-incrimination; speedy trial; defense counsel of the accused's choosing; right to examine witnesses, to have

---

[55] Statute Article 25.

[56] Statute Article 30.

[57] Statute Article 20.

[58] Statute Article 26.

[59] Statute Article 27.

[60] Statute Article 28. The matter of responsibility is somewhat further refined under Article 31 (grounds for excluding criminal responsibility may include mental disease, involuntary intoxication, self-defense, duress caused by threat of imminent death), Article 32 (mistake of fact or mistake of law, which precludes responsibility only if it negates either of the mental elements), and Article 33 [superior order and prescription of law, under which a person may be relieved of responsibility if (1) "(a) The person was under a legal obligation to obey orders; (b) The person did not know that the order was unlawful; and (c) The order was not manifestly unlawful." However, (2) "For the purposes of this article, orders to commit genocide or crimes against humanity are manifestly unlawful."]

[61] Statute Article 29. UN General Assembly, Resolution 2391 (XXIII) of November 26, 1968, "Convention on the Non-Applicability of Statutory Limitations to War Crimes and Crimes Against Humanity," entry into force November 11, 1970.

[62] Statute Article 66.

documents and testimony translated into a language of choice, and to receive exculpatory evidence from the Prosecutor.[63] Trial rules and processes are spelled out in additional detail in other Statute provisions and in the Rules of Procedure and Evidence and the Elements of Crimes adopted by the Assembly of States Parties.

New Justice Paradigm

While the Statute reflects old justice principles, it incorporates many elements of the new justice paradigm as well. These are not necessarily mutually exclusive, and many of the innovations rectify long-standing imbalances in justice procedures, particularly insofar as they have inadequately responded to gender inequalities. However, in going beyond improved implementation of traditional justice measures to include new justice objectives, the Statute's broad mandate is institutionally very challenging.

Rectifying Judicial Process Blindnesses

The Statute explicitly defines gender crimes under crimes against humanity and war crimes. It exhorts the ASP to select judges who are representative of the various major legal systems of the world, geographical areas, and male and female judges and recognizes the need for judges with expertise especially in the area of violence against women and children. These provisions demonstrate negotiators' heightened awareness of the problems of traditionally male- and Western-dominated courts in dealing with witness populations that are largely women, children, and people from non-Western countries. The Prosecutor, similarly, is instructed to "appoint advisers with legal expertise on specific issues, including but not limited to, sexual and gender violence and violence against children."[64]

Victims and Witnesses

In addition to mandating better balance in hiring Court staff, the Statute requires that in pursuit of its investigations, the Office of the Prosecutor particularly take into account the "interests and personal circumstances of victims and witnesses, particularly in regard to health, age, and gender, and to take into account the nature of the crime, particularly when involving sexual or gender violence or victimization of children."[65] These statutory

---

[63] Statute Article 67.
[64] Statute Article 42.9.
[65] Statute Article 54.1(b).

provisions reflect the victims' orientation of the new justice; however, they sit somewhat uncomfortably with some of the long-standing principles of justice, such as the presumption of innocence and the right to a fair trial.

The Statute also instructs the Registrar to set up a "Victims and Witnesses Unit" to "provide, in consultation with the OTP, protective measures and security arrangements, counseling and other appropriate assistance for witnesses, victims who appear before the Court, and others who are at risk on account of testimony given by such witnesses. The Unit shall include staff with expertise in trauma, including trauma related to crimes of sexual violence."[66] In trials, the judges are to "provide for the protection of the accused, witnesses and victims." [67] Thus, all three organs of the Court – the Office of the Prosecutor, the Registry, and Chambers – are responsible for protecting victims and witnesses, with particular attention to children and women, as well as providing protection and due process to the accused.[68]

More than merely providing protection, however, and as part of the set of restorative justice norms, the Court is enjoined to make possible the participation of victims in Court processes.[69] Victim participation is a more difficult problem than witness protection from the standpoint of traditional justice principles. Involving victims in Court proceedings before a conviction has been obtained could jeopardize the presumption of innocence. The Statute articulates the principles, but it is only in practice that the tensions among the Court's responsibilities will be worked out.

Victims' Trust Fund

Beyond protecting and involving victims, the Statute also directs the Court to "establish principles relating to reparations" including restitution, compensation, and rehabilitation.[70] The Statute directs the Assembly of

[66] Statute Article 43.6.

[67] Statute Article 64.6(e).

[68] Effective protection of witnesses is also crucial for the success of investigations and prosecution because (as was painfully and repeatedly discovered by the ad hoc tribunals) if victims and witnesses are too fearful of revenge to provide information to investigators or to testify, prosecutions falter.

[69] Statute Article 68.3: "Where the personal interests of the victims are affected, the Court shall permit their views and concerns to be presented and considered at stages of the proceedings determined to be appropriate by the court and in a manner which is not prejudicial to or inconsistent with the rights of the accused and a fair and impartial trial. Such views and concerns may be presented by the legal representatives of the victims where the Court considers it appropriate, in accordance with the Rules of Procedure and Evidence."

[70] Statute Article 75.

States Parties is to establish a trust fund for "victims of crimes within the jurisdiction of the Court, and of the families of such victims"[71] (see Chapter 4). The restorative justice objective is clear. The mechanisms for how it is to be pursued awaited implementation, and the dilemmas of upholding general principles of law and due process, while also incorporating victim interests, would have to be managed.

Incorporating traditional and new justice objectives, protecting sovereignty but mandating a wide range of responsibilities, seeking to end impunity and thus criminality, the Statute Conference successfully produced a treaty on which to construct the International Criminal Court. Elation swept the vast majority of participants in the Conference as it ended successfully two hours past its deadline, early in the morning of July 18, 1998. It remained to be seen whether adequate numbers of states would join and thus bring the treaty into effect. What would states gain by joining the Statute?

WHY DO STATES JOIN?

From the constructivist viewpoint, norm convergence drove a change in states' identities. Under pressure from domestic, transnational, and international advocates of countering impunity, domestic citizenries' concern over human rights converged with state decision makers' changing ideas about the proper realm of activities of the state, leading to a consensus on the creation of the ICC. New justice norms were incorporated into the Statute because state decision makers, informed by civil society, came to believe that a modern justice system had to take greater cognizance of victims' interests and social reconstruction following massive crimes than did traditional justice. Some of the Statute's provisions remained highly controversial even at the end of negotiations, most notably leading to active U.S. opposition to the Court, because the shift to new identities (incorporating the new norms of international criminal law) was not universal. Old understandings of the international system and appropriate behavior within it coexist, although uncomfortably, with newer ones.

Realist explanations for the creation of a new international organization tend to be circular. If states get together to sign a treaty creating a new organization, by definition it must be in their interests to do so. The harder question is what interests the organization serves. Since in the realist construct, gaining relative advantage (over other states) is the primary motive for

---

[71] Statute Article 79.

state behavior, a state would need to benefit relative to others by joining the ICC. It is conceivable a state concerned about its citizens being subject to international crimes, or convinced that genocide, crimes against humanity, and war crimes contribute to potentially costly regional threats, would join efforts to prosecute international criminals to deter future criminal behavior. A state might join the ICC succumbing to pressures exerted by other state supporters of the Court. Or a state might believe that it could manipulate the ICC's resources to contribute to its individual advantage. But these are weak explanations because the Court's resources are very small, relative to those of most countries, and relative gain is not clear.

Although realists would have difficulty explaining imperatives to join the ICC, their perspective could be useful to explain states' demurral from accession. Just as states pursue relative advantage, they should avoid relative disadvantage. States concerned that the ICC might constrain their independent behavior might oppose the Court more than states lacking such concerns. States worried that they would wind up disproportionately financing the Court might also be reluctant, unless there was some compensating advantage to joining. The United States has most vigorously opposed the ICC, mustering a series of arguments against the Court based both on power considerations and (ostensibly) on principle.

The United States asserts that the Court lacks oversight (so it could become overly politicized), and its operations could undermine U.S. constitutional protections for its citizens (by subjecting them to legal processes violating constitutional guarantees of due process). The United States objects to the Court's jurisdictional claim on the basis of territorial or suspect nationality, having sought suspect nationality to be an absolute requirement, charging that without suspect state acceptance of jurisdiction, were the Court to act against the national of a nonsignatory of the Statute, it would be applying a treaty to a state that hadn't accepted it (which contravenes international law standards).

U.S. objections generally boil down to concerns over maintaining state sovereignty, and echos of these concerns can be found in Chinese and Indian reticence to join the Statute. The Russian position has been less negative, and parliamentary consideration of joining seems to have moved further than among the other opposed UN Security Council members.

Neoliberal institutionalism doesn't require relative gain as a state interest: Absolute gain can suffice. If a general problem among states is more amenable to solution by collective action, neoliberal institutionalists would predict cooperative behavior, such as has taken place in the areas of international trade and finance, environmental protection, and human rights. Were states to believe that impunity is a threat to common welfare, cooperative efforts to counter it could be in the nations' interests. If an international court came to be a mechanism states viewed to be needed to counter impunity, just as, for instance, an international treaty and funding organization were deemed necessary to counter ozone depletion, states might join to create a court.

In neoliberal institutionalist terms, the Statute can be seen as evidence of an epistemic community in the overlapping areas of transitional and international criminal justice.[72] This community became convinced that impunity impedes international peace, security, and justice. For impunity most effectively and efficiently to be countered, an international organization needed to be created that would be more stable than would ad hoc tribunals established case-by-case by the UN Security Council. Serious controversies remained within the epistemic community about the degree of independence that the organization should have, and the crimes and people over which it would have jurisdiction. Particularly during the post–Cold War "institution-building" moment, however, conditions were ripe for creation of the ICC.

In the United States, some experts – particularly in the State Department – were members of the transitional justice/international criminal justice epistemic community and believed that joining the new institution would redound to collective and U.S. benefit. Others – particularly associated with civilian authorities in the Pentagon – were more concerned about U.S. vulnerabilities to the new Court; thus, they did not accept the beliefs of the epistemic community and hence vigorously opposed joining the Court. In the end, the interests of sovereignty outweighed the advantages of cooperation. The Clinton administration sought to keep the United States in a position to influence the shape of the new Court. The Bush administration withdrew

---

[72] The epistemic community literature mostly refers to cooperation in areas where scientific and/or technological knowledge is key to decision making. Haas "Introduction," (1992), 3, defines epistemic community as "a network of professionals with recognized expertise and competence in a particular domain and an authoritative claim to policy-relevant knowledge within that domain or issue-area." I use the term more loosely, as suggested by Sebenius, "Challenging Conventional Explanations of International Cooperation: Negotiation Analysis and the Case of Epistemic Communities" in the same volume: "an epistemic community can be understood as a special kind of de facto natural coalition of 'believers' whose main interest lies not in the material sphere but instead in fostering the adoption of the community's policy project. Initially, an epistemic community faces the problem of how to expand from a typically small, de facto natural coalition into a meaningful 'winning coalition.' Its actions can often be understood as changing the perceived zone of possible agreement in well-understood ways that are favorable to its objectives" (325).

completely, supported anti-ICC legislation, and viewed the Court as a threat to U.S. sovereignty.

CONCLUSIONS

Because the Court was conceived as a permanent institution to which any state's citizens might in theory become subject, states were very concerned about the ICC's challenge to sovereignty. The solution to the sovereignty problem was the principle of complementarity. Crimes that were too controversial (aggression, the use of weapons of mass destruction) were left for future negotiations. Jurisdiction (requiring a Security Council resolution or acceptance of the Court by the territorial or suspect state) and admissibility (proving that appropriate government authorities were unwilling or unable genuinely to prosecute crimes) criteria further defined the limits of the Court's reach, which is additionally constrained by its need for states' cooperation in order for it to carry out its activities and internally checked by the Prosecutor's need to receive approval from Pre-Trial Chambers before commencing official investigations and moving on to trials.

The consequence of wide participation in the Statute negotiations was inclusion of a broad range of objectives that flow from old and new justice norms. A carefully constrained Court is mandated to pursue an extremely broad range of goals. In that combination, of narrow constraint and broad mission, lurk the organizational and legal challenges that the ICC now faces in operation. As soon as it began operating, the Court began to confront the problems produced by its sometimes contradictory objectives and its inherently challenging tasks.

APPENDIX 3A: PREAMBLE OF THE ROME STATUTE
OF THE INTERNATIONAL CRIMINAL COURT

The States Parties to this Statute,

Conscious that all peoples are united by common bonds, their cultures pieced together in a shared heritage, and concerned that this delicate mosaic may be shattered at any time,

Mindful that during this century millions of children, women and men have been victims of unimaginable atrocities that deeply shock the conscience of humanity,

Recognizing that such grave crimes threaten the peace, security and well-being of the world,

Affirming that the most serious crimes of concern to the international community as a whole must not go unpunished and that their effective prosecution must be ensured by taking measures at the national level and by enhancing international cooperation,

Determined to put an end to impunity for the perpetrators of these crimes and thus to contribute to the prevention of such crimes,

Recalling that it is the duty of every State to exercise its criminal jurisdiction over those responsible for international crimes,

Reaffirming the Purposes and Principles of the Charter of the United Nations, and in particular that all States shall refrain from the threat or use of force against the territorial integrity or political independence of any State, or in any other manner inconsistent with the Purposes of the United Nations,

Emphasizing in this connection that nothing in this Statute shall be taken as authorizing any State Party to intervene in an armed conflict or the internal affairs of any State,

Determined to these ends and for the sake of present and future generations, to establish an independent permanent International Criminal Court in relationship with the United Nations system, with jurisdiction over the most serious crimes of concern to the international community as a whole,

Emphasizing that the International Criminal Court established under this Statute shall be complementary to national criminal jurisdictions,

Resolved to guarantee lasting respect for and the enforcement of international justice,

Have agreed as follows: ...

APPENDIX 3B: ROME STATUTE CRIMES

Article 5

Crimes within the Jurisdiction of the Court
1. The jurisdiction of the Court shall be limited to the most serious crimes of concern to the international community as a whole. The Court has jurisdiction in accordance with this Statute with respect to the following crimes:
   (a) The crime of genocide;
   (b) Crimes against humanity;
   (c) War crimes;
   (d) The crime of aggression.

2. The Court shall exercise jurisdiction over the crime of aggression once a provision is adopted in accordance with articles 121 and 123 defining the crime and setting out the conditions under which the court shall exercise jurisdiction with respect to this crime. Such a provision shall be consistent with the relevant provisions of the Charter of the United Nations.

Article 6

Genocide

For the Purposes of this Statute, "genocide" means any of the following acts, committed with intent to destroy, in whole or in part, a national, ethnical, racial or religious group, as such:

(a) Killing members of the group;
(b) Causing serious bodily or mental harm to members of the group;
(c) Deliberately inflicting on the group conditions of life calculated to bring about its physical destruction in whole or in part;
(d) Imposing measures intended to prevent births within the group;
(e) Forcibly transferring children of the group to another group.

Article 7

Crimes against Humanity

1. For the purpose of this Statute, "crime against humanity" means any of the following acts when committed as part of a widespread or systematic attack directed against any civilian population, with knowledge of the attack:
   (a) Murder;
   (b) Extermination;
   (c) Enslavement;
   (d) Deportation or forcible transfer of population;
   (e) Imprisonment or other severe deprivation of physical liberty in violation of fundamental rules of international law;
   (f) Torture;
   (g) Rape, sexual slavery, enforced prostitution, forced pregnancy, enforced sterilization, or any other form of sexual violence of comparable gravity;
   (h) Persecution against any identifiable group or collectivity on political, racial, national, ethnic, cultural, religious, gender as

defined in paragraph 3, or other grounds that are universally recognized as impermissible under international law, in connection with any act referred to in this paragraph or any crime within the jurisdiction of the Court;

(i) Enforced disappearance of persons;

(j) The crime of apartheid;

(k) Other inhumane acts of a similar character intentionally causing great suffering, or serious injury to body or to mental or physical health.

2. For the purpose of paragraph 1:

(a) "Attack directed against any civilian population" means a course of conduct involving the multiple commission of acts referred to in paragraph 1 against any civilian population, pursuant to or in furtherance of a State or organizational policy to commit such attack;

(b) "Extermination" includes the intentional inflection of conditions of life, *inter alia* the deprivation of access to food and medicine, calculated to bring about the destruction of part of a population;

(c) "Enslavement" means the exercise of any or all of the powers attaching to the right of ownership over a person and includes the exercise of such power in the course of trafficking in persons, in particular women and children;

(d) "Deportation or forcible transfer of population" means forced displacement of the persons concerned by expulsion or other coercive acts from the area in which they are lawfully present, without grounds permitted under international law;

(e) "Torture" means the intentional infliction of severe pain or suffering, whether physical or mental, upon a person in the custody or under the control of the accused; except that torture shall not include pain or suffering arising only from, inherent in or incidental to lawful sanctions;

(f) "Forced pregnancy"means the unlawful confinement of a woman forcibly made pregnant, with the intent of affecting the ethnic composition of any population or carrying out other grave violations of international law. This definition shall not in any way be interpreted as affecting national laws relating to pregnancy;

(g) "Persecution" means the intentional and severe deprivation of fundamental rights contrary to international law by reason of the identity of the group or collectivity;

(h) "The crime of apartheid" means inhumane acts of a character similar to those referred to in paragraph 1, committed in the context of an institutionalized regime of systematic oppression and domination by one racial group over any other racial group or groups and committed with the intention of maintaining that regime;

(i) "Enforced disappearance of persons" means the arrest, detention or abduction of persons by, or with the authorization, support or acquiescence of, a State or a political organization, followed by a refusal to acknowledge that deprivation of freedom or to give information on the fate or whereabouts of those persons, with the intention of removing them from the protection of the law for a prolonged period of time;

3. For the purpose of this Statute, it is understood that the term "gender" refers to the two sexes, male and female, within the context of society. The term "gender" does not indicate any meaning different from the above.

Article 8

War Crimes

1. The Court shall have jurisdiction in respect of war crimes in particular when committed as part of a plan or policy or as part of a large-scale commission of such crimes.

2. For the purpose of this Statute, "war crimes" means:

(a) Grave breaches of the Geneva Conventions of 12 August 1949, namely, any of the following acts against persons or property protected under the provisions of the relevant Geneva Convention:

(i) Willful killing;

(ii) Torture or inhuman treatment, including biological experiments;

(iii) Willfully causing great suffering, or serious injury to body or health;

(iv) Extensive destruction and appropriation of property, not justified by military necessity and carried out unlawfully and wantonly;

(v) Compelling a prisoner of war or other protected person to serve in the forces of a hostile Power;

(vi) Willfully depriving a prisoner of war or other protected person of the rights of fair and regular trial;

(vii) Taking of hostages.

(b) Other serious violations of the laws and customs applicable in international armed conflict within the established framework of international law, namely, in any of the following acts:

   (i) Intentionally directing attacks against the civilian population as such or against individual civilians not taking direct part in hostilities;

   (ii) Intentionally directing attacks against civilian objects, that is, objects which are not military objectives;

   (iii) Intentionally directing attacks against personnel, installations, material units or vehicles involved in a humanitarian assistance or peacekeeping mission in accordance with the Charter of the United Nations, as long as they are entitled to the protection given to civilians or civilian objects under the international law of armed conflict;

   (iv) Intentionally launching an attack in the knowledge that such attack will cause incidental loss of life or injury to civilians or damage to civilian objects or widespread, long-term and severe damage to the natural environment which would be clearly excessive in relation to the concrete and direct overall military advantage anticipated;

   (v) Attacking or bombarding, by whatever means, towns, villages, dwellings or buildings which are undefended and which are not military objectives;

   (vi) Killing or wounding a combatant who, having laid down his arms or having no longer means of defence, has surrendered at discretion;

   (vii) Making improper use of a flag of truce, of the flag or of the military insignia and uniform of the enemy or of the United Nations, as well as of the distinctive emblems of the Geneva Conventions, resulting in death or serious personal injury;

   (viii) The transfer, directly or indirectly, by the Occupying Power of parts of its own civilian population into the territory it occupies, or the deportation or transfer of all or parts of the population of the occupied territory within or outside this territory;

   (ix) Intentionally directing attacks against buildings dedicated to religion, education, art, science or charitable purposes, historic monuments, hospitals and places where the sick and wounded are collected, provided they are not military objectives;

(x) Subjecting persons who are in the power of an adverse party to physical mutilation or to medical or scientific experiments of any kind which are neither justified by the medical, dental or hospital treatment of the person concerned nor carried out in his or her interest, and which cause death to or seriously endanger the health of such person or persons;

(xi) Killing or wounding treacherously individuals belonging to the hostile nation or army;

(xii) Declaring that no quarter will be given;

(xiii) Destroying or seizing the enemy's property unless such destruction or seizure be imperatively demanded by the necessities of war;

(xiv) Declaring abolished, suspended or inadmissible in a court of law the rights and actions of the nationals of the hostile party;

(xv) Compelling the nationals of the hostile party to take part in the operations of war directed against their own country, even if they were in the belligerent's service before the commencement of the war;

(xvi) Pillaging a town or place, even when taken by assault;

(xvii) Employing poison or poisoned weapons;

(xviii) Employing asphyxiating, poisonous or other gases, and all analogous liquids, materials or devices;

(xix) Employing bullets which expand or flatten easily in the human body, such as bullets with a hard envelope which does not entirely cover the core or is pierced with incisions;

(xx) Employing weapons, projectiles and material and methods of warfare which are of a nature to cause superfluous injury or unnecessary suffering or which are inherently indiscriminate in violation of the international law of armed conflict, provided that such weapons, projectiles and material and methods of warfare are the subject of a comprehensive prohibition and are included in an annex to this Statute, by an amendment in accordance with the relevant provisions set forth in articles 121 and 123;

(xxi) Committing outrages upon personal dignity, in particular humiliating and degrading treatment;

(xxii) Committing rape, sexual slavery, enforced prostitution, forced pregnancy, as defined in article 7, paragraph 2 (f), enforced sterilization, or any other form of sexual violence also constituting a grave breach of the Geneva Conventions;

(xxiii) Utilizing the presence of a civilian or other protected person to render certain points, areas or military forces immune from military operations;

(xxiv) Intentionally directing attacks against buildings, material, medical units and transport, and personnel using the distinctive emblems of the Geneva Conventions in conformity with international law;

(xxv) Intentionally using starvation of civilians as a method of warfare by depriving them of objects indispensable to their survival, including willfully impeding relief supplies as provided for under the Geneva Conventions;

(xxvi) Conscripting or enlisting children under the age of fifteen years into the national armed forces or using them to participate actively in hostilities.

(c) In the case of an armed conflict not of an international character, serious violations of article 3 common to the four Geneva Conventions of 12 August 1949, namely, any of the following acts committed against persons taking no active part in the hostilities, including members of armed forces who have laid down their arms and those placed *hors de combat* by sickness, wounds, detention or any other cause:

  (i) Violence to life and person, in particular murder of all kinds, mutilation, cruel treatment and torture;

  (ii) Committing outrages upon personal dignity, in particular humiliating and degrading treatment;

  (iii) Taking of hostages;

  (iv) The passing of sentences and the carrying out of executions without previous judgement pronounced by a regularly constituted court, affording all judicial guarantees which are generally recognized as indispensable.

(d) Paragraph 2 (c) applies to armed conflicts not of an international character and thus does not apply to situations of internal disturbances and tensions, such as riots, isolated and sporadic acts of violence or other acts of a similar nature.

(e) Other serious violations of the laws and customs applicable in armed conflicts not of an international character, within the established framework of international law, namely, any of the following acts:

   (i) Intentionally directing attacks against the civilian population as such or against individual civilians not taking direct part in hostilities;

  (ii) Intentionally directing attacks against buildings, material, medical units and transport, and personnel using the distinctive emblems of the Geneva Conventions in conformity with international law;

 (iii) Intentionally directing attacks against personnel, installations, material units or vehicles involved in a humanitarian assistance or peacekeeping mission in accordance with the Charter of the United Nations, as long as they are entitled to the protection given to civilians or civilian objects under the international law of armed conflict;

 (iv) Intentionally directing attacks against buildings dedicated to religion, education, art, science or charitable purposes, historic monuments, hospitals and places where the sick and wounded are collected, provided they are not military objectives;

  (v) Pillaging a town or place, even when taken by assault;

 (vi) Committing rape, sexual slavery, enforced prostitution, forced pregnancy, as defined in article 7, paragraph 2 (f), enforced sterilization, and any other form of sexual violence also constituting a serious violation of article 3 common to the four Geneva Conventions;

 (vii) Conscripting or enlisting children under the age of fifteen years into the national armed forces or using them to participate actively in hostilities;

(viii) Ordering the displacement of the civilian population for reasons related to the conflict, unless the security of the civilians involved or imperative military reasons so demand;

 (ix) Killing or wounding treacherously a combatant adversary;

  (x) Declaring that no quarter will be given;

 (xi) Subjecting persons who are in the power of an adverse party to physical mutilation or to medical or scientific experiments of any kind which are neither justified by the medical, dental or hospital treatment of the person concerned nor carried out in his or her interest, and which cause death to or seriously endanger the heath of such person or persons;

(xii) Destroying or seizing the property of an adversary unless such destruction or seizure be imperatively demanded by the necessities of the conflict;

(f) Paragraph 2 (e) applies to armed conflicts not of an international character and thus does not apply to situations of internal disturbances and tensions, such as riots, isolated and sporadic acts of violence or other acts of a similar nature. It applies to armed conflicts that take place in the territory of a State when there is protracted armed conflict between governmental authorities and organized armed groups or between such groups.

3. Nothing in paragraph 2 (c) and (e) shall affect the responsibility of a Government to maintain or re-establish law and order in the State or to defend the unity and territorial integrity of the State, by all legitimate means.

4

Building the Court

Once the Statute was opened for signature on July 17, 1998, the ICC project faced a nebulous interregnum. Pessimists thought the Statute might languish without the requisite number of adherents for five or ten years, or even perhaps indefinitely. Optimists pressed for preparations to be made to establish the Court, believing that ratifications might snowball. The optimists were prescient. The needed 60 ratifications were in hand in April 2002, less than four years after the Statute had been completed – so quickly (as compared with the pessimists' vision) that practical preparations were rushed. (development of the Court was leisurely compared to the ad hoc tribunals' rapid genesis. From the adoption of the Yugoslavia Tribunal's Statute in May 1993, 18 months elapsed until the ICTY issued its first indictment.) For the ICC, the almost four-year hiatus between the Statute's being opened for signature and coming into force allowed negotiators to complete the Rules of Procedure and Evidence, Elements of Crimes, and other vital operational documents. Another year passed before the Court had a Prosecutor in place, and he first requested arrest warrants for suspects (in Uganda) in May 2005, almost seven years from the adoption of the Statute, three years after it took effect, just short of two years after the Prosecutor took office.

The Court that started operating on July 1, 2002, has less formal power than the ad hoc tribunals, since its jurisdiction is constrained by "complementarity" while theirs had "primacy," but it potentially has more to do, since their territorial and temporal jurisdictions were limited, but the ICC's are open-ended. The Statute and Preparatory Commission negotiators showed that they had learned much from the tribunals by, for example, subordinating the Registry to the Presidency, but many problems similar to those of the tribunals confront the Court. The tripartite structure is a management nightmare; judicial neutrality, prosecutorial independence, and organizational efficiency are not easily compatible; due process values clash with victims' interests; and operational environments are difficult. State cooperation is vital, but it also threatens to undermine the appearance (if not the reality) of Court neutrality.

This chapter is about how the ICC is hewing its operational path, a topic that most directly responds to the neoliberal institutionalist logic that links organizations' effectiveness and efficiency to the degree to which organizations can develop some independence from states even while they serve state interests. People who work for, or observe, the Court put it a different way. They say that if the ICC can demonstrate to its members that it is effective, efficient, and legitimate, states' support will continue and grow.

This chapter is long, and I hope, revelatory, incorporating information from interviews with participants. I describe sample conflicts within the ICC in considerable detail, intending to show how complicated the start-up has been, how tensions built into the organization's mandate and structure are manifested in internal organizational conflict and in organizational innovation. Aside from the larger international significance of the Court, I believe that its internal dynamics need to be understood in order for conclusions to be drawn about its likely future course, about where institutional evolution needs to take place, and about its chances for survival and success.

The chapter's first section describes the period preceding the Court's opening. It shows that the PrepCom resolved many uncertainties left by the Statute, but even with this strong underpinning, substantial discretion remained for the Court to develop its operations through practice. The second section discusses the development of the Office of the Prosecutor, often dubbed the "engine of the Court." In the transition to operations, the Prosecutor made controversial and high-stakes decisions that sought to maximize prosecutorial discretion, including on grounds that some observers found to be overly political. Since the Prosecutor realized that effectiveness defined in terms of trials and convictions could be a trap for the Court, he articulated alternative measures for success, while also seeking to set up his office to avoid the most troublesome of the tribunals' operational problems. The third section describes internal tensions in the Court among the OTP, Registry, and Chambers, produced by the amalgamation of civil- and common-law traditions, by the difficult tripartite structure of the Court, and by personal clashes. The fourth section describes Court innovations to implement its new (restorative) justice mandate and how the new justice mandate can clash with old (retributive) justice objectives. The chapter's fifth section discusses the Court's planning efforts.

FROM STATUTE TO COURT

The Rome Conference passed a Final Act,[1] along with the Statute, that established a Preparatory Commission to elaborate the rules and regulations that the ICC and its Assembly of States Parties would need for the Court to operate. In ten official sessions (1998–2002), with additional informal "intersessional" meetings, the PrepCom negotiated draft documents covering the Rules of Procedure and Evidence; Elements of Crimes; an outline for defining the crime of aggression; election procedures for the Assembly of States Parties to select judges, the chief and deputy prosecutor; agreements with the United Nations and with The Netherlands; a first-year budget for the Court; personnel and accounting policies; and more. While the PrepCom working groups toiled, signatures and ratifications of the Statute accumulated more rapidly than even most optimists had hoped, although the United States, Russia, China, Japan, India, and other states demurred.

The United States remained engaged with the PrepCom, and President Clinton signed the Statute in the waning days of his term of office, on December 31, 2000. When George Bush took office as President in January 2001, the official U.S. attitude flipped from critically engaged to actively hostile. During the year, the United States participated only in the PrepCom working group on the crime of aggression, because, the United States said, the issue was relevant to the UN Security Council.[2] In 2002, the United States abandoned the PrepCom meetings altogether, and in a May 2002 letter to UN Secretary-General Kofi Annan, the United States "unsigned" the Statute by informing him that it considered itself unbound by Clinton's signature.

States that had signed the Final Act and others invited to the Rome Conference (effectively, all states) were invited to join the PrepCom. The commission met its deadline of June 30, 2000, for the draft Rules of Procedure and Evidence and the Elements of Crimes, and continued work on the long list of other topics for which the Final Act had not specified

---

[1] United Nations Diplomatic Conference of Plenipotentiaries on the Establishment of an International Criminal Court, "Final Act" (July 17, 1998), Section F.

[2] Global Policy Forum, "Bush Administration Ponders Position Toward International Court" (2001).

deadlines. The PrepCom would go out of business at the conclusion of the first meeting of the Assembly of States Parties, which could take place only after the Statute had come into effect.

Preparing to Begin

By spring 2001, as states acceded to the Statute faster, PrepCom Chairman Ambassador Philippe Kirsch of Canada pushed for a "road map" of documents and actions necessary to bring the Court into being. Kirsch was supported strongly by NGOs, particularly in the person of William R. Pace, convener of the NGO coalition for the ICC. The PrepCom adopted the "Road Map Leading to the Early Establishment of the International Criminal Court" in September.[3] Moving the Court from Statute into operation required procedures and an agenda for the first ASP and documents governing the internal rules of the Court for initial operations (until final documents could be adopted by a later ASP). A mechanism needed to be developed so that the PrepCom could work with The Netherlands to find temporary quarters for the Court and to work on logistical arrangements.

Despite public goading from Pace, the Dutch government moved lethargically at first. The two Dutch Foreign Ministry officials responsible were convinced, on the basis of experience with prior treaties, that the ICC wouldn't materialize for at least ten years from 1998.[4] In June 2001, in an interview with a Dutch newspaper, Bill Pace predicted a "political catastrophe" when the Statute entered into force without proper preparations having been made.[5] In September, the government transferred then–Defense Ministry Director-General Edmond Wellenstein to become head of an ICC task force, and preparations intensified. As a result of Wellenstein's initiatives, a building was found for the Court in spring 2002.

On April 11, 2002, ten states[6] simultaneously deposited their Statute ratifications with the UN Secretary-General in New York, starting the clock ticking. On July 1, 2002, the first of the month following sixty days from the sixtieth ratification, after a gestation that could be measured back to the

---

[3] UN Preparatory Commission for the International Criminal Court, "Road Map Leading to the Early Establishment of the International Criminal Court" (2001); Martijn Groenleer, "Justice under Construction: The Birth and Early Development of the International Criminal Court" (2003), 46.

[4] Groenleer, ibid., 73.

[5] Ibid., 74.

[6] Bosnia and Herzegovina, Bulgaria, Cambodia, Democratic Republic of Congo, Ireland, Jordan, Mongolia, Romania, Slovakia, and Niger.

ILC draft of 1994, the Trinidad and Tobago proposal of 1989, the ILC draft of 1953, the Nuremberg Court of 1945, the founding of the Red Cross and the Lieber Code of the mid-nineteenth century, or perhaps the trial of Peter von Hagenbach in 1474, the first permanent international criminal court was born.

Filling the Empty Shell

The PrepCom created an advance team of five people to lay plans and make contacts for the Court's daily work. Initially housed in Dutch Foreign Ministry offices, next door to Dutch officials who were the liaisons to the new Court, the team soon switched to unfinished offices at "the Arc," the large office building on the outskirts of The Hague that Wellenstein had procured for the Court. At a news conference on July 1 in the reception area of the Arc, the team shielded press representatives from the unfurnished offices and incomplete wiring of the phone system. The Court was officially in business, housed in what one advance team member recalled was "an empty shell."[7]

The advance team, with its Dutch interlocutors, produced outlines for security measures, courtroom construction, and computer and communications requirements and initiated contacts with people and organizations that would be important to the ICC, including states, the media, defense counsel, NGOs, law enforcement, and other experts.[8] Meanwhile, the PrepCom completed arrangements for the first meeting of the Assembly of States Parties.

First Assembly of States Parties

The ASP[9] met in New York in September 2002 to adopt a budget and agree upon nomination and election procedures for the Court's judges and Prosecutor, officially adopting drafts from the PrepCom. The ASP appointed Bruno Cathala, a French former jurist who was ICTY Deputy Registrar, as the Court's first official, the Director of Common Services. The position was invented to carry out the functions of the Registrar after the Court was up and running. Since the Registrar was to be elected by the

---

[7] Interview, 2006.

[8] Interviews, 2006.

[9] The full term is "Assembly of States Party to the Rome Statute of the International Criminal Court." An individual state that has ratified the Statute is called a state party. In normal parlance, the plural can be states party, state parties, or states parties.

judges, and judges had not yet been selected, the Common Services post served as a transitional device. When the advance team's mandate ended on October 31, most of the team continued in Common Services. The ASP invited nominations for judges and Chief Prosecutor by December 8. States proceeded to nominate candidates for judges, but in mid-December ASP President Prince Zeid Riad Al Hussein of Jordan announced an extension of the deadline for nominations for a Prosecutor because none had yet been received.[10]

Electing Judges

The ASP reconvened February 3–7, 2003, and elected the Court's eighteen judges,[11] which was as political an operation as it had been in the ad hoc tribunals. Some states had suggested that a screening committee be established to scrutinize and compare judge nominees' qualifications prior to the elections; however, in the end, the elections became a matter of campaigns and vote trading among state representatives at the ASP meeting. A complicated voting system had been devised for the ASP by the PrepCom in which geographical representation, gender balance, and two categories of qualifications[12] served as the basis for the election of eighteen judges. After holding several practice elections to familiarize delegates with the balloting process, more than thirty rounds of voting were required to select the judges. Some observers were disappointed that qualities they thought most important for judges – experience in court presiding over criminal trials – were not apparently accorded the highest priority by the electors. Critics (including some of the ICC's judges themselves) argue that the elections as conducted are flawed because delegations pursue national honor by seeking to elect one of their nationals as a judge, rather than searching out the most qualified people. Election depends more on campaigning, bargaining, and vote trading, than on the issue- or experience-based characteristics of the candidates.[13]

The judges were sworn in at a ceremony at the Hague Peace Palace, seat of the International Court of Arbitration and the International Court of

---

[10] Human Rights First, press release, "Nominations for ICC Prosecutor Postponed" (2002).

[11] CICC Web site, "Building the Court." <http://www.iccnow.org/buildingthecourt.html>.

[12] "A: ... competence in criminal law and procedures, and the necessary relevant experience, whether as judge, prosecutor, advocate, or in other similar capacity in criminal proceedings; B: ... competence in relevant areas of international law, such as international humanitarian law and the law of human rights, and extensive experience in a professional legal capacity which is of relevance to the judicial work of the Court." ICC Web site, "Chambers."

[13] Interview, 2004, 2006.

Justice, on March 11, 2003. The judges then elected Ambassador Philippe Kirsch of Canada as President of the Court, Akua Kuenyehia of Ghana as the first Vice President, and Elizabeth Odio Benito of Costa Rica as the second Vice President. The judges elected Bruno Cathala as Registrar, over a Dutch candidate, moving him from Director of Common Services.

Finding a Chief Prosecutor

Recruiting the Chief Prosecutor proved to be more difficult than electing judges. The challenges and uncertainties of the job may have narrowed the field. The Office of the Prosecutor had yet to be created and its budget had yet to be determined. The Prosecutor's success would depend heavily on states' support, and there was no promise that such support would be forthcoming. Investigations would likely have to be undertaken in places lacking the very institutional characteristics that make national prosecutors' offices effective – a context of social stability, public support, effective police, governmental oversight, and executive mandate. It would be a tough job.

Political and professional requirements were both daunting. For election by the ASP, the new Chief Prosecutor should come from a state party to the Statute, but preferably not from a UN Security Council member. Because the two ad hoc tribunals were viewed as having been dominated by Anglo-American common-law heritage and personnel, many states sought to avoid similar domination of the ICC, although there was apparently also a concern that the Prosecutor should be someone with friendly relations with the United States, so as not to exacerbate the already rocky relationship. Professionally, the Chief should have experience in criminal prosecutions, be knowledgeable about human rights and international criminal law, have extensive management experience, and be capable of being an effective spokesperson for the Court.

According to the *New York Times*,[14] there were six or seven candidates considered, from Africa, Latin America, and Europe, "who have had the discreet backing of their governments" during a "quiet but intense" six-month search. Candidates publicly mentioned were Carla del Ponte, Chief Prosecutor of the ICTY, and Reginald Blanch of Australia, chief judge in New South Wales District Court .[15] The Associated Press referred as well to candidates from Canada and Gambia,[16] and there is evidence that candidates from Brazil and South Africa were considered in the running.[17]

---

[14] Simons, "Argentine Is Expected to Be Prosecutor for War Crime Court" (2003).
[15] *The Age*, "NSW Judge Candidate for International Court" (2003).
[16] CNN, "War Tribunal Starts Without US" (2003).
[17] Interviews.

Argentina's Luis Moreno Ocampo emerged as the consensus candidate in the spring of 2003. Moreno Ocampo, then a visiting professor at the Harvard Law School (and hence with an apparently friendly relationship with the United States), had been an assistant prosecutor in the trials of the former military junta in Argentina in 1985 that were terminated with Argentina's "full stop" law and amnesty. In 1986, he was again an assistant prosecutor in trials of police officers accused of political murders, kidnapping, and torture. In 1988, he became a main prosecutor in cases dealing with the 1987 military rebellion and against commanders of the Malvinas-Falklands war for military malpractice. From 1992 onward, he worked in a law firm dealing with criminal and human rights law, corruption control, and dispute resolution, consulting with a wide variety of governmental and nongovernmental international organizations on corruption issues and on human rights. He had presented seminars on these issues at Yale, Harvard, Stanford, NYU, and Columbia. Argentina is a civil-law country, although it is considered to have incorporated significant elements of common-law procedure. Moreno Ocampo was unanimously elected Chief Prosecutor on April 21, 2003, to begin work at the ICC on June 16. Although much of the legal groundwork for the Court's operations had been laid, it was up to the Chief Prosecutor to get the machinery in gear. This proved to be a contentious process.

CRANKING UP THE ENGINE

Major decisions confronted the Chief Prosecutor upon his arrival at the Court. While officials had been developing an operational code for his office, no final decisions could be made, and, as it turned out, his preferences differed from those who had been preparing the way. About two years had passed between the establishment of the ad hoc tribunals by the UNSC and the start of their first trials,[18] but their missions were clearer than that of the ICC: Although the particular cases they would pursue would have to be selected, their statutes defined the time periods and territories wherein they would look for crimes to prosecute. The ICC Statute spelled out Court jurisdiction and triggers, but the Office of the Prosecutor still had to develop the process by which these would be implemented, what the OTP's main focus would be, and how best the OTP could avoid the hindrances that slowed the tribunals' cases.

---

[18] The ICTY resolution passed in February 1993, and in April 1995, the trial of Dusco Tadic commenced. In November 1994, the UNSC chartered the ICTR, and the first trial, of Jean Paul Akayesu, began in January 1997.

Selecting where and how to involve the Court entails some of the most sensitive decisions that confront the ICC. Its actions needed to serve the antiimpunity and justice mandates of the Court, be legally defensible under the Statute, and, preferably, be politically palatable to the Court's constituencies. States, NGOs, international organizations, activists, and international lawyers held a variety of views about how best to implement the Prosecutor's duties. When the Prosecutor set up the OTP, he created what some observers consider to be a more politically, as opposed to legally, based decision structure for determining which situations to pursue and how to pursue them.

Protocols for Evaluating Jurisdiction, Admissibility, and Cooperation

Work to design the Office of the Prosecutor had begun well before the Rome Statute Conference convened, and the shape of the OTP was a major focus of negotiation at the Conference. Once the Statute was complete, the PrepCom took up the discussions in its development of the Rules of Procedure and Evidence. The original outline for the OTP, contained in the June 2002 PrepCom report on the coming year's budget and program,[19] proposed that the office consist of an Immediate Office of the Prosecutor with a deputy, two special assistants, a spokesperson, and secretarial staff, along with an administrative unit made up of a budget officer, a personnel officer, a programmer/analyst, and a language coordinator. This Immediate Office would supervise two divisions, one for investigations (with an information and evidence section, an investigation section, and an analysis section) and the other for prosecution (including a prosecution section, a legal advisory and policy section, and an appeals section). When the Statute came into effect, the advance team immediately began receiving communications seeking ICC investigations into alleged crimes. All the team could do was log in the communications and promise their senders that the Court would look into their claims. Meanwhile, planning continued in anticipation of the arrival of a Chief Prosecutor.

During the yearlong interim between the Statute's coming into force and the Chief Prosecutor's appointment, officials in the OTP developed draft regulations for how to proceed. Upon taking office, however, the new Chief Prosecutor suspended those early plans, and crafted a model for his office's operations that appeared to take diplomatic-political considerations into

---

[19] United Nations, *Assembly of States Parties to the Rome Statute of the International Criminal Court First Session* (2002), 265–70.

more immediate account than would have the implementation of the draft regulations, as outlined in the next section. The differences connote tension and a fundamental divergence of approach and analysis of how the Court should operate.

In August 2002, Morten Bergsmo joined the advance team from being legal adviser in the OTP of the ICTY. He had previously served as legal adviser to M. Cherif Bassiouni's Commission of Experts on the war crimes in former Yugoslavia, and went to the ICTY Prosecutor's Office when it came into being. Beginning in 1996, he served as an adviser and representative of the ICTY to the ICC Preparatory Committee, the Rome Conference, and the Preparatory Commission.

As the senior legal adviser and coordinator of the process to establish the ICC OTP, Bergsmo enlisted four international experts to develop draft regulations for the OTP. Adhering to the notion that the operation of the office should be as transparent as possible, and regarding decision criteria as being primarily legal in nature, the draft regulations assigned to the Deputy Prosecutor (investigations) the initial responsibility for examining incoming information "in close co-operation with the Deputy Prosecutor (Prosecutions)."[20] Once the new information was duly registered by the manager of the services section, the Deputy Prosecutor (investigations) would establish a "Preliminary Examination Team," which a legal adviser would instruct on "relevant legal issues, in particular on questions of jurisdiction, admissibility and other relevant legal matters, such as the contextual elements of the crimes."[21] The team would then assess the credibility of the information, describe the crimes, identify suspects, recommend investigation targets, and evaluate the likelihood that the investigation could be successful.[22] The team would report to the two Deputy Prosecutors.

If the deputies agreed that a matter did not merit starting an investigation, they would terminate the process. If the deputies agreed that the situation merited an investigation, they would develop a draft investigation plan[23] and

---

[20] ICC, "The Management of Preliminary Examination, Article 53(1), Evaluation, and Start of Investigation," *Draft Regulations of the Office of the Prosecutor* (annotated), Book 3, Part 2 Section 2, Regulation 3.1.

[21] Ibid., Regulation 4.1.

[22] Ibid., Regulation 4.5.

[23] Ibid., Regulation 6.5. The "draft investigation plan shall address and elaborate on, to the extent possible and appropriate, and in a tentative manner,the following: (a) an assessment of whether there is a reasonable basis to believe that a crime within the jurisdiction of the Court has been or is being committed (article 53(1)(a) of the Statute); (b) the relevant background of the situation, placing alleged offences in a broader geographical, social and cultural context; (c) an explanation of why the alleged offences warrant a full investigation

submit it with supporting material to the Chief Prosecutor.[24] They would recommend to the Chief Prosecutor whether to proceed, "paying specific attention to the interests of justice as specified by Article 53(1)(c) and Rule 48,"[25] and if the Chief Prosecutor decided to go ahead, the case would be submitted to the Pre-Trial Chamber for approval to commence an official investigation. If the deputies didn't agree on whether to proceed, they would go to the Chief Prosecutor before devising the investigation plan, and the Chief Prosecutor would decide whether to proceed.[26]

In the proposed process, the first question to be answered was whether it appeared likely that crimes under the jurisdiction of the Court had taken place and whether the situation would be admissible under the Statute. Then a recommendation including a preliminary evaluation of the "interests of justice" would be developed. The question of state cooperation was embedded in the evaluation, but not at a high priority.

Enter the Chief

At his inaugural ceremony, Moreno Ocampo pledged that the OTP would "undertake a participatory dialogue both in the policy-setting process and in the actual implementation of its policies." As he repeated in many venues in subsequent years, he was open to advice, hoped to hear from all constituencies – NGOs, state representatives, legal experts, and his fellow

against the backdrop of other alleged offences where such a step might not be recommendable; (d) an identification of the crime base incidents to be investigated and a description of likely suspects, together with the overall aim of the investigation; (e) a tentative indication of possible charges, modes of liability and potential defences,if any as provided for in article 31 of the Statute; (f) an explanation of the role and place of these likely suspects in the relevant chains of authority; (g) the whereabouts, if known, of the possible suspects and the likelihood to arrest them; (h) an assessment of the admissibility of a possible case under article 17 of the Statute; (i) a preliminary indication of resources, time and staff likely to be required to complete the investigation; (j) a preliminary indication of the main categories of evidence and the amount of evidence that is likely to be required to prove the possible charges; (k) matters of State co-operation and security; (l) an explanation of how the investigation and prosecution of the alleged crimes or perpetrators is expected to fit in with the broader context of cases pursued by the Office; (m) potential dangers to the integrity of the investigation or the life or well-being of victims and witnesses that could arise once the victims are informed of the intention of the Chief Prosecutor to seek authorisation, in accordance with rule 50(1) of the Rules of Procedure and Evidence; (n) any other mater that may be of relevance for a decision to start an investigation in the light of the specific situation."

[24] Ibid., Regulations 6.3, 6.5, and 6.7.
[25] Ibid., Regulation 6.7.
[26] Ibid., Regulation 6.4.

international prosecutors – and he wanted and needed help in developing ideas for how to operate this new international mechanism. Startling some observers, he said that the principle of complementarity "means that whenever there is genuine State action, the Court cannot and will not intervene" and therefore "the absence of trials before this Court, as a consequence of the regular functioning of national institutions, would be a major success." He paid tribute to NGOs' contributions to the creation of the Court and asserted that the OTP "needs to maintain the same level of interaction with civil society, through a policy of ongoing open dialogue." Reflecting his experiences pursuing corporate and government corruption in Argentina, he called upon business interests to help "improve, respect and defend human rights, peace, and social justice, and to work against violence" and noted that the media could contribute crucially by "exposing injustice and violence." In his closing remarks, he declared that protecting victims "is the objective of our mission," and that the attack on the Twin Towers in Manhattan showed that people's safety could not be protected solely by the state, but required that the international community be based on the rule of law. "We must learn: there is no safe haven for life and freedom if we fail to protect the rights of any person in any country of the world."[27]

Moreno Ocampo immediately began consultations about how to structure the office, and he rapidly began building his team. The OTP that emerged contrasted dramatically with Bergsmo's proposal. Critics of Bergsmo's proposal saw it as too rigid; critics of the Moreno Ocampo OTP say it's too political.

Upon becoming Chief Prosecutor, Moreno Ocampo hired as his chef de cabinet fellow-Argentinian diplomat Sylvia Fernandez de Gurmendi. Fernandez had long been associated with development of the ICC in her capacity as legal adviser in the Argentine Foreign Ministry delegation, first to the Preparatory Committee meetings (she was one of two vice chairs of the Prep Com prior to the Rome Conference), then to the Rome Statute Conference, and then in the PrepCom. At Rome she was one of two vice chairs of the Committee of the Whole. During the PrepCom period following the opening of the Statute, she headed the Working Group on the Crime of Aggression, and in the period just before the Statute came into force, she was involved in negotiations on behalf of the PrepCom with Dutch authorities over ICC premises and the ICC–host state agreement.

---

[27] ICC, "Statement made by Mr. Luis Moreno Ocampo at the ceremony for the solemn undertaking of the Chief Prosecutor of the ICC" (June 16, 2003).

The OTP that appeared in the fall 2003 report to the ASP was quite different from the OTP planned by the 2002 PrepCom report. The Immediate Office of the Prosecutor was expanded to twelve professionals (instead of the previous six), divided into an "External Relations and Complementarity Unit" and a "Public Information Unit." Reporting to the Immediate Office were the Services Section (Languages Unit and Information and Evidence Unit), the Legal Advisory and Policy Section, and the Knowledge-Base Section. The two Deputy Prosecutors (investigation and prosecution) would report to the Immediate Office of the Chief Prosecutor. The Chief's chef de cabinet, Fernandez de Gurmendi, was also the head of the External Relations and Complementarity Unit in the Immediate Office, and it was to this unit that incoming information and referrals were to be channeled, not to the Deputy Prosecutor (investigations) and preliminary examination team that the Bergsmo group had proposed. The communications intake work had thus been shifted from a unit defined by legal and criminal expertise to a unit defined by diplomatic (external relations and complementarity) expertise.

Moreno Ocampo continued to consult with legal and management experts about how to structure the office and was advised to keep the Immediate Office of the Prosecutor small and allocate responsibility for jurisdiction and complementarity screening to a separate division. Fernandez de Gurmendi became both chef de cabinet and head of the newly created Jurisdiction, Complementarity and Cooperation Division (JCCD). Jurisdiction meant that the unit would examine referrals to determine whether their allegations met the Statute's jurisdiction criteria.[28] Complementarity implied both the evaluation of whether a state was able and willing genuinely to prosecute (if crimes were suspected) and, more positively, the scope for Court support for state efforts. Cooperation meant making arrangements for cooperation between states and organizations and the ICC OTP. Skeptics about the role of JCCD called it the OTP's political office.

No final OTP rules of operation were publicized. Critics of the reorganization were concerned that a shift had taken place from primarily legal criteria driving the evaluation of referrals to a more political process, and one no longer outlined in specific, publicly available OTP rules. The draft rules remained posted on the OTP Web site, not modified, finalized, or replaced (as of June 2007), although an undated "annex" described the JCCD setup.[29]

---

[28] ICC, OTP, "Annex to the 'Paper on Some Policy Issues before the Office of the Prosecutor': Referrals and Communications" (2004).

[29] Ibid.

The Legal Advisory Section, headed by Bergsmo, shrank from seven officials in 2004 to three in 2005, and at the end of the year, Bergsmo left the ICC for a post at the University of Oslo.

Referrals Pour In

As soon as the Court came into existence in 2002, communications flooded in requesting the ICC's attention to alleged crimes. During the first year of existence, the Court received 472 communications. The Office of the Prosecutor reported that fifty of these referred to crimes that had taken place before July 1, 2002, and were thus not under ICC jurisdiction; thirty-eight referred to claims of state aggression, a crime not yet under ICC jurisdiction; sixteen claims were about U.S. actions in Iraq, but since neither Iraq nor the United States was a member state, the ICC had no jurisdiction. There were two communications about Israeli actions vis-à-vis Palestinians, but again, neither territorial nor national jurisdiction applied. Complaints outside the Court's jurisdiction were also received about alleged crimes in the Ivory Coast and about non-U.S. coalition forces in Iraq; some complaints pertained to crimes not under ICC jurisdiction, such as international drug crimes. On July 16, 2003, Chief Prosecutor Moreno Ocampo announced that he had decided to follow up reports of crimes taking place in Ituri, Democratic Republic of the Congo, a party to the Statute.[30]

A New Vision of Complementarity

As shown by the expansive tasks articulated in his inaugural speech, Chief Prosecutor Moreno Ocampo believed that the ICC in general, and the OTP in particular, could fight impunity in a variety of ways, and that state cooperation in his efforts would be crucial. His concept of complementarity implied more than that the ICC was only a backup to national jurisdiction. The ICC should, if possible, gain state cooperation, even that of the state(s) in which crimes were taking place, when it investigated a conflict situation. The ICC should encourage and support domestic authorities to act against impunity, but if a state could not conduct needed investigations and prosecutions, ideally, the state itself would refer its own situation to the Court, smoothing cooperation and reducing or eliminating the possibilities that the state would challenge the ICC's jurisdiction or cases' admissibility.[31] It was

---

[30] ICC, OTP, "Communications Received by the Prosecutor since July 2002" (2003).
[31] Interviews, 2005, 2006 with NGO and present and former OTP personnel.

a novel view of the ICC's relationship with states, and one that provoked widespread skepticism among the ICC "old hands." Nonetheless, the first situations that the Court pursued were in countries that had joined the Statute. Having met with OTP personnel, the governments of Uganda in December 2003 and the Democratic Republic of the Congo (DRC) in April 2004 requested that the ICC pursue investigations in their countries, saying they were unable to carry out necessary processes against suspected perpetrators of international crimes.

The conflicts in the Congo and Uganda were producing millions of casualties that had begun before the Court came into being but were continuing. The OTP's rationale for involvement based on government declarations of "inability" to prosecute struck some observers as problematic, but from the ICC OTP's standpoint, sufficient cause existed to begin investigations (see Chapter 7).

By initially pursuing cases in the (DRC) and Uganda at the governments' requests, the OTP focused on important international crimes but avoided challenging state sovereignty as it would have by opening the investigations *proprio motu* (under the Prosecutor's own authority). The third situation in which the OTP opened an investigation, in Darfur, western Sudan (in March 2005), skirted the issue of the Prosecutor acting *proprio motu* from an entirely different but also unexpected direction, a UN Security Council referral.

A Complementarity Spectrum

Moreno Ocampo's claim in his inaugural speech that the absence of ICC trials caused by state prosecutions would be a success for the Court shocked some observers, including some ICC judges: It sounded like a before-the-fact excuse for not being able to bring cases to Court. However, behind the statement was a creative idea. Moreno Ocampo and some JCCD officials proposed that encouraging national systems to improve their capacities to prosecute crimes that might fall under ICC jurisdiction by sharing information, training staff, and providing other forms of assistance could be included in the idea of ICC complementarity. They called the idea "positive complementarity," as contrasted with the "negative complementarity" of taking over prosecution when states proved unwilling or unable genuinely to do so themselves.

Complementarity can be imagined as a spectrum. On the negative end, suspecting that a state is not pursuing prosecutions in good faith, the Court carries out investigations, issues warrants, gains custody, and prosecutes suspects. At the positive end, the Court communicates its concerns about crimes, establishes legal and judicial training and cooperation mechanisms to bolster a weak justice system, and then monitors local judicial processes undertaken for crimes that would otherwise fall under ICC jurisdiction.[32] Critics have derided the positive complementarity idea as reimagining the Court as a (judicial) development assistance organization; however, enthusiasts argue that positive complementarity could become an important part of the ICC's work to counter impunity and would be a constructive and restorative measure, in contrast to the purely punitive orientation of traditional justice mechanisms.

ICC Prosecution Innovations

Because of ICC complementarity (as opposed to tribunal primacy), the ICC Chief Prosecutor pursued state cooperation differently than had the tribunals' prosecutors. Because of the tribunals' perceived shortcomings – such as their initial focus on too low-level suspects, their inadequate linkage of investigations to prosecution plans, and their unduly long cases caused by large numbers of charges against individual suspects – the Court's OTP implemented a series of innovations aimed at improving states' cooperation with the Court, tightening connections between investigation and prosecution, and focusing charges against suspects. The trials envisioned by the OTP would be optimized not only for bringing suspects to justice but also for demonstrating to observers that justice would and could be done expeditiously.

Seek Suspects Most Responsible for Crimes

At the beginning of the ICTY's operations, Prosecutor Richard Goldstone had brought Dusko Tadic to trial, transferred fortuitously from Germany, and had declared it policy to begin with lower-level transgressors and move up the ranks. Later, Goldstone and the tribunal were lambasted for failing early to grapple with those people at the top of the political and military hierarchies who were most responsible for the crimes that took place in the former Yugoslavia. Goldstone and his defenders pointed out that beginning with lower-level transgressors allowed the tribunal time to develop its procedures and pursue further investigations. Goldstone's successors, Louise Arbour and Carla del Ponte, focused increasingly on higher-level suspects, and as efforts were initiated to wind down the tribunal's

---

[32] Interviews, 2006, JCCD personnel.

operations, lower-level cases were increasingly dismissed, plea-bargained off the docket, or referred to newly created local tribunals as part of the overall completion strategy. ICTY President Claude Jorda's 1999 declaration that the tribunal should focus on the transgressors "most responsible" eventually became policy in both ad hoc tribunals (see Chapter 2).

The ICC OTP's 2003 policy paper announced the Court's intentions to "focus its investigative and prosecutorial efforts and resources on those who bear greatest responsibility, such as leaders of the state or organization allegedly responsible for those crimes."[33] The ICC's first arrest warrants – for leaders of the Lord's Resistance Army (LRA) in Uganda Joseph Kony and his four top henchmen – showed in October 2005 that the pursuit of the most responsible leaders, at least in this situation, was indeed the OTP's policy.[34]

Pursue Representative Cases of the Greatest Gravity

Having observed the problems of ICTY and ICTR prosecutions of individual suspects on large numbers of criminal charges, the ICC OTP intends to focus on small numbers of the worst crimes of its suspects, using carefully developed investigative and prosecution strategies to focus on representative, rather than comprehensive, criminal charges. In practice this means that the OTP analyzes information from conflict situations and ranks crime by gravity – from worst to less severe – and seeks first to investigate the worst crimes. Connecting the worst crimes to the persons most responsible, the OTP strategy is then to choose from among the individual incidents comprising such crimes to find a representative small sample and seek to develop information on those cases for which proof of the standard of "beyond a reasonable doubt" can most likely be obtained. As the Chief Prosecutor put it, he intends to proceed "sequentially," which means working on a very limited number of cases from each situation, pursuing them one at a time.

Although the Chief Prosecutor espouses this strategy as an efficiency measure, some victims' advocates have challenged it, arguing that all relevant charges and, if appropriate, multiple perpetrators should be pursued in order to show respect to the victims and to demonstrate the serious nature of an appropriately broad range of crimes. In particular, NGOs have argued in connection with the first case to come to Court, that of Thomas Lubanga Dyilo from the DRC, that prosecuting him for child recruitment but not mass rape and other gender crimes "reduces the number of victims able to

---

[33] ICC, OTP, "Paper on Some Policy Issues before the Office of the Prosecutor" (2003), 7.
[34] ICC, OTP, "Statement by the Chief Prosecutor on the Uganda Arrest Warrants" (2005).

obtain justice for the suffering or claim reparations."[35] Since the cases for warrants and charges come to the Pre-Trial Chambers from the OTP, Chambers too could question the OTP on the breadth of charges. The OTP will, however, generally be in the position to argue that it is pursuing those crimes for which it has most accurate information, and has decided what cases can best be made.

Aim Toward Efficient Cases through Effective Data Management

The inefficiencies of the ICTY and ICTR were notorious to the ICC's Statute negotiators. At the ICTY, Morten Bergsmo had helped bring order to the chaos of paper record keeping at the core of the ICTY's inefficiency. By the time the ICC became operational, the technologies of computer and Internet-based data management capabilities far outstripped what had originally been available to the tribunals. Bergsmo set about developing data management systems that would avoid the kinds of problems the ICTY had encountered. By the time of his departure from the ICC in December 2005, work on the Case Matrix data management system was largely complete, and the ICC was announcing that it would be made openly available to law enforcement organizations. Case Matrix is a data management system that provides a template for investigators to record, categorize, and cross-reference evidence in order to directly link it to elements of crimes for prosecution. Thus, when adequate evidence to demonstrate an element of crime has been accumulated, an investigator will know to move to another area for investigation, and when trial attorneys seek evidence to support a particular charge, the evidence will already be categorized and recoverable under the terms of the charges. ICC prosecutions should be much more efficient than those of the ICTY.

Integrate Investigation and Prosecution

The draft regulations for the OTP show that people involved in thinking about the ICC certainly recognized weaknesses produced by the separation between the ad hoc tribunals' investigation and prosecution teams. As a consequence, already during the transition phase prior to arrival of the Chief Prosecutor, draft rules brought the investigation and prosecution divisions together for initial screening of situations and proposed that prosecution personnel would join with investigators to develop the

---

[35] REDRESS, "International Criminal Court: Child Soldiers Prosecution Must Be Seen in Context" (2006); REDRESS, "Victims, Perpetrators, or Heroes: Child Soldiers before the International Criminal Court" (2006).

investigation plan. As the OTP has developed, integration has continued. Cases are now developed by teams that draw on the three divisions – JCCD, investigation, and prosecution – and these interdivisional teams flexibly shift personnel as processes continue. The prosecution division, rather than receiving a completed investigation dossier, is involved in cases "from the get-go," as Deputy Prosecutor for Prosecutions Fatou Bensouda put it.[36] In preparation for an investigation, the senior trial lawyer (prosecution) works with the lead investigator (investigations) to lay out a collection plan. Missions to the field are jointly planned and always include a prosecution team member.

A Sputtering Start

The engine of the court is running. The OTP has its critics, but observers during its first years were inclined to be patient, to see if warrants for arrest would be forthcoming, if cases could be brought to court, and if effective prosecutions would result. By the autumn of 2007, a record of accomplishment was accumulating. One suspect from the Congo was in court and another was in jail, but trial proceedings had not begun. Warrants for suspects in Uganda had been issued but were mired in the suspects' demand that the warrants be lifted as part of a peace deal. Warrants had been issued for two Sudanese suspects, but critics charged that the action was too slow and aimed too low. The OTP had announced the beginning of a formal investigation into large-scale sexual crimes in the Central African Republic (CAR), two and a half years after the CAR authorities had referred the situation to the Court. Those who considered the JCCD "too political" hoped that staff turnover would inject more criminal-law expertise into the intake end of the engine; others were concerned that investigative operations were underpowered. Moreno Ocampo's admirers argued that he was effectively learning on the job, that the OTP was gathering momentum, and that he was making the best of very difficult situations. Resistance to the engine came both from without, in extraordinarily challenging operational environments, and from frictions generated within the Court itself.

INTERNAL FRICTIONS

During its first five years, the ICC moved from a tiny advance team to a large operational organization, expanding while simultaneously pursuing investigations and initiating court proceedings. Under pressure to begin

[36] Interview, 2006.

operating quickly, the top staff experienced both the awkwardness of the Court's tripartite structure and confrontations among the three units as they sought to protect their roles. Three conflicts exemplified these tensions. First, the Registrar and Prosecutor clashed over administrative and communications responsibilities. Second, the OTP struggled to retain its independence against the Pre-Trial Chambers (PTCs) intent on fulfilling what they considered to be appropriate guidance responsibilities. Third, and in an additional demonstration of rivalry between the OTP and the PTC, after the Prosecutor raised questions about an appearance of possible bias on the part of the pretrial division, a long battle ensued over procedures for resolving the dispute.

OTP versus Registry

The Registry and OTP clashed on numerous occasions, leading to relations between the Chief Prosecutor and the Registrar that some observers described as poisonous. Among NGOs, it was reputedly the case that, for long periods of time, Moreno Ocampo and Cathala were not on speaking terms. The conflicts emerged from the structural characteristics of the Court and the efforts of its top leadership to preserve prerogatives of their offices and to pursue what they believed to be the imperatives of the Statute. Controversies arose over, among other things, how hiring processes would be implemented, how information would be transferred, and who would be the primary conduit of communications to states.

When the Chief Prosecutor began building up the office, he argued that, for the purposes of prosecutorial independence, all hiring activities should be undertaken by his own staff. At the same time, however, the Registry's Human Resources Section had overall responsibility for recruitment. The two offices clashed over how personnel recruitment would take place until an adverse report from the ASP's Committee on Budget and Finance rejected the Prosecutor's argument, on the grounds of bureaucratic duplication. Hiring was consolidated under the Registry. Under a negotiated agreement, the OTP would write the job descriptions and conduct candidate screening, while the Registry would carry out recruitment and other administrative functions. The final hiring decisions for the Prosecutor, of course, remained with the OTP.

As part of its duties, the Registry provides translation and record-keeping services, security, and data management technology and has the responsibility to record all transactions such as the transmission of documents between the prosecution and the Chambers. As the Lubanga (Congo) case got under-way in the spring of 2006, a dispute emerged over the proper role of the Registry in the area of evidence disclosure. Once Thomas Lubanga's defense counsel had been selected and began to work, the prosecution was required to turn over all evidence to the defense except for materials that might undermine witnesses' safety.

The Registry proposed a disclosure system under which all evidence to be turned over to the defense would first go to the Registry to be recorded, as the Registrar believed appropriate under the Rules of Procedure and Evidence. The OTP objected, proposing instead that materials be delivered directly to the defense, with a record of what was turned over to be delivered to the Registry. Wrangling before the judge demonstrated that what was at stake was the degree of involvement of the Registry in the substantive process of disclosure. The OTP sought to keep the Registry's role to a minimum; the Registry, acting perhaps in pursuit of the vision of a civil proceeding in which a "dossier" is developed that fully describes the case and evidence for eventual use by the judges, appeared to be inserting itself deeply into the substance of the proceedings.

The PTC ultimately approved the process by which the OTP would turn materials directly over to defense, with records of the transactions turned over to the Registry. Meanwhile, it was just one of several points of conflict between the OTP and Registry that characterized the early operations of the Court.

The Statute gives to the Registry the responsibility for arranging with governments the transfer of individuals to be brought for questioning or incarceration. When the Prosecutor requested of the PTC that an arrest warrant be issued for Lubanga, he also asked that the arrest warrant be kept secret until he was ready to publicize it, and that he be empowered to negotiate with the Congolese authorities for the transfer of the suspect to The Hague. The PTC decided to issue the arrest warrant but also to publicize it and to assign to the Registrar the task of arranging Lubanga's transfer to the Court. It appeared that the OTP had sought to increase its area of autonomy into a greater role interacting with the state, under the JCCD; however, the judges defended the Registry (see Chapter 7).

Common Law versus Civil Law and the Prosecutor versus Pre-Trial Chambers

In the inquisitorial, civil-law system, judges are actively engaged from early stages in a judicial proceeding and thus help to set the pace of the proceedings. They are expected to absorb large amounts of substantive information from the prosecution prior to the courtroom proceedings, which reduces the amount of time spent in open court. Investigating judges or magistrates help guide the collection of evidence, and judges in court may seek to verify evidence by asking witnesses questions. In the end, trial judges decide upon guilt or innocence on the basis of their expert evaluation of the facts of the case. Prosecutors are expected to provide exculpatory as well as incriminating evidence to the Court. Much of the case may be presented to the judge in a trial dossier consisting of evidence and written reports prior to court hearings. Evidentiary rules are less strict than the common-law system, with judges ruling on admissibility questions and balancing the weight given to particular evidence against its quality and mode of collection.

In contrast, in the common-law, accusatorial, adversarial process, judges are not exposed to the substance of cases prior to their appearing in court but are neutral "umpires" of a contest between prosecution and defense, making sure that the process is fair and legal in order that a jury can reach a decision about guilt or innocence. Cases are initiated and driven by prosecutors who exercise discretion about what to pursue, having received allegations of violation by victims or law enforcement officials. Prosecutors assemble and lead cases against alleged perpetrators, while defense lawyers seek to demonstrate that accusations cannot be proven "beyond a reasonable doubt." Since the jurors are not trained to evaluate the quality of evidence, evidentiary rules are very explicit, and evidence is presented in court in conjunction with direct testimony. No substantive pretrial or written evidence constitutes part of the trial record.

In the ICC's combination of the two systems, the Office of the Prosecutor drives the system by bringing cases to the Pre-Trial Chamber for approval of a formal investigation and then returns with a report of the investigation and possibly recommendations that warrants of arrest be issued. Thus, the PTC can exercise considerable control over the OTP. With the PTC dominated by civil-law judges, they sought to play larger roles than the OTP believed appropriate.

Former ICTY judge and President Claude Jorda, elected to the ICC judiciary in 2003, was appointed to the PTCs by Court President Kirsch. His chamber (PTC I) sat on the Democratic Republic of the Congo situation as it moved through ICC proceedings. Jorda had published and spoken eloquently from the time he was on the ICTY about the need to make trial procedures more efficient, stating at one point that "a trial should never last more than eighteen months total"[37] and calling for more vigorous monitoring and shaping of trial procedures by the judges.

A French judge with extensive trial experience, Jorda was quite explicit in his advocacy of civil-law mechanisms to control prosecutors, to speed trials, and to shift the emphasis toward victims. Dealing with the DRC situation, it soon appeared that the division of labor and authority between the PTC and the OTP would be a major area of contention in the development of the practice of the ICC. In general, the PTCs for both the DRC and Uganda sought much deeper involvement than the OTP appeared prepared to accept, but since the role of the PTCs had not been definitively spelled out in the Statute and rules, precedents established in Court – and possibly by the decisions of the Appeals Chamber – will determine future practice.

Judge Jorda wrote in June 2005 that the ICC PTC did not fit the mold of existing civil-law structures, being the equivalent of neither an investigating magistrate nor an investigating chamber. "It is difficult today to define the pre-trial procedure of the ICC within the context of an existing national or international procedural system,"[38] he observed, and went on to argue that the role of the PTC would be worked out in operation. In Jorda's view, the PTC was intended to help protect the interests of the states, the defense, and the victims, with the "ultimate goal" of ensuring the integrity of the proceedings.[39] As pretrial proceedings continued, PTC I took measures that appeared to interpret its duties broadly, including seeking to accelerate OTP activities, much to the apparent dismay of the Prosecutor. Jorda appeared to be pressing his idea that the Pre-Trial Chamber was the "embryo of a true Investigative Chamber"[40] that would play a large role in steering the Prosecutor.

It is conceivable that some form of consultation between judges and the OTP in advance of formal proceedings could have narrowed areas of difference between them; however, efforts in this direction failed. After formal proceedings began, OTP personnel explained the formalities as being more open for other potential parties to disputes (such as victims or defense attorneys) than informal agreements would have been.[41] The initial tool

---

[37] Petit, "Interview: Claude Jorda, Judge at the International Criminal Court" (2005), 4.

[38] Jorda and Saracco, "The Raisons d'etre of the Pre-Trial Chamber of the International Criminal Court" (2006), 1.

[39] Ibid., 2.

[40] Jorda, "The Major Hurdles and Accomplishments of the ICTY: What the ICC Can Learn From Them" (2004), 578.

[41] Interviews.

used by PTC I was the "status conference," a meeting to which it summoned the OTP to report on the progress of its investigations. As described further in Chapter 7, the OTP has complied with these requests with something less than enthusiasm, finding them to be PTC interference with the OTP's independence. The status conference was used frequently by the ICTY judges to gain information about the Prosecution's intentions. While the mechanism isn't foreseen in the ICC Statute or rules, judges with ICTY experience brought it with them and began scheduling such conferences when they felt that the information flow from the OTP was too sparse.

In the late spring of 2006, PTC I used another device, this one based in the ICC Statute, to increase its role in directing prosecution activities. Out of mounting frustration that, despite a year of investigations following the OTP's receipt of the report of the Commission of Inquiry on Darfur, ICC investigations were not yet taking place in Darfur and warrants of arrest did not appear to be close, the PTC asked for comments from two *amicus curiae* (friends of the court) known to be critical of the ICC's slow progress, in effect pressurizing the OTP to accelerate its activities (see Chapter 7).

Judges Have the Last Word

Interorgan tensions that bear upon cases before the Court ultimately wind up coming before the judges. As these matters are sorted out, accumulated judicial precedents and standardized procedure should reduce the level of internal strife and confusion, and the Court should be able more efficiently to expend efforts on its investigations and cases. However, there is no guarantee that such conflicts themselves will be decided expeditiously, as shown by a controversy that began in early 2006 involving the OTP, the Uganda and Congo PTCs, and the Presidency. The prosecution charged that since the newly appointed senior legal adviser to the Pre-Trial division (all the pretrial judges), Gilbert Bitti, had previously worked for the OTP, he should be barred from being in any way involved in the Uganda and Congo cases because such involvement would raise the appearance of a potential lack of PTC judicial neutrality. After eleven months of acrimonious legal briefs, no definitive decision was reached.

Bitti had been a member of the French delegation to the Rome Conference, and subsequently to the PrepCom. Soon after the ICC began operating in July 2002, he joined the Court, serving first in the Registry and, from January 1, 2004, as Morten Bergsmo's deputy in the OTP legal advisory section. In October 2005, Bitti left his position with the OTP to become the senior legal adviser to the Pre-Trial division, working on legal matters assigned to him by the judges of the division.

On January 6, 2006, the OTP sent a memorandum to Court President Kirsch requesting that Bitti's duties as senior adviser to the Pre-Trial division be limited to prevent the appearance of judicial partiality, since Bitti had been heavily involved in matters concerning the Congo and Uganda situations that were likely to come before the judges of PTC I (Congo) and PTC II (Uganda).[42] A few days later, the OTP notified PTC I and PTC II that it had sent a request to the Presidency regarding Bitti, but didn't copy the note's text. The OTP also informed Judge Hans-Peter Kaul, President of the Pre-Trial division[43] and Bitti's ultimate superior at the time, of the request. In late January, Court President Kirsch informed the Prosecutor that the Presidency had no standing to decide the matter nor to send it on to the judges sitting together as a plenary of the judges.

In February, there was more back-and-forth between the OTP and the Pre-Trial division, and in March Judge Kaul indicated to the OTP that the pretrial judges had decided that their division could not act upon the request. In May, Kaul declined to respond to the Prosecutor's inquiry whether the senior legal adviser was still rendering advice to the division. Meanwhile, the Prosecutor informed Jean Flamme, defense counsel to Congolese defendant Thomas Lubanga, of his concerns about the matter, and Flamme added his voice to the Prosecutor's request to the Pre-Trial division president to keep Bitti away from the case.

In August, the Prosecutor submitted a formal "Application to Separate the Senior Legal Adviser to the Pre-Trial Division from Rendering Legal Advice Regarding the Case" to both PTC I and PTC II.[44] In October, the pretrial judges decided temporarily to relieve Bitti of his functions in connection with the Lubanga (Congo) and Kony et al. (Uganda) cases. The PTC judges argued, however, that since the Prosecutor kept referring to possible damage to the appearance of judicial impartiality, he was implicitly challenging their impartiality. Since this could imply a case for disqualification of the two PTCs' judges, they asked President Kirsch to assemble the uninvolved judges in plenary to decide whether indeed the Prosecutor's request amounted to a request for their disqualification, and if so to decide the matter.

---

[42] ICC, Pre-Trial Chamber II, "Prosecutor's Application to Separate the Senior Legal Advisor to the Pre-Trial Division form Rendering Legal Advice Regarding the Case" (2006), 11ff.

[43] Each division of the Chambers – Pre-Trial, Trial, and Appeals – has its own president, in addition to the President of the Court as a whole.

[44] ICC, Pre-Trial Chamber 1 "Prosecutor's Application to Separate the Senior Legal Adviser to the Pre-Trial Division from Rendering Legal Advice Regarding the Case" (2006).

Meanwhile, PTC I declared that it lacked jurisdiction to entertain the Prosecutor's request (to separate Bitti from work on the Congo),[45] and PTC II dismissed the request (to separate Bitti from work on Uganda).[46] The pretrial judges urged the Presidency to act with dispatch, since an important hearing (confirmation of charges for Thomas Lubanga) was upcoming in early November.

On November 7 (two days before the confirmation hearing for the case against Lubanga), President Kirsch informed all concerned that he had consulted with the eleven (uninvolved) judges. They determined that the application by the OTP did not amount to a request for the disqualification of any judge; therefore, there were no grounds to call a meeting of judges under the statutory process for considering judicial disqualification.[47] The OTP's challenge remained unanswered, Bitti remained adviser to the PTC, and as the Congo and Uganda cases moved forward, the proscription against his involvement became moot.

Leadership

Aside from the particulars of the Bitti matter, outside observers of the Court were concerned that the Court suffered from a lack – or a surplus – of leadership. Although the President is the formal head of the ICC, and although President Kirsch was generally credited with outstanding service as the diplomatic emissary of the Court, critics argued that his quest to retain judicial neutrality and his impulses as a diplomat led him to play more of a "facilitator" role than a decisive one in seeking to resolve clashes between the Prosecutor and Registrar. Following the second round of judicial elections in 2006, the judges again voted to elect a president (to a three-year, once-renewable term). The election was contested, and Kirsch won by only a single vote, with almost half of the judges favoring another candidate with greater judicial, courtroom, and administrative experience.[48] In 2009 a new president will be elected.

While Moreno Ocampo headed the engine of the Court, he was criticized by some for seeking too political a role externally, preferring the bright

---

[45] ICC, Pre-Trial Chamber I, "Decision on the Prosecutor's Application to Separate the Senior Legal Advisor to the Pre-Trial Division from Rendering Legal Advice Regarding the Case" (2006).

[46] ICC, Pre-Trial Chamber II, "Decision on the Prosecutor's Request to Separate the Senior Legal Adviser to the Pre-Trial Division from Rendering Legal Advice Regarding the Case" (2006).

[47] Ibid., Annex, "Internal Memorandum from the President to the President of the Pre-Trial Division" (2006).

[48] Interviews.

lights of international exposure to the nitty-gritty of investigation and prosecution, and also for micromanaging his division internally, stifling initiative and orderly procedure. The Registrar came in for criticism as an empire builder. At the same time, all three men had strong defenders. They argued that Kirsch was putting the Court on the map and managing a fractious bureaucracy; Moreno Ocampo was making headway against the huge difficulties of building and operating the OTP while under crushing pressure to avoid political missteps but to stride boldly against a wide range of crimes and criminals; and Cathala had an enormous span of responsibilities – from personnel security to information technology to arranging for a suspects' defense and victims' representation – and had to knit together an intentionally diverse personnel complement.

NEW JUSTICE INNOVATIONS

While the old (retributive) justice mandate of the Rome Statute was clearly being carried out as the OTP began investigations, the Court struggled to implement its new (restorative) justice mandates as well. Four influences converged to produce ICC innovations in victim orientation. First, from the mid-1980s, interest in victim welfare among legal scholars and practitioners grew, and international efforts followed.[49] Concern for victims and the connection of trials to social healing became so accepted by the international justice community that the question of whether to include victim-oriented innovations into the Statute was not controversial: The question was how these concerns should be included. The rather vague provisions in the Statute remained to be worked out.[50]

Second, the dominance of common-law traditions, and their perpetrator focus, in the ICTY and ICTR grated especially upon representatives of European civil-law states, most notably France, in which the turn toward victims was particularly strong.[51] France generally wanted the Rome Statute to include more of its civil-law tradition than had the tribunals, flowing

---

[49] Bassiouni, "International Recognition of Victims' Rights" (2006), 203–79.

[50] For example, how would the ICC handle the complexities of potentially mass claims for aid and/or reparation; how would it include victims in the legal process without compromising due process rights for defendants and without overwhelming the Court; how would it identify victims for reparations purposes, as individuals and/or groups; and how could victims' interests be served without infringing on the independence of the prosecution? See ibid., 245–6.

[51] Interviews, French participants in Rome Statute negotiations and French ICC officials.

from genuine conviction of the value of victim representation at court and perhaps as well from national pride considerations.

Third, the experiences of the ICTY and ICTR showed that local populations in the areas where the crimes had taken place had very low opinions (if any) of the tribunals because of their remoteness, their unfamiliar legal processes, and the fact that they really had no role or potential offer of reparations for the victims.[52] The ICTR and ICTY belatedly developed institutional capacities to improve witness protection and handling and outreach programs to counteract the antitribunal propaganda that prevented the tribunals from gaining local legitimacy.

Last, NGOs pressed hard for substantial provisions favoring victims, flowing from their long advocacy in domestic and international contexts of human rights and humanitarian concern.

Implementing the Victim-Orientation Mandate

The Statute directs the Pre-Trial Chambers to evaluate OTP measures to guarantee that witnesses and victims connected with investigations are properly protected. Chambers are mandated as well to make it possible for victims to be involved in proceedings,[53] and the Registry is instructed to implement Statute provisions to "protect the safety, physical and psychological well-being, dignity and privacy of victims and witnesses."[54]

Under the Statute, victims have the right to have "their views and concerns to be presented and considered at stages of the proceedings determined to be appropriate by the Court and in a manner which is not prejudicial to or inconsistent with the rights of the accused and a fair and impartial trial."[55] From the OTP's standpoint, victims and witnesses are primarily important as providers of information for the investigation, and witness protection is vital in order that witnesses and victims feel safe enough to come forward. Presenting victims' "views," in contrast, is a less clear-cut objective, and one that may run at cross purposes to the OTP's independence in pursuing its investigations. Some observers of the OTP argue that views could mean perceived inadequacies of an investigation, and those are views the OTP might rather not valorize; therefore, the OTP

---

[52] Bassiouni, op cit., footnote 335, points out that drafters of the Statutes of the two ad hoc tribunals deliberately minimized (ICTY) or rejected (ICTR) provisions regarding victim reparations.

[53] Statute Article 68.3.

[54] Statute Article 68.1.

[55] Statute Article 68.3.

objective in investigations and the PTC objective of gaining appropriate victim participation may be in conflict.[56]

According to Judge Jorda, the PTC is the earliest appropriate recipient of communications from victims concerning Court proceedings, the earliest stage of "proceedings" being OTP investigations;[57] the OTP didn't consider its investigations to be proceedings, and the matter ultimately had to be tested in Court (see discussion on Congo in Chapter 7). In the Darfur situation, PTC I used its responsibilities toward victims to bring into Court the criticism that the Prosecutor was proceeding too gingerly (see discussion on Sudan in Chapter 7).

The Registry's Victims and Witnesses Unit (VWU) and Victims Participation and Reparations Section (VPRS) are deeply, though separately, involved in the Court's responsibilities toward victims. In these capacities, the Registry comes into direct contact with the OTP because investigators need to carry out field operations to gain information from witnesses and collect documents and other information in the areas where crimes have taken place; the OTP and the Registry jointly pursue "outreach" programs to inform local communities about the Court and the opportunities it presents for people to report on crimes and to seek reparations or representation in ongoing judicial processes.

Witness Protection

Civil-law systems include victims of crimes in the legal processes much more centrally than do common-law systems. Bruno Cathala, Registrar of the ICC, argues that from his (French, civil-law) perspective there is no tension between a victim orientation and prosecution objectives; rather, he attributes the belief in an opposition between retributive justice and victims' interests to be the product of a common-law paradigm.[58]

---

[56] Victims can communicate to the Pre-Trial Chamber when the Prosecutor initiates criminal proceedings *proprio motu* (Rome Statute Article 15), the PTC can decide to ask for more information from the Prosecutor and from victims (Statute Article 15), and victims may make submissions when the PTC considers jurisdiction and admissibility (Article 19(3)). Moreover, the PTC must authorize warrants upon application by the Prosecutor, and therefore has a role in how and when those warrants become public, one criterion of which in the Uganda case was measures taken by the OTP and Victims and Witnesses Unit for protection of witnesses and victims prior to public unveiling of the warrants (discussed in Chapter 7).

[57] Jorda and Saracco, "The raisons d'etre of the Pre-Trial Chambers of the International Criminal Court" (2005), 10.

[58] Interviews.

The ICTY's Statute Article 22, "Protection of Victims and Witnesses," rather vaguely says, "Protection measures shall include, but shall not be limited to, the conduct of in camera proceedings and the protection of the victim's identity." The tribunal's judges, in their Rules of Procedure and Evidence, expanded upon the article, instructing the Registry to establish a victims and witnesses section to recommend protective measures and to provide counseling and support for them.[59] This was the precedent for development of the ICC Registry's VWU, but it has developed much further. It seeks to coordinate with the Prosecutor to enable witnesses to be available to the Court without fear of retribution and, if needed, to support potential witnesses with counseling and psychological assistance, travel aid to come to The Hague, and so on.

The ICC's VWU is mandated to be active as early as the investigation stage (not just at the trial phase as in the tribunals) and is conceived by its staff as a "service provider" to make participation possible; to provide support, assistance, and protection; and to provide advice to the OTP when needed. The VWU's services can be requested by prosecutors or defense counsel, or ordered by Chambers. OTP investigators can make known the availability of the unit but cannot promise any services; thus, the Court seeks to avoid creating any incentive for people to make up stories of victimization in order to gain aid.

The VWU has held training sessions for OTP investigation teams to instruct them in best practices for dealing with victims and witnesses and to impress upon them that the well-being of witnesses is key to their (prosecution) interests, since if witnesses find that it is too dangerous to cooperate with the Court, the OTP will have an impossible task of investigation and trial. The ability of investigators to find witnesses will depend upon witnesses' confidence that they'll be relatively safe even as they are in contact with the ICC. Each person served by the VWU needs to have a "protection plan," and these are individually developed by the VWU and approved by the Registrar.

Extensive contact with local NGOs aids the VWU in getting its message out and learning about potential problems; NGOs are also key in pressing victims' and witnesses' rights and demanding improved services from the ICC (see Chapter 5).

Victim Participation and Reparations
The VPRS of the Registry implements the Statute mandate to take into account the views of victims throughout the Court's processes. The practice

---

[59] Rule 34 A(I–ii).

and law of this new inclusive mandate are a major area of operational and legal development for the ICC. Operationally, the VPRS is closely linked to the activities of NGOs in the field and is (along with the Victims' Trust Fund, discussed later in this section) the focus for their pressure on the ICC to become much more fully engaged than its predecessors in victim-oriented justice activities.

A major uncertainty of the VPRS operation is that the idea of "participation" has not been fully defined in practice nor is there a clear definition of what constitutes a "victim." Since the Registry in general, and the VPRS within it, is mandated to serve the needs of the Court, it depends upon the Court – that is, the Chambers – to establish definitions and parameters within which to work. In practice, these criteria are being developed in the context of legal wrangling between victims' counsel and the OTP in front of the Pre-Trial Chambers, as the victims seek to participate at early stages in Court proceedings (see Chapter 7; this has been the subject of extensive consideration in the case of Thomas Lubanga Dyilo of the Democratic Republic of the Congo).

In 2006, the VPRS developed and issued forms for victims, as individuals [60] or organizations,[61] seeking participant status, on which they (or a representative) can indicate how they consider themselves victims, the crimes by which they believe they have been victimized, and the kind of participation that they seek. Use of the form is not mandatory, and in fact the first requests for participation (in the DRC case) were filed by the NGO International Federation of Human Rights Leagues (Fédération Internationale des Ligues des Droits de l'Homme, FIDH) before the form was issued.

In the field, the VPRS sought to identify and work with NGOs and other local groups to inform and assist victims about how they could participate in the ICC's proceedings. VPRS personnel generally did not go to victim communities, but worked through people with local contacts such as NGOs, local authorities, and religious and traditional leaders. In the late winter of 2006, the staff consisted of seven people at headquarters in The Hague, and they were seeking to add about two people in each country where investigations were under way. The aim was to have VPRS staff on the ground as soon as the OTP initiated serious investigations.

[60] ICC, "Standard Application Form to Participate in Proceedings before the International Criminal Court for Individual Victims and Persons Acting on their Behalf."

[61] ICC, "Standard Application Form to Participate in Proceedings before the International Criminal Court for Victims Which are Organizations or Institutions."

VPRS staff were traveling frequently to the situation countries Uganda and the DRC in 2005 and 2006, seeking to improve contacts with victim communities. The ICC's active engagement is mandated by the Statute but also spurred by contrary pressures. On one hand, NGOs are pressing for greater involvement of victims with the ICC and for the Court's eventual heavy engagement in reparations and restorative justice programs. On the other hand, the ICC itself is concerned not to raise victim expectations too high, since disappointed high expectations could undermine ICC legitimacy as much or more than under-attention to victims in the first place. The VPRS was working closely with the Registry's public information/outreach office to develop and disseminate information about the ICC into local communities, a challenging task given that most of the target communities have high levels of illiteracy and operate in local languages. In addition, VPRS staff were holding daylong information and training sessions for magistrates and lawyers in Uganda and the DRC. The idea of victim participation was easier to explain in the DRC, which followed civil-law and French traditions, as compared with Anglo common-law Uganda, where victim participation was alien to justice traditions.[62]

Under the Statute, the Court (judges) were instructed to "establish principles relating to reparations to, or in respect of, victims,"[63] requiring restitution from convicted persons or awards from or through a Victims' Trust Fund (VTF) established for the purpose by the Assembly of States Parties.[64] The Statute left the details for future elaboration. A board was appointed for the VTF at the first ASP in September 2002. Because of disagreements among states over the rival objectives of serving victims' rights and maintaining due process standards for suspects, it took until the end of the fourth ASP in the fall of 2005 to reach agreement on the VTF rules (see Chapter 6), and the agreement left to the judges the final determination of how to strike the appropriate balance. In November 2006, the board of the VTF announced its intention to begin considering requests for assistance.[65] By January 2007, the trust fund had received 2.3 million Euros in contributions.

Outreach

The isolation of the ICTY/ICTR from the areas in which crimes were committed and the inadequacy of the broadcasting of trials by the ICTY

---

[62] Interviews.
[63] Statute Article 75.
[64] Statute Article 79.
[65] ICC, "Communique from the Chair of the Board of Directors of the Trust Fund for Victims of the International Criminal Court" (2006).

led to the gradual establishment in the ICTY of an "outreach" program, as described in Chapter 3. Outreach was another aspect of "new justice" that evolved in the tribunal context and informed discussions in the ICC development process, but has only begun to be explicitly addressed in operations of the Court – not written into the Statute or rules. Outreach is pursued both by the Registry and the OTP, in the context primarily of the field offices. NGOs pressed hard for an improvement in the Court's outreach activities. At the 2005 ASP, they were critical of the Committee on Budget and Finance's (CBF) reduction of financial allocations to Registry outreach; they were much relieved in 2006 when a similar CBF recommendation was rejected by the ASP, and the budget for out-reach significantly increased (see Chapter 6). Court personnel from all three organs traveled with increasing frequency to situation areas as well as states contemplating accession to the Statute to explain the Court's purpose and operations. Many of the meetings were organized by NGOs (see Chapter 5). Recognizing a lack of coordination among the separate organs' outreach activities, following a recommendation from the CBF, the Court developed a consolidated plan for outreach that was presented to the fall 2006 Assembly of States Parties (see following discussion).

COORDINATION AND PLANNING

In March 2004, the Committee on Budget and Finance of the Assembly of States Parties reported "concern over a certain fragmentation between the three organs" of the Court.[66] Worried that the ICC might fall prey to the ad hoc tribunals' schizoid conflicts between their Presidents, Prose-cutor, and registrars, the Court declared a "one-court principle," at once verifying the CBF's concerns and seeking to rectify the problem. In addition, as had the tribunals before it,[67] the Court formalized the existence of discussions among the Presidency, Registry, and OTP, referring from the spring of 2004 to the Coordinating Council (Coco), which intended to iron out administrative coordination problems. Moreover, in the fall of 2004, the CBF recommended that the Court initiate a deliberate planning process, and this turned into a project to develop a strategic plan for the Court[68] and this turned into a project to

---

[66] ICC, Assembly of States Parties, Third Session,"Report of the Committee on Budget and Finance," ICC-ASP/3/CBF.1/L4 (2004).

[67] See ICTY Rules of Procedure, amended in 2000, Chapter 2, Rule 23*bis*.

[68] ICC, Assembly of States Parties, Third Session, "Report of the Committee on Budget and Finance" ICC-ASP/3/18 (2004), Para. 46.

develop a strategic plan for the Court. Separately, a financial planning model and an outreach plan were being developed. The plans were presented to the fall 2006 ASP, showing that the Court had completed its initial formative phase and had taken shape as a continuing and stable organization.

Battling a Split Personality

Administrative leadership conflicts in the ICC have to be worked out among the three top officials, and this is affected by the officials' personal relations as well as by their formal roles. While major aspects of overlapping and contested responsibilities that bear on the conduct of judicial proceedings are being sorted out in formal proceedings, Court officials are trying to improve internal administrative coordination with administrative innovations.

The Court's three main organs are organizationally largely independent. The judges are elected by the ASP (to nine-year, nonrenewable terms) and, in turn, elect from among themselves their President (to a three-year, once-renewable term). The President has overall responsibility for the functioning and administration of the ICC. The Registrar is elected by the judges[69] (a five-year, once-renewable term) and is to "exercise his or her functions under the authority of the President of the Court."[70] The Prosecutor is elected by the members of the ASP (to a nine-year, nonrenewable term)[71] and "shall have full authority over the management and administration of the Office, including the staff, facilities and other resources thereof."[72]

The clash between the Registry and OTP over personnel recruitment was an early example of the fractious nature of the Court's structure. Other matters have been more difficult to resolve.

Since the President is a judge who sits in judicial chambers (the first President, Philippe Kirsch, placed himself on the Appeals Chamber), there is something of a role conflict for the President when, as the top official of the Court, he is confronted with Registry–OTP disputes whose outcome may bear upon a particular case in Court. For example, were the Registrar and OTP to disagree over administrative control of activities connected

[69] Statute Article 43.4.
[70] Statute Article 43.2.
[71] Statute Article 42.4.
[72] Statute Article 42.2.

to victims and witnesses in a particular case, the President could come to believe that coming down on one side or the other would entail taking a position that favored, for example, victims over the accused, or vice versa, in matters that could hypothetically also come before the Appeals Chamber. President Kirsch's actions in response, according to people close to the Court, has been to attempt to mediate disputes and facilitate agreements between the Registry and Prosecution, rather than authoritatively to intervene. Thus, although the Registrar is statutorily subordinate to the President, in practice the Registrar remains largely independent.

Because OTP press releases and other kinds of outreach activities were not being effectively coordinated with similar activities originating in the Registry's External Relations Office, in 2004 the Coco established its External Communications Working Group made up of representatives of the Presidency, the Registry, and the OTP. These officials meet frequently to coordinate the activities and statements of the three organs in order to present a consistent external message.

When in 2004 the Committee on Budget and Finance recommended, and the ASP adopted, a resolution calling for development by the Court of a strategic plan, an interorgan working group, called the Strategy Group, was established in response. Additional working groups were established to help coordinate budget development (the Budget Steering Committee), and the External Communications Group was assigned the job of drafting an overall strategic plan for "outreach."[73]

Planning

In its first years, the Court expanded prodigiously. Like any international organization funded from state contributions, the ICC had to develop a budget that would meet with states' approval, and the states' approval hinged on the willingness of their governments (generally foreign affairs and finance ministries) to support it. The PrepCom had prepared an initial draft budget, and the first Assembly of States Parties duly approved expenditure levels and assessed members for contributions. Worried about the high rate of growth, particularly in light of the unexpectedly large size and costs of the ad hoc tribunals, the ASP's Committee on Budget and Finance recommended in 2004 that the Court "prepare a set of over-arching objectives and expected accomplishments for the court as a whole

---

[73] Wennerstrand, "Presidency Promotes 'One Court'" (2005), 4.

reflecting the collective plans for advancing the aims of the Rome Statute ... underpinned by the objectives of each of the organs,"[74] and the recommendation was adopted by the third ASP. The ad hoc tribunals had developed their completion plans under pressure from the Security Council; the Court would develop its Strategic Plan with the strong encouragement of a nervous ASP.

ICC Budget, 1,000 Euros (% Growth)

Budget Year	2002–3	2004	2005	2006	2007
ICC Requested		55,089[a]	69,564[b]	82,464[c]	93,458[d]
			(26)	(19)	(13)
Approved by ASP	30,894[e]	53,072[f]	66,784[g]	80,417[h]	88,872[i]
		(72)	(26)	(20)	(11)
Actual Expenditure	21,479[j]	43,510[k]	63,830[l]	64,107[m]	
		(102)	(47)	(0.4)	

[a] ICC-ASP/2/10, "Draft Resolution of the Assembly of States Parties on the 2004 Draft Programme Budget ... in 2004," Annex I, 155.

[b] ICC-ASP/3/2, Draft Programme Budget for 2005, ASP Third Session, Official Records, 3.

[c] ICC-ASP/4/5, Proposed Programme Budget for 2006, ASP Fourth Session, Official Records, 3.

[d] ICC-ASP/5/9, "Proposed Programme Budget for 2007, ASP Fifth Session, Official Records, 3.

[e] ICC-ASP/1/3, "Budget Appropriations for the First Financial Period ... " Resolution ICC-ASP/1/Res.12, in ASP, First Session, Official Records, 349.

[f] Resolution ICC-ASP/2/Res.1, "Programme Budget for 2004," ICC-ASP/2/10, Second Session, Official Records, 202.

[g] Resolution ICC-ASP/3/Res.4, "Programme Budget for 2005," ICC-ASP/3/25, 323.

[h] Resolution ICC-ASP/4/Res.8, "Programme Budget for 2006," ASP Fourth Session Official Records, 350.

[i] Resolution ICC-ASP/5/Res.4, "Programme Budget for 2007," ASP Fifth Session Official Records, 383.

[j] ICC-ASP/4/9 Statement I "International Criminal Court Statement of Income and Expenditure ... for the Period Ending 31 December 2004," 7 September 2005, 32.

[k] ICC-ASP/4/5, 139. "Proposed Programme Budget for 2006" Annex V, Summary Table by Object of Expenditure. Statement I.

[l] ICC-ASP/5/9/corr.1, 3. "Proposed Programme Budget for 2007," Table Annex VI, 8 September 2006.

[m] ICC-ASP/6/3, "Report on Programme Performance of the International Criminal Court for the Year 2006" (2007), 9.

Aware of the sensitivity of the states to the rapid growth of the court's budget, ICC officials were also concerned that the budgetary process needed to be based on some realistic idea of how much the Court could do at any

[74] ICC, Assembly of States Parties, op cit.

level of resources. They sought to develop a method to predict costs and to determine where in their organizational processes difficulties were likely to arise under different planning assumptions. These ideas were developed concurrently with the Strategic Plan[75] and called the "Court Capacity Model." The plan and model were completed during the summer of 2006, and sent to the ASP at its fifth session in November.

Strategic Plan

The strategic planning process was hindered partly by the crush of other business and partly by the range of responsibilities and objectives pursued by different parts of the Court. The final overall plan embraced a broad range of goals providing little new focus; the OTP plan rearticulated the principles that had come to guide the office over the preceding three years; and the outreach proposal incorporated many of the objectives of NGOs and "new justice" advocates within the Court, but was accorded a lower apparent priority than core OTP activities.

Representatives to the ASP are diplomatic representatives of their states; because of the normal rotation of diplomatic staff, the ASP audience to whom the Strategic Plan was addressed included few people who were involved in negotiating the Statute – thus, it sought to inform them about the Court, its context, and its overall mission as well as its immediate and longer-term objectives.

The Strategic Plan was extensively negotiated among the Court's organs. A somewhat anodyne document, it is a useful basis on which the Court can inform new ASP representatives and others about the Court's aims and priorities. The Strategic Plan's mission was stated in traditional, rather than new justice, terms, to "Fairly, effectively and impartially investigate, prosecute and conduct trials of the most serious crimes; Act transparently and efficiently; and Contribute to long-lasting respect for and the enforcement of international criminal justice, to the prevention of crime and to the fight against impunity."[76] Within the mission, the plan states three strategic goals,[77] each one having priority objectives for the coming three years, and additional ten-year objectives. The first goal is to "conduct fair, effective and expeditious public proceedings in accordance with the Rome Statute and with high legal standards, ensuring full exercise of the rights of

---

[75] ICC, Assembly of States Parties, Fifth Session, "Strategic Plan of the International Criminal Court" ICC-ASP/5/6 (2006).

[76] Ibid., p. 4.

[77] Ibid., p. 5.

all participants."[78] The second is for the Court to gain support by enhancing awareness, a correct understanding, and increased support for the Court.[79] The third goal is for the Court to be "a model of public administration," efficient, flexible, and accountable, with a qualified and motivated staff working in a caring environment and a "non-bureaucratic culture."[80]

The real priority-setting activity remained in the budgetary process, and the Court Capacity Model was a more instructive device for this.

Court Capacity Model

Even before the strategic planning got seriously under way, Court officials were talking about developing a "Court Capacity Model."[81] The idea was that the Court's activities could be thought of as a production operation, built up from distinct phases of activity, each of which could be pursued at larger or smaller scale, needed to dovetail with prior and successor operations, and which, if implemented at the wrong scale, could create excess capacity, and thus waste, or become a bottleneck in the operation.

Devising the model in advance of experience with a full cycle – from investigation through trial outcome – had to be a largely hypothetical exercise, but information was being produced even as the Court began its operations, and precedents could be found in the ad hoc tribunals'

---

[78] Priority objectives for goal 1 included conducting four to six new investigations of existing or new situations over the next three years; putting in place a system to address all security risks; developing policies to protect all participants in proceedings and persons otherwise affected by the Court's activities; completing the Court Capacity Model and initiating discussions with the Assembly of States Parties on the number of cases the court will be able to pursue each year; and developing options for field offices as well as the permanent premises. Ibid., pp. 6–8.

[79] Priority objectives for goal 2 included cultivating awareness and understanding of the Court in affected communities; developing cooperation mechanisms, in particular for suspects' arrest and surrender; increasing support for the Court by improved communication and mutual understanding with stakeholders; and developing and implementing ways to publicize all proceedings for local and global audiences. Ibid., pp. 8–9.

[80] Priority objectives included establishing and clarifying roles of and decision-making processes within and between the Court's organs; becoming a nonbureaucratic administration focused on results rather than processes; deploying programs to achieve "identified optimal levels of quality with maximum efficiency"; submitting sound, accurate and transparent budget proposals; recruiting a diverse staff of the highest standards; providing maximum possible security, safety, and welfare for all staff; developing a supportive and ethical staff culture; and becoming an "e-institution" that provides high information security. Ibid., pp. 9–11.

[81] ICC, Assembly of States Parties, Fifth Session, "Court Capacity Model," ICC-ASP/5/10 (2006).

operations. The model could be useful not only in deciding how to build the Court, but also in explaining to the donor countries how the scale and speed of the Court's operations would depend upon the amount of resources donated. International justice would have to be purchased at a price. While the Strategic Plan presented the Court's mission, goals, and objectives, the Court Capacity Model, unveiled at the same time, presented a dynamic indicator of how much activity could be undertaken, how the Court's officials conceptualized its processes, and how the process could be monitored. The model depended upon the assumptions built into it about, for instance, the number of personnel needed for the particular tasks enumerated in it, but with any set of assumptions, the model could be used to show the ASP how much justice activity could be bought for how much money.[82] It would be useful not only as a management and budgeting tool, but also to make the point to the ASP that it was up to the states to decide how much Court, how much international justice, they wanted.

Strategic Plan for Outreach

Experience from the ad hoc tribunals and strong, consistent messages from nongovernmental organizations brought home to ICC officials the need for a coordinated public relations presence. The primary public relations and information responsibilities fell under the authority of the Registry, which, according to the Rules of Procedure and Evidence, includes among its many activities the duty ("without prejudice to the authority of the Office of the Prosecutor") to "serve as the channel of communication of the Court."[83] The Registry's Public Information and Documentation Section includes a Library and Documentation Center and a Public Information Unit (PIU), the latter being the primary information/outreach office for the ICC. The Prosecutor's immediate office has its own public information adviser, who also serves as the Prosecutor's spokesperson. As the Prosecutor played an increasingly public role, coordination between the Registry's PIU and the OTP became difficult, so to coordinate the Court's overall public information and outreach activities, a committee was established in 2004 including representatives from the PIU, OTP, and the Presidency.[84]

Because of the wide range of audiences that the Court seeks to address, from government officials and legal scholars to victims of atrocities in remote locations, and with the urging and examples of networks of

[82] Ibid.
[83] Rule 13.1.
[84] Interviews.

international and local NGOs, like many other areas in the Court, officials decided that a plan and some objectives needed to be worked out. The resulting Strategic Plan for Outreach, presented to the fall of 2006 ASP, explains in detail the multiple efforts needed to reach a broad spectrum of audiences and various components that the Court will include as it develops outreach programs specific to its activities in each field.[85]

OTP Report on Prosecutorial Strategy

The OTP's 2006 report stated five strategic objectives for the coming three years.[86] First, it would seek to "further improve the quality of the prosecution, aiming to complete two expeditious trials." Second, it would "conduct four to six new investigations of those who bear the greatest responsibility in the Office's current or new situations." Third, it sought "to gain the necessary forms of cooperation for all situations to allow for effective investigations and to mobilize and facilitate successful arrest operations." Fourth, it would "continuously improve the way in which the Office interacts with victims and addresses their interests." The OTP's fifth objective was to "establish forms of cooperation with states and organizations to maximize the Office's contribution to the fight against impunity and the prevention of crimes."[87]

The OTP reiterated the "one-court principle," showed in a chart how its strategy lined up with the ICC strategic goals 1 and 2 (discussed previously), and then stated three principles of prosecutorial strategy: "positive complementarity," "focused investigations," and "maximizing the impact."

The Prosecutor's strategy precluded none of the objectives built into the office from the Statute, and gave little evidence for how efforts would be allocated among them; however, for readers seeking to acquaint themselves with the challenges facing the office, it would be an instructive document. After three years, objectives could be clearly articulated, even if the internal mechanisms for attaining them remained in flux.

CONCLUSIONS

Despite the four-year gap between completion of the Statute and the initiation of Court operations, when the ICC opened for business in 2002, its form was still largely undetermined. As the new organization came into

---

[85] ICC, Assembly of States Parties, Fifth Session, "Strategic Plan for Outreach of the International Criminal Court," ICC-ASP/5/12 (2006).
[86] ICC, OTP, "Report on Prosecutorial Strategy" (2006), 1.
[87] Ibid., 3.

being, the consequences of earlier decisions became clearer. Exhortations in the Statute notwithstanding, selection of the judges appeared more a political campaign by states than a selection based on merit. Sensitivities to the Prosecutor's powers, and the difficulty of the position, made this a surprisingly narrow recruitment.

Once the Chief Prosecutor took office, the OTP's operational code appeared to shift from a formal, civil-law-informed, legalistic approach to a looser, more politically conceived structure. "Positive complementarity" and "self-referrals" reduced the Court's challenge to sovereignty and thus should ease its acquisition of cases and improve its ability, even without cases in court, to promote states' actions against impunity.

Tensions among the organs of the Court stimulated administrative innovations, but these innovations did not resolve the division of labor. This will be worked out only in practice and by judicial decisions. The President of the Court staffed the Pre-Trial Chambers mostly with civil-law judges. The disputes that have so far emerged between the PTCs and the Prosecutor revolve around rival visions of their relative power, the independence of the Prosecutor, and the roles of the PTCs. These will ultimately be resolved by the Appeals Chamber, which includes a mixture of civil- and common-law judges. Early decisions seem to be leaning in the direction of PTC judicial discretion, thus toward the civil-law approach.

The Presidency of the Court may be a position with too many duties. The President is the formal head and chief external representative of the Court as a whole and a judge member of the Appeals Chamber and is responsible for the administration of the Court. Particularly as appeals activities increase, these three roles may be more than any individual can fully serve.

Operations of the Court also demonstrate how traditional justice and new justice objectives are melding. Extensive concern over victims' participation in the Congo case show that the Court is embracing new justice objectives in the legal process. Less progress has been made toward incorporating the restorative objectives embodied in the Trust Fund for Victims, where a slow start and limited collection of donations implies that its operations will not soon become a materially significant part of the Court's operation. Unlike the legal process, the Trust Fund falls less under the control of the judges and is much more subject to the preferences of states (see Chapter 6).

Planning and modeling efforts revealed in the fall of 2006 what Court officials could agree upon regarding the ICC's direction and the connection between the breadth and intensity of its actions, on the one hand, and the resources they would require, on the other. The Strategic Plan demonstrated that the Court is largely fixated on organization building – the majority of its objectives were in its category of being a "model of public administration," the area where challenges to the Court's officials were most immediate. The Court Capacity Model will inform the states how much Court activity they can buy for how much money: Decisions about how much justice to purchase belong to the states, and policy control remains essentially budgetary.

Realists assert that states are paramount in the international system. The domination of politics over pure expertise in election of the Court's judges and Prosecutor, Court officials' quest for organizational legitimacy, and their aversion to antagonizing states demonstrate their sensitivity to the power dynamics that realists emphasize. But the relevance of state power to the Court does not vitiate the possibility that the Court will be found useful and supported by states for reasons other than relative advantage over other states, verifying the neoliberal institutionalists' vision of potential positive-sum outcomes of international cooperative behavior and also potentially verifying the constructivists' contention that shifting identities at the international level – pressed by civil society organizations upon national decision makers through domestic politics – lead to the evolution of international institutions.

The importance and legitimacy of the Court also depend upon the priority states accord to the norms on which it is built. Future constructivists may look back upon the ICC as an organization that provided a new channel for action within an increasingly coherent normative consensus. Alternatively, they may see the Court as an organizational innovation that failed because its normative basis was misunderstood or fell apart, or because it was organizationally incapable of carrying out the agreements that led to its creation. Nongovernmental organizations continue to be vital to the Court in pressing upon states the normative framework of international criminal law and, more immediately, by being directly involved in publicizing the Court, pressing for state adherence to the Statute, and carrying out activities directly in support of its operational activities. The next chapter discusses this complex ICC–NGO relationship.

5

NGOs – Advocates, Assets, Critics, and Goads

Nongovernmental organizations cajoled, lobbied, and in myriad ways pushed hard for the birth of the International Criminal Court, and now they are nurturing it, criticizing it, and sometimes acting as the Court's surrogates or agents, extending its reach. At once the ICC's most vigorous champions and its most demanding taskmasters, NGOs closely monitor the organization's declarations and actions. They do not speak to the ICC with one voice because they pursue a range of objectives. However, through the NGO Coalition for the International Criminal Court (CICC), they coordinate with each other on the objectives they share. From the Statute Conference onward, the relationship between the ICC and the NGOs has probably been closer, more consistent, and more vital to the Court than have analogous relations between NGOs and any other international organization.

By mid-2006 the CICC claimed more than 2,000 member organizations worldwide, ranging from major international NGOs such as Human Rights Watch (HRW) and Amnesty International (AI) to local peace and justice organizations. Many of the NGOs with which the Court interacts are members of the CICC. Some are closely affiliated with governments, such as the International Criminal Law Network, founded and largely funded by The Hague municipality and the Dutch Ministries of Defense and Foreign Affairs. Some are themselves federations, such as the International Federation of Human Rights Leagues (FIDH). Although the NGOs seek to shape the actions of the Court, the Court must manage the pressures exerted by the NGOs. This chapter explains the Court's symbiotic relationship with the NGOs and how they moved from being crucial to the Court's creation to being vital to its operations.

INTERNATIONAL RELATIONS THEORY AND NGOS

Realists minimize the role of NGOs. Because the realist model is one in which states are the paramount actors, domestic, transnational, and global NGOs don't make it onto structuralist or neorealist radars. To the small extent that domestic politics might influence policy making, and domestic politics might be influenced by nongovernmental organizations, there may be some link from NGOs to policy; however, the national interest to which states' rational decision makers respond exists apart from the claims that domestic organizations might make about it. In neoliberal institutionalists' views, the states remain paramount actors, but they are joined at the international level by organizations that manifest international institutional commitments. Insofar as NGOs might assist in reducing transaction costs for states and international organizations (by, for instance, providing information or informal communications channels), they may have some role to play at the global level. However, as argued in the Introduction, the basis for institutionalism, like realism, tends to be material rather than normative. It is in the normative realm that NGOs have had their most pervasive effects. The constructivists are most concerned with normative change, and since NGOs can be key transmitters of normative values, constructivists tend to be more interested in NGOs than other varieties of analysts.

Constructivist scholars argue that nongovernmental organizations[1] publicize and build support for norms at the domestic and international levels, calling them "norm entrepreneurs."[2] The number of these organizations has exploded since World War II, particularly in fields associated with global issues such as human rights and the environment.[3] From the 1980s onward, Amnesty International, Human Rights Watch, and other NGOs advocated international organizational measures against criminal

---

[1] Nongovernmental organizations are commonly thought of as organizations other than government and profit-oriented ones. They are sometimes also called civil society organizations. One definition holds that NGOs are voluntary organizations whose objectives include consulting, educating, mediating, participating in government action, and acting as catalysts to government action. Shestack, "Sisyphus Endures: The International Human Rights NGO" (1978).

[2] Finnemore and Sikkink, "International Norms and Political Change" (1998), 887–917.

[3] For example, NGOs accorded consultative status by the UN Economic and Social Council (ECOSOC) grew from 41 in 1948 to 2,500 in 2002. Karns and Mingst, *International Organizations: The Politics and Processes of Global Governance* (2004), 231. If domestic NGOs are included, depending upon definitions, the number probably runs to the millions.

impunity, converging in support of an international criminal court by 1995 in the CICC.

From the constructivist viewpoint, national leaders' identities come to necessitate the appearance of respect for international norms, and the practice of presenting the appearance eventually modifies their behavior. As noted earlier, the behavioral changes can accumulate into a "norms cascade."[4] The move in the 1990s from discussion of an ICC to negotiation of the Statute could be seen as the result of the cascade passing a tipping point. At the global level, NGOs convey information and analyses, promote exchanges of ideas across borders, and can focus international attention on otherwise obscure events. Publicity may inhibit perpetrators and deter some of the deal making that can lead to impunity. Governments that begin by ignoring or rejecting NGO calls to uphold international standards often come to pay at least rhetorical respect to human rights norms, thus strengthening domestic demands for greater compliance.[5]

GROWTH OF NGO INVOLVEMENT

Until the 1990s, the idea of an International Criminal Court was primarily developed by international legal experts. In the background during the 1970s and 1980s, international human rights and humanitarian NGOs multiplied and expanded. Finally, what had long survived as an esoteric quest by international lawyers to establish a mechanism for punishing international crimes reached the mainstream of international human rights activism. Nuremberg-style retributive old justice converged with the increasingly vigorous new, restorative justice movement that embraced social reconciliation, with a focus on victims and reparations.

NGOs commented extensively on the International Law Commission draft of July 1994 (see Chapter 3).[6] In the fall, they pressed the General Assembly's Sixth (legal) Committee to recommend that the General Assembly pass a resolution to create an ad hoc committee that would discuss the draft and move toward a statute conference. The resolution passed on December 10, 1994.[7] In February 1995, as momentum built, World

---

[4] Finnemore and Sikkink, op cit., 895.
[5] Risse, Ropp, and Sikkink, *The Power of Human Rights: International Norms and Domestic Change* (1999).
[6] For example, Amnesty International, "Memorandum to the International Law Commission: Establishing a Just, Fair and Effective Permanent International Criminal Tribunal" (1994).
[7] UN General Assembly, "Establishment of an International Criminal Court," Resolution 49/53, (1994).

Federalist Movement (WFM) Executive Director Bill Pace convened a meeting in New York to establish a steering committee of what came to be the NGO CICC.[8] The CICC steering committee included representatives from the WFM, the International Commission of Jurists, Amnesty International, the Lawyers Committee for Human Rights, Human Rights Watch, Parliamentarians for Global Action, and No Peace Without Justice.[9] (By mid-2006, the steering committee had expanded to include eleven organizations.)[10]

From the first meeting onward, the CICC served as an umbrella and coordinating organization for a steadily growing raft of NGOs interested in the creation of the ICC. CICC members now ascribe to three principles: (1) promoting worldwide ratification and implementation of the Rome Statute of the ICC; (2) maintaining the integrity of the Rome Statute of the ICC; and (3) ensuring the ICC will be as fair, effective, and independent as possible.[11] These very general principles permit organizations with broadly varying objectives to participate in the coalition. Most of the organizations involved with the ICC pursue broader agendas than just the Court, for example, more general human rights issues, victims' rights, gender rights, rule of law, conflict mediation, and peace. The CICC coordinates their efforts to improve the efficiency of NGOs' contributions to the Court and to pool their influence on major common issues. From the ICC side, it has been extremely useful to have the CICC channel NGO contacts with the Court so that its officials don't have to interact individually with thousands of separate organizations.[12]

NGOS AND THE STATUTE

During the preparatory phase before the Statute Conference, CICC member organizations, as well as the expanding CICC Secretariat itself, produced

---

[8] The WFM had been formed in 1947 as the World Movement for World Federal Government, and went through several subsequent names before becoming the WFM. It has member and associated organizations and individual supporters in many parts of the world, linked together by the idea that global peace requires some form of world government.

[9] Stoelting, "NGOs and the ICC" (1999).

[10] Amnesty International, Asociación Pro Derechos Humanos, European Law Students Association, Fédération Internationale des Ligues des Droits de l'Homme, Human Rights First, Human Rights Watch, No Peace Without Justice, Parliamentarians for Global Action, Rights and Democracy, Women's Initiatives for Gender Justice, and the World Federalist Movement. NGO CICC, CICC Web site, "Steering Committee."

[11] NGO CICC, CICC Web site, "Membership Request Form."

[12] Interviews.

information materials, lobbied members to express support for an ICC, organized regional meetings with NGO and governmental representatives to promote their ideas about the Court, and produced newsletters and position papers on a multitude of aspects of the ICC and affiliated issues in international law and human rights. The NGOs devoted extensive effort to researching, writing, and disseminating information and position papers throughout the preparatory process and in advance of the Rome Conference. Close contact with national delegations meant that many NGO positions were articulated in national positions as well.

At formal and informal meetings and in their publications, the NGOs supported proposals for an ICC radically different from the International Law Commission draft. They sought to maximize Court independence from the UN Security Council, and they emphasized a new justice victim orientation. They tended to agree on both of those objectives but differed in their focuses. Some sought a longer list of crimes to be included in the Court's jurisdiction, others wanted to stress a narrower range that could command greater agreement among the negotiating states. Some NGOs vigorously supported including the crime of aggression in the Statute's purview; others viewed it as being politically too divisive. A similar division arose over explicitly criminalizing the use of weapons of mass destruction.

The highly organized NGO coalition, which by the time of the Conference included more than 800 members of which 236 were actually represented at Rome,[13] played a pivotal role in the Statute negotiations. CICC members divided into three kinds of groups – regional caucuses that met with state representatives from their own regions; issue-based groups focused, for example, on victims, peace, children, gender justice, and religiously based organizations; and teams of NGO representatives working on the subjects into which the state delegations had divided the work of the conference: Establishment (of the Court); Definitions (of terms, crimes); State Consent (jurisdiction); Trigger Mechanism and Admissibility (referrals, Security Council, complementarity); General Principles (of law); Composition and Administration (of the Court); Investigation (the Prosecutor); Trial, Appeal, and Review (rules); Penalties; and Cooperation (with states and other organizations).[14]

The CICC vastly increased the transparency of the negotiations by providing daily updates of states' positions based on public comments and conversations with delegates. Groups not attending at Rome could receive a

---

[13] Glasius, *The International Criminal Court: A Global Civil Society Achievement* (2005), 27.
[14] NGO CICC, *The Rome Treaty Conference Monitor* (1998), 1.

daily digest of events called *On The Record*, which the CICC helped distribute but did not write.[15] The Inter-Press Service, a nonprofit journalists' association with NGO consultative status at UNESCO, published a newspaper called *Terra Viva* supported by contributions from the European Union through the NGO No Peace Without Justice (NPWJ) and the CICC, in which the *CICC Monitor* was an insert.[16] These helped maintain momentum in the negotiations and enabled state representatives to know what was going on in areas other than those in which they were directly involved. The daily updates also served as a running "straw vote" on the major topics of the conference, enabling in particular the smaller and like-minded states to recognize the extent of their agreement even as the more powerful states sought to reopen areas of negotiation and divide opposition (Chapter 3).

Some state representations recruited NGO personnel to be members of their delegations, so in some cases NGO positions became state positions. The CICC's innovative use of electronic communications enabled it to become the fastest and most comprehensive source of information to Conference participants. Observers and participants agreed in retrospect that the NGO role at the Statute Conference was more influential in the progress of the Conference than had NGO participation been at any prior large international negotiation. CICC convener Bill Pace emerged as one of the major founding influences of the Court.

The final Rome Statute strongly reflected NGOs' efforts although the NGOs didn't get everything they wanted. For example, while most of the participating NGOs and a majority of states were sympathetic to arms control objectives being pursued by the "Peace Caucus," a coalition of groups seeking to criminalize the use of weapons of mass destruction and of landmines, the clear rejection of this position by the members of the Security Council – the nuclear weapon states – ultimately made it an unattainable objective.[17] Because human rights organizations didn't want the negotiations to collapse, they were willing to let the weapons issue go, but they pressed hard to create a highly independent prosecutor and a Court as free as possible from future Security Council control.

A coalition of women's groups pushed successfully to focus the new court on the victimization of women. The Women's Caucus for Gender

---

[15] Ibid., p. 3.

[16] Inter-Press Service, *Terra Viva* (1998), 2.

[17] Burroughs and Cabasso, "Confronting the Nuclear-Armed States in International Negotiating Forums: Lessons for NGOs" (1999), 470–4.

Justice had been founded at the February 1997 Statute Conference Preparatory Committee meeting. From a small group of organizations, the Caucus grew to hundreds of members from all over the world by the time of the Statute Conference itself, and the Caucus joined the CICC steering committee.[18] The Caucus brought gender issues into the mainstream of the CICC's aims and was represented consistently by a 12- to 15-person team at the Rome Conference, among the hundreds of NGO representatives.[19]

Women's advocacy groups had accomplished major breakthroughs in both the ICTY and the ICTR in the few years prior to the Statute Conference during which the tribunals' trials had begun. Building upon the Yugoslavia and Rwanda tribunal precedents (Chapter 2), the Women's Caucus infused gender concerns throughout the Statute. In addition to writing gender crimes[20] into the Statute as crimes against humanity and war crimes, the ASP is to elect judges including "a fair representation of female and male judges"[21] and judges having legal experience including with violence against women or children.[22] The Prosecutor is instructed to appoint advisers with legal expertise including sexual and gender violence and violence against children,[23] and the Registry's Victims and Witnesses Unit is to include staff with expertise in trauma, "including trauma related to crimes of sexual violence."[24]

At the Statute Conference, some NGOs were concerned that the gender focus could support an agenda antithetical to values upheld by the Catholic Church, Muslim countries, and "pro-family" organizations. They feared that the sexual crime definitions might appear to legalize abortion. Their opposition to the gender crimes definitions forced a painstakingly negotiated compromise that inserted into the Statute a clause noting that the definition (of enforced pregnancy) "Shall not in any way be interpreted as affecting national laws relating to pregnancy."[25] There was considerable wrangling as well over terminology that these groups feared might lead to some implied approval of other than heterosexual gender identities, so under the crimes against humanity definitions, a clarifying paragraph was included that stated: " 'Gender' refers to the two sexes, male and female,

---

[18] Glasius, op cit., 78–81.

[19] Ibid., 80–1.

[20] Statute Article 7.1(g), "rape, sexual slavery, enforced prostitution, forced pregnancy, enforced sterilization or any other form of sexual violence of comparable gravity," and similar language in 8.2(b)(xxii), 8.2(e)(vi).

[21] Statute Article 36.8(a)iii.

[22] Statute Article 36.8.b.

[23] Statute Article 42.9.

[24] Statute Article 43.6.

[25] Statute Article 7.2(f).

within the context of society. The term 'gender' does not indicate any meaning different from the above."[26]

In addition to including women's concerns in the Statute, NGOs pursuing new justice objectives focused more widely on the welfare of victims and witnesses. Article 68, "protection of the victims and witnesses and their participation in the proceedings," was a major victory that built upon the lessons learned from the Yugoslavia and Rwanda tribunals. The Court is instructed to protect witnesses and victims involved in its procedures and, drawing on the civil-law tradition, establishes that the Court "shall" permit victims' and witnesses' "views and concerns to be presented and considered" in its proceedings.[27]

Another area in which NGOs exerted tremendous effort at the Conference was in bolstering the majority of countries' drive for a highly independent ICC, free from the need for the UN Security Council to bring it into action. NGOs generally supported Germany's proposal that would have amounted to universal jurisdiction. As described in Chapter 3, the NGOs and most like-minded states sought a jurisdictional regime under which the Court would have been empowered to prosecute any suspected perpetrator of the crimes defined by the Statute. Since the United States, in particular, sought an ICC that would only be triggered by a Security Council resolution, states seeking to gain U.S. support for the Statute sought to compromise, which led to a more limited jurisdictional regime.

ADVOCACY, ADVICE, AND OUTREACH

With completion of the Statute, the NGOs remained highly engaged. CICC members continued to pursue discussions and negotiations in the Preparatory Commission as it developed the Rules of Procedure and Evidence and the Elements of Crimes. They pushed for states to support the emerging organization's budget. They continued national campaigns for states' signature and ratification of the Statute, and urged the states that had joined to develop and adopt implementing legislation for their domestic legal codes.

Promoting the Rome Statute and Staffing the Court

Once the ICC came into being, the NGOs that had expended such huge energy to create the Court believed further effort would be needed for it to

---

[26] Statute Article 7.3.
[27] Statute Article 68.3.

succeed. The theory of norm cascades and tipping points may imply irreversibility; however, real organizations can fail; states' commitments can waver, wane, or evaporate; and the organization's resources could be supplemented by NGOs' efforts. Even though political support for the ICC among its members is fairly solid, states still guard their sovereignty jealously, and they have rival priorities as they calculate their foreign policies and financial commitments. NGOs can be advocates for the Court in ways that Court officials can't: They campaign for states to accede to the Statute, they push for legislation in member states to bring their laws into conformity with ICC obligations, and they can urge the Assembly of States Parties to expand the ICC's budget. Connecting at an operational level with the Court, they provide information to the Office of the Prosecutor, assist the Court's outreach efforts, and bring local people into contact with the Court either directly or through legal procedures such as helping them to petition the Court for official victim status.

NGO personnel are in close contact with the Court at policy and operational levels. Court officials seek both to gain from the knowledge and ideas of the NGOs and to protect the Court's freedom of operation. NGO officials are sometimes critical of what they see as insufficiencies or failings of the Court, but in these early years, they have been reluctant to criticize too stridently as they seek to give the ICC and its officials time to consolidate the organization and to develop its operations.

Advocating Adherence

The CICC and its members, notably the Parliamentarians for Global Action, advocate state adherence to the Rome Statute by arranging informational seminars and national and regional meetings of parliamentarians, other NGOs, legal experts, and local leaders. As the rate of new adherences declined, the CICC inaugurated a project targeting a new state each month to be the recipient of focused efforts to promote awareness of, and action on, the Rome Statute. In fall 2005, Mexico became the 100th member of the Rome Treaty, despite adverse pressure from the United States. By fall 2006, the number had grown to 104, with new members St. Kitts and Nevis, Comoros, Montenegro, and Chad.[28] Ratification is only one of the CICC's objectives, however. Even when a state has ratified the Statute, more steps are necessary to bring it fully into effect.

---

[28] NGO CICC, CICC Web site, "States Parties to the Rome Statute of the ICC, According to the U.N. General Assembly Regional Groups."

To cooperate with the Court, a state that has joined the Statute needs to have legal authority to transfer arrested individuals to the Court. This means the crimes subject to Court prosecution generally must be criminalized explicitly in domestic law, so that the arrest of a suspected individual will fall under the authority of national law enforcement officials. Similarly, for states to fulfill their side of the complementarity bargain – in which suspects are to be tried by the Court only in the event that states with jurisdiction prove unwilling or unable genuinely to prosecute – states must have the legal and institutional capacity to carry out such prosecutions on their own.

So little is known in most countries and their legal establishments about the Rome Statute and the Court that there is tremendous scope for informational activities. As employees of an international organization who are officially nonpolitical, ICC officials do not proselytize on behalf of the Court,[29] and the ICC's own official outreach activities are aimed at states where the Court is involved. Although Court officials' availability may decline as courtroom activities increase, the Prosecutor, Registrar, President, judges, and top staff were traveling frequently in the ICC's early years to training and information sessions in member and nonmember states, usually sponsored by academic institutions, legal organizations, and NGOs and frequently aided by CICC coordination. The NGOs thus bear the organizational burden for sponsoring and organizing such meetings, and ICC officials can appear as providers of information rather than as advocates. The NGOs' involvement also helps replace the possible impression that the ICC people are self-important and condescending outsiders with the friendlier image that they come at the behest of NGOs seeking with local people to expand human rights and rule-of-law initiatives.

In addition to the ICC staff, an international group of academic and legal experts, many of them participants at Rome and affiliated with NGOs, also circulate to seminars for legal professionals, legislators, scholars, and activists helping to work on draft legislation, sharing model legal codes with national authorities in states that have signed the Statute, and engaging officials in countries considering signature and/or ratification in discussion about what the domestic legal requirements and ramifications will be.[30]

NGOs have also led in efforts within the United States to counteract American hostility to the Court. As U.S. opposition to the Court congealed

---

[29] Interviews.
[30] For example, Regional Human Security Center, Regional Workshop, "The International Criminal Court and the Arab World" (2005).

under the Bush administration (see Chapter 6), CICC members denounced U.S. pressure against signatory and potential signatory states intended to thwart Statute ratification or force acceptance of U.S. bilateral immunity agreements. U.S. NGOs dispute government allegations that the Court is a threat to U.S. interests.[31]

Electing Court Officials

During the 2003 process of nominating and electing judges (and during the 2006 second round of elections), the CICC organized meetings between NGOs and those running for judgeships. Following those meetings, NGO representatives communicated to national delegations about their preferences and priorities, quite likely influencing the votes that were eventually cast. The Women's Caucus again appeared influential. In the first round of balloting in 2003, six women and one man emerged as the first elected judges. The single victorious male candidate described his campaigning as having been focused largely on NGO meetings, in contrast to some other competitors who spent no time with the NGOs. He believed that his selection was also aided by his experience in his home country as the head of a children's welfare-oriented NGO.[32] It took twenty-nine more ballots to select the rest of the Court's eighteen judges.

In addition to his credentials as a prosecutor of the Argentine generals implicated in the "dirty war" of the 1970s, Chief Prosecutor Moreno Ocampo was the founder of an anticorruption NGO in Argentina and was a board member of the international anticorruption NGO Transparency International. As nominee for Chief Prosecutor, he met in New York with NGO representatives prior to his election-by-acclamation by the Assembly of States Parties.

The speakers list at the installation of the new Chief Prosecutor also shows the importance of NGOs to the ICC. The speakers included President of the Assembly of States Parties H. R. H. Prince Zeid Ra'ad Zeid Al Hussein of Jordan; Court President H. E. Judge Philippe Kirsch; the new Chief Prosecutor, Mr. Luis Moreno Ocampo; former Nuremberg prosecutor and long-time advocate of an international criminal court Professor of Law Benjamin Ferencz; and three NGO representatives: Secrétaire générale

---

[31] For example, see NGO CICC Web site, "US and the ICC," and the Web site for the American Non-Governmental Organizations Coalition for the International Criminal Court.

[32] Interview.

du Comité des victimes des Khmers Rouges Mme. Billon Ung Boun-Hor; Secretary General of the Pan African Lawyers Union Mr. Getachew Kitaw; and NGO Coalition for the International Criminal Court Convener Pace. It has become routine as well for Pace to address the plenary session of the annual meeting of the Assembly of States Parties.

THE NGOS AND ICC OPERATIONS

Like the ICC, NGOs collectively straddle the dilemmas of reconciling justice and peace, international legal norms and local political expediencies, prosecutorial and victim orientations, long- and short-term perspectives. The ICC Statute is a universalist document espousing global norms. The crimes that the Court prosecutes are crimes that may shock the conscience of humankind, but they are visited upon real people in actual places. There is no guarantee that upholding the international norms necessarily maximizes local interest, at least in the short spans of potential victims' lives. As the Court began pursuing investigations and prosecutions, NGOs became vital assets to its operations and constructive, but critical, commentators on its behavior.

NGOs had extensive experience in the domestic and international contexts in which the ICC began operating. While an ICC-centered view might regard the NGOs as adjuncts to the Court's operations, the perspective from the NGOs' standpoint is that the ICC is a new international organization trying to fit into a large NGO and international governmental organization community. The objectives of the NGOs include shaping and ultimately promoting the ICC, but their activities predate the ICC, and their mandates are generally quite different than those of the Court. Promoting human rights, women's issues, victims' rights, peace, or justice can all be connected with the ICC's mandate, but they are not bounded by it. Similarly, the ICC's mandate is not coextensive with any NGOs because it is ultimately a judicial institution.

Initiating Referrals

Under the ICC Statute, anyone can send a letter to the Prosecutor calling for investigation into suspected crimes. The Statute requires the Prosecutor's Office to screen these submissions and respond to them. The communications about suspected crimes can come from government representatives, NGOs, or individuals. Long before the ICC came into being, human rights and humanitarian NGOs had been collecting the kinds of information upon which such letters can be based. Now NGOs are major sources of information for the ICC Prosecutor.

The Office of the Prosecutor reported on February 10, 2006, that it had received 1,732 communications from individuals and organizations, three referrals from states parties to the Statute, and one referral from the UN Security Council. The 1,732 messages, the OTP said, came from individuals or groups located in at least 103 countries. With 60 percent of the messages coming from the United States, Great Britain, France, and Germany, it can be concluded that many originated with human rights NGOs. Crimes were alleged to have taken place in 139 countries.[33] (The OTP deemed 20 percent [346 communications] to be worthy of further analysis.)[34]

Providing Local Contact

Despite the creation of regional offices (by mid-2006, there was one for Uganda in Kampala and one in Kinshasa and one for the Congo in Ituri), the ICC has very little continuing presence in the situation areas. In contrast, the local NGOs are part of the scene, working not only (and in many cases not even primarily) on international justice matters but also engaging in peace, mediation, humanitarian, development, and other kinds of efforts.

The Court depends upon local NGOs and leaders for contact with local populations. In efforts to explain the ICC's role and rules and the opportunities for victims to make their views known, Registry Public Information Office personnel and Victims Participation and Reparations Section officials hold seminars for local leaders and legal professionals, meet with local NGOs, and develop information for use in radio and print media to spread the word about the Court. These events are often planned and presented in cooperation with local NGOs and include NGO representatives as conduits to local groups. Much as there can be difficulties in distinguishing legitimate journalists from others, the Court faces challenges in picking trustworthy and credible local intermediaries and information sources. CICC regional representatives can sometimes help the ICC to screen organizations to determine which are legitimate and most likely to be useful.

These NGOs, community organizations, and local leaderships vary in their views of the ICC, and their attitudes both reflect and shape local responses to the Court as it pursues its activities. ICC officials are aware of

---

[33] ICC, Office of the Prosecutor, "Update on Communications Received by the Office of the Prosecutor of the ICC" (2006).
[34] Ibid.

the difficulties that the ICTR and ICTY experienced in their relations with local populations and of the strong suggestions from NGOs and others that vigorous outreach and local representation programs be developed in the situation areas. Exhortation and implementation, however, are very different things. For the ICC as an organization with limited resources, budgetary trade-offs must be made. So far, the budget lines for outreach and regional offices, as approved by the Assembly of States Parties, have been small. In the fourth ASP in the fall of 2005, for example, one of the contentious issues was whether to permit the Registry to expand its outreach personnel component, adding eleven staff people including eight who would work at field offices. The Committee on Budget and Finance targeted this line item for reduction in the ICC's proposal, recommending only five for field activities. In the end, the Registry budget was reduced as recommended by the CBF but left with the flexibility to reprogram resources from other budget components into outreach. At the next ASP, in November 2006, under pressure from NGOs and despite a similar recommendation from the CBF, the ASP voted to significantly expand the outreach budget from €1.4 million in 2006 to €2.7 million in 2007 (for all public information and documentation section expenditures).[35]

Serious contradictions are built into the ICC's operations at the local level. NGOs and local organizations pursue a broad spectrum of activities in their own societies, so NGOs exist on most sides of these contradictions. A primary divide is between peace-oriented and justice-oriented NGOs. A second dilemma is how the ICC can gain government cooperation but appear unbiased. NGOs and local organizations might be thought of in this context as pressure groups as well as resources for the ICC; the problem for the organization is to be responsive and convincing enough that the NGOs do not oppose, and preferably assist it, and that the Court's legitimacy as an organization is increased at local and international levels.

Acting simultaneously at these two levels is itself fraught with problems. International human rights—oriented organizations, such as Human Rights Watch and Amnesty International, call for suspected perpetrators of statutory crimes to be indicted and prosecuted. They advocate a narrow understanding of the Statute's criteria under which the "interests of justice" might be cited as a reason not to prosecute.[36] In contrast, some local NGOs

---

[35] Boyle, "ICC Outreach Budget Gets Big Boost" (2006).

[36] Amnesty International, "Open Letter to the Chief Prosecutor of the International Criminal Court: Comments on the Concept of the Interests of Justice" (2005); Human Rights Watch Policy Paper: "The Meaning of 'The Interests of Justice' in Article 53 of the Rome Statute" (2005).

view situations very differently. They claim, for example, that for the northern Uganda peace negotiations to succeed, the government's offer of amnesty to Lord's Resistance Army fighters must be upheld. They charge that when the ICC issued arrest warrants against leaders of the LRA, it acted against local interests (see Chapter 7).

To operate in a country requires some degree of cooperation from the government. The Chief Prosecutor solved this problem in Uganda and the Congo by gaining referrals from those governments to pursue investigations. But those agreements make the ICC appear to be working with the government in conflicts in which government forces and personnel are also suspected by local populations of engaging in criminal activity. As a consequence, in both Uganda and the Congo, the ICC sought NGO assistance in reaching out to local populations and has been criticized by the same organizations for disrupting peace efforts or neglecting government-related crimes. In the Congo, various local organizations pressed the ICC for additional (or different) arrests following the arrest and transfer from DRC custody in Kinshasa of Union of Congolese Patriots leader Thomas Lubanga Dyilo to stand trial in The Hague (see Chapter 7). In Uganda, in addition to some calls for the ICC to suspend its activities and/or respect the government's amnesty offer, some groups called for the Prosecutor to demonstrate impartiality by issuing warrants against the government Uganda People's Defense Force (UPDF) as well as the rebel LRA forces.

Reconciling Divergent Agendas

The International Center for Transitional Justice (ICTJ), in collaboration with the Berkeley Human Rights Project, carried out research in northern Uganda to determine what local people really wanted in connection with peace and justice efforts. They found complex answers that favored both prosecution and conciliation; as a consequence, they recommended that the ICC continue its prosecution efforts but expand its outreach program to explain to the local people what its mandate is and how prosecutions were intended to promote peace.[37]

The more the ICC can focus and clarify its objectives, the more clearly it should be able to explain its decisions. However, since its mandate is broad and not entirely coherent, this remains a difficult challenge, one compounded by the limits of its resources, the difficulty of outreach in the

---

[37] International Center for Transitional Justice, "New Study Finds Ugandans Favor Peace with Justice" (2005).

areas of its operations, and the complexity of the situations in which it is involved. Again, it seeks NGO help to resolve the problem. It organizes visits to The Hague by local leaders and NGO representatives from situation states. The visitors typically also spend time with international NGO people organized by the CICC.

The information flow needs to work in the other direction too – from the local areas back to the ICC – in order for full implementation of the Statute's mandate for ICC attention to victims and witnesses. NGOs have been central to this process. For example, in the DRC situation, affiliates of the FIDH held local meetings to explain to local groups the ICC in general, and victims' rights in particular. As a result, some victims asked to participate in the Court's proceedings regarding the Congo. Even before the ICC Registry had completed work on a form for victims to use to seek participant status, the FIDH assisted a group of five victims to petition the Court for representation. The victims (whose numbers grew as the case moved toward the fall 2006 confirmation hearing) were thereafter represented by a lawyer, so FIDH did not take part in actual Court proceedings. As described in Chapter 7, the submission will set precedents for the form and timing of victim representation at the ICC, once disagreements between the Prosecutor and the Pre-Trial Chamber are worked out, possibly through the appeals process.

Ensuring the High Quality of Justice

The ICC Statute has very little to say about the defense of suspects, making the Registry responsible for defense counsel, while the Chambers guard due-process rights and the presumption of innocence. The Registrar created a Division of Counsel with sections for defense and for victims representation. Both sections depend upon NGOs to help carry out their responsibilities.

Concerned about the lack of any structure to provide an "equality of arms" (a defense strong enough to balance the Prosecutor's capabilities), Advocats sans Frontiérs (ASF) and the Union Internationale des Advocats, as well as representatives of national bar associations came together in 2002 to create the International Criminal Bar (ICB) to make available counsel for defendants before the two ad hoc tribunals and, especially, the ICC. The ICB was founded on June 15, 2002, at the Conference of Montreal. It held its first general assembly in Berlin on March 21 and 22, 2003, at which 400 people from more than 50 countries attended. Its governing council includes representatives from five continents and represents all of the world's legal systems; four members are regional coordinators for Asia, Latin America and the Caribbean, Sub-Saharan Africa, and the Arab World. The ICB's members include national and regional bars, the largest international organizations of counsel, and individuals who have been deeply involved in the development of international criminal law. As its Web site proclaims, "Through the membership of non-governmental organizations, the ICB has the benefit of the experience and perspective which these groups have developed through many years of working towards the creation and implementation of the ICC."[38]

The ICB presents joint training courses with the ICC for counsel interested in practicing before the Court, and it assists the ICC in developing lists of counsel authorized for that practice. The Court can assign "duty counsel" from its lists to defendants until they either hire their own lawyers or choose an alternative from the Court's list, and it also maintains a list of counsel available for victim representation.

THE EVOLVING NGO–ICC RELATIONSHIP

From the time of the Preparatory Committee's (post-ILC 1994 draft Statute) work through the first year of the Court's existence, the group of state representatives, NGO personnel, and Court officials involved with negotiating, planning, and beginning to operate the ICC was remarkably stable. An identifiable community, first centered in New York, but then adding The Hague as a second locus of activity, negotiated and began to implement the consensus that developed over the period of their involvement. In contrast, by late 2005, the NGO community had greater personnel continuity than either state representatives to the ICC or, because of its rapid recent growth, the Court itself. Once the Court came into being, located in The Hague, the state representations began to be subject to the more normal rotational effects of diplomatic service postings – people long involved with the ICC's creation as government representatives moved to other activities, and diplomats in The Hague were assigned to deal with the ICC and transferred the portfolio to their successors as they shifted to other posts.

Early Court employees left for other jobs, and many new Court employees were hired from outside of the community. NGO personnel involved with the Court were not subject to the same rotational forces. Still heading the CICC in 2006, Bill Pace counted that overall, from 2003 to the 2005 Assembly of States Parties, around 85 percent of the national

---

[38] International Criminal Bar Web site.

delegates were new and had not been part of the Rome process, the Preparatory Committee, or participants in the development of the Rules of Procedure and Evidence.[39]

The turnover in personnel meant that until the ICC settled into paths established by a more stable personnel roster that had accumulated experience through a whole cycle of a "situation," from referral to conviction, the long-involved NGO personnel would have greater institutional knowledge – and thus be better potential agents of socialization for new members of the ICC community – than many ICC staff. Some of the NGO people worried that new ICC personnel didn't share the values of the old community and, with many new officials coming from other international organizations, believed that the Court threatened to become another bureaucratized, politicized, UN-like organization.

Both sides generally refrain from criticizing each other publicly or very strongly, although NGOs have occasionally issued advisory and cautionary messages concerning the Court. ICC officials are publicly grateful for NGO support in its activities, and NGO representatives, while concerned about some aspects of the Court that they see developing ineffectively or too slowly, avoid taking positions that would give the Court's adversaries – particularly the United States – ammunition to support attacks on the new organization. Interactions between the Court and NGOs are frequent, some are formalized, and they take place at many organizational levels. Bill Pace, convener of the CICC, is a frequent visitor and interlocutor with the top leadership. The Prosecutor has regularized semiyearly briefings with NGO representatives. In field operations, in headquarters consultations, and during the annual ASP meetings, the NGOs are vigorously represented and generally welcomed by Court officials. Like officials of the states party to the Statute, the NGOs are willing to give the Court running room before evaluating it too stringently in public.

This does not mean that the NGOs are uniform in their praise of the Court or that ICC people are uncritical of some NGO statements and positions. NGO officials, for example, view Prosecutor Moreno Ocampo's handling of the announcement of the Uganda referral, where he appeared in a joint news conference with President Museveni, to have been a major mistake[40] (see Chapter 7). Some NGO officials believe that the Court takes for granted NGO assistance to contact local populations and to promote the Court in areas where investigations are being carried out, without

---

[39] Interview.
[40] Interviews.

appreciating the difficulties that the NGOs face or the limits of their resources.[41] NGO officials question whether the President has managed to exert enough management control over the Registrar. They argue that the antipathies between the Office of the Prosecutor, the Registry, and the Pre-Trial Chambers show more than just the need for a shakeout period of running the Court but that they are instead manifestations of personal rivalries that could damage the Court. Some NGOs worry that the new justice objectives of the Court – particularly victim participation (see Chapter 7), outreach, and operation of the Victims' Trust Fund – are underemphasized by the Court in favor of old justice objectives.[42] Other NGO personnel are concerned that, in pursuit of the old justice objectives, the OTP has been inefficient and too slow. Some NGOs have criticized the Prosecutor for being "too political" in his timing of investigations and publicizing of warrants, but others have criticized him and the Court for being insensitive to the Court's potentially disruptive effect upon peace efforts.

NGOs criticized the Report on Prosecutorial Strategy (Chapter 4) for lacking analysis of the effects of OTP policies and strategies.[43] Human Rights Watch applauded the Strategic Plan but called for greater emphasis on victim participation and reparations, outreach and communications with local populations, and promotion of positive complementarity objectives.[44]

Some ICC officials, generally after expressing appreciation for all the NGOs have done for the ICC, gently explain that, by 2006, the NGOs possessed exaggerated senses of their "ownership" of the organization and, having been vital to and successful in promoting the Court, were not managing to redefine their roles to permit the Court its necessary independence. The differences between human rights organizations and peace-oriented organizations, moreover, meant that ICC officials understood that it would be impossible to keep all of their NGO interlocutors satisfied simultaneously.[45] ICC officials recognize that the NGOs pursue their own agendas, and that they will seek to pressure the ICC in the direction of their own priorities rather than necessarily understanding or being fully sympathetic to the myriad constraints and pressures under which the Court operates.

[41] Interviews.
[42] Human Rights Watch, "Memorandum on the Strategic Plan of the International Criminal Court" (2006).
[43] NGO CICC, "The Office of the Prosecutor: Taking Stock Three Years On," *Monitor*, No. 33 (2006), 3.
[44] Human Rights Watch, op cit.
[45] Interviews.

CONCLUSIONS

From the Statute to the budget, from referral to defense, NGOs have been crucial to the ICC. They helped create the normative climate that pressed states to take seriously creation of the Court. Their legal experts helped shape the Statute, while their lobbying efforts built support for it. They advocate Statute ratification around the world and work at expert and political levels within member states for passage of necessary domestic legislation. They are strongly represented at the meetings of the Assembly of States Parties and, continuing the pattern of their interaction at the Statute Conference, use the ASP meetings to press for decisions promoting their priorities in the budget discussions and provide their views whenever possible to policy discussions in the Court. They have good access to high officials at the ICC, having worked with the veterans of the Statute process since the beginning and being a prime constituency for the Prosecutor from the time of his selection through to current operations. Local and international NGOs are closely engaged in monitoring, commenting upon, and assisting in the ICC's activities in the situation countries.

The NGOs are at once assets for the organization and sources of criticism, exhortation, and pressure upon it. Perhaps more than for any other international organization, the ICC depends upon NGOs for its operations. Although NGOs and states can't directly affect the judicial core of the organization, they provide information about crimes, help locate victims and witnesses, promote and organize victim participation, and so play an important role in shaping the context for trials. NGOs comment publicly on the Court's actions, push for expansion of its activities especially in the new justice areas of outreach in conflict areas, in victims' participation and reparations, and in upholding due-process standards and defense "equality of arms" and so implicitly set an agenda for the future evolution of the ICC.

The continuity of NGO involvement with the ICC and the different career patterns of NGO personnel (which can leave individuals within organizations for long periods of time or may entail their moving between organizations or even into the ICC itself) and those of national diplomats means that the NGOs have become repositories of more institutional historical knowledge about the ICC than have national representatives to it and have greater expertise than some of the organization's employees themselves. As NGOs seek to shape the ICC to conform to the interests and priorities that they have pursued since the early 1990s, they inevitably press against the limits imposed upon the ICC by the states that are members of the organization. The NGOs have the luxury of pursuing their own clearly identified mandates – which may not be fully compatible with those of other NGOs – whereas the ICC must seek to respond to the complexities of its own mandate and the welter of demands from states and NGOs.

The constructivist vision of "norm entrepreneurs" is upheld quite concretely by the efforts of NGOs to promote Statute accession. Perhaps less obviously, and relevant more to a neoliberal institutionalist's concerns about NGO–IGO relations, the NGOs are serving as operational extensions of the ICC in some of their work, especially in the areas where the Court is carrying out investigations. In the ICC's dependence upon NGOs to help navigate among local organizations and to spread the word about the Court, the boundaries between the official organizational structures of the Court and the NGOs are blurring.

6

ICC–State Relations

So far, states that are party to the Statute have willingly supported the ICC, but the Court's most vigorous supporters fret that the states are not dedicated enough to its effectiveness. States' views differ on how interventionist they should be in the operations of the Court, recognizing that its judicial operations must appear free from political influence. But given the leadership problems inherent in the tripartite structure of the Court and statutory ambiguity about the role of the Assembly of States Parties, ICC proponents argue that the states could condemn the Court to irrelevance if they don't more vigorously promote further accessions to the Statute, more actively engage in charting the Court's future, and much more energetically provide cooperation in the investigation and arrests of suspects.

Acutely aware the states are watching them, Court officials strive to convey images of judicial seriousness, procedural excellence, and administrative efficiency. But a sneaking fear persists that without much greater state involvement, the ICC's ability to bring suspects to the Court and try them will prove inadequate to the task of retaining states' financial and political support. This realization may be what motivated the Prosecutor initially to point out that the Court's success will be found partly in broader undertakings than just trials, for instance in a decline of impunity due to domestic prosecutions promoted by the ICC. The OTP is, however, under great pressure from states, NGOs, and Chambers to accelerate the pace of investigations, requests for warrants, and moves toward trials. Because much of what the OTP does is shrouded in appropriate secrecy, it is very difficult to evaluate the extent of state cooperation.

U.S. opposition to the Court has raised the price of Statute ratification to states that accept assistance from the United States. U.S. legislation confronts ICC member states with the difficult decision of whether to accede to U.S. demands to accept bilateral agreements that immunize U.S. citizens from ICC jurisdiction or to stand on principle and pay an economic price. Paradoxically, however, U.S. opposition may also have helped build the Court's credibility. The early opposition by the United States undermined the image of the ICC as an extension of Neocolonial influence or a tool of Western domination. Meanwhile, the U.S. antipathy appears to be softening.

This chapter is divided into three substantive sections and a conclusion. The first section discusses the intricacies of support for, and opposition to, the Court. I argue that the normative basis of the Court's appeal is what made negotiation of the Statute possible in the first place, and that converging international normative commitments against impunity continue to be the ICC's primary basis of support. The conflict between the universal nature of the Statute's normative claims and the particularistic nature of national sovereignty is at the root of opposition to the Court, as shown by the U.S.–ICC relationship. Realist calculations, institutional inertia, and the untenableness of the United States indefinitely swimming against the normative tide all imply that U.S. policy will continue to change.

The chapter's second section describes how states that have joined the Rome Statute Treaty relate to the Court. As members of the Assembly of States Parties, they have a quasi-legislative role, although they have viewed this role as quite limited. Because member states differ in their preferred image of the Court, consensus has not emerged on policy directions for the Court, and because the Court was created as an independent organization, they are anyway reluctant to assert policy primacy. On important issues they have tended to return leadership to the Court, rather than to make constraining policy decisions in areas such as the balance between civil and common law, the Trust Fund for Victims, the ICC's budget, Strategic Plan, and Court Capacity Model. Under its current mandate, the ICC has a lot of running room, which is also to say that there is something of a leadership vacuum at the level of the Assembly of States Parties. Addition of aggression as a prosecutable crime to the Court's purview would strengthen the ICC's normative basis but would create a reaction from states most concerned about maximizing sovereign prerogatives, particularly the members of the UN Security Council.

The third section explains the consequences of states' obligations under the Statute to cooperate with the Court. Most countries need to revise their legal codes so that they are able to cooperate with the Court. States' adherence to the Statute thus has the effect of aligning their legal codes with an international set of norms and standards – a progressive development of international law. The requirements for cooperation with the Court, rather than the Court's operations themselves, may be the aspect of the Rome Statute that contributes most to changing the international environment of criminal impunity.

THE COURT'S SUPPORTERS AND OPPONENT(S)

Previous chapters argued that the Rome Statute creates a broad mandate lacking clear priorities for the Court, in pursuit of both traditional and new justice paradigms. The mandate responded to a broad range of states' normative commitments, from countering impunity for criminal acts to transitional justice victims' orientations to the outlawing of aggression, and the overall package made it possible for a range of states to sign on. States acceding to the Statute doubtless vary in their commitment to its various objectives, but they agree over the basic idea of creating a standing court to pursue perpetrators of the most heinous crimes. States remaining outside the Statute find it excessively challenging to state sovereignty.

Even when states accede to the Statute, they still face choices about the level of support they will extend to the Court. Statute principles may rank highly among normative commitments of state decision makers without necessarily commanding significant resources: The objectives of the Court may be subordinated to alternative political objectives and alternative demands upon limited financial resources.

The Court's activities remain mostly within the ambit of states' foreign affairs and justice ministries (with finance ministries holding the purse strings). ICC relations with individual states are relatively simple because the range of interests connecting states to the Court is small. Given the Court's limited jurisdiction, once a state decides that countering impunity is a worthy international function, and that the ICC is an important instrument to express and pursue this objective, contestation and clashes of interest between governmental institutions (for instance, between foreign and defense ministries) ends. Extensions of jurisdiction could raise the salience of the Court for states: Should a Statute amendment enable the Court to prosecute an individual crime of aggression, the stakes will rise.

Because of the need for legal expertise to deal with ICC matters, states' representatives to the ICC in The Hague tend to be people with backgrounds in law, often seconded to foreign ministries from justice ministries and sometimes with some background in criminal law.[1] Many of them are

---

[1] Interviews.

responsible as well for other legal institutions in The Hague such as the ICTR, the ICJ, and the International Court of Arbitration: The Court may be important, but it commands only the limited attention of most foreign ministries and diplomatic representations. Since the Court opened in 2002, a congenial group has developed in The Hague among the personnel of international organizations such as the ICTR, International Court of Justice (ICJ), International Court of Arbitration, ICC, NGOs, and the academic community that shares an enthusiasm for international institutions and international law. With encouragement from the Dutch government and The Hague municipal authorities, frequent seminars, conferences, briefings, and workshops bring the community together, but it is a group whose interests are tangential to the main focus of most of their countries' diplomatic endeavors.

For states unengaged with the ICC or opposed to it, contact with the community is limited. U.S. representatives were largely prohibited by Washington from getting too close to ICC events and officials for the first few years of the Court's existence. Russian and Chinese representations in The Hague have had limited contact with the Court. Japanese contact increased in 2006 as parliamentary interest in completing legislative requirements for joining the Statute moved forward, and the government stated its intention eventually to join. On April 27, 2007, the Japanese Diet approved accession to the Statute, and officials indicated that final steps to pass relevant legislation and to deposit ratification with the UN were expected by October 1.[2]

There is a curious mixture of limited state attention and support, great personal interest among those involved with the Court, and a propensity to defer to ICC officials for directing the development of new organization. According to people involved with the Court, states' representatives to the Court are often more reluctant for states to become involved in the Court's policy decisions than some of the Court's officials are. In its formative years, the ICC has had plenty of latitude.

Normative Commitments and the Court

Because the parties to the Statute support the Court, opposition is externalized. Internationally, only the United States has pursued vigorous opposition to the ICC, according to one Court official, thereby paying more respect to the powers of the Court than the many countries that view it as

---

[2] Leopold, "Japan Expects to Join New Criminal Court in Oct" (2007).

benign and generally weak. The United States' Security Council colleagues Britain and France joined the Statute along with the rest of the European Union states, but nonsignatory UN Security Council permanent members China and Russia expressed cautious support for the Court's objectives.

Russia signed the Rome Statute in September 2000 and by 2003 had engaged cabinet ministries in a discussion of its compatibility with the Russian Constitution, with the stated intention of moving toward ratification. Russian sources indicated that President Vladimir Putin would decide sometime in 2004 whether to move a ratification bill into the Duma;[3] however, by the end of 2006, ratification had still not come up for consideration. In the Security Council, Russia voted in favor of the Sudan referral, asserting that the referral "would promote an effective solution to the fight against impunity."[4]

Publicly, China is more negative.[5] China abstained on the Darfur referral. It declared its support for a political solution to the conflict, "deplored deeply the violations of international humanitarian law and human rights law and believed that the perpetrators must be brought to justice," but believed that "the question before the Council was what was the most appropriate way to do so." The Chinese representatives said that China would prefer trial before Sudanese courts and did not favor a referral without Sudanese acceptance of the Court's jurisdiction. It noted, as a nonsignatory of the Rome Statute, that China "had major reservations about some of its provisions."[6] Nonetheless, there is considerable interest in China among academics and legal specialists about the Court, shown by frequent invitations to Court officials to participate in seminars and conferences there.

[3] No Peace Without Justice, "Kremlin Int'l News Broadcast-Press Conference with Kirsch and Kolodkin" (2004), 224.
[4] UN Press Release SC/8351, "Security Council Refers Situation in Darfur, Sudan, to Prosecutor of International Criminal Court" (2005).
[5] China's Foreign Ministry Web site states: "Though it is hard to anticipate the operation of the Court, if the Court can get the general support and cooperation by its effective operation, it will be undoubtedly positive and useful to the international community and is also what China wants to see. As to the question of acceding to the Statute, the Chinese Government adopts an open attitude and the actual performance of the Court is undoubtedly an important factor for consideration. We do not exclude the possibility of considering the accession to the Statute at an appropriate time. In future, the Chinese Government will, as an observer state, continue to adopt a serious and responsible attitude to follow carefully the progress and operation or the International Criminal Court. China is willing to make due contributions to the realization of the rule of law in the international community." People's Republic of China, Ministry of Foreign Affairs, "China and the International Criminal Court" (2003).
[6] UN Press Release SC/8351, op cit.

States that support the ICC vary considerably in their enthusiasm. For example, even though the European Union as an organization has been very supportive of the ICC and holds out the prospect of deepening cooperation in areas of investigation and arrests of suspects, by mid-2007, nine of the twenty-five EU countries, including France, hade not yet passed legislation necessary to bring their domestic penal codes into conformity with the Statute.[7] At the fourth ASP, a Working Group on Ratification and Implementation of the Rome Statute was established. At the fifth ASP, in the fall of 2006, the Working Group's Plan of Action was adopted, but no resources were allocated to the (tiny) ASP Secretariat to implement it.[8]

The United Kingdom was very active at the Rome Conference and sought to intermediate between the like-minded states and the United States in the treaty negotiations (see Chapter 3). The degree of U.K. support for the Court in operation, however, is less clear. Foreign Secretary (2001–6) Jack Straw was reportedly less enthusiastic about the ICC than his predecessor, Robin Cook, and U.K. officials were concerned about what they considered slow progress toward trials.[9]

The U.S. Position

The United States endorses the objective of ending impunity. According to Ambassador David Scheffer, former U.S. Ambassador at Large for War Crimes Issues (1997–2001), the Clinton administration "strongly supported the establishment of an international criminal court."[10] U.S. experts were heavily involved in the Statute discussions as legal experts and sought to protect U.S. interests. The United States appeared willing to support the Court as long as it remained subordinated to the UN Security Council, as it was in the original ILC proposal. Once it became clear that the ICC would be independent of UNSC permanent members' veto powers, however, the United States found increasing fault with the Court. Negotiators sought compromises in the hopes that the United States would join, but their efforts ultimately failed. At the end of the Rome Statute Conference, the United States rejected the Statute on pragmatic grounds as well as principled and constitutional grounds.[11]

---

[7] Chicon and Bibas, "Europe Supports the ICC without Fail and without Zeal" (2007), 4.
[8] Amnesty International, "International Criminal Court: Implementing the Assembly's Plan of Action for Achieving Universality and Full Implementation of the Rome Statute" (2007), 2.
[9] Waugaman, "London's Confident Realism" (2006), 3–4; interviews, spring 2006.
[10] Scheffer, "The Future U.S. Relationship with the International Criminal Court" (2005), 163.
[11] Elsea, "U.S. Policy Regarding the International Criminal Court" (2002), 4–7.

The U.S. government argued that U.S. officials and military forces should be exempted from the Court's jurisdiction because the country's military activities were crucial to international peace and security. U.S. global involvement would expose its officials more to others' accusations than those of other states, and its adversaries might try to thwart it by lodging spurious charges against it. The consequent dampening effect on U.S. actions would be bad for international peace and security. Although the United States thus claimed that immunity for its officials would therefore be of general benefit, opponents argued that this was mere hypocrisy. They argued that adequate protections had been built into the Court to prevent baseless charges, particularly in the form of the complex series of actions necessary for the Prosecutor to proceed with investigations *proprio motu* or in pursuit of state referrals. Furthermore, since the Court would be intent on preserving its own legitimacy, the Prosecutor and pretrial judges would screen out frivolous charges.

U.S. representatives argued that the Statute threatened to violate international law by subjecting nonsignatory states to the Court's jurisdiction (that is, individuals from a state that hadn't joined the ICC could still be subject to it if arrested under the Court's territorial jurisdiction). Court proponents countered that the ICC has jurisdiction over individuals, not states. People worldwide are subject to arrest and trial in countries other than their own under local laws, and the United States does not view this as a challenge to sovereignty. Similarly, transfer of a U.S. citizen to the ICC by another country would not challenge U.S. sovereignty.

On constitutional grounds, U.S. negotiators argued that U.S. constitutional protections would not be available to U.S. citizens should they become subject to Court proceedings, and the Court as designed would lack the democratic "checks and balances" fundamental to U.S. values. The counterargument stressed the heavy involvement of U.S. legal experts in drafting the ICC Statute and rules.

All the U.S. objections were the subject of negotiation and measures in the Statute that sought to ameliorate them. The objections have all been disputed by international legal experts, including experts of high standing in the United States. Ambassador Scheffer, who negotiated at Rome and was instructed to vote against the Statute, later argued that in order to assuage U.S. concerns, changes in the Rules and Procedures, even short of Statute amendments, could reduce U.S. opposition to ratification,[12] but he urged U.S. accession to the Treaty in its existing form.

---

[12] Scheffer, op cit.

Objections to the Statute were strongest among the civilian leadership of the Pentagon and among right-wing U.S. politicians and thinkers. Given the broad interpretive latitude possible over constitutional and international legal matters, had U.S. politicians, policy makers, and decision makers *wanted* to accede to the Treaty, principled and constitutional justifications could readily have been found.

Invade The Hague!

When the Statute passed and was opened for signature, its U.S. opponents in Congress acted to thwart signature. Testimony before Jesse Helms's Senate Foreign Affairs Committee featured, among other speakers, the American Enterprise Institute's John R. Bolton, who castigated the nascent Court as an international organizational threat to U.S. sovereignty. Helms declared that should the Statute be submitted to his committee, it would be "dead on arrival."[13]

The Clinton administration managed to prevent legislation attacking the ICC from being passed by Congress, but the strength of congressional opposition to the Court deterred Clinton from bringing the Statute to the Senate for ratification. On June 29, 1999, the "Protection of United States Troops from Foreign Prosecution Act of 1999"[14] was submitted to the House of Representatives. Vigorously opposed by the Clinton administration, the bill did not pass, but its advocates kept trying. In June 2000, the similar American Servicemembers Protection Act (ASPA) of 2000[15] was introduced in the House. The bill would have outlawed cooperation with the Court and authorized the President to use all means necessary to release from the custody of the Court U.S. military personnel or elected or appointed officials of the U.S. government. The new version of the bill proposed preventing participation by U.S. personnel in peacekeeping operations unless they were immunized from Court jurisdiction. Again, the bill failed.

Despite U.S. congressional opposition to the Court, lawyers from the Justice and State Departments continued to participate in developing the Court's Rules of Procedure and Evidence. According to Ambassador Scheffer, "we worked very hard ... in 1999 and 2000 to address our remaining concerns about the Rome Statute, and the U.S. voted in favor of the Rules of Procedure and Evidence and the Elements of Crimes" in June 2000.[16] Under

---

[13] Cited in Bolton, "No, No, No to International Criminal Court" (1998).
[14] 106th Congress, 1st Session, H.R. 2381.
[15] 106th Congress, 2nd Session, H.R. 4654.
[16] Scheffer, op cit., 163.

the Statute, states could sign the Treaty without ratifying it until December 31, 2000. Thereafter, signature and ratification had to be accomplished in one step, constituting accession to the Treaty. States that had participated in the Rome Conference were welcome to participate in the Preparatory Commission meetings even if they hadn't signed, until December 31, 2000; thereafter, participation was limited to signatory states, but states signing thereafter had to go all the way and ratify.

Because President Clinton basically supported the idea of the Court and sought to continue U.S. participation in the preparatory process in the hopes that further compromises might be reached that would ease U.S. entry, the United States signed the Statute on December 31, 2000. Nonetheless, in January 2001, the Bush administration entered office unalterably opposed to the Court, with its policy spearheaded by newly appointed Under Secretary of State for Arms Control and International Security John R. Bolton.

In early May, the ASPA of 2001[17] was introduced in both the House and the Senate. Essentially the same as the ASPA of 2000, the legislation would have prohibited any U.S. government cooperation with the ICC unless the United States ratified the Rome Treaty. Now that the United States had signed the Statute, the legislation would have required actions counter to the normal obligation under the Vienna Convention on the Law of Treaties (1969), according to which states that have signed but not ratified treaties are considered bound nonetheless not to contravene them.[18] The act did not pass in 2001, although weaker legislation preventing cooperation with or funding to the Court was approved.[19]

On May 6, 2002, shortly after the required 60 ratifications for the Statute to come into effect were obtained, Under Secretary of State for Arms Control and International Security Bolton sent a letter to UN Secretary-General Kofi Annan, in the latter's role as the depositary for the Rome Statute, announcing that the United States did not intend to become a party to the Treaty, thus had no legal obligations arising from its signature, and requesting "that its intention not to become a party ... be reflected in the depositary's status lists relating to this treaty."[20] Later in the month,

---

[17] H.R. 1794/S. 857 (2001).

[18] Vienna Convention on the Law of Treaties, May 23, 1969 (entered into force January 27, 1980), Article 18. The United States has not signed the Convention, but its provisions are generally considered to be customary international law, even by the United States.

[19] NGO CICC, CICC Web site, "Updates on the United States through December 2005."

[20] U.S. Department of State, Press Statement, Richard Boucher, Spokesman, Letter to UN Secretary General Kofi Annan from Under Secretary of State for Arms Control and International Security John R. Bolton (2002).

the ASPA of 2002 was introduced with strong support from the Bush administration, and it passed in August as part of an appropriations bill dealing with terrorism.[21] Since its original introduction in 1999, the bill had expanded in coverage, and waivers had been added so that, should the President so decide, its requirements could be suspended in the interests of national security. It is known colloquially by its detractors as the "Invade The Hague Act" because it calls upon the President to use any necessary means to free U.S. personnel from the custody of the Court.

U.S. Bilateral Agreements for Immunity

The new administration's objectives for policy toward the ICC went beyond staying out of the Statute to actively seeking to guarantee that U.S. citizens would be immune to the Court and to thwart other states from acceding to the Statute without taking U.S. concerns into account. The United States vigorously pressed states to conclude agreements with the United States that would guarantee its citizens immunity from the Court's jurisdiction, threatening to cut off aid to states that refused to agree.

Article 98 of the Rome Statute prohibits the Court from requesting assistance or the surrender of a person to the Court if to do so would require the state to "act inconsistently" with its obligations under international law or international agreements either regarding its own or third-party states unless the state or the third-party state waives the immunity or grants cooperation. The United States has interpreted this article to mean that its citizens cannot be transferred to the ICC by any state that has signed a bilateral agreement with the United States prohibiting such a transfer, even if the state is a member of the Rome Statute. The United States actively pressures states to conclude such so-called Article 98 or bilateral immunity agreements (BIAs). By spring 2006, such agreements had been accepted by approximately one hundred governments and were under consideration by approximately eighteen more.[22] According to the CICC, fifty-four countries "rejected U.S. efforts to sign BIAs despite unrelenting U.S. pressure and the threat and actual loss of military assistance" under the ASPA.[23] Under the ASPA, unless a state party to the Rome Treaty agreed to a BIA, it would

---

[21] U.S. Public Law No. 107-206, 116 Stat. 820, "American Servicemembers Protection Act of 2002." Title II of "2002 Supplemental Appropriations Act for Further Recovery from and Response to Terrorist Attacks on the United States."

[22] NGO CICC, "Summary of Information on Bilateral Immunity Agreements (BIAs) or so-Called 'Article 98' Agreements as of April, 2006."

[23] NGO CICC, "Countries Opposed to Signing a U.S. Bilateral Immunity Agreement (BIA): U.S. Aid Lost in FY04 & U.S. Aid Threatened in FY05."

become ineligible for military assistance (unless the President waived application of the law or the country was a NATO member or a "major non-NATO ally"). In addition, under a later piece of legislation – the 2005 and 2006 Nethercutt Amendment to the Omnibus Appropriations Bill[24] – no Economic Support Fund assistance could go to countries party to the Rome Treaty that had not concluded a BIA (subject to the same waivers as the ASPA). EU and South American Common Market (MERCOSUR) members collectively rejected the U.S. interpretation of Article 98, and most of them individually refused to sign BIAs.[25]

The U.S. stance on the ICC is a consistent irritant in relations with its European allies as well as with the countries potentially subject to the cutoffs of aid prescribed by the ASPA. Along with its refusal to participate in the Kyoto accords on global climate change, its strident position on the ICC is a symbol of its rejection of principled multilateralism (as the Europeans see them) in favor of unilateralist hegemonism.

Signs of a Change in U.S. Policy

By 2005–6, evidence emerged of divisions within the administration's position on the ICC. On September 9, 2004, then–U.S. Secretary of State Colin Powell stated in testimony to the U.S. Senate Committee on Foreign Relations that genocide was taking place in the western Sudan region of Darfur.[26] The United States pushed for UN Security Council economic sanctions against Sudan and the creation of a commission to investigate the situation. When the commission reported back to the Secretary-General in January 2005,[27] it concluded that a finding of genocide could not be made because there was no evidence of government intent, a government policy, to commit genocide. "No genocidal policy has been pursued and implemented in Darfur by the Government authorities," the commission stated, but this did not in any way detract from "the gravity of the crimes perpetrated in that region. International offences such as the crimes against humanity and war crimes that have been committed in Darfur may be no less serious and heinous then genocide."[28]

---

[24] H.R. 4818 (2005); H.R. 3057 (2006).

[25] Under the ASPA and Nethercutt Amendment waivers, the effect of the legislation is to target U.S. pressure on weak and poor countries. NATO and "major non-NATO" allies are automatically exempted from sanctions, and the President can waive their application on an annual basis to other states on national security grounds.

[26] BBC, "Powell Declares Genocide in Sudan" (2004).

[27] UN, "Report of the International Commission of Inquiry on Darfur to the United Nations Secretary-General Pursuant to Security Council Resolution 1564 of 18 September 2004."

[28] Ibid., 4.

Because of its antipathy to the ICC, the United States argued that the Sudan situation should be assigned to the Rwanda tribunal, or that another new ad hoc tribunal under either UN or African Union auspices should be established to pursue the Sudan situation. Other Security Council states argued that the ICC was already established to deal with just such a situation. In a move generally attributed to the relative pragmatism of newly appointed Secretary of State Condoleeza Rice, over the objections of ideologically fired opposition from Ambassador Bolton, in March 2005, the United States abstained from the Security Council vote that referred the Darfur situation to the ICC. The United States made sure that the costs of involvement of the ICC would be borne by the ICC or by voluntary contributions, not by the UN regular budget (so U.S. funds would not find their way to the ICC). Upon adoption of the resolution, the United States reiterated its objections to the ICC, said the United States would have preferred a hybrid tribunal, noted that the resolution would prevent the ICC from acting against citizens of states that were not party to the Statute (such as U.S. citizens), and tacitly threatened that the United States would withhold its dues to the UN if the UN furnished funds to the ICC.[29] The United States had nonetheless tacitly recognized that the Court might be useful and that there were diplomatic and practical costs to opposing it.[30]

Other evidence accumulated that the U.S. position toward the ICC was under pressure. Military and diplomatic officials publicly stated that the anti-ICC policy – particularly the BIAs – might be damaging U.S. relations with other countries and causing them to turn to U.S. rivals for assistance. U.S. Army Southern Command Commander General Bantz Craddock testified to the House Armed Services Committee in March 2005 that the ASPA had the unintended consequence of "restricting our access to and interaction with many important partner nations." He said that of the twenty-two nations worldwide affected by ASPA sanctions prohibiting international military education and training (IMET) funds from going to some Rome Statute parties,

11 of them are in Latin America, hampering the engagement and professional contact that is an essential element of our regional security cooperation strategy.... Extra-hemispheric actors are filling the void left by restricted U.S. military engagement

---

[29] UN Press Release SC/8351, op cit.
[30] Cryer, "Sudan, Resolution 1593, and International Criminal Justice" (2006), 195–222, argues inter alia that some of the Resolution's paragraphs that reflect U.S. demands may not be legal.

with partner nations. We now risk losing contact and interoperability with a generation of military classmates in many nations of the region, including several leading countries.[31]

While the military realities of opposition to the ICC began to sink in, Ambassador to the UN Bolton still pressed strident diplomatic opposition to the Court. In fall 2005, the United States forced deletion of references to the ICC in the documents of the 2005 United Nations Reform Summit at the General Assembly.[32] Similarly, in negotiations at the end of 2005 and the beginning of 2006, the United States insisted on expunging references to the ICC from the draft Security Council Resolution on the Protection of Civilians in Armed Conflict.[33]

On February 2, 2006, the Pentagon released its Quadrennial Defense Review. In the interest of improving the United States' ability to cooperate with other countries in pursuing national security goals, it declared that the Department of Defense would "consider whether the restrictions on the ASPA on IMET and other foreign assistance programs pertaining to security and the war on terror necessitate adjustment as we continue to advance the aims of the ASPA."[34]

In March, a Pentagon official argued that the costs of the ASPA might be overwhelming its value. "One has to weigh the hypothetical benefits of this policy in the future against the very real damage it is inflicting on our important relationships in the region." He was particularly concerned about Mexico's recent ratification of the Statute and its refusal to sign a BIA. "In the case of Mexico, which is one of our most important relationships, there's no question this is a setback. Suddenly we find we are in this glass box where we can't reach out to them."[35]

Secretary of State Rice appeared to agree with the Pentagon view. On March 10, on her way to the inauguration of Chile's new President Michelle Bachelet, she was asked about whether ASPA cutoff provisions might come up during discussions with Chilean authorities, and she seemed to indicate an understanding that the policy might be counterproductive. She said:

---

[31] Craddock, Testimony, "Fiscal Year 2006 National Defense Authorization Budget Request" (2005).

[32] NGO CICC, "International Criminal Court Must Remain in Final U.N. Reform Document" (2005).

[33] UN Security Council Report, "Update Report No. 4: Protection of Civilians in Armed Conflict" (2006).

[34] U.S. Department of Defense, "Quadrennial Defense Review Report" (2006), 91.

[35] Robert Pardo-Maurer, the Deputy Assistant Secretary of Defense for Western Hemisphere Affairs, quoted in Diehl, "A Losing Latin Policy: Are We about to Punish Democratic Allies?" (2006).

As to Chile and the ICC, we do have certain statutory requirements concerning the ICC. I think you're probably aware of, as I testified yesterday, that we're looking at the issues concerning those situations in which we may have, in a sense, sort of the same as shooting ourselves in the foot, which is, I guess, what we mean. By having to put off aid to countries with which we have important counterterrorism or counter drug or in some cases, in some of our allies, it's even been cooperation in places like Afghanistan and Iraq. And so I think we just have to look at it. And we're certainly reviewing it and we'll consult with Congress about it. But I think it's important from time [*sic*] that we take a look to make sure that we're not having a negative effect on the relationships that are really important to us from the point of view of getting our security environment – improving the security environment.[36]

Two further incidents showed that the United States was factoring the ICC into its policies as a potentially useful instrument. In April, Nigerian officials delivered former President of Liberia Charles Taylor to the Special Court for Sierra Leone in Freetown in connection with an arrest warrant issued by the Court in 2003. The operation was carried out with the consent of Liberia's new President, Ellen Sirleaf Johnson, who according to observers sought assurances from the United States and other countries that Taylor would be removed from the region and tried elsewhere, possibly in The Hague. The United States played an important behind-the-scenes role in negotiations to transfer Taylor to The Hague for a trial to be conducted by the Sierra Leone Court, but on the premises of the ICC.[37] Taylor arrived in The Hague on June 20, 2006. The United States accepted the idea that ICC facilities could be used and paid for by the Sierra Leone court and directly discussed the details with ICC personnel. In addition, in May, Assistant Secretary of State for African Affairs Jendayi Frazer, asserting the United States' dedication to ending the Lord's Resistance Army's depredations in Northern Uganda, declared in a speech to the Royal Institute of International Affairs in London, "And as I say, as ICC indicted war criminals, they need to be captured and turned over to the Court."[38]

Perhaps most tellingly, in spring 2006, having had its proposals for contacts with the ICC repeatedly rebuffed by Washington, the U.S. Embassy in The Hague was permitted for the first time to send a representative to an

---

[36] U.S. Department of State, Trip Briefing, Secretary Condoleezza Rice (2006).
[37] Negotiations over Taylor's trial location grew increasingly complicated when Dutch authorities sought guarantees that after the trial Taylor would become the responsibility of some other state and as a rising chorus of civil society organizations in Sierra Leone objected that Taylor should be tried in the region where he committed his crimes – at the Special Court.
[38] Clarke, "U.S. Wants to Rid Uganda of LRA Rebels This Year" (2006).

ICC diplomatic briefing and to invite ICC officials to its annual July 4, Independence Day, celebration.[39]

In September, the House and Senate approved amendments to the ASPA, repealing the ban on IMET funding to ICC state parties that had failed to sign a BIA, and in October the White House announced that the President had issued waivers on prohibitions to IMET aid to twenty-one states. Foreign military funds and economic support funds were still banned for those ICC member states that had not signed BIAs, but efforts were afoot further to roll back the aid restrictions of the ASPA in legislation to be proposed in the upcoming (newly Democratically controlled) 2007 legislative session.[40]

The U.S. Decision Calculus

If U.S. policy makers seek immunity from international jurisdiction over genocide, crimes against humanity, and war crimes, their due-process and constitutional arguments against joining the Statute are irrelevant. Supporting impunity for U.S. citizens can be justified only on the grounds that other (strategic) U.S. national interests override interests in an international rule of law. From this viewpoint, the United States should not join the Court. This is a choice wherein sovereignty overrides legality, and historically most countries and certainly the United States have readily taken this position.[41]

If, on the other hand, policy makers decide that adherence to the Statute would benefit the United States (by winning friends, by strengthening deterrence against international crimes, and by making available a new institution for serving U.S. interests), then the legal arguments are also irrelevant, but the United States should join. To join would strengthen neoliberal institutionalist imperatives in favor of the ICC's survival and growth and might at least imply a growing U.S. acceptance of the idea of an international society bounded by consensual law.

If one exchanges the realist's focus on material interests, such as leadership impunity or broadening international support for U.S. policy within what Hedley Bull called an international system, for a vision of international society, then the U.S. position based on exceptionalism and national advantage is untenable. In Bull's model of society, anarchy's destructive effects can be ameliorated by, among other actions, states accepting international law to which states must be equally subject. There could be an

---

[39] Interviews.
[40] NGO CICC, "Are the United States' BIAs on the Way Out? New U.S. Legislation Points to a Possible Change in Direction" (2006), 20.
[41] See Krasner, *Sovereignty: Organized Hypocrisy* (1999).

international societal interest in suppressing genocide, crimes against humanity, and war crimes. Decisions about the U.S. position on the Court are thus less questions of legal technicality than of choices between alternative visions of the world. If the international society model became predominant in U.S. politics, it would behoove the United States to accept it as a new framework for multilateral behavior.

Consequences of the U.S. Position for the Court

U.S. alienation from the ICC has been costly for the Court in at least three ways. First, since the ICC is funded by assessed contributions from its member states calibrated (as is the UN's regular budget) to the donor's wealth, having the world's wealthiest country outside of the Court reduces the resources available to it and increases the burden upon the member states. Second, perhaps more importantly, because of the Court's reliance on state cooperation to, for instance, apprehend suspects and provide information, having the world's most powerful country with the most widely spread military and greatest intelligence capability hostile to it means that the challenges it faces are even greater than those faced, for instance, by the ICTR. Even with the (sometimes halfhearted) support of the United States, NATO, and UN peacekeeping forces, the Yugoslavia tribunal had trouble bringing suspects to Court. Lacking U.S. support and facing even more difficult situations, the prognosis for the ICC is guarded at best. Third, declared opposition to the Court and threats of aid cutoffs under the ASPA may also be deterrents to some states that would otherwise consider acceding to the Rome Statute.

There may be positive sides to U.S. opposition, however. First, U.S. hostility may have improved the Court's image in some countries. Court officials and NGO personnel engaged in seeking additional accessions to the Statute report that in some national capitals, the fact that the United States opposes the Court attracts officials to sign on.[42] Second, U.S. antipathy might help the Court establish a reputation for independence that largely eluded the Yugoslavia and Rwanda tribunals. Unlike the tribunals, which have been staffed primarily by U.S. and British employees, a more internationally diverse staff at the ICC lends at least the appearance of greater neutrality, although some critics argue that Anglo-American influence remains strong directly and through surrogates in the ICC.[43]

---

[42] Interviews.

[43] In particular through officials from the Anglo-American, common-law-dominated countries Australia, Britain, Canada, Ireland, New Zealand. Interviews.

Despite U.S. opposition to the Court, the ICC is operational. More states would likely join the Statute if the United States did so, the budget would be shared more broadly were the United States a contributor, and it would be easier for the Court to acquire information and cooperation were the United States a member. Still, even as an institution beginning with a narrower base than it might desire, leaning more heavily for funds on member states than it would if it added some additional wealthy countries to its membership, with the ICC in operation, it is building institutional inertia.

STATES' POLICY OVERSIGHT

States affect the ICC by their adherence or opposition to the Statute, as discussed previously, but once they join, there is still a broad range of possible forms that their participation can take. Adherents to the Statute become members of the Assembly of States Parties to the Rome Statute, the ICC's legislative body, and thus can play some role in the oversight and guidance of the Court's governance. Chapter 4 already described the ASP's role in approving the Rules of Procedure and Evidence and the Elements of Crimes, in electing Court officials, and in urging the Court to develop a strategic plan. In this section, ASP considerations about the Court's budget, and particularly permanent premises for the Court; the Victim's Trust Fund, which has important implications for implementation of the new (restorative) justice mandate; and extension of jurisdiction over the crime of aggression, which may affect states' support and opposition to the Court generally, illustrate how important the ASP can be to the Court. The ASP thus has major responsibilities toward, and power over, the Court, but in the ICC's early years, the ASP did not assert control strongly.

Budget as Policy

The Court itself, led by the Registry, develops the organization's draft budget, which is then considered (and, if so decided, modified) and approved by the ASP. The ASP created a Committee on Budget and Finance, to which members (who are not necessarily part of states' delegations to the ICC) are elected for their expertise in budgetary and financial matters, to work with the Court to develop the budget and to report its recommendations on the Court's proposals to the ASP at its annual meeting.

From the Court's first year, the CBF has been heavily involved with the Registry to craft an increasingly transparent and orderly budget development process and has subjected the Court's proposals to painstaking line-by-line scrutiny. The CBF issues a report to the fall ASP meeting making recommendations on approval and denial of proposed budget items. (Similarly, the CBF reacted to the Strategic Plan and the Court Capacity Model (Chapter 4) in fall 2006, calling for more explicit expenditure targets and clear evaluation processes.) The ASP has largely shied away from directly guiding Court policy, but the CBF's recommendations and ASP actions on the budget constitute a strong policy influence–for example, in CBF recommendations that new expenditures for outreach programs and field offices be smaller than those requested by the draft budget and urged by NGOs in 2005 and 2006,[44] and by ASP adoption of the CBF position in 2005, but its rejection in 2006 and replacement with a large increase in outreach funding (as pushed by NGOs), from €1.4 million to €2.7 million for 2007.[45]

ASP decisions about the funds and plans for the Court's permanent premises will also have huge policy consequences. The Dutch government promised financing and facilities for temporary premises for the ten-year period 2002–12. Given the long lead-time needed for architectural studies, fundraising, planning, and construction, decisions about the location, size, and characteristics of the permanent premises rapidly became pressing. Those decisions require a long-term vision of the Court.

The ASP created a Working Group on the Permanent Premises, and along with the CBF, Court personnel, and Dutch government officials, discussions were already under way in 2004. Three alternatives were presented to the fall 2005 ASP: expansion of the current temporary premises, location of an alternative existing facility to which the Court could be moved, or construction of wholly new facilities. The Dutch government proposed to assist the Court with financing and architectural services for permanent facilities on the grounds of a disused military facility on the outskirts of The Hague, the Alexanderkazerne. The fall 2006 Assembly of States Parties decided to proceed on the basis of the Alexanderkazerne proposal.

The new premises represent a huge financial investment (on the order of hundreds of millions of Euros) and critical policy choices for the ASP. Planning the new premises requires making assumptions about the number and occupations of people who will work in the Court when it reaches its

---

44 ICC, ASP, Fourth Session, "Report of the Committee on Budget and Finance on the Work of Its Fifth Session" ICC-ASP/4/27 (2005), para. 68, recommended reduction of the Registry's request for eleven new positions in outreach to eight such positions; ICC, ASP, Fifth Session, "Report of the Committee on Budget and Finance on the Work of Its Seventh Session" ICC-ASP/5/23, 2006, para. 77, also reduced Registry requests.

45 Boyle, "ICC Outreach Budget Gets Big Boost" (2006).

steady-state size, thus how much the Court can do, and about whether the Court will do most of its work at headquarters or become decentralized to facilities closer to where crimes took place and where victims would have an easier time seeing justice done. In May 2007, the CBF indicated that planning was proceeding on the basis of two scenarios: a "target" scenario of the needs of the Court as of the year 2012 and a "growth" scenario for expansion thereafter. The "target" staff size was estimated at 1,137; the "growth" staff, at 1,364;[46] both were comparable to the ICTY at its largest. Already in 2006, Court and NGO officials and some state representatives to the Court were worried that progress toward the permanent premises was too slow, and that the Court might face an interregnum between expiration of Dutch support for the temporary facilities and completion of a permanent headquarters that would add confusion and expense to the Court. They pressed for accelerated ASP action.

Clarifying the Mandate – the Trust Fund for Victims

Under the Statute, the Court is directed to establish a Trust Fund for Victims (VTF) in response to restorative justice, victim-oriented principles promoted by NGOs, and civil-law states. The Statute left to the ASP determination of how the VTF would operate. Unlike the Statute's extensive specification of legal principles and judicial processes, the victim-oriented aspects of the Court were sparsely addressed. The ASP's decisions ultimately tilted slightly more toward a civil-law and victim-oriented position than to common-law principles, but they also demonstrated the ASP's preference to leave final determinations to the Court's judges and to the VTF board of trustees. The outcome of the VTF debate did not demonstrate decisive ASP leadership of the Court. Rome Statute Article 79 called for the establishment of a Trust Fund "by decision of the Assembly of States Parties for the benefit of victims of crimes within the jurisdiction of the Court, and the families of such victims."[47] The Court (judges) may order money and other property from the fines or forfeiture exacted against convicts to be transferred to the Trust Fund.[48] The Court can also acquire other funds, but Article 79 doesn't indicate what those sources of funds might be. The details of fundraising and management were left to the ASP.[49]

---

[46] ICC, ASP, Sixth Session, "Report of the Committee on Budget and Finance on the Work of Its Eighth session," ICC-ASP/6/2 (2007), 11.

[47] statute Article 79.1.

[48] Statute Article 79.2.

[49] Statute Article 79.3.

The Statute refers to victims of crimes over which the Court has jurisdiction, but it does not specify how such a victim officially becomes one from the standpoint of the Court. For civil-law states and those concerned to enhance the victim orientation of the Court, victims should come under the purview of the Court as soon as possible once crimes have been determined to have occurred. Civil-law and victims' advocates argued that the VTF board should be able to begin operations as soon as situations had been specified, early in the Court's proceedings.

For common-law states, victims are people who have suffered from crimes the perpetrators of which had been convicted. With conviction comes certainty. Common-law states viewed the VTF with concerns about due process and fairness. How could the VTF determine that victims existed before a trial was completed? If it did so, couldn't this prejudice the rights of a defendant? Furthermore, if victims were disconnected from specific perpetrators, did this mean that they were victims of the general situation – in which case huge numbers of people might have claims to pursue from the Court? Given the likely limited resources of the Court, wouldn't this be a formula for frustration of victims and failure of the Court, rather than a boon to its legitimacy?

In 2002, the ASP adopted a Preparatory Commission recommendation to establish the trust fund for victims mentioned in the Statute[50] and created a board of directors to set up and run the fund.[51] The Court's Registry was to help the VTF board, but the ASP also envisioned appointing an executive director and staff for the fund.[52] It still needed to name a board and for the new board to develop its rules of operation. The rules had to be approved by the ASP.

Former President Oscar Arias Sanchez of Costa Rica, former Polish Prime Minister Tedeusz Mazowiecki, Queen Rania al-Abdallah of Jordan, Archbishop Desmond Tutu of South Africa, and former Minister of Health of France and President of the European Parliament Simone Veil were elected to the board at the September 2003 second ASP. During 2004, NGOs proposed draft regulations for the fund and pointed out, among other concerns, that the Statute's designation of victims as people who had suffered from crimes over which the Court had jurisdiction was quite vague.[53]

---

[50] ICC, ASP, "Establishment of a Fund for the Benefit of Victims of Crimes within the Jurisdiction of the Court and of Families of Such Victims," First Session, Official Recards (2002), ASP/1/Res. 6.

[51] Ibid., Annex, para. 1.

[52] Ibid., para. 6.

[53] For example, REDRESS and Forensic Risk Analysis, "The International Criminal Court's Trust Fund for Victims: Analysis and Options for the Development of Further Criteria for the Operation of the Trust Fund for Victims, Discussion Document" (2003).

Following extensive consultations, draft regulations presented to the Third Assembly of States Parties did not gain approval, and the matter was held over until the next ASP. Victim-oriented NGOs continued to hold meetings, seminars, and consultations and to propose modified regulations. At the fourth ASP in November 2005, along with the debate over defining victims, controversy emerged over how and whether voluntary contributions to the VTF could be "earmarked" for particular victims or situations. Board member Mme. Simone Veil gave impassioned speeches to the ASP, and at a meeting of the NGOs, she pressed states to resolve their differences and allow the VTF to begin operation and expressed her impatience and frustration.[54] At the end of the session, the regulations were adopted.

The agreed VTF regulations distinguish between funds collected from awards for reparations (that is, from perpetrators by order of the Court) and all other sources.[55] Funds collected through awards can benefit only victims "affected directly or indirectly by the crimes committed by the convicted person."[56] Modeled on common-law procedures, the judges, as part of a sentence, can decide to claim reparations from a convict and then turn over acquired resources to the VTF for distribution.

The VTF board can draw upon other, voluntarily donated resources to support more broadly defined victims and their families even before a trial has begun, as long as the judges, once informed of the board's intention, determine that it would not be prejudicial to the trial to do so. What qualifies the victim for the voluntary funds is not direct connection with a perpetrator, but with being defined by the VTF board as having suffered from crimes under the Court's jurisdiction in general. Thus, the ASP didn't solve the problem of definition but left the determination to the VTF board. The VTF is to notify Pre-Trial Chambers of its decision to act, and

---

[54] At the 2005 ASP, it was announced that VTF board member Oscar Arias was resigning from his seat. He was subsequently elected president of Costa Rica and took office in May 2006. Later in May, former President of Trinidad and Tobago Arthur N. R. Robinson was elected to the VTF board. It had been President Robinson's call for the creation of an ICC in 1988 that restarted serious consideration of the matter by the UN General Assembly and International Law Commission. During 2006, Queen Rania of Jordan indicated that she would no longer serve on the board. The fall (2006, fifth) ASP left the position open when nominations were not forthcoming from the Asian region; the hope was that someone would be found by the time of the January continuation of the fifth ASP.

[55] ICC, ASP, Fourth Session, "Regulations of the Trust Fund for Victims," (2005) ICC-ASP/4/Res. 3 Annex, Part II, Chapter IV, para. 34.

[56] Ibid., Part III, Chapter I, para. 46.

the rules give the PTCs a limited period of time during which they can raise objections.[57]

Victim advocates extolled this outcome that permitted the VTF to become something like an insurance fund for victims of atrocity crimes. From the civil-law/victim-oriented viewpoint, it brought the ICC further into the business of reparative or restorative justice, away from retribution. Common-law advocates still feared that the process could compromise the presumption of innocence and were concerned that the judges would find it very difficult to come to a dispassionate decision about whether engaging the VTF might be prejudicial because to delay VTF action would appear to be acting against victims in favor of the accused – an unpopular position.[58]

Extending Jurisdiction – Aggression as a Crime

Aggression is the most controversial crime in the Statute. There was over-whelming sentiment at the Rome Conference to include aggression in the Statute, but there was also adamant opposition to it, particularly from the United States and other Security Council permanent members. When negotiators recognized their inability to reach consensus, they compromised by extending the Court's jurisdiction over aggression and creating a seven-year grace period (in practice, to the 2009 Statute Review Conference) during which to develop the Statute amendments.[59] Jurisdiction can be exerted once provisions define the crime and set out the conditions under which the Court shall exercise jurisdiction, "consistent with the relevant provisions of the Charter of the United Nations."[60] Because the UN Charter delegates to the Security Council responsibility for responding to

---

[57] Dealing with the questions of when the fund could take action, the regulations declare that to implement the "activities and projects" of the VTF (Part III, Chapter II), the Trust Fund "shall be considered to be seized" when the board "considers it necessary to provide ... rehabilitation or material support for the benefit of victims" (para. 50(a)(I)), and (this is where the ball was kicked over to the judges) the board has informed the Court (judges) and the "relevant Chamber" (not specifying pretrial or trial chamber, since there is no direction in the regulations as to when this can take place, leaving open the possibility that the board might decide to seek to initiate reparations or assistance to victims even while a case is at the pretrial stage) has not (with various deadlines and time periods) responded to the board that the proposed activity would "pre-determine any issue to be determined by the Court," including jurisdiction, admissibility, the presumption of innocence, "or be prejudicial to or inconsistent with the rights of the accused and a fair and impartial trial" (para. 50(a)(ii)).

[58] Interviews.

[59] Statute Article 123.1.

[60] Statute Article 5.2.

aggression,[61] such Statute provisions will need explicitly to delineate the relationship between the Court and the Security Council.

The Preparatory Commission began discussions on aggression in 2002 and then shunted the matter over to the Assembly of States Parties, which then established the Special Working Group on the Crime of Aggression (SWGCA). The working group is special in that it invites participation by ICC Statute parties as well as all members of the United Nations, since the questions at hand involve the UN Charter as well as the ICC. Beginning in summer 2004, the SWGCA has met annually in Princeton under the sponsorship of the Woodrow Wilson School and the Liechtenstein Institute on Self-Determination in what the ASP calls the "informal inter-sessional meeting" of the SWGCA. Participants have also established an electronic "virtual working group" to pursue development of the needed statutory and other language.

There are four main areas of technical difficulty, underlying which is the basic problem of whether an individual crime of aggression can be reduced to legalities or whether the matter is so politically embedded as to make "legalization" impossible. The SWGCA has proceeded on the basis of a discussion paper produced by the Preparatory Commission's coordinator of the Working Group on Aggression.[62]

The first challenge is to define aggression. A 1974 General Assembly resolution defines the state crime of aggression,[63] but it does not establish

---

[61] UN Charter, Chapter VII.

[62] ICC, Preparatory Commission for the International Criminal Court, Working Group on the Crime of Aggression, "Discussion Paper Proposed by the Coordinator" (2002), PCNICC/2002/WGCA/RT.1/Rev. 2.

[63] Article 1: "Aggression is the use of armed force by a State against the sovereignty, territorial integrity or political independence of another State, or in any other manner inconsistent with the Charter of the United Nations, as set out in this definition." Article 2 indicates that first use of armed force in contravention of the Charter constitutes prima facie evidence of an act of aggression but reserves the Security Council's right to decide whether such an act might be justified or "not of sufficient gravity." Article 3 enumerates acts that, regardless of a declaration of war, qualify as acts of aggression (invasion, annexation by force, bombardment, or use of weapons against a state's territory; port blockage; attack on the land, sea, or air forces or marine and air fleets of another state; use of armed forces within a state contravening an agreement on their stationing; allowing a state to be used for perpetrating aggression against a third state; sending of armed bands, groups, irregulars, or mercenaries to carry out acts of force against another state). Article 4 indicates that the UN Security Council can add acts to this list. Article 5 establishes that there are no political, economic, military, or other justifications for aggression; that a war of aggression is a crime against international peace and gives rise to international responsibility; and that no territorial acquisition or advantage resulting from aggression is to be recognized as lawful. Article 6 retains Charter supremacy. Article 7 notes that the right to self-determination, freedom, and independence is to be maintained. Article 8 notes that all of the provisions must be considered together in interpretation. UN General Assembly, Resolution 3314(XXIX) (1974).

an individual crime. In order for the ICC to be able to prosecute a crime of aggression, the material elements (what actually happened) and mental requirements (intent, motive, understanding of consequences) of an individual person's crime must be defined, and its relationship to the state crime will have to be determined. The discussions at SWGCA revolve in part around how specific or generic such a description should be. The individual crime will likely be defined as the act of participating in the planning, preparation, initiation, or execution of an act of aggression as defined in the UN General Assembly resolution.

A second area of discussion is how a new aggression provision of the Statute would come into force. Would states parties to the Statute automatically be subject to accepting it were the amendment procedure (which requires a supermajority of parties) fulfilled, or would they in contrast either have to "opt in" or have the right to "opt out" of the new provision?

A third topic is how the legal principles of the Statute that apply to the existing crimes (such as complicity in attempted crime, command responsibility, higher orders) apply to the new crime, which is inherently a "leadership" crime and thus something of a special case, and whether these need to be spelled out or should be left to the Court to determine.

The fourth and by far most sensitive set of issues is over *who* decides when aggression has taken place (or been planned!). Can the ICC pursue a suspected perpetrator of aggression without the Security Council having first found that such an act has taken place? Must the ICC act if the Security Council has found aggression? Could the General Assembly and/or the International Court of Justice trigger ICC investigations? Related to that question of "trigger," once an act of aggression has been determined to have happened, how does the Court proceed with an investigation of individuals while protecting the due-process rights of the accused?

With regard to the role of the Security Council, according to a CICC report on SWGCA meetings of 2005, there are two general lines of thought. The first line is that UN Charter Article 39 gives the Security Council the exclusive authority to make such a determination. A second line of thought is that a Security Council finding of aggression is not required. Within this view, there are several alternatives: (a) the UNSC has no role to play – Chapter VII is for enforcement, and the ICC can independently determine whether the elements of the crime appear to have been perpetrated (after all, the Nuremberg and Tokyo trials took place without the UN); (b) the UNSC does not have exclusive responsibility, but primary responsibility, and if the Security Council fails to act, the ICC could go ahead; or (c) the UNSC does not have exclusive responsibility, and if it fails to act, the General Assembly or International Court of Justice would need to do so.[64]

Will states jealous of their sovereign rights to the use of force be willing to subject their leaders to a rule of law in which aggression is explicitly defined and criminalized? Consensus on the question wasn't even close at the Statute Conference. Even though the intersessional discussions have been described as constructive and friendly, British and U.S. representatives have not participated, and for the most part the discussions are among technical experts not representing settled state policies. The rationale for inviting all UN member states to the SWGCA is strong – failing agreement with the permanent members of the Security Council, such amendment of the ICC could lead to a confrontation between the Court and at least some of the permanent members of the Security Council. Would the establishment of formal jurisdiction over the objections of major states be worth the risk to the Court of such a confrontation?

The arguments in favor of proceeding (if possible) even against the views of the United States and/or other Security Council permanent members are that aggression has already been identified as a state crime, that state crimes have individual perpetrators, as the United States and its allies were willing to argue at Nuremberg, and that the current development of international society is such that the vast majority of states (as shown in Rome in 1998) are prepared to move forward with international law in this direction. Even setting down the markers of international norms is a constitutive act that may serve to modify behavior and reduce the likelihood of criminal acts such as aggression. The arguments against are that international society still reserves to the state the ultimate capacity for the use of force, and that "self defense," enshrined in the Charter of the UN, may still be a rather flexible concept. Why risk institutional credibility over the issue of aggression? Enforcement may not only be impossible but likely be actively opposed by the most powerful state(s) should aggression be pursued. In addition, all the information needed for the investigation will reside in the country least likely to cooperate – the country of origin of the officials in question.

STATESIDE COMPLEMENTARITY: COOPERATING WITH THE COURT

This section discusses the dependence of the Court upon cooperation from states, particularly those that have joined the Statute. Chapter 4 discussed

---

[64] NGO CICC Team on the Crime of Aggression, "Informal Inter-sessional Meeting ... from 13 to 15 June 2005" (2006).

complementarity – positive and negative – in the context of ICC operations in states where crimes may have taken place. A lively policy debate simmers over the extent to which the ICC should be engaged in judicial assistance to states and over criteria by which to determine a state's willingness and ability to prosecute. However, ICC prosecution should be the exception rather than the rule. Prosecution of the Statute's crimes should usually take place at the domestic level, and only failing this (when a state with jurisdiction is genuinely unwilling or unable) is the Court to become involved.

When a state accepts an obligation to cooperate with the Court by acceding to the Statute,[65] it formally obliges itself to become able to prosecute Statute crimes. Nonetheless, it remains sovereign, and it can implement (or not) prosecution and cooperation obligations according to its own decisions. The most that the ICC can do in response to noncooperation is to notify the Assembly of States Parties or (if the situation was referred by the Security Council) the Security Council of the failure to comply with a request to cooperate.

For states to comply with the Statute, their legal codes must enable them to prosecute the Statute's crimes, and they must be able to cooperate with the Court. For these purposes, they must bring their domestic legislation into line with the Statute.[66] For example, in order for a state to cooperate with the Court in apprehending suspects, its own legal system must criminalize the crimes declared illegal under the Statute and provide for domestic enforcement capabilities.[67] Aligning domestic law with Statute obligations often requires constitutional adjustments, changes in legal codes, or both,[68] not only to make enforcement possible but also to uphold the due-process standards and legal principles embraced by the Statute. NGOs, including Parliamentarians for Global Action, Amnesty International, the International Committees of the Red Cross, and many other national and international organizations,[69] have been crucial in helping states to develop

---

[65] Rome Statute Article 86: General obligation to cooperate. "States Parties shall, in accordance with the provisions of this Statute, cooperate fully with the Court in its investigation and prosecution of crimes within the jurisdiction of the Court."

[66] Relva, "The Implementation of the Rome Statute in Latin American States" (2003), 331–66.

[67] Statute Article 88: Availability of procedures under national law. "States Parties shall ensure that there are procedures available under their national law for all of the forms of cooperation which are specified under this Part."

[68] Statute Article 87.7.

[69] Parliamentarians for Global Action, "Parliamentary Kit on the International Criminal Court (ICC)," New York and Rome (2006); the CICC posts extremely useful materials of their own and from other NGOs regarding implementation on its Web site, <http://www.iccnow.org/?mod=romeimplementation>.

legislation for Statute implementation. Some states have assisted in this regard too by directly, or through NGOs, funding conferences, workshops, and seminars for parliamentarians and others.

By joining the Rome Statute, states agree to grant to the Court on their territory "such privileges and immunities to the Court as are necessary for the fulfillment of its purposes,"[70] made official by the state signing the Agreement on Privileges and Immunities of the ICC. This agreement establishes the Court as a legal entity within the state, accords its top officials diplomatic immunity, makes it tax exempt, protects its records and property, permits it communications facilities at least as favorable as those of any diplomatic mission or intergovernmental organization, prevents censorship of such communications, and grants personal immunity to States Parties' representatives to the Assembly, victims, witnesses, and experts before the Court, among other things. The agreement establishes the ICC and its personnel as the equals of other international organizations and their employees within the territory of member states and is closely comparable to the UN Agreement on Privileges and Immunities that serves the same purpose.[71]

Cooperation also entails an obligation to assist the Court in collecting information and apprehending suspects when a state is in a position to do so – clearly actions over which domestic authorities are supposed to have complete control. In addition, states can cooperate indirectly with the Court by aiding other states or organizations, notably NGOs, in their support for the Court, and they may serve as international advocates for the Court, its Statute, and its operations.

Well aware of the need for aligning national systems with the Statute, the Court, friendly states, and nongovernmental organizations have made assistance to states in developing their laws major projects in support of the Rome Statute.[72] As of February, 2007, 139 countries had signed the Statute, and 104 had ratified or acceded; 62 had signed the Agreement on Privileges and Immunities, and 48 had ratified it.[73]

Under the complementarity doctrine, the ICC has jurisdiction only in the event that a state is unable or unwilling genuinely to prosecute perpetrators

---

[70] Statute Article 48.

[71] Nilsson, "Contextualizing the Agreement on the Privileges and Immunities of the International Criminal Court" (2004), 559–78.

[72] See; NGO CICC, "Implementation of the Rome Statute" (2007), for model cooperation agreements, domestic legislation campaigns, etc. On difficulties in the process of implementation, see Amnesty International, "The Failure of States to Enact Effective Implementing Legislation" (2004).

[73] Ibid.

of Statute crimes. Ability is indicated, in part, by the legal system of the state: Has it criminalized Statute crimes and enabled its own judicial system to try appropriate cases? The more willing and able a state is domestically to prosecute Statute crimes, the less likely crimes within its jurisdiction would be taken up by the Court. Thus, ironically for the United States, bringing the U.S. code into compliance with the Statute would *decrease* the likelihood that U.S. citizens would fall afoul of the ICC. Since the U.S. legal code has not been brought into conformity with the Statute, should other states apprehend a U.S. citizen suspected of perpetrating Statute crimes, they might either try them themselves or transfer them to the ICC (unless a BIA prevented such an action), fearing that the U.S. legal system would not be engaged appropriately in prosecution should the suspected transgressor be returned home.

CONCLUSIONS

Constructivist, realist, and neoliberal institutionalist images of states' motivations each explain parts of ICC relations with states. A constructivist lens focuses upon ideological support or rejection of the Court. Thus, both the affection for the Court expressed by NGOs and supportive states and the stridency of conservative U.S. politicians' antipathy fit well into the constructivist logic. U.S. opposition to the Court's deleterious effects on the country's global standing and regional alliances is primarily ideological, as is now being demonstrated by a realist backlash. Aid cutoffs are too costly in the view of U.S. foreign policy realists who seek the benefits of assistance even to states that acceded to the ICC Statute but refuse to conclude a U.S. (BIA) bilateral immunity agreement.

Realists could argue that the low level of diplomatic representation to the ASP and states' limited willingness to finance the Court reflect its limited relevance to their relative power. They could explain U.S. opposition to the Court, and Chinese, Russian, and Indian reluctance to join by powerful states' inclination to preserve maximum flexibility in the use of military power and disinclination to subordinate themselves to cooperative structures that do not aid in promoting material objectives. The generally higher regard for the Court exhibited by middle and weaker states would confirm for realists the effort of the weak to employ international institutions to trammel the power of the strong. These arguments imply a Court with more coercive potential than is likely, but realism nonetheless provides a useful framework to explain states' general propensity to protect sovereignty and thus to limit the ICC's capabilities. The realist argument thus does explain the difficulty and risk involved in extending exercise of ICC jurisdiction over the crime of aggression. Not only is there disagreement among Statute parties over how far the Court should go regarding aggression, but action on aggression will likely increase UN Security Council permanent members' antipathy to the Court, unless the amendments grant the UNSC primary responsibility for determining when aggression has occurred. Given the record of the Statute negotiations, the grant by the states parties of so much discretion over the Court to the UNSC appears unlikely; therefore, a formula will most likely be found to postpone action on aggression beyond the 2009 Review Conference.

To maximize the chances of organizational survival and growth, ICC officials seek to serve the Court's constituencies by fully implementing the mandate, gaining legitimacy through exemplary implementation of its procedures, and doing so efficiently. This is the realm of neoliberal institutionalism. It is possible that the Statute's primary effect will be in the standardization of domestic law, in judicial assistance to countries developing their legal systems, and in deterrence of crime; however, these likely will not be adequate to justify the Court's infrastructure and personnel costs if it isn't seen to be doing a lot of what it was originally conceived to do – put people on trial. The retributive justice mandate is paramount; restorative justice is an increasingly important secondary objective. The next chapter shows the complexities and difficulties of implementing the Court's core objectives.

7

The First Situations

The ICC has become deeply enmeshed in four African countries experiencing massive criminal law violations in a web of conflicts ranging from Rwanda in the south to Sudan in the north and the Central African Republic and Chad in the west. By mid-2007, the ICC had four "situations"[1] on its docket. The governments of Uganda, the Democratic Republic of the Congo, and the Central African Republic referred their own situations to the Court. The Darfur, Sudan, situation was referred by the UN Security Council.

The four situations raised common challenges and unique problems for the Court. The sections of this chapter begin with a description of each conflict's background and the sequence of events leading to the Court's involvement. The exposition that follows focuses on aspects of each situation that illuminate particular characteristics of the Court's processes and problems. Uganda, the DRC, and the CAR are all adherents to the ICC Statute, so their self-referrals skirted the problem of situation–state non-cooperation with the Court; however, there was the possibility that their governments were seeking to use the ICC for their own purposes in internal conflicts. The Court would need to strive for impartiality even though it had been invited into the countries by their governments. This problem is sometimes called the threat of instrumentalization of the Court. Could the Court carry out investigations and prosecutions under self-referrals without being used by the governments?

Different forms of instrumentalization were at work in the Sudan situation. On the one hand, as in the earlier creation of the two ad hoc

---

[1] The Statute uses the term "situation" to describe a conflict in which crimes are alleged to have taken place. See "Triggers," Chapter 3.

tribunals, the UN Security Council was turning a conflict over to the Court about which it had been able to do very little on its own, raising the possibility that the Court was being used as a symbolic smokescreen for UNSC inaction. On the other hand, NGOs hoped that ICC involvement, and the threat that officials might be labeled as suspects, would help to pressure the Sudanese government to alter its behavior in Darfur.

In all four situations, NGOs were vigorous in their demands for international involvement to thwart alleged large-scale crimes. Nonetheless, NGOs themselves disagreed over the relationship between establishing peace and pursuing justice. The tension between these objectives was most visible in the Uganda situation, where some (especially local) NGOs charged that ICC involvement was interfering in a peace process. The problem appeared to be exacerbated when officials of the Lord's Resistance Army, for whom warrants had been issued by the Court, demanded that the warrants be lifted as a condition for ending the violence.

Tensions over the Court's internal division of labor and between civil- and common-law mechanisms surfaced in each of the situations, with the Pre-Trial Chambers and the Office of the Prosecutor jockeying for primacy. In the Sudan and CAR situations, the PTCs publicly pressurized the OTP; the OTP resisted what it saw as interference and continued to seek maximum independence. In the DRC and Sudan situations, critics inside and outside the Court argued that the Prosecutor was inadequately vigorous in his investigations and too narrow when he eventually issued warrants. Then, just as Prosecutor Richard Goldstone of the ICTY had been criticized for pursuing a target of convenience and apprehending a low-level official when he brought Dusko Tadic from German custody to the ICTY, so some critics belittled the OTP's achievement in March 2006 when it brought the first suspect, Thomas Lubanga Dyilo, to the ICC from a Congolese prison. Similarly, critics argued that the Sudan warrants avoided the most important suspects, and that the CAR investigation was proceeding too slowly. The Prosecutor's consistent response was that he was following appropriate investigation procedures and would bring cases to Court when the evidence warranted.

UGANDA

Conflict Background

In November 2003, United Nations Undersecretary-General for Humanitarian Affairs and Emergency Relief Coordinator Jan Egeland stated, "I cannot find any other part of the world that is having an emergency on the scale of Uganda, that is getting such little international attention."[2] Conflict in Uganda extends back to Colonial times, pitting northern against southern groups and their organizations, over ethnicity, religion, and economic interests.

In January 1986, the southern-dominated National Resistance Movement/Army (NRM/A) under Yoweri Museveni overthrew northern-based Tito Okello's government after a five-year guerilla war. In May, the NRM/A ordered former (largely northern) government soldiers to report to barracks. Since the old army had been dominated by Acholis from the north, who had fought against Museveni's forces, they were deeply suspicious of the command.[3] Instead of complying with Museveni's order, many of the former soldiers fled to southern Sudan.

With Sudanese government support, former Okello government officials and soldiers built a rebel organization initially called the Holy Spirit Movement (HSM) under the leadership of Alice Auma Lakwena, "a self-styled prophetess who claimed to be a spiritual medium with the power to perform miracles,"[4] including making her soldiers immune to bullets. After her forces took major casualties in battle against the NRM/A in November 1987, Lakwena fled to Kenya. In 1988, Joseph Kony, a young relative and follower of Lakwena,[5] re-formed the remnants of the HSM into what came to be called the Lord's Resistance Army.[6]

Under Kony's leadership, the LRA adopted more standard guerilla tactics, attacking civilian targets to demonstrate the government's inability to protect its people. In March 1991, the government's army, the Ugandan People's Defense Forces, began "Operation North," attacking the LRA and supporting local defense groups mostly armed with bows and arrows. These "arrow groups" were organized by Acholi Government Minister Betty

---

[2] Agence France-Presse, "War in Northern Uganda World's Worst Forgotten Crisis: UN" (2003).

[3] There was also a troubling echo of the past, since in 1971 when Idi Amin took power in Uganda, he had ordered Acholi and Langi officers to report to barracks, whereupon they were massacred. Ssenyojo, "Accountability of Non-State Actors in Uganda for War Crimes and Human Rights Violations: Between Amnesty and the International Criminal Court" (2005), 410 and footnote 36.

[4] Akhavan, "The Lord's Resistance Army Case: Uganda's Submission of the First State Referral to the International Criminal Court" (2005).

[5] Allen, *Trial Justice: The International Criminal Court and the Lord's Resistance Army* (2006), 37, questions whether Kony and Lakwena are really related. The book is a superb exploration of the Uganda/LRA/ICC interaction through early 2005.

[6] Akhavan, op cit., 407.

Bigombe, who had been assigned to end the insurgency. The arrow groups and Operation North failed.

The LRA established bases in southern Sudan, supported by the Khartoum government that believed LRA pressure on Uganda would undermine Ugandan support for the secessionist Sudanese People's Liberation Army (SPLA) in its conflict (1983–2005) with Sudanese governmental forces. With an estimated 3,000 to 4,000 fighters, the LRA claimed to be opposing Museveni's government, but its continuing attacks in northern Uganda mostly targeted Acholis, its fighters looting and pillaging villages, raping women, and abducting many child "recruits."[7] Kidnapped children reportedly ranged in age from eight on up, mostly fourteen to sixteen, although the proportion of children to adult abductees was not extraordinary in the context of conflict in the region. Those abducted were used as soldiers, laborers, sexual slaves, and "wives" of LRA commanders.[8]

The government's UPDF was also accused of massive abuses as it sought to remove civilians from the areas in which the LRA was active, to rob the LRA of material support. Beginning in 1996, the army herded civilians into "protected villages" intended to isolate them from the conflict and enable freer military movements, much as the British had created concentration camps during the Boer War and the United States had sought to create "strategic hamlets" during the Vietnam conflict. The "internally displaced persons" (IDP) camps reproduced the worst aspects of their earlier precedents – they were terminally dangerous for their inmates due to poor health conditions, inadequate nutrition, and lack of infrastructure. They also became targets for LRA attacks.[9]

By 1998–1999, Sudanese support for the LRA was subsiding. The government was negotiating peace with the SPLA in the south and seeking to improve relations with the United States in the wake of the bombing of the U.S. embassies in Nairobi and Dar es Salaam by Al Qaeda, whose leader Osama Bin Laden had resided in the Sudan for several years. Following the U.S. Department of State's designation of the LRA as a terrorist organization in December 2001, Sudan agreed to stop supplying aid to it.

From 2000, after an offer of amnesty, which some LRA fighters accepted, the LRA seemed quietly to be residing in southern Sudan. Believing that the LRA was weak, in March 2003, the UPDF sought finally

---

[7] Ssenyojo, op cit., 412.
[8] Allen, op cit., 64–5.
[9] Ibid. 53–60.

to destroy the LRA, with Sudanese permission. The effort failed, however, and LRA attacks in northern Uganda resumed.

Observers estimate that from 1986 through 2005, the LRA abducted more than 38,000 children, including 12,000 after the entry into force of the Rome Statute on July 1, 2002.[10] The UN Office for the Coordination of Humanitarian Affairs estimated that, in early 2006, because of their fear of abduction, 40,000 children were commuting from their rural homes into towns and IDP camps at dusk to sleep in areas more protected from the depredations of the LRA.[11] Massive insecurity had disrupted farming, herding, trading, and schooling and consequently caused severe regional economic decline.

Referral

In late 2003, informal conversations between lawyers representing Uganda at the International Court of Justice in The Hague[12] and ICC personnel led the ICC OTP to believe that the Ugandan authorities might be interested in referring the LRA conflict situation in northern Uganda to the Court.[13] On December 16, 2003, Ugandan President Museveni sent a confidential letter to the Chief Prosecutor[14] referring the conflict to the Court. In January, the two met in London to discuss how to proceed, and Museveni and Moreno Ocampo jointly held a news conference to announce the referral on January 29, 2004. Museveni's statements, as reflected in the Ugandan press, appeared to focus the ICC on the LRA, and Moreno Ocampo's response reinforced that impression. According to a news report,

Museveni invited the ICC to probe the LRA for terrorism and committing the most barbaric atrocities against Ugandans.

"They should answer for kidnaping children and conscripting them into the LRA and for raping young girls and infecting them with HIV/AIDS," Museveni said. Ocampo said these terrorists use telephones, buy and receive weapons from individuals and countries that could be traced.

---

[10] Akhavan, op cit., 407.

[11] IRIN, "Uganda: Too Scared to Return Home" (2006).

[12] Uganda was accused before the International Court of Justice in The Hague by the Democratic Republic of the Congo of various violations during the Congo conflict of 1998–2003. International Court of Justice, "Armed Activities on the Territory of the Congo (Democratic Republic of the Congo v. Uganda)" (2005).

[13] Interviews, spring 2006.

[14] Akhavan, op cit., 403; ICC, Presidency, Letter from Chief Prosecutor Moreno Ocampo to President Kirsch, ICC-02/04-1 06-07-2004(2004), appendix to "Decision Assigning the Situation in Uganda to Pre-Trial Chamber II" (2004), 4; ICC, "Facts and Procedure Regarding the Situation in Uganda" (2005).

Museveni said he was grateful that Ocampo had received Uganda's complaint and was willing to act and apprehend the Kony terrorists.

"The Uganda Government is using its capacity to fight these terrorists within the country's borders but those beyond our reach deep inside our neighbouring countries will be dealt with by the special prosecutor," Museveni said.

"A key issue will be locating and arresting the LRA leadership. This will require the active co-operation of states and international institutions in supporting efforts of the Ugandan authorities. ... This will require the concerted support of the international community – Uganda and the Court cannot do this alone," a statement read.[15]

The Sudanese ambassador to Uganda signaled his country's turn away from supporting the LRA on February 17, stating that should the Court ask for Sudan's aid in arresting Kony, "Sudan will readily comply with the ICC request," and particularly because of attacks by the LRA in southern Sudan, he predicted that Kony and his henchmen would soon be apprehended.[16]

Instrumentalization

President Museveni's referral to the ICC appeared to serve his own political objectives. Even though his forces were free to act inside Uganda, ICC involvement could help gain Sudanese and DRC permission for UPDF forays across borders to attack the LRA. By calling upon the ICC to act against the LRA, he could shift attention away from UPDF misdeeds. His embrace of the ICC could help legitimate his government, especially in the eyes of European leaders. Moreover, the ICC's appeal for international cooperation in apprehending LRA suspects could help lead to their capture. However, Museveni's dedication to international criminal justice seemed variable. Once ICC warrants were issued against top LRA leaders, Museveni used the Court as both carrot and stick, alternatively dangling the possibility of lifting the ICC warrants if the LRA would negotiate an end to hostilities and calling for the leaders' prosecution at The Hague.

Uganda's referral served the ICC Prosecutor's purposes as well. The OTP had been evaluating the Uganda situation in response to communications received from 2002 onward. Chief Prosecutor Moreno Ocampo recognized that a self-referral would vastly simplify his task by making Uganda's cooperation much more likely than would have his proceeding *proprio motu*. In addition, public announcement of the self-referral could help build

[15] Price, "Kony Probe Begins June" (2004).
[16] Allio, "Sudan Predicts Kony End" (2004).

the credibility of the Court, since critics often wondered what the chances were that the ICC would gain necessary cooperation from situation states. The ICC Prosecutor responded eagerly to Uganda's interest and was immediately drawn into countervailing pressures of human rights norms, humanitarian values, and Ugandan internal politics. Although self-referral eased the Court's practical problems, it raised the possibility that the ICC was being enlisted on one side of the internal conflict. The way in which the referral was announced buttressed observers' suspicions.

Moreno Ocampo's appearance on a platform with Museveni set off alarms among international NGOs concerned about the appearance of ICC partiality. Amnesty International welcomed the announcement but asserted that the investigation "must be part of a comprehensive plan to end impunity for all such crimes, regardless of which side committed them and of the level of the perpetrator," cautioning that Uganda appeared to have sought to limit the referral "to crimes committed by one party to the conflict." In a rather harsh statement, Amnesty International emphasized that a referral could not "limit the scope of any investigation," and urged the independence of the Prosecutor, citing Article 42(1) of the Rome Statute.[17]

Human Rights Watch praised the opening of the investigation. In its press release, the director of its international justice program, Richard Dicker stated:

Human Rights Watch has documented many shocking abuses by the LRA in Uganda, but the ICC prosecutor cannot ignore the crimes that Ugandan government troops allegedly have committed. ... President Museveni's referral does not limit the prosecutor's investigation only to crimes allegedly committed by the LRA. The prosecutor should operate independently and has the authority to look at all ICC crimes committed in Uganda.[18]

---

[17] Amnesty International, "Uganda: First Steps to Investigate Crimes Must Be Part of Comprehensive Plan to End Impunity" (2004). Statute Article 42(1) says: "The Office of the Prosecutor shall act independently as a separate organ of the Court. It shall be responsible for receiving referrals and any substantiated information on crimes within the jurisdiction of the Court, for examining them and for conducting investigations and prosecutions before the Court. A member of the Office shall not seek or act on instructions from any external source."

[18] Human Rights Watch, "ICC: Investigate All Sides in Uganda – Chance for Impartial ICC Investigation into Serious Crimes a Welcome Step" (2004). When Moreno Ocampo announced in October 2005 that the Court was issuing arrest warrants for five LRA leaders, he emphasized the fairness of his investigation. The OTP "had analyzed the gravity of all crimes in Northern Uganda committed by the LRA and Ugandan forces" and found that the LRA's crimes were "much more numerous and of much higher gravity than alleged crimes by the UPDF." ICC, "Statement by the Chief Prosecutor on the Uganda Arrest Warrants" (2005), 2, 3.

The HRW press release raised the issue of victims' interests when it "cautioned that the prosecutor should conduct his investigation in a way that does not jeopardize the security of the children who are still in LRA captivity or escalate the risk of further abductions." Some local Ugandan organizations expressed concern about the effects of ICC involvement upon ongoing peace negotiations.

Peace versus Justice

Once the Chief Prosecutor and President Museveni announced the referral, the ICC was plunged into the dilemmas of peace versus justice and subject to Museveni's ever-shifting strategems. Moreno Ocampo struggled to find a balance between carrying out his statutory responsibilities to pursue the alleged crimes and his concern for the interests of victims. Those interests, particularly in the eyes of humanitarian local NGOs, included not just being included in judicial procedures, but ending the killing and kidnapping.

The ICC Statute's preamble asserts that countering impunity contributes to prevention of crimes. If this is correct, then the operations of justice should enhance peace. Peace negotiators argued, however, that by threatening the LRA leadership, the ICC reduced their incentive to lay down their arms. Skeptics about the LRA's sincerity countered that only the LRA leaders' arrests or their military defeat would truly end the conflict. President Museveni came down on all sides. He variously called for crushing the LRA militarily, arresting its leadership, and supporting the ICC's efforts, but he also repeatedly implied that he had the power to suspend ICC prosecutions if the LRA would negotiate an end to hostilities. While his peace initiatives drew support from humanitarian organizations, his apparent willingness to endorse LRA impunity roused protests and warnings from international human rights organizations. The Court was stuck in the middle.

Following the referral, many Ugandan peace organizations argued that ICC involvement would make peace less likely. For example, Acholi Religious Leaders' Peace Initiative negotiator Father Carlos Rodriguez warned, "The issuing of such international arrest warrants would practically close once and for all the path to peaceful negotiation as a means to end this long war, crushing whatever little progress has been made during these years."[19] Other Ugandan groups and the Amnesty Commission (created by the Amnesty Act of 2000) "voiced concern that the investigation

---

[19] *The New Vision*, "Probe Army Too, Amnesty Tells ICC" (2004).

could worsen the conflict," according to an analyst at the University of British Columbia's Liu Center.[20]

The amnesty of 2000 had succeeded in luring significant numbers of LRA commanders to trade their weapons and military pursuits for peace during the intervening years; however, Kony and his top leaders were not responsive. Even though they were in periodic contact with government and other negotiators, their demands remained unclear and their raids, abductions, and attacks continued. Skeptics were convinced that they had no real intention of negotiating peace. The government continued to oscillate between a policy of negotiation and force, frequently stating that the only way to end the conflict was by complete military victory.

On July 29, 2004, the Chief Prosecutor announced that, having completed its preliminary inquiry, the OTP was opening a formal investigation into the situation in northern Uganda.[21] He later maintained that, in deference to ongoing peace efforts, the investigation was pursued with a "low profile."[22] In November, President Museveni announced a partial cease-fire with the LRA so that its leaders could gather, with international observers if they so desired, and discuss how to take up the amnesty offers. The President said that if the leadership reached agreements with the Acholi community for some kind of settlement, "the state could then withdraw its case and we could inform the ICC that we have a solution to the Kony problem. That is what the ICC wants. No cover-up, no impunity."[23] In early January 2005, Executive Director James Otto of the Gulu-based Human Rights Focus urged the government to drop charges filed with the ICC against Kony,[24] and in mid-February the Catholic Church charged that the ICC's involvement was counterproductive. "Their officials seem to lack serious grasp of the fact that to start war crimes investigations at a time when the war is not yet over risks having, in the end, neither justice nor peace delivered."[25] In late February, as another cease-fire expired, the ICC came under continued criticism from local and international NGOs as well as Britain's ambassador to Uganda. Representatives from Christian Aid, Conciliation Resources, and Uganda's Concerned Parents Association, the Ugandan peace initiative Kacoke Madit ("big meeting" in Acholi), argued

[20] Huß, "Human Security Update: Northern Uganda" (2004), 5.

[21] ICC, "Prosecutor of the International Criminal Court Opens an Investigation into Nothern Uganda" (2004).

[22] Interviews.

[23] Quoted in *The New Vision*, "ICC May Drop LRA Charges" (2004).

[24] *The New Vision*, "Drop Kony ICC Case, Say NGOs" (2005).

[25] *The New Vision*, "ICC Threats Might Mar Peace Talks, Church Says" (2005).

that threats of arrest and prosecution undermined LRA inclinations to participate in peace talks. "The ICC has committed a terrible blunder," said Bryn Higgs, Uganda Program Development Officer for Conciliation Resources. "The irony is that the ICC is there for a humanitarian purpose, it wants to discourage terrible crimes with impunity, but instead it pushes the LRA back in the bush and this leads to a continuation of the atrocities." U.K. Ambassador Sir Emyr Jones Parry said, "This is about sequencing. First you need to put an end to the conflict and move into peace. After this comes justice and reconciliation."[26]

Speaking for the ICC, JCCD Legal Officer Darryl Robinson argued that the rate of defections from the LRA did not appear to have been slowed by ICC involvement, and he noted that, under the Statute, an investigation couldn't be suspended unless it could be shown to not be in the interests of justice.[27]

Aware of the beating it was taking from local commentators in Uganda, in March 2005, the ICC OTP brought Acholi representatives to ICC headquarters for consultations. Government supporters criticized the visit.[28] Local distrust of the LRA, of the ICC, and of the government's seriousness meant that the situation was very complicated. Intentionally or not, the ICC had become politically significant locally. In March, the OTP indicated that it would soon seek arrest warrants for Kony and some of his top commanders.[29]

On April 16, following another meeting at ICC headquarters, the ICC Chief Prosecutor and "the visiting Delegation of Lango, Acholi, Iteso and Madi Community Leaders from Northern Uganda" issued a statement noting that they had agreed to work together "to achieve justice and reconciliation, the rebuilding of communities and an end to violence," calling on "local communities, the Government of Uganda, national and international actors to join this common effort" and urging the LRA's members "to respond positively to the appeal to end violence." They sought the Sudanese government's cooperation with Uganda, the ICC, international actors, and "all stakeholders" in peace efforts, and they agreed "to continue to integrate the dialogue for peace, the ICC and traditional justice and reconciliation processes."[30]

---

[26] Volqvartz, "ICC under Fire over Uganda Probe" (2005).
[27] Ibid.
[28] *The New Vision*, "Acholi MPs Denounce for Hague Delegation" (2005).
[29] *The New Vision*, "Acholi Leaders to Meet ICC" (2005).
[30] ICC, "Joint Statement by ICC Chief Prosecutor and the Visiting Delegation of Lango, Acholi, Iteso and Madi Community Leaders from Northern Uganda" (2005).

According to a report on the meeting, Moreno Ocampo indicated some flexibility, saying he could "suspend planned prosecutions ... to enable peace moves to succeed."

"As soon as there is a solution to end the violence and if the prosecution is not serving the interest of justice, then my duty is to stop investigation and prosecution," he said. "I will stop but I will not close," he added. "Timing is possible but immunity is not possible .... The main interest of the victims now is their life," he said, not ruling out a resumption of prosecutions even in several years' time.[31]

It was an ambiguous statement that appeared designed to assuage peace organizations' concerns but veered close to endorsing a political role for the Court. Inside the ICC, concerns harking back to the internal debate over the OTP's operational rules were reinforced. Was the OTP proceeding according to legal standards or flirting with a political calculus?

Warrants and Politics

Inside the Court, the Prosecutor sought maximum maneuvering room for the timing of his announcements to allow him to pursue a broad interpretation of the interests of justice and the interests of victims. Having ventured into the minefield of political exigencies, his actions were open to criticism from both sides. Commentators partial to a human rights perspective, such as Human Rights Watch and Amnesty International, called for the immediate broad indictment of suspects on the basis of criminal law criteria. On the other side, humanitarian organizations seeking to ameliorate violence through peace negotiations believed that justice should await peace.

On May 6, 2005, the Office of the Prosecutor (under the rules of the Court, secretly) applied to Pre-Trial Chamber II for arrest warrants for five LRA leaders.[32] On July 8, the PTC decided that the warrants should be issued but kept under seal until further steps for victim and witness protection were taken, and permission for publication was issued by the Chamber. The Pre-Trial Chamber refused the Prosecutor's request that he be the one to communicate with the states, holding to the Statute's designation of the Registry as the appropriate channel of communications.[33] The warrants sought the arrest of top LRA leader Joseph Kony on twelve counts of crimes against humanity and twenty-one counts of war crimes, Kony's

---

[31] *The New Vision*, "Court Rules Out Kony Immunity" (2005).
[32] ICC, PTC II, "Decision on the Prosecution's Application for Warrants of Arrest Under Article 58" (2005).
[33] Ibid., 6–7.

second in command Vincent Otti for eleven counts of crimes against humanity and twenty-one counts of war crimes, and three other members of the top LRA command, Raska Lukwiya, Okot Odhiambo, and Dominic Ongwen.[34]

The PTC noted that under the Statute and rules issuance of warrants is to be justified "on the basis of circumstances and evidence existing at the time of the application, and is not dependant or conditional on future circumstances," thus showing its concern that the OTP might be using unstated and possibly political criteria in its decisions about when to publicize the warrants of arrest.[35]

From July until October 14, 2005, the warrants remained under seal. Teams from the Registry and OTP traveled repeatedly to Uganda to develop protection schemes for witnesses and victims. Meanwhile, the Prosecutor continued to seek control over announcement of the warrants, thwarted by the Pre-Trial Chamber's continued rejection of his arguments and denial of his request for leave to appeal.[36]

The way in which the warrants finally became public demonstrated that the ICC hadn't yet perfected the coordination of public announcements. During the week of September 26, William Swing, head of the UN mission in the DRC, told a closed session of the Security Council that the arrest warrants had been issued, and on October 6 he announced the warrants again at a press conference. On October 7, the Prosecutor called and then, due to PTC objections, canceled a press conference to announce the warrants, but a Ugandan official confirmed that they had been sent to Uganda, Sudan, and the DRC on September 27. Wrangling with the Pre-Trial Chamber continued over what parts of the warrants could be made public, while the Pre-Trial Chamber restricted publicity in the interests, it said, of victim and witness protection. On October 13, the Pre-Trial Chamber finally unsealed the warrants, and Moreno Ocampo held his delayed press conference. A longtime observer of the ICTY and ICTR commented, "The first steps on the road to a Uganda trial before the ICC have thus shown not so much an independent prosecutor as a prosecution under guardianship."[37]

[34] ICC, "Statement by the Chief Prosecutor on the Uganda Arrest Warrants" (2005).
On March 2, 2007, the Prosecutor subsequently requested that the PTC withdraw the warrant for Raska Lukwiya due to Lukwiya's death.
[35] Ibid., 7.
[36] ICC, PTC II, "Decision on Prosecutor's Application for Leave to Appeal in Part Pre-Trial Chamber II's Decision on the Prosecutor's Applications for Warrants of Arrest Under Article 58" (2005).
[37] Stuart, "Uganda: Reasons for a Bumpy Start" (2005).

Leverage or Blockage?

Once the warrants were issued, they appeared to help pressure the LRA leadership to sue for peace. Paradoxically, the warrants then also became a major impediment to reaching an accord between Uganda's government and the rebel organization. Betty Bigombe, the former Ugandan government minister who had been serving as an intermediary with the LRA, said that the warrants would end mediation efforts: "There is now no hope of getting them to surrender. I have told the court that they have rushed too much."[38]

The Sudanese government agreed to cooperate in efforts to apprehend the LRA suspects, and it appeared from subsequent news stories that new pressures on the LRA leaders forced them out of safe havens in Sudan. They were tracked around northern Uganda, into the DRC and Central African Republic, and they divided into several groups. They continued to be dangerous to both civilians and military forces, which they demonstrated by killing eight Guatemalan UN peacekeepers in an ambush in the eastern Congo in late January 2006.[39] Ugandan government spokesmen referred to the LRA as no longer a serious force, but continued military efforts by the Ugandan People's Defense Forces to defeat them failed. Humanitarian agencies continued to describe effects of the long-running conflict as among the most dire in the world.[40]

ICC proponents argued that the Court's involvement had positive results. Sudan agreed not to provide the LRA with safe havens[41] and permitted the UPDF to pursue the LRA into Sudanese territory. With the LRA's freedom of operations increasingly constrained, it lost any hope of victory. ICC involvement raised international awareness of the conflict [42] and prompted some lower-level LRA leaders to separate themselves from the indicted top leadership and to accept the amnesty offer.[43] Contrarily, a late March 2006 NGO report asserted that the ICC arrest warrants for LRA leaders had not appeared to improve the situation "and may indeed have jeopardised the security of civilians, sparking increases in LRA violence and attacks on humanitarian organizations."[44] As 2006 progressed, however, the situation began to change.

---

[38] *The New Vision*, "LRA Talks Over, Says Bigombe" (2005).
[39] *The New Vision*, "Kony Flees into Congo" (2006).
[40] Civil Society Organizations for Peace in Northern Uganda, "Counting the Cost: Twenty Years of War in Northern Uganda" (2006).
[41] Akhavan, "The Lord's Resistance Army Case," 416.
[42] Ibid., 420.
[43] Ibid., 417.
[44] Civil Society Organizations for Peace in Northern Uganda, op cit., 12.

Following amendment of the 2000 amnesty law to bring Ugandan law into conformity with obligations under the ICC Statute,[45] in April 2006, the Ugandan government announced that those individuals subject to ICC warrants would not be entitled to amnesty. Other rebel fighters could gain amnesty, and the government would still seek to negotiate the conflict's settlement. A Parliament member from Gulu, Regan Okumu, objected that the peace process would be disrupted by the new law. Human rights activist James Otto asserted that changing the amnesty law would be "to the detriment of the children still in [rebel] captivity."[46]

In May, President Museveni announced agreement with Sudanese authorities that if the LRA's Kony didn't respond positively to a government peace offer, Uganda and Sudan would jointly undertake to "handle him militarily."[47] At the same time, Museveni appeared to offer Kony a friendly inducement, again demonstrating his proclivity to use the Court for leverage, riding roughshod over the ICC's legal obligations. "The President said much as Kony and four of his cohorts had been indicted by the International Criminal Court, if he got serious about peaceful settlement, the Government of Uganda would guarantee him safety."[48]

Museveni's apparent promise of immunity from the ICC warrants evoked an immediate response from Chief Prosecutor Moreno Ocampo in a restrained but clear declaration that ICC procedures would not be held hostage to the President's negotiating tactics: "The governments of Uganda, Sudan and Democratic Republic of Congo are obligated to give effect to the arrest warrants, and we are confident they will honour their commitment to do so," he was reported as saying,[49] and Court spokesperson Sandra Khadouri said, "It's the government of Uganda that referred the situation to the International Criminal Court in December 2003 ... they are now under obligation and made a commitment."[50] With his statement, Chief Prosecutor Moreno Ocampo, who before the warrants were issued had asserted that the timing of prosecution activity was flexible, had hardened his position. " 'The defendants could challenge the admissibility of the arrest warrants,' Moreno Ocampo told journalists. 'But the prosecutor can do nothing. The case is in the hands of the judges.' "[51]

---

[45] IRIN, "LRA Leaders Not Entitled to Amnesty – Minister" (2006).
[46] Ibid.
[47] *The New Vision*, "Museveni Gives Joseph Kony Final Peace Offer" (2006).
[48] Ibid.
[49] BBC, "New Overture to Uganda's Rebels" (2006).
[50] Frank Nyakairu & Agencies, "International Criminal Court Opposes Museveni Peace Offer to Kony" (2006).
[51] Anderson, "World Court Faces Biggest Challenge" (2006).

While the Chief Prosecutor sought to demonstrate his lack of maneuverability, UN Undersecretary General for Humanitarian Affairs Jan Egeland said in September that he would report to Secretary-General Kofi Annan and to ICC Prosecutor Moreno Ocampo that "I have been told by the people that the ICC indictment is a stumbling block to the peace process. ... The predominant feeling among all the stakeholders in the peace process is that the ICC warrant of arrest should be dropped against the LRA leaders so that a peaceful conclusion to the talks can be reached."[52] In October 2006, contravening an August 26 cease-fire agreement with the government, the LRA leadership threatened to renew the war unless the ICC warrants were scrapped.[53]

President Museveni continued to issue confusing messages. In late October he declared that the ICC warrants should be upheld, but he seemed also to indicate that there were other possibilities. News reports quoted him as saying, " 'The ICC is actually very good for us (Uganda) because it makes the terrorists (rebels) come up to seek peace and end impunity. ICC was created to fight impunity.' " Holding out the possibility of later concessions, he reportedly continued:

"To ask the ICC to withdraw the warrant without any remedy is to condone impunity. ... Here is a terrorist you have not reconciled with and you throw away the stick? We need to first create a new situation then we can talk to the ICC. I'm told it can review it." The President said since it is Uganda that complained to the ICC, in case the rebels came out for peace, the government would tell the world court that "a new situation has arisen and the people have found an alternative method of conflict resolution."[54]

The August truce was extended on November 1,[55] and again in December when the Sudanese mediator, southern Sudan Vice President Reik Machar, announced that an LRA delegation would visit the ICC in The Hague to "plead for the lifting of the indictment the court placed on the top rebel commanders."[56] At the end of the month, Kony sent a message to Museveni, quoted in press reports saying, "The ICC should leave Uganda to handle the issue of accountability since Uganda has a functional justice system with jails in Luzira, Lugore etc."[57] It appeared that the LRA was becoming acquainted with the legal details of ICC admissibility criteria. The

[52] Matsiko et al., "Kony Charges a Stumbling Block, Says U.N. Chief" (2006).
[53] Kwera, "Uganda Violence" (2006).
[54] Muyita et al., "Museveni Insists on Kony ICC Arrests" (2006).
[55] *The New Vision*, "The New LRA-Uganda Truce" (2006).
[56] Mukasa, "LRA Truce Extended for 2 Months" (2006).
[57] IRIN, "IDPs Unlikely to Meet Deadline to Vacate Camps" (2006).

truce expired in February, was renewed in April and again at the end of May 2007. Peace advocates argued that local justice mechanisms could be engaged to bring the LRA fighters back into the Acholi community; however, some local and major international human rights groups argued that the proposed "traditional" form of reconciliation (called *matu oput*) would not fulfill international justice standards and was not appropriate for the kinds and scale of crimes with which the LRA leadership was charged.[58] LRA and local peace spokesmen continued to assert that the ICC warrants were the main sticking point preventing a peace agreement.[59]

The ICC warrants initially appear to have done just what Museveni sought – to promote regional cooperation between the Sudan, Congo, and Uganda to end the LRA's freedom of maneuver and to thereby raise the threat level against Kony and the LRA. The same cooperation should have made arrest of the LRA leaders possible, fulfilling Moreno Ocampo's objectives. But then, given Kony's demand that the warrants be lifted as a condition for peace, Museveni's and Moreno Ocampo's objectives appear to have diverged. How could the conflict be ended without violating the ICC's commitment to prosecute crimes under its Statute? Museveni's many maneuvers seemed to imply that some formula might be found whereby a domestic solution to countering impunity could be offered to ICC judges; who might then find proceeding with a Court trial to be against the interests of justice. The dilemma remained, however, that after the warrants were issued, such a finding could be made only after the suspects were arrested, turned over to the Court, and appeared before the Pre-Trial Chamber for confirmation of the charges. The Prosecutor, meanwhile, had seemed to turn from statements about his flexibility toward the shelter of a narrower understanding of his judicial responsibilities, leaving to the judges any decisions about whether the "interests of victims" or the "interests of justice" might be served in ways other than bringing the suspects to trial.

For the ICC, the Uganda referral appeared to be a great first opportunity. The conflict situation had produced massive casualties and civilian displacement, the alleged suspects were internationally reviled, and the friendly government's request for help avoided a clash with sovereign prerogatives. Once involved, however, the OTP discovered escalating complexities. The Prosecutor roused the suspicions of human rights groups when he appeared to focus on the LRA rather than crimes generally in northern Uganda,

[58] Human Rights Watch, "Benchmarks for Assessing Possible National Alternatives to International Criminal Court Cases Against LRA Leaders" (2007).
[59] Okeowo, "LRA and Ugandan Government Renew Truce" (2007).

including the government's UPDF. Making upholding the appearance of ICC neutrality even more difficult, President Museveni never seemed quite to grasp – or perhaps to respect – the Court's ultimate purpose of serving as an agent of international justice, as opposed to a source of leverage for his own machinations. Despite apparent popular northern Ugandan support for the idea of accountability, local peace groups increasingly accused the ICC of obstructing peace. The OTP responded with an increasingly vigorous outreach program, including bringing Ugandan NGO representatives to The Hague while the search went on for some way to reconcile the LRA leaders' quest to have the ICC warrants lifted with the Ugandan government's duty to implement its obligations under the ICC Statute. In its first situation, the Court continues to face the dilemmas of promoting peace to save civilian lives while seeking to uphold accountability during an ongoing conflict.

CONGO

On March 17, 2006, the ICC received its first suspect into custody when Thomas Lubanga Dyilo was transferred from the Democratic Republic of the Congo to the Court's prison facility in Scheveningen, outside The Hague; the case instantly became historic and subject to close international scrutiny. As the Court's processes slowly unfolded, the tensions deepened between the Pre-Trial Chamber and the Office of the Prosecutor, and NGOs became increasingly impatient with the slow pace and narrow scope of the case. Despite the cavils and disappointments, the case broke new ground even before it reached trial stage. Criteria for granting victim status even at early stages in the proceedings were developed in decisions of the Pre-Trial Chamber, and routines for sharing information between the prosecution and defense were worked out.

Conflict Background

According to a 2006 report in the medical journal *The Lancet*, civil and international conflict in the Democratic Republic of the Congo from 1996 claimed approximately four million lives.[60] (For comparison, the 2005 estimated population of the country was approximately sixty million people, so 7 percent of the country's population can be considered war casualties.)[61]

---

[60] Brennan et al., "Mortality in the Democratic Republic of Congo: A Nationwide Survey" (2006), 44–51.
[61] CIA, The World Fact Book online. Democratic Republic of Congo.

The human costs were produced by direct combat, large attacks against civilians, malnutrition, and the collapse of medical facilities and other secondary effects of the long-running conflict.

The war, one of the deadliest since World War II, swelled in part from the regional population movements and rivalries that boiled over from the 1994 genocide in Rwanda and in part from the disintegration of the regime of President Mobutu Sese Seko. As the Tutsi Rwandan Patriotic Front conquered Rwanda, ending the genocide, Rwandan Hutus, including Interahamwe genocidaires, fled into Zaire, where they were housed in huge refugee camps that themselves became centers of conflict and coercion. The inability of Mobutu's government to secure the region led the new Rwandan authorities to be very concerned about controlling violence that could spill back into Rwanda. In 1996, with Rwandan and Ugandan support, prominent Zairian opposition leader Laurent Kabila led a revolt and military takeover that toppled President Mobutu after more than thirty years of dictatorial rule. Kabila's forces captured the capital of Kinshasa on May 17, 1997, and Kabila renamed the country the Democratic Republic of the Congo. During the next two years, his Ugandan and Rwandan Tutsi supporters turned against him. Forces from surrounding countries entered into the conflict, all sides seeking to control the region's mineral wealth. Angola, Namibia, and Zimbabwe supported Kabila; Rwanda and Uganda supported antigovernment militias, including those led by Thomas Lubanga Dyilo and by future coalition government Vice President Jean-Pierre Bemba. While Lubanga resided in prison, Bemba was the leading opponent of Joseph Kabila in the DRC's 2006 presidential election, a role that some observers suspected might have prevented action against him by the ICC in connection with forces under his control in the Congo and in the Central African Republic.[62]

On July, 10, 1999, a cease-fire was signed in Lusaka, Zambia, by the six countries. By then, the anti-Kabila forces controlled most of the northeastern half of the country, and the cease-fire had little effect. At the end of September, UN Security Council Resolution 1279 created the United Nations Mission in the Democratic Republic of the Congo (MONUC) to enforce the agreement. In February 2000, the UN Security Council approved deployment of 5,537 peacekeepers to monitor the cease-fire.

Meanwhile, on January 17, 2001, Laurent Kabila was assassinated in a failed coup attempt, and his son Joseph emerged as President. Throughout the period, ethnic conflict was rampant in the northeast, most intensely in

---

[62] Penketh, "Extermination of the Pygmies" (2004); Kajee, "World Court Probes Ex-African Leader" (2006).

the Bunia and Ituri districts, where Rwandan- and Ugandan-supported militias operated. In December 2002, a peace agreement was signed among government, rebel, and opposition groups at Sun City, South Africa, establishing a power-sharing arrangement for a transitional government that then took office in July 2003. Although the general level of violence declined, serious local outbreaks continued as militias jockeyed for political position and control of mineral-rich areas.

Referral

The DRC government deposited its ratification of the ICC Statute along with nine other states on April 2002 whose joint action started the sixty-day clock ticking to bring the Statute into effect. In July 2003, the newly appointed Chief Prosecutor announced that, having studied the submissions, he would "closely follow the situation in the DRC," and in September he reported that he would be prepared to seek authorization from a Pre-Trial Chamber to start an investigation under his *proprio motu* powers but would prefer to work with the Congolese authorities.[63] Moreno Ocampo urged President Kabila to refer the DRC situation to the Court, and in April 2004, Kabila sent Moreno Ocampo a letter seeking ICC investigation of possible crimes within the jurisdiction of the Court committed anywhere in the territory of the DRC. The Uganda referral had come in January; now the ICC had its second situation.

Instrumentalization?

Like Museveni's, Kabila's decision to refer the DRC situation to the Court appears to have been motivated significantly by his own political calculations. He had entered politics after the assassination of his father in January 2001 and had little record until then of participation in the conflicts ravaging the country.[64] The ICC's temporal jurisdiction began on July 1, 2002, so only crimes committed after that date could come under its purview. Compared with other DRC political and military leaders, Kabila had little to fear from the Court.

His referral to the ICC apparently came about because he saw that he could gain from it both domestically and internationally. "The ICC was

---

[63] ICC, "Prosecutor Receives Referral of the Situation in the Democratic Republic of Congo" (2004).

[64] Burke-White, "Complementarity in Practice: The International Criminal Court as Part of a System of Multi-level Global Governance in the Democratic Republic of Congo" (2005), 565, citing Edgerton, *The Troubled Heart of Africa: A History of the Congo* (2002).

exploited right from the start. It suited Kabila as a weapon against his adversaries," said a lawyer from the region quoted anonymously in 2004.[65] The transitional government included vice presidents and ministers from a broad spectrum of political parties within the DRC, including former enemies in the conflict. Because of the others' reputations and records – and the continuing violence in the northeast after July 1, 2002 – ICC involvement threatened them. Their indictment would likely impair their political chances or even remove them from electoral contention, strengthening Kabila.

Because of the weakness of the Congolese judicial and police systems, Kabila could not be sure that the local justice system would operate effectively against his powerful adversaries, nor that the courts would be or appear impartial. The ICC could provide a surer route to trials. His willingness to engage international justice could improve his international standing particularly with the European Union and France, which had strongly encouraged him to accept ICC jurisdiction.[66]

The referral appears to have had some cautionary effect. In an interview in 2003, Thomas Lubanga Dyilo, head of the Union of Congolese Patriots (UPC), an Ituri-region political and (allegedly) militia organization, said that "the Court has been a pressure on the political actors who were killing people ... these people are very afraid today to commit such slaughter."[67] Another regional leader, Xavier Ciribanya, said, "Many here in the East are afraid the Court will come. ... We all now are thinking twice. We do not know what this Court can and will do."[68]

The referral also apparently affected internal Congolese political dynamics. Following the Prosecutor's announcement, some government officials launched reforms of the national judiciary and sought to establish a truth and reconciliation commission.[69] From the standpoint of the Prosecutor's office, however, the reforms did not firmly establish a basis on which to terminate investigations, particularly as Kabila's government continued to support the Court's involvement.

Cooperation

To carry out investigations, the OTP sought help from organizations on the ground in the area – the United Nations's peacekeeping force, MONUC,

---

[65] Cruvillier, "ICC Joins the Congolese Chess Game" (2004).
[66] William Burke-White, personal communication (3/21/06).
[67] Interview cited in Burke-White, op cit., 588.
[68] Ibid.
[69] Ibid., 570.

and local and regional NGOs. MONUC could help to provide ICC officials with transportation, communications, and security, but relations between MONUC and the ICC were not simple.

Traditional UN peacekeeping rests on the presumption of force neutrality. Once peacekeeping forces are perceived not to be neutral, they become potential targets of combatants who believe their interests threatened or damaged by the peacekeepers' actions. To the extent that the ICC seeks the arrest of leaders, it may be a threat to local political actors and to the impartiality of organizations that support its efforts. UN officials were concerned that should the ICC become identified with their peacekeeping efforts, peacekeepers' neutrality might be doubted. MONUC's initial mandate, established by the UNSC well before the ICC had come into existence, had not included the pursuit of international justice.[70]

When MONUC was reauthorized by the Security Council in October 2004, its mandate was expanded to include efforts to assist in countering impunity and bringing serious violators of human rights and international humanitarian law to justice.[71] Presumably out of deference to U.S. opposition to the Court, the new mandate language did not mention the ICC at all, but it could be used by the UN and MONUC to justify their interactions

---

[70] The MONUC mandate under Security Council Resolution 1291 (2000) of February 24, 2000, focused on the cease-fire, disengagement, monitoring of forces, control of military supplies, aid in humanitarian measures, *"with particular attention to vulnerable groups including women, children and demobilized child soldiers"* [emphasis added], in close cooperation with other United Nations agencies, related organizations, and nongovernmental organizations; it was to cooperate closely with the facilitator of the national dialogue, help with de-mining, and protect its own and related UN forces and personnel.

[71] Under Resolution 1565 (2004) of October 1, 2004, the Security Council revised the mandate and increased MONUC's force level to 17,175. New aspects of the mandate were to establish links with the UN Operation in Burundi (ONUB) and with the governments of the DRC and Burundi, to coordinate monitoring efforts and discourage cross-border movements of combatants between the two countries, and to monitor the arms flow on the lakes, inspect aircraft, and other transport vehicle cargoes in the ports, airports, airfields, military bases, and border crossings in North and South Kivu and Ituri.

The Security Council extended the mandate to support the DRC Government of National Unity and Transition, declared its intention to support security efforts and help provide security for government-affiliated institutions and officials in Kinshasa until the Kinshasa police could take over, help Congolese authorities to maintain order in other strategic areas, support completion of the electoral process, and "assist in the promotion and protection of human rights, with particular attention to women, children and vulnerable persons, investigate human rights violations to put an end to impunity, and continue to cooperate with efforts to ensure that those responsible for serious violations of human rights and international humanitarian law are brought to justice, while working closely with the relevant agencies of the United Nations."

with the Court. The ICC undertook extensive communication and negotiation with MONUC, and although official agreements were rarely cited by officials, a working relationship developed on the ground whereby MONUC did assist the ICC in establishing security, communications, and transport for ICC personnel.[72]

At the same time, OTP and Registry personnel connected with NGO intermediaries to contact potential witnesses to help in the investigation and to carry the Court's messages to victims. The NGOs were also crucial in publicizing to victims, witnesses, and the general population what the ICC was doing and that it was a constructive and trustworthy new arrival in the area.

The Court's Internal Tensions

In June 2004, the Chief Prosecutor announced that the OTP was formally opening investigations into the DRC. In July, Court President Philippe Kirsch assigned the DRC situation to Pre-Trial Chamber I, made up of judges Claude Jorda, Akua Kuenyehia, and Sylvia Steiner, with Jorda presiding. On July 26, the Court announced:

The International Criminal Court will pay its first official visit to the Democratic Republic of Congo from 26 July to 30 July 2004. Officials of the Office of the Prosecutor and the Registry will hold closed meetings with representatives of the national authorities, civil society, and international organisations present in the country. The aim of the visit is to evaluate the possibilities for future cooperation.[73]

Once the investigation became official, the PTC had a combination of responsibilities toward suspects, victims, and witnesses and possibly for general oversight that remained to be defined in operation. The OTP sought to maximize its independence and autonomy in pursuit of its investigative strategy, dealing with victims and witnesses, and establishment of the range of its discretion leading up to presenting a case in court. The Pre-Trial Chamber didn't await communications from the OTP but sought to prod the Prosecutor; push for streamlined cases; protect defendants, victims, and witnesses; and stretch the boundaries of its oversight of the OTP. Their exchanges became rather testy.

On October 15, 2004, PTC I invited the prosecution to an "informal meeting." The meeting was held on November 9, but the Prosecutor insisted that the meeting be recorded and transcribed in order that the record be

---

[72] Interviews.
[73] ICC, "The International Criminal Court to Send Its First Official Visit to the Democratic Republic of Congo" (2004).

available for later defense or appeals purposes. At the meeting, the PTC requested a copy of the agreement between the OTP and the Congolese authorities and President Kabila's letter of referral, but the Prosecutor objected that these were outside of the judges' authority and raised confidentiality problems, and refused to turn them over. Thereafter, the discussions between the OTP and PTC were carried out in formal meetings and documents. Advocates of inquisitorial (civil-law), judicially led procedures view the adamancy of the PTC as improving the balance between it and the OTP; [74] adversarial (common-law), prosecution-oriented observers worry that the OTP's freedom of action is being overly constrained.[75]

On February 15, 2005, the PTC issued a decision informing the Prosecutor that it was calling a "status conference" for March 15, 2005, because communications to the PTC from the OTP during and following the informal meeting indicated to the PTC that matters needed to be considered that would enable the PTC "to provide, *inter alia*, for the protection of victims and witnesses and the preservation of evidence through the holding of a status conference."[76]

On March 8, the OTP responded, arguing that the PTC was acting beyond its mandate in "deciding" to call a status conference without first apprising the OTP that it was considering such an action and that the OTP should have the opportunity to "present arguments on the Chamber's authority to convene a status conference during an investigation, a matter that raises fundamental issues of high institutional importance."[77] The Prosecutor argued that the Statute, Rules of Procedure and Evidence (RPE), and the regulations of the Court "do not provide any support for a status conference to be convened during an investigation," that, procedurally, such a conference could raise concerns about the PTC's appearance of impartiality and, that substantively, the information so far supplied to the PTC did not support the PTC's conclusion that a status conference was necessary for the purposes of protecting victims and witnesses or providing the preservation of evidence. The next day, the PTC rejected the OTP's arguments and reaffirmed the date of the status conference.[78]

---

[74] Miraglia, "The First Decision of the ICC Pre-Trial Chamber: International Criminal Procedure Under Construction" (2006).
[75] Interviews.
[76] ICC, PTC I, "Decision to Convene a Status Conference" (2005).
[77] ICC, PTC I, "Prosecutor's Position on Pre-Trial Chamber I's 17 February 2005 Decision to Convene a Status Conference" (2005).
[78] ICC, PTC I, "Decision on the Prosecutor's Position on Pre-Trial Chamber I's 17 February 2005 Decision to Convene a Status Conference" (2005).

This peevish exchange showed the Prosecutor striving to reduce the PTC's oversight of his investigation process, and the PTC seeking to take an active role at an early stage in Court procedures, justifying this by its statutory responsibility to protect the rights of possible suspects, victims, and witnesses. The Prosecutor's office tried again, filing on March 11 for "leave to appeal" the rejection of its request to meet on the matter of the status conference. On March 14 the PTC rejected the request on the grounds that the OTP had not shown that the matter was significant from the standpoint of the fairness or expeditious conduct of the proceedings or the outcome of the trial,[79] and the status conference was held on March 15 as scheduled.

On May 26, 2005, the PTC received applications filed on behalf of six victims of the Congo conflict with the assistance of the International Federation of Human Rights Leagues. A series of hearings took place regarding requests for anonymity and other protective measures in which the PTC decided, apparently with some contestation by the ad hoc counsel for the defense, to supply records to the OTP but not to the defense that included identifying information about the victims.

From May 2005 until January 17, 2006, the PTC considered the application for victim representation. For the PTC, the central questions were whether the Statute, RPE, and regulations of the Court "accord victims the right to participate in the proceedings at the stage of investigation of a situation and, if so, what form such participation should take." It was also up to the PTC to decide whether the applying six people could actually be considered victims under RPE Rule 85.[80] The OTP challenged the applications on the grounds that, first, investigations were not "proceedings" within the meaning of the relevant Statute article[81] since "investigations" appeared under the "Trial" section of the Statute; second, that participation of victims at the investigation stage would be inappropriate; and third, that the applicants hadn't shown that their personal interests were affected at the investigation stage.[82] The PTC was seeking to define its role as protector of victims and witnesses from the earliest stages of the Court's activities in a situation, while the OTP strove to preserve its freedom to conduct its investigation – and relations with potential witnesses – as it saw fit.

[79] ICC, PTC I, "Decision on the Prosecutor's Application for Leave to Appeal" (2005).
[80] ICC, PTC I, "Public Redacted Version, Decision on the Applications for Participation in the Proceedings of VPRS 1, VPRS2, VPRS3, VPRS4, VPRS5, and VPRS6" (2006), 7.
[81] Rome Statute Article 68(3).
[82] ICC, PTC I, "Public Redacted Version," op cit., 8.

The PTC rejected the OTP's arguments, finding that the word "proceedings" in the Statute could refer to any activities of the Court. Further, there was no inherent reason why victims wouldn't have an interest already at the investigation stage. In addition, it found that at the Statute Conference and in international law in general, there was clear sentiment to include victims directly in such processes as shown by precedents set by the European Court of Human Rights and the Inter-American Court of Human Rights. The PTC also found that the applicants had, according to information they provided, suffered from crimes under the jurisdiction of the ICC within the DRC situation, including the murder of spouses and other family members, loss of property and houses, severe harm as a consequence of a victim's abduction and enslavement, torture, lasting physical suffering, and emotional suffering.

Once again, the Prosecutor requested leave to appeal the PTC's decision,[83] challenging the idea that there could be "situation victims," as opposed to victims affected personally by a 'case' and the accused of such a case. The Prosecutor was concerned that such a wide interpretation of the Statute would imply that anyone who had been victimized in the course of crimes under the Statute's definitions since the Court came into existence could be considered a victim, thus leading potentially to thousands of people seeking to "participate" even before a particular case or suspect had been identified. "Given the massive scale of alleged criminality in the DRC, this ruling could result in tens of thousands, or hundreds of thousands of individuals, having the right to participate in the investigation stage."[84] The OTP was also concerned that, by approving people as victims, the PTC was prematurely concluding, "without any application by the Prosecution for an arrest warrant or request for confirmation of charges, that crimes within the Court's jurisdiction had likely occurred, seemingly a usurpation of the OTP's leading role in specifying a case."[85] There were back-and-forth filings from the victims' representative and the OTP on leave for permission to appeal,[86] and then the PTC found in favor of according victim status to the

---

[83] ICC, OTP, "Prosecution's Application to Leave to Appeal Pre-Trial Chamber I's Decision on the Applications for Participation in the Proceedings of VPRS 1, VPRS 2, VPRS 3, VPRS 4, VPRS 5 and VPRS 6" (2006).

[84] Ibid., 2.

[85] Ibid.

[86] ICC, PTC I, "Observations of the Legal Representative of VPRS 1 to VPRS 6 Following the Prosecution's Application for Leave to Appeal Pre-Trial Chamber I's Decision on the Applications for Participation in the Proceedings of VPRS 1 to VPRS 6" (2006); ICC, PTC I, "Prosecutor's Reply to 'Observations of the Legal Representative of VPRS 1 to VPRS 6'" (2006).

applicants at the investigation stage of the proceedings, rejecting essentially all of the OTP's arguments.

In February, while considering the OTP's application for a warrant, the PTC still sought to steer the OTP's investigation. A colloquy during the February 3, 2006, PTC hearing on the OTP's request illuminated the senses of duty felt by both sides. PTC judge Jorda asked:

Where is the office of the Prosecutor heading? We are at the beginning of these proceedings and this is a very central issue. Do you intend to prosecute individuals with national-level responsibilities? Or do you intend to limit your action to individuals who are leaders of militias? As you have said in your own submissions, there are many militias. It is an inter-ethnic conflict .... So there is a risk that your Prosecutions and investigations may become – your efforts may become rather diffuse, and result in many requests for arrest warrants from this Chamber. I think it is important that we gain further clarity on this issue at this stage.[87]

Prosecution senior trial lawyer Ekkehard Withopf responded that the mid- and long-term intentions of the prosecution "do not form part of the decision-making process of this Pre-Trial Chamber in respect to the application." He went on to explain, however, the importance of Lubanga's UPC, its armed wing the Patriotic Front for the Liberation of the Congo (FPLC), and the OTP's conviction that this armed group was "responsible for the gravest grimes committed in Ituri." He noted that the OTP was investigating other crimes of other armed groups in the region. Judge Jorda thanked Withopf, asserting that "all international courts face this issue [the course of the prosecution's investigations]," but granting that "it is no direct concern of mine. The Office may do what it wants."[88] The application was successful, the warrant was issued, and the PTC seemed to recognize some limits to its oversight of the prosecution's operations.

As in the case of the Uganda warrants, the OTP sought to control the contacts with the DRC, rather than working through the Registry, but the PTC rejected the request, confirming that, as stipulated in the Statute, communications with the government on the practicalities of the warrant were the duty of the Registrar. The Chief Prosecutor and the Registrar, according to some Court employees, were not on speaking terms.[89]

---

[87] ICC, PTC I, "Redacted Version of the Transcripts of the Hearing Held on 2 February 2006 and Certain Materials Presented During that Hearing"(2006), 32.

[88] Ibid., 29–30.

[89] Interviews.

Lubanga: War Criminal, Target of Opportunity, Harbinger?

From eastern Congo, Thomas Lubanga Dyilo came to Kinshasa, the DRC's capital, in August 2003 to participate in peace talks, but he continued to reside there, according to media reports, "under virtual house arrest." Nonetheless, he claimed that he was in control of his FPLC forces.[90] On March 11, 2005, by order of President Kabila, he was placed under formal house arrest in the Grand Hotel in Kinshasa along with three other warlords on charges of genocide and crimes against humanity under the DRC military code. He was also accused by the United Nations of having masterminded the murder of nine Bangladeshi MONUC peacekeepers killed in an ambush in the Ituri district on February 25. On March 29, the DRC authorities issued another arrest warrant against Lubanga, alleging crimes of murder, illegal detention, and torture.[91] Lubanga was already notorious, according to Human Rights Watch, for having commanded Hema (tribe) militias of the UPC to carry out atrocities.

In the rich gold town of Mongbwalu and surrounding villages they slaughtered some 800 civilians in 2002 and 2003, mostly targeting those who were Lendu. After their battles, the UPC militia carried out house-to-house searches looking for Lendu civilians to arrest, torture, and then execute. In one massacre in the town of Kilo, Hema militiamen killed their Lendu victims – including women and children – by hitting them over the head with a sledgehammer.[92]

HRW applauded the arrests but chastised President Kabila for appearing to value the Bangladeshi peacekeepers' lives more than those of Ituri civilians, urging him immediately to "order the arrest and investigation of all the armed group leaders implicated in killing civilians sitting at the Grand Hotel in Kinshasa, not just the ones who may have killed U.N. peacekeepers."[93]

As Tadic's incarceration in Germany had offered an opportunity to the ICTY, so Lubanga's being in jail in Kinshasa presented the ICC OTP an opportunity to avoid the problems associated with organizing the arrest of a suspect. Even if the transfer was opportunistic, however, the Prosecutor argued that it was compelled by events. Under DRC law, Lubanga could be

---

[90] Anderson, "ICC Enters Uncharted Territory" (2006).
[91] ICC, Pre-Trial Chamber I, "Decision Concerning Pre-Trial Chamber I's Decision of 10 February 2006 and the Incorporation of Documents into the Record of the Case against Mr. Thomas Lubanga Dyilo" (2006), para. 33.
[92] Woudenberg, "Arrest All Ituri Warlords" Le Potentiel (2005).
[93] Ibid.

held for up to a year with month-to-month renewals of the detention by order of the regional DRC prosecutor's office. After the year (which would have ended in mid-March 2006), however, the case would need to be reviewed and renewed by a judge. The ICC Prosecutor feared that Lubanga would be released because the DRC authorities had not compiled a record that would justify continued detention. Moreno Ocampo argued to the Pre-Trial Chamber that the file on Lubanga in the Congo was "literally empty," asserting that "any judge who has to decide on the extension of detention ... will have a very difficult time ... knowing that there is no investigation being done,"[94] and on January 13, 2006, requested that the PTC issue an arrest warrant for Lubanga.[95] The PTC examined the OTP's application in order to determine whether indeed the case conformed to the ICC's criteria that the judicial system appeared unable or unwilling to prosecute crimes under the jurisdiction of the Court, that the case was of sufficient gravity, and that the suspect a "most responsible" leader of large-scale crimes.

Because of what it called "certain changes" in the DRC national judicial system since the time of the original referral, particularly in Ituri, the PTC viewed skeptically the OTP's argument that the case was admissible on the grounds that the DRC justice system was inadequate to provide appropriate judicial measures for the crimes under the Statute.[96] However, the PTC accepted the OTP's argument that the DRC warrants contained no references to child conscription and thus were not acting on the "specific case before the court."[97]

The PTC also analyzed the admissibility of the case from the standpoint of its "sufficient gravity."[98] It agreed that prosecuting Lubanga would contribute to the deterrent mission of the ICC. The arrest warrant was issued, conveyed by the Registrar to the DRC, and Lubanga was flown out of Kinshasa on a French military aircraft. He arrived on Friday, March 17, 2006, the day before former Yugoslav President Slobodan Milosevic was laid to rest in his home town following his death from a heart attack a week

---

[94] ICC, PTC I, "Redacted Version of the Transcripts of the Hearing Held on 2 February 2006," op cit., 35.

[95] ICC, PTC I, "Warrant of Arrest" (2006).

[96] ICC, PTC I, "Decision Concerning Pre-Trial Chamber I's Decision of 10 February 2006 and the Incorporation of Documents into the Record of the Case against Mr. Thomas Lubanga Dyilo, Annex I: Decision on the Prosecutor's Application for a Warrant of Arrest, Article 58"(2006), para. 36.

[97] Ibid., para. 38–9.

[98] Ibid., para. 64–75.

before in his ICTY jail cell in The Hague. A new chapter in international criminal prosecutions began just as an old one ended.

Lubanga was brought to the ICC on charges of enlisting, conscripting, and using children younger than age fifteen in his army.[99] Upon Lubanga's arrival at The Hague, Moreno Ocampo stressed that this was only a first step:

This is important, it's a sequence. We will investigate crimes committed by other militias and other persons – this is the first case, not the last.

We are totally committed to staying in Congo – to make sure justice is done. ... Our investigation is our contribution to building a stable democracy in Congo.

As I have said, this is only the beginning. I am committed to continuing to work for the people in Ituri and in Congo as a whole. This arrest is a step forward in realizing the Rome Statute vision – to end impunity and atrocities all over the world.

For 100 years, a permanent international criminal court was a dream – this dream is becoming a reality.[100]

A warrant for a second suspect was apparently requested by the OTP later in 2006 but rejected by the PTC on grounds allegedly having to do with the inadequate level of responsibility of the suspect. The rejection was appealed by the OTP, but no public traces of the matter appeared by the middle of 2007.[101]

Moving Toward Trial: Victim Participation, Scope of Charges, Defense

Thomas Lubanga appeared before the Pre-Trial Chamber in open court for the first time on March 22, 2006, where he confirmed his identity, acknowledged the charges against him, and received a court-appointed defense attorney, Belgian Jean Flamme. The next step in the Court's procedures called for a "confirmation hearing" before the PTC, for arguments between prosecution and defense over whether there was sufficient reason to proceed to the trial phase. More new machinery had to be developed and engaged, as the prosecution, Registry, and defense, working directly with each other and through the Pre-Trial Chamber, developed routines for the disclosure of information to the defense while still seeking to protect victim

---

[99] War crimes under either Statute Article 8(2)(e)(vii) (for a noninternational conflict) or Article 8(2)(b)(xxvi) (an international conflict), Ibid., para. 25.

[100] ICC, Statement by Luis Moreno Ocampo to the Press Conference in Relation with the Surrender to the Court of Mr. Thomas Lubanga Dyilo (2006).

[101] Interviews.

and witness identities. The OTP and defense filed repeated motions for PTC resolution over the content and nature of document "redactions," while the defense and OTP collaborated to smooth the information flow and reduce Registry participation in the document exchanges. The Registry had argued that all documents should be transmitted through it from prosecution to defense; however, the prosecution and defense argued that this would unreasonably delay the process, and that the Registry had no reason to have custody of substantive information. The PTC resolved the issue by permitting direct transfer of the information, with notification to the PTC and Registry of each transfer, so that the Registry could keep a log of all materials.

With support from NGOs, and then the appointment by the PTC of counsel to represent victims, additional claimants to victim status and participation in the process were filed with the Court, and this prompted a second long series of hearings and filings, as each victim's status was to be adjudicated by the PTC.

The original date for the confirmation hearing was set for June 23, but it was postponed by the PTC in order to allow sufficient time for the defense to acquire and study the materials being transferred to it from the prosecution. On June 28, the OTP informed the PTC that due to problems with the security situation in Ituri, further investigations into the case were being suspended, and thus the planned September confirmation hearing would be limited to charges against Lubanga for enlisting, conscripting, and using children as soldiers.

Concerned that the charges against Lubanga were too narrow, on July 31, Human Rights Watch and seven other NGOs issued a "joint letter" to the Chief Prosecutor: "We are disappointed that two years of investigation by your office in the DRC has not yielded a broader range of charges against Mr. Lubanga."[102] The NGOs argued that the narrow charges threatened to reduce the possibility of appropriate victim representation, since victims of other crimes would not be directly connected to the case, and that the suffering of victims of other crimes would not be validated or exposed. They hoped that additional suspected perpetrators would be brought to court. The NGO Women's Initiative for Gender Justice meanwhile filed a request

---

[102] Human Rights Watch, "D.R. Congo: ICC Charges Raise Concern: Joint Letter to the Chief Prosecutor of the International Criminal Court" (2006). The other NGO signatories were Avocats Sans Frontières, Center for Justice and Reconciliation, Coalition Nationale pour la Cour Pénale Internationale – RCD (the CICC chapter in the DRC), Fédération Internationale des Ligues des Droits de l'Homme (FIDH), International Center for Transitional Justice, Redress, and Women's Initiative for Gender Justice.

to participate in the case as an *amicus curiae* ("friend of the court"), a request that the OTP and defense both opposed.

Local NGOs were reportedly angry and disappointed about the progress of the case. " 'There is too much amateur work at the office of the prosecutor. It's not that the charges don't exist; it's that the prosecutor has done mediocre work ... and we in Ituri will be the ones to pay the price.' "[103] According to a report from Bunia, eastern Congo, a lawyer there said, "Investigating cases of child soldiers in Ituri is like picking a ripe mango that fell at your feet. It could not be any easier."[104]

Confirmation hearings for the Lubanga case finally took place November 9–28, 2006, and on January 29, 2007, the Pre-Trial Chamber decided to send the case to the Trial Chamber.[105] The prosecution contended that Lubanga had overall responsibility for his armed organization that recruited and used child soldiers, and that he was aware of the practice. The defense portrayed the prosecution case as being based on a misunderstanding of Lubanga's role, presence, and activities in eastern Congo. Movement toward trial was delayed when Jean Flamme, Lubanga's defense attorney, resigned from the case, and a replacement had to be found, assigned, and begin work. The Presidency established Trial Chamber I and assigned the Lubanga case to it, but in light of a request from Lubanga's temporary counsel, the transmission of the records of the pretrial phase to the Trial Chamber were suspended until a new defense counsel was appointed and could become familiar with the case.[106] Requests to the PTC for permission to appeal various aspects of the charges against Lubanga filed by both Flamme and the Office of the Prosecutor were denied by the PTC on May 24.[107] As events unfolded in summer 2007, the case appeared to be on track to come before the Trial Chamber sometime in early 2008.

The fifth Assembly of States Parties convened in The Hague while the confirmation hearings were still taking place in the fall of 2006. In accord with his previous statement about proceeding "sequentially," Chief Prosecutor Moreno Ocampo reported to the ASP that a second investigation was under-way in the Congo and that the OTP was considering opening a third.

[103] Anonymous quote, in Petit, "Minimalist Investigation in Lubanga's Case" (2006), 1.
[104] Ibid.
[105] ICC, PTC I, "Decision on the Confirmation of Charges" (2007).
[106] ICC, The Presidency, "Decision Constituting Trial Chamber I and Referring to It the Case of The Prosecutor v Thomas Lubanga Dyilo" (2007).
[107] ICC, Pre-Trial Chamber I, "Decision on the Prosecution and Defence Applications for Leave to Appeal the Decision on the Confirmation of Charges" (2007).

He said that his office expected to seek arrest warrants in the second case during the first half of 2007.[108]

With its first suspect in custody, the ICC's judicial operations ground forward, developing information-sharing routines, screening methods for victims seeking representation at the Court, and establishing that victims could participate even before charges had been confirmed. The ICC OTP's intention to avoid what observers considered the overly broad charges that had been pressed by the ICTY and ICTR resulted in a case focused on the recruitment and use of child soldiers in Ituri, a charge that NGO commentators found significant but too narrow. Even with the PTC's intention to limit the length of court proceedings, the pretrial phase lasted for approximately a year, and it appeared that the actual trial would perhaps begin, but likely not end, within the eighteen-month period that Judge Jorda had long before indicated was his target for the maximum duration of court proceedings (see Chapter 4). The Prosecutor's intention to proceed sequentially meant that major suspects in the DRC had not been publicly named at all by the time that the first trial proceedings were to begin in the Lubanga case, leading to impatience on the part of NGO observers.

On October 18, 2007, the ICC announced that, pursuant to an arrest warrant requested on June 25 by the Presecutor and issued secretly by the PTC on July 2, Congolese authorities turned Mr. Germain Katanga over to the Court on October 17 for crimes associated with an attack on the Ituri village of Bogoro on February 24, 2003.[109] Katanga was the alleged commander of the Force de Résistance Patriotique en Ituri (FRPI), a militia that, according to HRW, had "helped lead one of the largest massacres in Ituri, that at Nyakunde Hospital in September 2002," and at other massacres in various locations in 2002 and 2003.[110] While hailing Katanga's transfer to the ICC, Human Rights Watch and the International Crises Group nonetheless called upon the OTP to pursue higher government officials whose complicity allegedly would have been required for violence and arms supplies to have continued untrammeled in the Ituri

[108] ICC, Luis Moreno-Ocampo, "Opening Remarks" to the Fifth Session of the Assembly of States Parties (2006).

[109] ICC, Pre-Trial Chamber I, "Urgent Warrant of Arrest for Germain Katanga," ICC-01/04-01/07-1-US-tENG (September 27, 2007).

[110] Human Rights Watch, "D.R. Congo: Army Should Not Appoint War Criminals: Congolese Government Must Investigate and Prosecute Warlords, Not Reward Them"(2005); "ICC/DRC: Second War Crimes Suspect to Face Justice in The Hague: Investigation Should Expand to Include Senior Officials in the Region" (2007).

region.[111] Chief Prosecutor Moreno Ocampo indicated that the DRC investigations were continuing, focused on a third case.[112]

SUDAN

On March 31, 2005, the United Nations Security Council referred the Darfur, Sudan, situation to the International Criminal Court.[113] For the Court, it was a momentous event. The referral had been unimaginable only a few months before, given U.S. opposition and the lukewarm attitudes of Security Council members China and Russia. For the ICC, this unexpected Security Council referral was a boon and a threat – a boon because it showed that the Court could be an asset to the Security Council; a threat because without Sudanese cooperation and vigorous assistance from other countries, the ICC faced major difficulties in implementing an investigative strategy and apprehending suspects.

Four aspects of the ICC's involvement with Sudan are particularly salient – the significance of the Security Council Resolution for the Court; the scope of the ICC's operational capabilities in situations of state non-cooperation; the continued friction between the Pre-Trial Chamber and the Prosecutor; and efforts to use the Court to pressure the government, whose officials were suspected of committing crimes, even as the ICC sought the government's cooperation in investigating those same crimes.

Conflict Background

Long-standing feuds in the western Sudan region over resources, political representation, and economic development boiled into military confrontations in late 2002 and spring 2003, as two primarily Nilotic, African-tribal-based groups, the Sudan Liberation Movement/Army (SLM/A) and Justice and Equality Movement (JEM), attacked local installations and personnel of the ethnic Arab Khartoum government which the Nilotic Sudanese held responsible for Darfur's marginalization. Still extracting itself from a twenty-year war in the south, the government was slow to react, and then called upon Arab tribes to fight the rebels. To its summons came the mostly

---

[111] Bibas, Chicon, and Petit, "Germain Katanga, Second Congolese Transfer to the ICC" (2007), 1.
[112] UN News Center, "Congolese War Crimes Suspect Turned over to International Criminal Court" (2007).
[113] UN Security Council, Resolution 1593 (2005).

nomadic local Arabs who, under the effects of long-term drought, were seeking land on which to settle.[114]

The government paid Arab tribal leaders with grants and gifts based on how many soldiers they provided. Africans who volunteered were apparently turned away as the government selectively enlisted tribes it felt would remain loyal, including people from neighboring Chad, Libya, and other states.[115] These recruits became the forces identified by locals and outsiders as the "Janjaweed," a term long used in Darfur to describe armed horse- or camel-mounted bandits.

Several rounds of mediated talks were convened beginning in August 2003, but by the end of the year, Human Rights Watch estimated that 600,000 civilians had been displaced and needed assistance, hundreds of villages had been burned down, and 70,000 refugees had fled to Chad from attacks mostly perpetrated by the Janjaweed.[116]

While the Darfur situation was deteriorating, a long-running war between northern and southern Sudan was ending. In 2004, after more than two decades of fighting, under pressure from an international community motivated by humanitarian concern and growing interest in oil discoveries,[117] the Comprehensive Peace Agreement (CPA) between the (southern) Sudan People's Liberation Army and the Khartoum government established a shaky peace and the prospect of a coalition government in which the SPLA's long-time leader, John Garang, became a vice president of Sudan. The cessation of combat in the south allowed the government to shift additional attention to the Darfur region, and violence escalated as army and air attacks were coordinated with the Janjaweed.[118] The UN Security

[114] UN Secretary-General, "Report of the International Commission of Inquiry on Darfur to the United Nations Secretary-General" (2005), 24. For background on the conflict, see Prunier, *Darfur: The Ambiguous Genocide* (2007).

[115] UN Secretary-General, "Report of the International Commission of Inquiry on Darfur," op. cit., 24.

[116] Human Rights Watch, Annual Report, January 2004, "Summary of Situation in Darfur."

[117] Lado, "The Political Economy of Oil Discovery and Mining in the Sudan: Constraints and Prospects on Development." Discoveries of oil in the south beginning in 1980 contributed to the north's interest in controlling the region and to outsiders' desire that the conflict be settled. Further discoveries in the 1990s and construction of oil pipelines added to Canadian, U.S., Chinese, and Malaysian companies' pressure on their governments to help resolve the conflict. In 2005, oil was discovered in the Darfur region as well. Gidley, "Oil Discovery Adds New Twist to Darfur Tragedy" (2005). See also Reeves, *A Long Day's Dying: Critical Moments in the Darfur Genocide* (2007), 138–9, 283–4.

[118] UN High Commissioner for Human Rights, Report of the United Nations High Commissioner for Human Rights and Follow-Up to the World Conference on Human Rights: Situation of Human Rights in the Darfur Region of the Sudan (2004), para. 6.

Council, in a "presidential statement" in April 2004, expressed its "deep concern about the massive humanitarian crisis" in Darfur.[119] In June, the Security Council condemned "all acts of violence and violations of human rights and international humanitarian law by all parties,"[120] and in its July Resolution 1556 (2004), under Chapter VII of the UN Charter, the Security Council again condemned the violence, declaring the Darfur conflict a threat to international peace and security.[121]

Meanwhile, in June, the U.S. Department of State commissioned a study of Sudanese refugees in Chad, which was completed in August[122] and repackaged for public presentation.[123] On September 9, Secretary of State Colin Powell testified to the Senate Foreign Relations Committee, "When we reviewed the evidence compiled by our team, along with other information available to the State Department, we concluded that genocide has been committed in Darfur and that the Government of Sudan and the jinjaweid [sic] bear responsibility – and genocide may still be occurring."[124]

At Powell's urging, the Security Council sought a full report from the Secretary-General.[125] The Secretary-General appointed Italian judge and Professor of International Law Antonio Cassese to head the commission. Cassese had been the first President of the ICTY and is an authority on the International Criminal Court. His Commission of Inquiry delivered its 176-page report[126] on January 25, 2005. It estimated that there were 1.65 million civilian displaced persons in the Darfur region and another 200,000 across the border in Chad, "largescale destruction of villages throughout the three states of Darfur," and that

the Government of the Sudan and the Janjaweed are responsible for serious violations of international human rights and humanitarian law amounting to crimes under international law. In particular, the Commission found that the Government forces and militias conducted indiscriminate attacks, including killing of civilians, torture, enforced disappearances, destruction of villages, rape and other forms of sexual violence, pillaging and forced displacement throughout Darfur. These acts

---

[119] UN Security Council, Press Statement on Darfur, Sudan, by Security Council President (2004).
[120] UN Security Council, Resolution 1547 (2004).
[121] UN Security Council, Resolution 1556 (2004).
[122] Goldberg, "Khartoum Characters" (2005).
[123] U.S. Department of State,"Documenting Atrocities in Darfur" (2004).
[124] U.S. Department of State, "Powell Reports Sudan Responsible for Genocide in Darfur" (2004).
[125] UN Security Council, Resolution 1564 (2004).
[126] Secretary-General, "Report of the International Commission of Inquiry on Darfur," op cit.

were conducted on a widespread and systematic basis, and therefore may amount to crimes against humanity.[127]

In contrast to the government's claims that its actions were for counterinsurgency purposes, the commission stated that it found most attacks were "deliberately and indiscriminately directed against civilians." The rebel forces were also responsible for serious violations of international human rights and humanitarian law "which may amount to war crimes," but there was not "a systematic or a widespread pattern to these violations."[128]

Referral

Judge Cassese had been closely involved with the negotiations of the Rome Statute and its Rules of Procedure and Evidence, and subsequently coedited a major (2,018 page) commentary upon it. Along with the commission's review of conditions in Darfur and characterization of the crimes taking place there, it considered alternative means to bring suspected Sudanese perpetrators to justice, such as an ad hoc or hybrid tribunal, but decided, "The prosecution by the ICC of persons allegedly responsible for the most serious crimes in Darfur would contribute to the restoration of peace in the region."[129]

The United States was strongly opposed to the referral and pressed for alternatives in the weeks prior to the Security Council decision.[130] Frank about U.S. motives, U.S. Ambassador-at-Large for War Crimes Issues Pierre-Richard Prosper said on January 28, 2005, "We don't want to be party to legitimizing the ICC."[131] U.S. antipathy to the ICC sailed under the flag of reinforcing regional authority. Prosper sought to convince Security Council members that a Sudan tribunal should be created under African Union auspices using the facilities of the ICTR in Arusha, thus reinforcing the AU's role in the region and economizing on court costs. According to the United States, the ICC wouldn't be a good alternative because it remained remote from the Sudan (in The Hague) and in any case was preoccupied with the situations in the DRC and Uganda.[132]

---

[127] Ibid., 3.
[128] Ibid., 3–4.
[129] Ibid., 5.
[130] See also Cryer, "Sudan, Resolution 1593, and International Criminal Justice" (2006), 195–222.
[131] Hoge, "U.S. Lobbies U.N. on Darfur and International Court" (2005).
[132] Aita, "African Union Tribunal Proposed for War Crimes in Darfur" (2005).

GOs, governments friendly to the ICC, and the media piled on to
est that the United States threatened to sacrifice the welfare of hundreds
of thousands of Sudanese, to preserve perpetrators' immunity, to undermine
principles of justice, and to subvert humanitarian values on the altar of
ideological antipathy to the Court.

On March 31, the Security Council referred the situation to the ICC with
eleven affirmative votes, no negative votes, and Algeria, Brazil, China, and
the United States abstaining.[133] Acting U.S. Permanent Representative
Ambassador Anne Patterson's statement to the Security Council demonstrated that even though new Secretary of State Condoleeza Rice had
apparently convinced President Bush to take a pragmatic position on the
referral, ICC opponents (such as the soon-to-be-nominated permanent
representative to the UN, John Bolton) had extracted their pound of flesh in
the form of caveats and conditions that sought to make life harder for the
Court.

The U.S. Position

U.S. fingerprints are all over Security Council Resolution 1593. The resolution announces that all states shall cooperate with the Court under the
UN Charter, while noting that for Rome Statute nonparties, their obligation
arises only from the Charter and not from the Rome Statute.[134] It
announced that, other than Sudanese, people from nonparty states involved
in referral-related activities in the Sudan would themselves be subject only
to jurisdiction of their own ("the sending") states and not to the ICC unless
they explicitly accepted the ICC's jurisdiction.[135] The Security Council
decreed that none of the expenses of the referral would be paid by the UN,
but would be borne by voluntary contributors and the parties to the Rome
Statute.[136]

In her statement to the Security Council, U.S. Ambassador Patterson
"strongly supported bringing to justice those responsible for the crimes and
atrocities that had occurred in Darfur and ending the climate of impunity
there," but indicated that the United States would have preferred a hybrid
tribunal in Africa. She claimed that the resolution was "precedent-setting"
because, she believed, in the future, "absent consent of the State involved,

---

[133] UN Security Council, Resolution 1593 (2005).
[134] Ibid., para. 2.
[135] Ibid., para. 6.
[136] Ibid., para. 7.

any investigations or prosecutions of nationals of non-party States should come only pursuant to a decision by the Council." This was an effort to claim victory for the United States' position that a citizen of a nonstate party could not be subject to the ICC unless the state of citizenship permitted jurisdiction – a position clearly at odds with the jurisdictional regime of the Rome Statute, under which such a person could be subject to the Court if the crime took place on the territory of a state party to the Rome Treaty.[137]

She was glad that the resolution "recognized" that no ICC expenses would be borne by the UN (fulfilling a U.S. demand but contravening Rome Statute Article 115(b), under which the costs of situations referred by the Security Council were to be financed by the UN), threatening that "any effort to retrench on that principle by the United Nations or other organizations to which the United States contributed could result in its withholding funding or taking other action in response."[138]

Relations between the United States and ICC remained distant at a formal level; however, there were some signs that a thaw was possible. Assistant Secretary of State for African Affairs Jendayi Frazer testified to a congressional committee hearing on Sudan in late 2005 that Deputy Secretary of State Robert Zoellick "has signaled that if the ICC requires assistance, the United States stands ready for any assistance. But they haven't asked us for any assistance in developing their list [of suspects] or getting the government to adhere to any ICC charges."[139] When, during the hearing, Congressman Donald Payne of New Jersey urged cooperation between the Department of State and the ICC, the ambassador reiterated, "Deputy Secretary Zoellick has made very clear that if we were asked by the ICC for our help, we would try to make sure that this gets pursued fully, to use his words, because we don't want to see impunity for any of these actors. So they haven't asked, but if they did, we stand ready to assist."[140] Oddly, the Court thereafter did not seek U.S. help.[141]

---

[137] Rome Statute Article 12.2(a).

[138] UN Security Council, Statement of Anne Woods Patterson, United States, following the vote. UN Security Council, Resolution 1593 (2005). As Cryer, op cit., 206, points out, there is a UN constitutional issue here because the General Assembly, not the Security Council, has exclusive authority over budgetary matters under UN Charter Article 17.

[139] U.S. House of Representatives, Committee on International Relations, Subcommitte on Africa, Global Human Rights and International Organizations, "Sudan: Losing Ground on Peace?" (2005), 29.

[140] Ibid., 32.

[141] Interviews.

China abstained from the vote, according to its representative's statement to the Security Council, because of "major reservations" regarding some of the provisions of the Rome Statute and because it believed that the perpetrators should be tried in Sudanese courts. The Algerian representative would have preferred an African Union–devised solution to the problem of Sudanese impunity as well as to resolve the conflict itself.[142] The Brazilian representative indicated strong support for the ICC and the referral but objected to the resolution's paragraph 6, which proclaimed the U.S. view on the selective jurisdiction of the Court and thus "would not strengthen the role of the International Criminal Court."[143]

The good news for the ICC was that the United States had abstained. The United States' desire to support humanitarian interests, counter impunity in the Sudan, and avoid the approbation of other states, particularly those of the European Union, overcame its objections to the Court. The bad news for the Court was that, with the referral, the ICC faced a huge challenge: Sudan had not agreed to its jurisdiction, and although bound under the UN Charter to fulfill Security Council resolutions, the government showed no signs of willingly cooperating with the Court. The ICC may have been handed a task that it was bound to fail.

The good news from the standpoint of impunity in the Sudan was that the Security Council referral denoted an international commitment to pursuing the perpetrators of large-scale crimes. The bad news was that, like the situation in Yugoslavia at the time of the ICTY's creation, the international community showed little willingness to take more vigorous action to protect the victims of the ongoing crimes, and assignment to the Court could be seen as a fig leaf for inaction.

Countering impunity and supporting humanitarian law were only two of the outside powers' multiple objectives in Sudan. The United States, Great Britain, Russia, and China were all interested in the oil concessions Khartoum controlled. In addition, the United States and Great Britain were in close contact with the government on measures to monitor and counter suspected Al Qaeda terrorist operations in the area. Perhaps most flagrantly, the head of Sudan's national security agency, Major-General Salah Abdullah Gosh, generally considered by observers to be one of the architects of the government's activities in Darfur, was welcomed in London and at the CIA for

---

[142] UN Security Council, Statement of Abdallah Baali, Algeria, following the vote. UN Security Council, Resolution 1593 (2005).
[143] Statement of Council President Ronaldo Mota Sardenberg, Brazil, following the vote. UN Security Council, Resolution 1593 (2005).

discussions with intelligence officials about Al Qaeda as well as Darfur. In 2005, Gosh said, "We have a strong partnership with the CIA. The information we have provided has been very useful to the United States." [144] Given the mixed motives of the major powers, it remained unclear how much international cooperation the ICC would receive.

Sudan's Reaction

Immediately after the Security Council announced the referral on April 3, 2005, the Sudanese Cabinet lambasted the Security Council resolution. President Uma al-Ashir stated that his government would not hand over any Sudanese citizens to be tried outside the country, and the Council of Ministers "declared its 'total rejection' of U.N. resolution 1593." [145] Acting Information Minister Abdul-Basic Sandarac told state-run Radio Omdurman that the Cabinet had appointed a committee to work out "how to deal with this situation," asserting that the resolution violated Sudanese sovereignty and would "further complicate the problem in Darfur and give the wrong signals to the rebels." [146]

The president further announced that Sudan's judiciary was prepared to try those accused of violations in Darfur, demonstrating that the Sudanese authorities understood ICC admissibility criteria. The government created a Special Criminal Court to prosecute crimes committed in Darfur. In June, Justice Minister Ali Mohamed Oman Yasmin stated that the government considered the new court "a substitute to the International Criminal Court," and announced that on June 18 it had begun hearing the first cases of 160 people accused of committing crimes in Darfur. [147]

In response to Sudan's moves, successive reports by the ICC Chief Prosecutor asserted that the special court was not focused on leaders of the crimes of concern to the ICC, and that very small numbers of prosecutions were actually underway. Sudan had indicated that by December 2005, of 160 individuals who had been identified for prosecution for crimes in Darfur, 26 defendants had been tried in six trials, but these were neither for the kinds of mass crimes over which the ICC had jurisdiction nor of the kind

[144] Silverstein, "Official Pariah Sudan Valuable to America's War on Terrorism Despite Once Harboring Bin Laden, Khartoum Regime Has Supplied Key Intelligence, Officials Say" (2005); Beaumont, "Sudan's Gosh Holds Talks in London on Darfur and Terror" (2006).

[145] IRIN, "Sudan: Darfur War-Crime Suspects Won't Go to ICC, Government Says" (2005).

[146] Oman, "Sudan's Cabinet Rejects U.N. Resolution on ICC Trials" (2005).

[147] IRIN, "Sudan: Judiciary Challenges ICC over Darfur Cases" (2005).

of high-level decision makers – persons most responsible – that the ICC seeks to prosecute.[148]

The ICC in the Sudan

On April 5, 2005, ICC Chief Prosecutor Moreno Ocampo announced that he had received thousands of documents from the Special Commission plus its final report and a confidential annex. The annex included a list of fifty-one individuals and the Commission's reasons that it suspected them of committing crimes under ICC jurisdiction. The Chief Prosecutor opened the sealed envelope with his Cabinet – the two Deputy Prosecutors (Brammertz and Bensouda) and the head of the Jurisdiction, Complementarity and Cooperation Division (Fernandez) on April 7. After they studied the list, the Prosecutor's Office resealed it to maintain confidentiality. The OTP publicly stated that "the list is advice to the Prosecutor and not mandatory for him to follow."[149] Under the OTP's understanding of the Statute, it was up to the OTP to conduct its own inquiries and analyses in order to decide whether to pursue a formal investigation into the Darfur situation.

On June 1, Moreno Ocampo informed the Pre-Trial Chamber and the President of the ICC that he had decided to go ahead with the formal investigation.[150] Announcing the decision on June 5, the OTP press release said that in addition to the Special Commission's report, the OTP had requested information "from a variety of sources, leading to the collection of thousands of documents. The Office also interviewed over 50 independent experts." Moreno Ocampo said that the investigation would focus on "the individuals who bear the greatest responsibility for crimes committed in Darfur" and would "require sustained cooperation from national and international authorities. It will form part of a collective effort, complementing African Union and other initiatives to end the violence in Darfur and to promote justice."[151] Optimists regarding the ICC involvement argued that it would provide some deterrence to ongoing crimes in Darfur. Former Clinton administration official and International Crisis Group Africa analyst John Prendergast asserted, "Regime officials are very worried about the long-term ramifications of the ICC investigation" and added that

---

[148] ICC, Second Report of the Prosecutor, Mr. Luis Moreno Ocampo, to the Security Council, Pursuant to UNSC 1593(2005) (2005), 5.

[149] ICC, "List of Names of Suspects in Darfur Opened by the ICC OTP" (2005).

[150] ICC, Office of the Prosecutor, Letter from Luis Moreno Ocampo to Judge Claude Jorda, Presiding Judge, Pre-Trial Chamber I (2005).

[151] ICC, "The Prosecutor of the ICC Opens Investigation in Darfur" (2005).

those "indicted by the ICC will become international pariahs. . . . Justice will not come quickly in Sudan. But it will come."[152]

A vigorous but beleaguered NGO community in Khartoum had pressed for Sudanese ratification of the Rome Statute; engaged with international counterparts in bringing information about the Court to media, legal experts, and government representatives; and met with ICC officials in Khartoum and at The Hague. The United Kingdom and Khartoum-based Sudan Organization Against Torture (SOAT), affiliated with the FIDH, chronicled human rights abuses in Sudan generally and Darfur in particular, aided in victim rehabilitation, and pressed for Sudanese acceptance of an expanded UN and African Union peacekeeping presence in Darfur.[153]

The OTP assembled an investigation team of approximately twenty-six people who carried out their efforts outside Sudan, since the Sudanese authorities refused to cooperate with the investigation on site. The safety of the investigators, much less witnesses and victims, could not be guaranteed inside Sudan. On June 29 and again on December 13, 2005, Moreno Ocampo reported to the Security Council on the investigation's progress. The reports indicated that documents and other evidence continued to be collected, cooperation had been requested and obtained from states and from NGOs, and witness statements were being taken.[154]

Descriptions of the ICC's progress in Sudan from ICC insiders indicated that the investigation faced debilitating difficulties. They claimed that lack of a consistent investigation and prosecution strategy was undermining progress toward warrants. High personnel turnover sapped momentum. Tensions with the Registry were inhibiting operations on the ground. A deteriorating security environment in 2006 led the Registry Security Division to determine that OTP missions into the area were becoming overly risky, and the investigation slowed. Some participants in the missions argued that investigations required taking risks and that the ICC shouldn't be seen to be among the first international organizations to leave when situations became threatening. The lack of Sudanese cooperation increased the challenge to the ICC to tenaciously build cases that could stand up in

[152] Ford and McLaughlin, "Global Law Claims New Turf in Sudan" (2005).
[153] FIDH, Khartoum Centre for Human Rights and Environmental Development, Sudan Organization Against Torture, "International Criminal Court Programme Sudan: The International Criminal Court and Sudan: Access to Justice and Victims' Rights Roundtable, Khartoum, 2–3 October 2005"; *Sudan Tribune*, "Peace and Justice in Darfur: Victims' Rights Hijacked" (2006).
[154] ICC, "Report of the Prosecutor of the International Criminal Court, Mr. Luis Moreno Ocampo, to the Security Council Pursuant to UNSCR 1593(2005)" (2005); ICC, "Second Report of the Prosecutor," op cit.

Court. The task was feasible, some Court personnel argued, but internal problems were hampering the effort.

ICC representatives visited Khartoum in the spring of 2006 but described their activities there as investigating what the Sudanese courts were doing rather than investigating the crimes in Darfur. There was no indication that ICC teams would be permitted access to Darfur or given access to victims and/or witnesses in Sudan of the crimes they sought to investigate.

Presidential adviser Salah al-Addin threatened that ICC involvement in the Sudan would undermine peace efforts:

> Those who feel threatened by the ICC, at a certain point, it will be a matter of life and death to them. They could block the C.P.A. (Comprehensive Peace Agreement). The situation is so fragile. We shouldn't be complacent. Sudan is a very dangerous place. Your Somalia would be a picnic if Sudan degenerates into chaos. It would draw in the elements you fear most. It would require an influx of U.S. troops just like Afghanistan.[155]

Ongoing negotiations between the Sudan government and the rebel organizations mediated by Nigerian representatives in Abuja, Nigeria, produced a cease-fire agreement on May 5, 2006, between the government and one faction of the Sudan Liberation Movement/Army. A second SLM faction and the Justice and Equality Movement held out, arguing that the peace did not adequately address underlying and major sources of conflict. The Khartoum authorities agreed to meet with UN representatives to discuss a peacekeeping effort, but no guarantees were made.[156] A few weeks later, UN Undersecretary-General for Humanitarian Affairs Coordinator Jan Egeland called 2006 the worst year of the conflict in Darfur.[157] Khartoum continued to bar humanitarian organizations from entering the area. Negotiations over UN augmentation of the African Union force dragged on. Civilian casualties mounted while ICC investigations continued on the periphery of the region. Peace was elusive. The effects of the Security Council 1593 referral remained murky.

---

[155] Rubin, "If Not Peace, Then Justice" (2006), 52. The identification of al-Addin in the article as a "moderate Islamist" was challenged by experts on the Sudan who noted that the National Islamic Front (NIF), of which he is a member, was not moderate from the standpoint of the Darfur conflict. The NIF had routinely threatened that outside intervention would not only undermine peace efforts but also result in high casualties for intervening forces. Nonetheless, the comment demonstrated the poor prospects for ICC access to Darfur and its ability to protect witnesses unless the situation changed significantly. Personal communication, April 5, 2006.

[156] Kessler, "Sudanese, Rebels Sign Peace Plan for Darfur" (2006), 1.

[157] Reeves, "Why Abuja Won't Save Darfur" (2006).

At a May 31, 2006, press roundtable, the Chief Prosecutor previewed his third report to the Security Council to be delivered on June 14. He stated that his investigators had questioned victims and witnesses in fourteen countries, interviewed hundreds of witnesses, analyzed thousands of documents, and collected expert evidence. Asked about whether warrants could be issued without access to the area in which the crimes had actually taken place, Moreno Ocampo simply responded that his office was doing a good investigation. The investigations' details remained confidential and would continue to be so until warrants were issued.

PTC I Tries to Light a Fire under the OTP

On May 11, 2006, the UN High Commissioner for Human Rights (UNHCHR), former ICTY Prosecutor Louise Arbour, implicitly criticized the ICC Prosecutor when, following a trip to Darfur, Sudan, she told a news conference, "I believe we must call on the ICC to act more robustly, and visibly discharge the [Security Council] mandate" in order to bring to trial those guilty of war crimes.[158] In July, Antonio Cassese, the ex-Chairman of the UN Commission of Inquiry on Darfur, similarly criticized the Prosecutor for acting too cautiously in Sudan.[159] Cassese wrote that the Prosecutor should have requested Sudanese cooperation immediately after he had decided to open an investigation, on July 1, 2005, rather than declining to do so. Had he issued such a request, he would have been refused, but then he could have gone to the UN Security Council to seek its assistance in pressing for cooperation. Cassese described observers as mystified by Moreno Ocampo's reticence. Further, Cassese suggested that had the Prosecutor focused upon establishing the Sudanese chain of command, which presumably would not require investigations at the crime scenes, having determined that crimes were taking place and that they were perpetrated by the Sudanese military, warrants could have been considered under the principle of command responsibility. Cassese argued that the UN Security Council's action placing four Sudanese nationals involved in Darfur on the list of people against whom member states must adopt sanctions amounted to the UNSC acting politically in lieu of judicial acts that should be undertaken by the ICC.[160]

---

[158] Waddington, "Arbour Urges ICC to Act on Darfur Crimes" (2006).
[159] Cassese, "Is the ICC Still Having Teething Problems?" (2006), 434–41.
[160] Ibid., 439–41.

Acting under a rule permitting requests for *amicus curiae* submissions from individuals or organizations,[161] PTC I invited Arbour and Cassese to submit "observations concerning the protection of victims and the preservation of evidence in Darfur."[162] In essence the two prominent and experienced international officials were being asked to comment upon the Chief Prosecutor's course of action, each of them having recently been critical of those actions. Under the rules, the OTP (and defense) had a right to reply.[163]

Cassese's response to the Pre-Trial Chamber asserted that the Court's responsibility toward victims and witnesses could be divided into two aspects: first to protect them so that they could testify; and second, to "see to it that serious offences against victims are terminated," particularly against civilians, women, and children, "in accordance with the general purpose of criminal law and procedure, namely to forestall or impede the perpetration of crimes." Cassese pointed out that the Chief Prosecutor had endorsed this objective for the Court in his third report to the UN Security Council on ICC activities in Darfur.[164]

Cassese pressed the OTP to collect evidence about the Sudanese military's criminal responsibility and chain of command, as well as those of the rebel groups. He suggested that the OTP should directly or through the Pre-Trial Chamber seek the appearance before the Chamber of Sudanese officials to report on measures taken to protect witnesses and victims and directly or through the Chamber request the President of the Court to ask the Sudanese authorities to protect victims, and he recommended that since the OTP claimed that the situation was too dangerous for its personnel to undertake large-scale investigations in Sudan, the OTP could seek permission from Sudan to conduct interviews of victims in the main towns of Darfur. Cassese also suggested that the ICC request that the rebels guarantee during such investigations that they would temporarily suspend armed activities. Cassese thought that Sudanese officials as well as victims could be brought to The Hague to give testimony, and should the government resist, its refusal could be reported to the Security Council.[165]

---

[161] Rules of Procedure and Evidence, Rule 103: Amicus curiae and other forms of submission, para. 1, 2.

[162] ICC, PTC I, "Decision Inviting Observations in Application of Rule 103 of the Rules of Procedure and Evidence" (2006).

[163] Rules of Procedure and Evidence, Rule 103.2, op. cit.

[164] ICC, PTC I, "Observations on Issues Concerning the Protection of Victims and the Preservation of Evidence in the Proceedings on Darfur Pending Before the ICC" (2006).

[165] Ibid.

UN High Commissioner for Human Rights Louise Arbor told the Pre-Trial Chamber that the UNHCHR believed from experience that there had been very limited retaliation against victims for "interacting with the international community," and that such investigations always entail risks, but that those can be minimized. She called for "an increased visible presence of the International Criminal Court in Sudan" both to carry out investigations and to contribute to the international presence that increased the protection of civilians in the area.[166] After a lengthy review of UNHCHR activities in Sudan, Arbour asserted that the ICC needed to step up its activities in Darfur to help deter continued criminality, to take advantage of victims' willingness, even at risk to themselves, to come forward with evidence, and to contribute to protection simply by the presence of unarmed ICC personnel in the area. She stressed that since the ICC's mandate came from the UN Security Council under UN Charter Chapter VII (Peace and Security), Sudan and all other states were obligated to cooperate with the ICC, including ensuring that victims and witnesses could freely and without fear of retribution come forward to testify to the Court.[167]

The Chief Prosecutor responded to both *amicus* briefs, arguing to Cassese that the OTP prosecution strategy was appropriate, ongoing, and oriented not toward general protection of Sudanese civilians but toward the development of information on which criminal cases could be based. In response to Arbour, he argued that the ICC's mandate was not for general humanitarian assistance or protection but, again, for specific judicial activities, and that the UNHCHR was misunderstanding the role of the Court and the OTP. Regarding both Cassese's and Arbour's briefs, the OTP noted that since it was not interviewing victims in Darfur, no protective mechanisms were appropriate to pursue under the Statute; because the OTP was bound by the Statute's standards of protection for witnesses and victims, the experiences of the Commission and the UNHCHR in their own operations was irrelevant. Furthermore, since the ICC investigations could lead to legal action, he asserted that resistance to ICC activities in Darfur would likely be much stiffer than it had been to the mere information-gathering activities with which Arbour and Cassese were familiar.[168]

---

[166] ICC, PTC I, "Observations of the United Nations High Commissioner for Human Rights Invited in Application of Rule 103 of the Rules of Procedure and Evidence" (2006).
[167] Ibid.
[168] ICC, PTC I, "Prosecutor's Response to Cassese's Observations" (2006); "Prosecutor's response to Arbour's Observations of the United Nations High Commissioner for Human Rights" (2006).

Arrest Warrants

Chief Prosecutor Moreno Ocampo reported to the UN Security Council on December 19, 2006, that his investigations into the Darfur situation were continuing productively.[169] He said that since the start of the investigation, the OTP's Darfur team had conducted more than seventy missions to seventeen different countries, "screening hundreds of potential witnesses and conducting more than 100 formal witness interviews, many of which were with victims of the crimes in Darfur currently under investigation."[170] The Prosecutor asserted that the evidence proved that various crimes under the jurisdiction of the Court had been committed, and that grave crimes continued. In four missions to Khartoum, the OTP investigated whether it appeared that domestic proceedings obviated the need for ICC involvement, and this effort was continuing, although it did not appear that the cases currently pursued by the OTP would be inadmissible due to Sudanese actions. Moreno Ocampo indicated that he expected the OTP's examination of domestic proceedings to be completed by February 2007, with a planned visit to Khartoum in January.[171]

On February 27, the Prosecutor submitted to PTC I an application for summonses to be issued to two Sudanese officials, Ahmad Muhammad Harun, who had been Minister of State for the Interior and head of the "Darfur Security Desk," allegedly involved in recruiting the Janjaweed, who "knowingly contributed to the commission of crimes against humanity and war crimes, including murder, rape, torture, inhumane acts, pillaging and the forcible transfer of civilian populations," and Ali Kushayb, a local commander allegedly responsible for leading Janjaweed attacks.[172] The request for summonses, rather than warrants of arrest, implicitly invited the Sudanese authorities to cooperate with the Court and turn over the two suspects. The Prosecutor's application noted at its end, however, that should Sudan indicate its unwillingness to comply with ICC efforts, the PTC would be justified in issuing warrants for arrest rather than summonses. According to a press account following the Prosecutor's filing, "Sudan's justice minister, Mohammed Ali al-Mardi, rejected the allegations and said Khartoum would not hand them over for trial. 'We are not concerned with,

---

[169] ICC, "Fourth Report of the Prosecutor of the International Criminal Court to the U.N. Security Council Pursuant to UNSCR 1593" (2005).
[170] Ibid., 3.
[171] Ibid., 7.
[172] ICC, PTC I, Prosecutor's Application under Article 58(7) (2007).

nor do we accept, what the International Criminal Court prosecutor has opted for,' al-Mardi said in Khartoum."[173]

NGOs welcomed the Prosecutor's February announcement, calling both for Sudanese cooperation with the Court and for the OTP to continue its investigations. HRW's Richard Dicker said, "While the individuals identified today are important, the ICC prosecutor should move up the chain of command to target those senior Sudanese government and military officials responsible for the most serious crimes in Darfur."[174] Antonio Cassese admired the Prosecutor's thoroughness in the warrant requests but was "surprised by the fact that the prosecutor started with mid-level individuals," which he saw as an indication that Moreno Ocampo "has decided to adopt the small step strategy, a very gradual strategy, not to go directly looking for the major players who did the planning." He pulled back from criticizing Moreno Ocampo, however, stating his belief that the Prosecutor "has good reasons" for his approach.[175] On April 27, 2007, the PTC issued warrants for the arrest of Ahmad Harun and Ali Kushayb,[176] leading to repeated Sudanese government denunciations.[177]

When the Security Council referred the Darfur situation to the ICC, even with U.S. reluctance and conditions, a major milestone had been reached. The PTC's subsequent approval of warrants for Ahmad Harun and Ali Kushayb was a second major step: For the first time, the Court had managed to carry out major investigations without cooperation from the state on whose territory the alleged crimes had taken place. Actually gaining custody of the suspects, of course, would be much more difficult, unless the two individuals were to travel outside the country and be arrested by authorities in other states. During the interplay between the PTC and the OTP, the tussle over prosecutorial strategy and the Court's role in conflict continued. NGOs and others (such as Louise Arbour and Antonio Cassese) hoped that the actions of the Prosecutor would raise pressures on the government, or at least contribute maximally to international pressures on the government to force a change in policy. The twenty-month investigation prior to the warrants and the naming of suspects that observers believed were not at top levels of the government showed both the independence of

---

[173] Associated Press, "International Criminal Court Names Former Sudan Minister in Darfur War Crimes Case" (2007).

[174] Ibid.

[175] Petit, "The Small Steps Strategy of the ICC in Darfur" (2007).

[176] ICC, PTC I, "Decision on the Prosecution Application under Article 58(7) of the Statute" (2007).

[177] BBC, "Sudan 'Will Defy Darfur Warrants'" (2007).

the Prosecutor and, perhaps, his caution, if not an excess thereof.[178] The implicit message that might unfortunately be gleaned from both the DRC and Sudan cases is that for top political actors, the threat from the Court remains low.

THE CENTRAL AFRICAN REPUBLIC

Conflict Background

In March 2000, United Nations Mission in the Central African Republic (MINURCA) peacekeeping forces departed the Central African Republic, having assisted in maintaining order through economic upheaval and mutinies against the government of President Félix Patassé. Patassè had first been elected in 1993 and was reelected in September 1999. In May 2001, he had enlisted the aid of militias from Libya, Chad, and the Congolese Movement for the Liberation of the Congo (MLC) to quash an attempted military coup. Another coup attempt in 2002 led to Patassé's removal from office in March 2003, and his replacement by the coup leader, former CAR Army Chief of Staff François Bozize.

According to the FIDH, in the fall of 2002's fighting, Patassé, "suspicious of his regular army of which a great number of members left with the former putchists, ... surrounded himself for protection with a few well armed Libyans, with the support of Jean-Pierre Bemba's [MLC] men and with troops of the Chadian mercenary, Abdoulaye Miskine."[179] The FIDH, supported by the Central African League for Human Rights, learned of what it called "flagrant violation of the laws and customs of war" during the fighting, constituted by large-scale rapes and murders. The FIDH's February 13, 2003, report was the first it sent to the ICC, arriving well before a Chief Prosecutor had been appointed. In September 2003, Amnesty International sent a research team to Bangui, CAR, and carried out its own study of the conflict and, like the FIDH, reported "widespread and systematic rapes" primarily carried out by MLC members.[180]

---

[178] Antonio Cassese uses the term "exceedingly prudent," in a negative sense, in his introduction to International Justice Tribune, *ICC in 2006: Year One: Legal and Political Issues Surrounding the International Criminal Court* (2007), 13.

[179] FIDH, News Release, "War Crimes in the Central African Republic: FIDH Formally Brings Its First Case before the International Criminal Court" (2003).

[180] Amnesty International, "Central African Republic: Five months of War against Women" (2004).

Referral

On December 22, 2004, the government of the Central African Republic referred the conflict in its territory to the ICC OTP for investigation, following a finding by its high court (Cour de Cassation) that the national justice system would be incapable of prosecuting the crimes. In January 2005, the Court's Presidency assigned the CAR situation to Pre-Trial Chamber III. The Office of the Prosecutor indicated that it was undertaking informal investigations in the CAR. It took from the time of the CAR's referral in December 2004 until late May 2007 for the OTP to decide that events in 2002–3 warranted a formal investigation. Once again, a PTC sought to speed the OTP's considerations.

On September 27, 2006, the Registry forwarded a request to PTC III from the CAR "including, inter alia, a request that the Prosecutor provide information on the alleged failure to decide, within a reasonable time, whether or not to initiate an investigation," and on November 30, the judges requested information from the OTP on the status of its preliminary examination of the CAR situation. About two weeks later, the OTP responded, arguing that there was no prescribed period of time within which the conclusion of a preliminary evaluation should be expected, and that the CAR situation had some unique characteristics that explained the elapse of time. It noted, moreover, that the referring state had the right to question a decision about whether to proceed or not, but that no decision had been made, so that there was no OTP duty to report.[181]

Nonetheless, the OTP reported to the Chamber that it had received communications from the FIDH alleging crimes, and the OTP was evaluating these and other information. It sought and received further information from the CAR authorities, and the OTP's Jurisdiction, Complementarity and Cooperation Division was analyzing the material received. Representatives from the OTP had traveled to Bangui, Central African Republic, particularly to evaluate domestic proceedings, and met with CAR representatives, NGO representatives, and local diplomatic missions. A report had been drafted in the OTP in July 2006, but then further allegations were communicated to the OTP, and new information was conveyed that dealt with the period 2002–3. The OTP indicated to the PTC that it was "committed to completing its analysis of the CAR situation as expeditiously as possible and informing the

---

[181] ICC, PTC III, "Prosecution's Report Pursuant to Pre-Trial Chamber III's 30 November 2006 Decision Requesting Information on the Status of the Preliminary Examination of the Situation in the Central African Republic" (2006).

relevant parties in a timely fashion," but it could not say when this was likely to occur.[182]

At the November 2006 Assembly of States Party to the Rome Statute, the Chief Prosecutor indicated that his planning was based on the idea that an additional situation would come under formal investigation during the coming year, and on May 22, 2007, he announced initiation of a formal investigation into the CAR situation, estimating that it would take approximately eighteen months to complete. Moreno Ocampo stated that the massive sexual crimes of 2002–3 "cannot be ignored under international law" and that since current conditions in the country were deteriorating, his office supported efforts by the UN and others to stabilize the situation. He expressed the hope that the Court's involvement would help to deter future violence and to promote enduring regional peace.[183] International human rights organizations, including Human Rights Watch and Women's Initiatives for Gender Justice, welcomed the emphasis on sexual crimes, particularly in the wake of their disappointment that similar crimes had not been charged in the DRC and Uganda cases.[184] Some activists remained disappointed that the Court had taken so long to act,[185] although HRW's Richard Dicker pointed out that the OTP, with four situations under investigation, was understaffed.[186]

The CAR investigation announcement demonstrated the crucial connection between NGOs and the ICC, and in particular their role in drawing attention to sexual crimes. The long delay in the Prosecutor's announcement might best be attributed to a triage strategy wherein the OTP, with limited resources and still developing its capacities and routines, sought to address first the crimes that it considered to have the greatest gravity. The CAR announcement showed that the NGOs' efforts at the ICTR, and Judge Pillay's evocation of women's testimonies in the Akayesu case (see Chapter 2), had irreversibly altered the terrain of international prosecutions.

OTHER POSSIBLE SITUATIONS

In annual reports to the Assembly of States Parties and in comments to the press, the OTP indicated that it had other situations under review. Court

---

[182] Ibid.
[183] ICC, "Prosecutor Opens Investigation into the Central African Republic" (2007).
[184] Glassborow, "CAR Case to Focus on Sexual Violence" (2007).
[185] Polgreen and Simons, "Hague Court Investigating Rights Violations in Central African Republic" (2007).
[186] Human Rights Watch, "Central African Republic: ICC Opens Investigation" (2007).

personnel and observers have repeatedly pointed out that all the situations currently under investigation and prosecution are in Africa, and some NGOs have gone so far as to indicate that, in order to demonstrate balance, the Court should consider situations elsewhere. The OTP's response has been that it proceeds according to its "gravity" criteria, which, simply put, boil down to casualty levels, and that the conflicts in Africa at present overwhelm any others over which the Court (by virtue of territorial or national jurisdiction) might extend its purview. Nonetheless, Court officials have been in frequent contact with officials in Colombia, and the OTP and other personnel have visited there several times.[187]

Communications to the OTP, of course, have covered crimes from many parts of the world. On its Web site, the OTP has twice summarized and categorized requests for investigation and in some cases has indicated why it decided not to pursue them.[188] In particular, it responded to suggestions that it investigate crimes in Venezuela and in Iraq by detailing reasons why they did not constitute admissible situations, in public statements posted on its Web site. Regarding accusations in Venezuela, the OTP indicated that its jurisdiction could be triggered, since Venezuela is party to the Statute, but that the allegations did not appear to be of the nature or level of crimes that would require ICC examination.[189] Regarding Iraq (where, since Iraq is not an ICC signatory, only crimes committed by a party state – namely the United Kingdom – would fall under its consideration), the OTP did not find that crimes had taken place that would justify an investigation.[190]

CONCLUSIONS

The ICC generally, and the Prosecutor's office most directly, faces contradictory compulsions. To gain situation states' cooperation, close interactions with governments are necessary, but these governments also seek to use the Court to their own advantage. Working too closely with situation governments risks destroying the appearance of the Court's impartiality; too distant a relationship might scupper prosecutions. In the ICC's case in Uganda, although LRA depredations appeared more serious than those of the UPDF, observers wondered whether the ICC would bring a case against government officials. Particularly because of Chief Prosecutor Moreno

---

[187] Interviews.
[188] ICC, OTP, "Update on Communications Received" (2006).
[189] Ibid., Annex, Venezuela Response.
[190] Ibid., Annex, Iraq Response.

Ocampo's appearance with President Museveni, the Court was suspected of bias.

In the DRC, the Lubanga prosecution raised questions about the OTP's focus. Particularly as the transitional government carried out elections in which some candidates (for example, Jean-Pierre Bemba) had been suspected by human rights organizations of crimes similar to Lubanga's, it appeared that political considerations might have trumped ICC neutrality. These kinds of dilemmas had faced the ad hoc tribunals, and they will continue to be facts of life for the ICC. Chief Prosecutor Moreno Ocampo faced the same problem in Uganda and in the DRC that his ICTR counterparts Carla del Ponte and Hassan Jallow faced in Rwanda: The need for government cooperation cuts hard against investigation and indictment of suspects closely connected to the government.

The problem of cooperation in the Sudan situation is even more complicated, since the Sudanese authorities do not recognize the ICC's right to be involved at all. The Security Council's referral of the Sudan situation to the Court demonstrated limits to U.S. opposition to the Court, but because of major states' economic and security interests, little international leverage was exerted either to promote Sudan's cooperation with the Court or for it to end the Darfur violence. Sudan's willingness to accede to the OTP's requests for meetings in Khartoum to discuss the status of national judicial measures, however, was perhaps a weak indicator of pressure to appear respectful of the Court. Partial and dilatory as this cooperation was, it could be evidence to support the constructivists' idea that shame has some compelling international effect.

The necessary secrecy of prosecution investigations makes evaluation of criticisms difficult. Nonetheless, credible critics such as Louise Arbour and Antonio Cassese argued in the Sudan situation that the OTP could have taken measures that would likely have accelerated investigations and perhaps also served positive humanitarian purposes. The OTP's operational code is still a work in progress. The Prosecutor consistently maintains that he is proceding with due speed, given the requirements for legality, but critics argue that more could be done faster, even, as in Sudan's case, facing situation state opposition. In the Uganda situation, critics question the lack of warrants for UPDF officials. In the DRC, they ask why only Lubanga, and why are the charges so narrow? In Sudan, even with the spring 2007 warrants for Harun and Kushayb, the Prosecutor was criticized for not aiming at the highest levels of responsibility.

In all four situations, NGOs were vital to the ICC's investigations and outreach, but they also pursued their own visions of Court operations sometimes at cross purposes with each other and with the Court. In Uganda and Sudan, humanitarian, peace-oriented NGOs worry that arrest warrants will damage the possibilities for peace, while human rights organizations call for rigorous implementation of the law. Humanitarian and legal imperatives may converge over the longer run, when threats of arrest may help deter crimes. In the short run, however, peace and justice appear to remain in tension.

Inside the ICC, the division of labor and the balance of prerogatives between civil-law-like oversight of the Prosecutor by the Pre-Trial Chambers and the Prosecutor's independence were slowly being established by precedent. The OTP was pushed to accelerate and deepen investigations, on the one hand, while also being required to accept an expansive role for victims and their representatives at early stages of the confirmation process.

In all four situations, the Court's involvement was only a part – and perhaps a small one – of efforts to ameliorate conflict. Issuing warrants in northern Uganda added pressure to the LRA and provided a vehicle for Sudanese–Ugandan cooperation, but the changing constellation of relations between Sudan, Congo, and Uganda made progress against the LRA possible. In the Congo, the gradual development of the transitional mechanisms that led to democratic elections would have proceeded regardless of the Court; the threat of ICC action, however, appears to have accelerated efforts to reconstruct the domestic justice system. The Lubanga case will test the Court's ability to efficaciously carry out trial procedures; meanwhile, additional warrants against high-profile suspects might improve the Court's reputation. In the Sudan, everything appears to hinge on the amount of outside pressure that can be brought to bear on the government. In the Central African Republic, the Prosecutor noted that the ICC was working within the context of other UN organizations in efforts to stabilize the country, and that the Court hoped to contribute to the deterrence of additional crimes.

8

Conclusions

The Politics of the International Criminal Court

Flowing from sources traceable back at least to the Old Testament and classical Greece, the river of justice traversed a norms cascade at the Rome Statute Conference in 1998. States accepted the Nuremberg principles that individuals are culpable for international crimes, that an individual is responsible whether or not domestic law criminalizes the international crime, that superiors are responsible for the acts of subordinates and subordinates are not relieved of responsibility due to superior orders, and that suspects have rights to fair trials. States granted that genocide, crimes against humanity, and war crimes are international crimes worthy of prosecution. They inscribed both retributive and restorative justice objectives into the Statute. Victims gained status as subjects, not mere objects, of justice. Gender crimes were recognized as among humanity's most heinous acts.

Debate over international crimes and individuals' potential culpability for them is over. International criminal law is a set of ideas whose time has come, and the International Criminal Court is the organizational manifestation of this consensus. Just because the norms command considerable agreement, however, does not mean that agreement exists over how to implement them, or that they are simple to put into operation. The ICC's mandate and structure as outlined in the Statute are fundamental to the organization, representing its cognitive architecture. Its operational characteristics combine that architecture with the practical limitations of a real organization.

MANDATE

The Statute is a compromise document. Complementarity protected sovereignty, and jurisdiction was limited to just three crimes and two jurisdiction principles. Pre-Trial Chambers check the independence of the Prosecutor, and the Security Council was given the ability to refer cases to the Court and to suspend its activities. States that join are obliged to bring their domestic legal systems into congruence with the Statute and to cooperate with the Court, but no sanctions or enforcement capacity were created to ensure either of these.

The Statute formally recognizes the objectives of both retributive and restorative justice paradigms, presenting the Court with a broad and challenging mandate. Because the retributive model dominated the tribunals and the Statute drafting process, that part of the ICC's operation is spelled out much more explicitly than were the restorative side's institutional innovations. Restorative justice in the ICC is still evolving, largely under the tutelage of the Pre-Trial Chambers and the Registry.

Since construction of the Statute was ultimately a diplomatic-political activity, not an exercise of rational design, the Court's objectives may not be mutually compatible. Priorities among objectives must be developed in operation, by Court officials functioning within the structure devised by the Statute negotiators.

STRUCTURE

The ICC's organizational structure evolved in negotiations based on the 1994 International Law Commission draft, informed by the experiences of the ICTY and ICTR. The tribunals' tripartite structure of Chambers, Prosecutor, and Registry, with the distant oversight of the UN Security Council, shared its heritage with the ICC Statute, having emerged from experts' long contemplation of an international criminal court and from the ICC designs drafted by the International Law Commission.

The tribunals showed that they could function but also exposed serious structural and operational problems. The Rome Statute negotiators tweaked the model, subordinating the Registry to the Chambers, separating the Court from the UN, and establishing the Assembly of States Parties, but the skeleton remained visible. Tensions between the Chambers and the OTP persisted, and the Registry, even though subordinated to the Presidency, remained vigorous but with a somewhat ambiguous role. The ASP provides membership input to the Court but has so far been reticent to supervise the ICC's development closely. In the Court itself, there is either an excess or a deficit of leadership: The President, Chief Prosecutor, and Registrar all lead aspects of the Court's operations and external relations, but deference to the organs' independence, difficulty in devising a division of labor, and personal differences mean that despite the slogan of the "one-court principle," interlocutors often experience more than one Court, and final decisions in the Court are hard to reach. Efforts continue to improve administration and coordinate the organs without compromising their requisite independence.

The tribunals were crafted largely around common-law legal patterns, but they evolved to include civil-law expediencies and greater judicial activism. The ICC began where the tribunals had arrived (as of 1998), combining a common-law-style independent prosecutor (capable of undertaking cases *proprio motu*) with embryonic civil-law judicial constraints (in the form of the Pre-Trial Chambers), a compromise devised to protect states from feared "frivolous" prosecutions.

The tribunals' judges wrote their own rules as they went along, since the Security Council's statutes for them focused on establishment rather than operation. With more time available and seeking to divide the legislative responsibility from operations, the Statute negotiators wrote a much more ornate statute and reserved for the Preparatory Commission and the Assembly of States Parties the right to compose and approve rules for the Court, creating a surrogate international form of separation of powers that the tribunals didn't have.

The ICC Statute negotiators brought as many of the tribunals' experiences into their considerations as possible; however, their negotiations ended before the full lessons of the tribunals had been grasped. Full responses to the tribunals' lessons fell to the Preparatory Commission as it hammered out the Court's rules, and to the organs of the Court as it undertook operations.

OPERATIONS

For the ad hoc tribunals, learning how to operate was an adventure, forcing the judges to develop their rules on the fly and successive prosecutors to turn their official responsibilities into workable routines. Faced with monumental challenges, they were investigating crimes while being obstructed by local governments and neglected by the major states that had spurred their creation in the first place. The kind of international prosecution that they were mandated to carry out had not been undertaken since Nuremberg. Nonetheless, they developed institutional momentum and legitimacy more credibly than their detractors had imagined possible, eventually mounting serious and precedent-setting court cases. The tribunals eroded the traditional international law distinction between internal and international conflict, raised the profile of sexual crimes, and demonstrated the difficulties of prosecuting genocide.

They revealed important pitfalls that their ICC successors strove to avoid. Overly broad charges created prosecution problems, motivating the ICC Prosecutor to define charges narrowly. In the tribunals, separation of investigation from prosecution activities produced case information inefficiently, and it was often unusable for the prosecution. So the ICC OTP integrated prosecution personnel into its investigation teams from the start. The ICC learned from the tribunals' inadequate attention to outreach and witness protection and early created victims' units and outreach capabilities.

Selection of judges for the Court disappointed observers who had hoped for a less political selection process than occurred for the tribunals. Recruiting a Chief Prosecutor proved to be much more difficult than expected. The first Chief Prosecutor has many qualifications for the position from the standpoint of the ASP, but as with the political selection process for the judges, questions remain about his expertise in the areas most needed by an international criminal court.

When the Chief Prosecutor arrived, he overrode civil-law-oriented experts' proposals for the review structure for the Court's intake work. Detractors charge that the resulting Jurisdiction, Complementarity and Cooperation Division is more political-diplomatic than legal in its orientation; supporters argue that the legalistic alternatives would not adequately have taken into account political realities and, in any case, once the Chief Prosecutor was selected, it was his job to determine the best structure for his own operation. The Prosecutor has been under tremendous pressure from inside the Court, from enthusiastic governments, and from NGOs to move cases rapidly into court. The Pre-Trial Chambers have been aggravated about what they see as the slow pace of investigations and, in the Democratic Republic of the Congo and Sudan cases, the choice of suspects and narrow range of alleged crimes. The PTCs and OTP have struggled with each other to delineate their roles, with the OTP believing that Chambers are intruding on prosecutorial prerogatives, and Chambers concerned over the OTP's investigations and protection of victims and witnesses. The Appeals Chamber has mostly sided with the PTCs.

The Prosecution and Registry have come into conflict over evidence disclosure and control of communication with situation states. Both issues required judicial decisions to establish operational precedents; in the case of disclosure, defense and prosecution successfully argued to minimize the Registry's role. In communications with the situation states, the PTCs upheld statutory language establishing the Registry's leading role, constraining the

Prosecutor's ability to time announcements and to negotiate arrangements with the states.

Pre-Trial Chambers, NGOs, bureaus of the Registry, and the board of the Victims' Trust Fund have been working to implement restorative justice objectives, and some actions have already borne fruit. NGOs helped organize victims' requests for participation in the DRC (Lubanga) case's pretrial phase, and resultant litigation among the OTP, Pre-Trial Chambers, defense, and Appeals Chambers has begun to provide the definitions and criteria under which victims will participate. The Victims' Trust Fund is beginning to operate with a small secretariat. Case-by-case board decisions about when and how to aid victims will have to be made, with Pre-Trial Chambers having an oversight responsibility. The fund depends on voluntary donations, so donors will govern the magnitude of reparative measures; it can be expected to remain small in comparison with the humanitarian needs of the victims of the kinds of mass crimes that the Court is empowered to prosecute. Thus, while operational balance between retributive and restorative justice is not yet settled, the emphasis appears to remain heavily on the retributive side.

Convinced by the tribunals' experience that outreach should be an important function of the Court, both the Registry and the OTP developed external relations capabilities that were largely uncoordinated at the start. Particularly with pressures from NGOs to bring information about the Court to the situation states, the Court's officials established a coordination committee and a strategic plan for outreach. While the coordinating council, "one-court principle," and outreach plan show important organizational innovations to reduce internal conflict and smooth the Court's operations, they are also testaments to the problems of achieving these objectives.

So far, the Court has had an easy time acquiring financial resources from the Assembly of States Parties. From 2002 to 2007, its budget expanded rapidly. The ASP Committee on Budget and Finance has worked with the Registry to improve financial reporting and control. The CBF exerts pressure on the Court in the form of recommendations to the ASP for budgetary limitations in response to the Court's draft budget; however, with the rapid growth of the Court and relatively generous annual budget, the Court has not run up against serious reactions to redundancy and inefficiency. The Court has also benefited from pressures brought to bear on the ASP by nongovernmental organizations that press for budgetary expansion in areas of their concern (such as outreach and victim reparations) but do not call for retrenchment in other parts of the budget.

NGOS

Nongovernmental organizations played a larger role at the ICC Statute negotiations than at any previous international conference. They used electronic technologies to great effect at the conference, provided information and reacted to unfolding events rapidly through their umbrella coalition, the CICC, and kept pressure on national delegations. Combined with the compelling quality of the norms they were championing, their involvement at Rome is generally credited with helping to create the final agreement. Continuing on a path established in their relations with the tribunals, NGOs pressed successfully for raising consciousness about gender crimes and inscribing them in the Statute, along with an emphasis on restorative justice. Once the Statute was complete, they pursued campaigns for accession to the Treaty and are actively involved with the ASP, pressing their agendas.

At operational levels of the Court, NGOs have also been crucial. They participated vigorously in the Prosecutor's hearings about how to set up his office, and they continued to comment on the actions of the Court as its operations got under way. The Prosecutor regularized NGO contacts with semiyearly consultations on policy. Much of the information flowing into the OTP regarding alleged crimes has come from NGO sources. On the ground in the situation states, NGOs have played such vital roles in providing information about the Court and helping Court officials to set up local contacts that they can be seen almost as extensions of the Court itself.

NGOs' objectives vary, however. Particularly as the Court has become involved in the situation states, humanitarian and human rights objectives of NGOs have been in some tension with each other. In Uganda, for example, NGOs focused on humanitarianism have suggested that the ICC find some way out of the impasse over the warrants it issued to LRA leaders so that peace agreements could move forward. In contrast, human rights organizations have stressed the importance of carrying out the Court's judicial processes, in order to clearly establish the message that impunity cannot be tolerated even (or perhaps especially) when suspected transgressors hold potential victim populations at risk. NGOs have been reluctant to criticize the Court, although they have expressed discomfort when the OTP has appeared to identify too closely with governments (as in Uganda and the DRC), has narrowed charges against suspects too much (Lubanga), or has aimed too low (in Sudan).

STATES

Accession to the Statute is most easily explained by states' desires to demonstrate opposition to impunity and to create a mechanism at the international level to counter it. Most of the states that join would expect not to be the scenes of international criminal law violations or the home states of international criminal law transgressors, and they would expect that, should such crimes occur, their domestic legal institutions would deal with them. Thus, the impulse to join must, for most countries, either be to support antiimpunity in other states or to demonstrate adherence to the norms for some other reason, such as the compulsions of identity or a quest for prestige. These motives fit the constructivist proposition that states can pursue quests for nonmaterial and absolute gains. The positions of states opposed to the Court can also be explained by constructivists. Dedication to absolute sovereignty is just as much based on ideas as is dedication to alternative norms, as would be decision makers' belief in their own exceptional right to carry out the kinds of acts criminalized by the Statute.

U.S. motives in opposing the ICC appear mixed. Some U.S. opponents of the Court apparently fear that the Court might constrain the use of U.S. military force and thus undermine national or international security. Others are ideologically opposed to the idea of subjecting the United States to an organization it does not control. Regardless of the reason for U.S. enmity toward the ICC, as it began to experience the foreign policy costs of its opposition (in Europe, Latin America, and with regard to Sudan), it moderated its opposition, as a realist would predict.

States' accessions to the Statute do not establish their degree of support for the Court in practice (aside from their assessed financial contribution). States' tepid support for the ICC so far is shown by the slow implementation of the domestic legal reforms necessary to bring signatory state's penal codes into compliance with Statute requirements. Members of the Assembly of States Parties, while encouraging additional states to sign the Statute, do not accord accession a high priority in their bilateral relations with nonsignatories. The relatively low level of priority accorded to ICC matters by states is also evident in the level of diplomatic representation that many countries accord the Court in The Hague and in the annual meetings of the ASP. Although U.S. opposition to the Court appears to be waning, active cooperation remains a distant prospect. Meanwhile, the discussions about the crime of aggression carry the potential for rousing greater opposition from the major powers who are currently outside the Court.

THE SITUATIONS

Core judicial functions define the ICC and enable it to defend itself against pressures to politicize its role; however, the Statute leaves considerable leeway for Court officials to explicate that role and its limits. In developing procedures for selecting situations to investigate, the OTP shifted emphasis from a legalistic approach to a somewhat more political-diplomatic one. In practice, when the OTP opted for negotiated self-referrals, thus avoiding the problem of noncooperation by situation states, the Prosecutor risked appearing partisan.

The Court is experiencing hazards common to the tribunals, as well as some new ones of its own. Like the Yugoslavia tribunal, the Court is pursuing crimes perpetrated in ongoing conflicts; thus, the Court itself becomes embroiled in the politics of the conflict. Much as Serbian authorities vilified the ICTY, so (for instance) the Sudanese government is decrying the ICC in its investigation of Darfur. Like the Rwanda tribunal which has found it impossible to prosecute individuals associated with the current government's party because of the need for government cooperation, the ICC has been accused of going easy on the military forces of President Museveni in Uganda and the political figures in the DRC who were vital to its transitional election process.

The threat of instrumentalization has been more immediate to the ICC than it was to the tribunals, since the Court's complementarity doctrine requires it to cooperate more closely with sovereign authorities. President Museveni engaged the Court in part to build support among other, particularly European, states, and to add the ICC's clout to his efforts against the LRA. Ugandan and external critics argued that the Court was being coopted by the government and, as a consequence, would overlook crimes of the Ugandan military (UPDF). This image was exacerbated by the Prosecutor's appearance with Museveni in London and Moreno Ocampo's later statements that implied that investigations would be sensitive to ongoing political efforts. After the warrants were issued, the Prosecutor argued that he would pursue criminality whatever the source, including the UPDF, but that the Lord's Resistance Army's crimes were much greater than those of the UPDF. President Museveni exacerbated the problem by repeatedly appearing to use the Court for leverage against the LRA, making claims that he could get the Court to lift its warrants if his negotiations with the LRA leadership succeeded.

Meanwhile, just as advocates of a negotiated settlement in Bosnia pressured the Yugoslavia tribunal not to indict officials with whom negotiations were taking place, humanitarian organizations worried that the ICC's arrest warrants for the LRA would damage chances for peace, raising the perennial question of whether peace and justice could or should be simultaneously pursued. They pressed for the Court to lift the warrants, which the Prosecutor firmly rejected as not within his power. Should it come to such a decision, the judges will have to decide what to do. The Statute thus gave the OTP cover for staying out of the political fray, but the Court as a whole cannot avoid it. The Court's image has been battered, at least among humanitarian and peace-oriented observers.

In the Congo, President Kabila appears to have used the Court to discredit potential opposition and build external support for his government too. Issuing a warrant for only one suspect, and appearing to hold off until a first round of elections took place in the DRC for a new government, opened the Prosecutor to charges that he was timing his actions according to political, not judicial factors. Victim-oriented NGOs wanted warrants to be issued for additional suspects and wider charges against the first suspect, Thomas Lubanga Dyilo. Cooperation with the authorities enabled the ICC to bring Lubanga into court, but deference to the government may have limited the range of suspects the OTP pursued. The appropriate secrecy of OTP operations makes evaluation of the instrumentalization of the Court very difficult, although should a pattern emerge of only second-tier miscreants being subject to Court warrants, an adverse conclusion about the political orientation of the Prosecutor could appropriately be drawn. On the other hand, ICC involvement seems to have spurred DRC authorities to build their domestic judicial capacities, which, if genuine, would be a highly positive result of Court involvement.

In the Sudan, after a two-year investigation, the ICC issued two warrants. Humanitarian NGOs welcomed the addition of ICC pressures to others being exerted upon the Sudan government to moderate its genocidal actions in Darfur; however, other observers regarded the OTP's progress as sluggish and aiming too low. Because the initial information turned over to the OTP from the Special Commission included many more names and much higher officials of the state, the Prosecutor's claim that the warrants issued were based on the best evidence and lodged against the most serious perpetrators was not found convincing by some closely involved with the situation. Similarly, announcement after two and a half years of consideration of a formal investigation into the Central African Republic struck some commentators as a rather slow response.

In all four situations, Pre-Trial Chamber judges sought to channel prosecution activities toward greater concern for victims, with swifter investigation procedures to bring suspects before the Chambers. The early years of the ICC in these ways mirror the tribunals, where the first few years were also characterized by judges' dissatisfaction with the prosecution's slow progress and efforts by the Chambers to exert increasing influence over the OTP.

BUILDING JUSTICE

The ICC is the organizational manifestation of new institutions of international criminal justice built on norms advocated by international lawyers and by NGO activists commanding the consensus of an epistemic community that coalesced at the Rome Statute Conference. The insights of constructivist theorists – that ideas matter and that decision makers can be motivated by moral commitments, desires for enhanced reputation, prestige, and the fear of embarrassment, and thus that nonmaterial goals can become national interests – are verified by the creation of the ICC. Limited Court jurisdiction (over only genocide, crimes against humanity, and war crimes) and protections of sovereignty (the Security Council's role, the need for voluntary state cooperation, checks on the Prosecutor from Chambers) accord with realist insights; moreover, realists can explain the potential material costs of state opposition. States' delegation of limited authority to an international organization, reciprocal influences of the organization upon the states, and vice versa, and their consequences for the organization's autonomy, survival, legitimacy, and growth fit the neoliberal institutionalists' vision.

The normative consensus and organizational machinery have largely been established, but the Court is still young. States remain capable of instituting single-purpose tribunals to pursue international criminal justice, in the patterns of the ad hoc tribunals, domestic–international mixed truth commissions, and a variety of other special courts.[1] The ICC was intended in part to make such ad hoc arrangements unnecessary; nevertheless, they also represent alternative organizational species that could coexist with, or supplant, the ICC. The Court's survival and vitality can be demonstrated only as it accumulates a record of operation, through the 2009 Statute Review Conference and beyond, including completion of full judicial cycles from referral to conviction (and/or acquittal) of suspects, engagement of its

---

[1] Such as the Special Court for Sierra Leone, Extraordinary Chambers in the Courts of Cambodia (Khmer Rouge tribunal), and the Iraqi High Tribunal (*Dujail* trial of Saddam Hussein and others).

machinery for restorative measures, and resolution (or shelving) of the aggression debate.

Internally, routines for coordination remain fluid even as the organization generates massive tomes of operational rules. Because the Court's original President, Registrar, and Chief Prosecutor remain in place, the degree to which coordination and leadership problems are structural, as opposed to personal, remains to be seen. Future leaders of the Court will have the advantage that they will not be faced with the challenges of bringing the entire organization into being. The early years of the Court are nonetheless establishing precedents that will shape the Court for years to come. The challenges to the Court come from all directions – it pursues its cases in very difficult operational environments; its retributive, restorative, civil-law/common-law, peace, truth, and justice objectives reside together, but not comfortably, in its organizational mandate. Court officials assert that the touchstone of their organization's reputation and legitimacy is its judicial (nonpolitical) nature, even as they juggle the political pressures to which they are subject.

During a visit to Japan in December 2006, ICC President Kirsch demonstrated his concern about the Court's reputation:

There's not a shred of evidence after three-and-a-half years that the court has done anything political. The court is operating purely judicially ... and that, in turn, has had clearly an effect of relaxation on the part of states that were initially very opposed to the court and now are much more sympathetic and interested in the court.[2]

This encomium to legal objectivity understates the complexity of challenges to the Court. While incorporating design elements contributed by legal experts, the Statute is ultimately a document of political compromise, establishing an organization with tensions built into it by a broad mandate, that operates in highly politicized environments. Political choices abound at all levels – international, organizational, and among the Court's organs and personnel. Its decision mechanisms cannot be comprehensively legal. Even though its core activities are primarily judicial, its broad mandate, administrative complexity, and intricate connections to states and other organizations inevitably involve it in nonjudicial decisions, political in their ramifications. The boundaries between judicial and political choices cannot be sharp. The timing and substance of Court interactions with international organizations, arrangements for cooperation with states in and out of the

---

[2] Quoted in Herman, "Japan's Expected to Support International Criminal Court" (2006).

ASP, with situation and other states, and with local and international NGOs require more than purely judicial decision making. The Court's course will be determined by officials' judicial decisions, administrative choices, and political judgment as it strives to fill the organizational niche created by converging international criminal law norms. Rather than non-political, the Court must be politically constructive or, at least, non-threatening, by virtue of its modes of action. Its record in this regard is promising so far, but its secure establishment as a significant operational organization will take a considerably longer period.

Its success so far is indicated indirectly by states' continuing support. States have bestowed generous budgets upon the Court and appear willing for its staff to grow to approximately the largest size of the Yugoslavia tribunal (planning for the ICC's permanent headquarters is based on a staff size of about 1,250). Survival and growth are ensured in the short run. For long-run solidification of the ICC's position, the Court will need to show ASP members that it continues to contribute to their objectives. This requires successful, respectable, reasonably efficient trials and constructive cooperation with states as they pursue suspects on their own. The Court's success would also be shown by further accessions to, and members' adoption of domestic legal codes in compliance with, the Rome Statute.

International NGO support for the Court too depends on the ICC's ability to implement activities across the range of its somewhat internally contradictory mandate. The Court's service to humanitarian and human rights objectives, retributive and restorative justice goals, would sustain NGOs' enthusiasms for the Court, although these objectives are not easily compatible. NGO support for the ICC could continue to raise the embarrassment threat against states contemplating opposition to, lack of cooperation with, or only feeble support for the ICC, additionally aiding in securing the Court.

Norm convergence enabled the constitution of a new institution of international criminal justice at a propitious moment in international history between the fall of the Berlin Wall and the fall of the Twin Towers, enabling states prodded by international lawyers and NGOs to produce the Statute of the International Criminal Court. From a constructivist's standpoint, the creation of the ICC denotes a pivotal historical moment in the development of international society. From a realist's standpoint, further complexity has been added to the anarchic international system without fundamentally changing it. For neoliberal institutionalists, states added to the panoply of organizational mechanisms intended to mitigate anarchy and enable collective gains. From all three standpoints, the future of the organization rests upon its ability to navigate political currents while being responsive to states' interests yet resisting their pressures, as humanity builds a court to try individual perpetrators of its worst crimes, to bring recognition to their victims, and to restore the rule of law and help heal societies.

Web Sites for Further and Ongoing Information

The Frederick K. Cox International Law Center War Crimes Research Portal (Case Western Reserve University): http://www.law.case.edu/war-crimes-research-portal/. This Web site provides a massive set of further links, arranged by topic.

The Hague Justice Portal: http://www.haguejusticeportal.net/. This Web site contains links to academic institutions and events in The Hague, relevant journals, etc.

The ICC's "Legal Tools" page: http://www.icc-cpi.int/legal_tools.html. The Legal Tools include the Rome Statute of the ICC, under the "Access to the Tools," "Basic ICC Documents" link, and a treasure trove of preparatory and other documents.

International Criminal Court English homepage: http://www.icc-cpi.int/home.html&l=en

International Justice Tribune: http://www.justicetribune.com/index.php?page=v2_une. A newsletter and archive (by subscription) with superb reporting from and about various courts and tribunals are included on this Web site.

International Criminal Tribunal for the Former Yugoslavia homepage: http://www.un.org/icty/.

International Criminal Tribunal for Rwanda homepage: http://69.94.11.53/default.htm.

NGO Coalition for the International Criminal Court: http://www.iccnow.org/. This is an excellent source of news and analysis about current issues regarding the ICC, with materials from a wide variety of NGOs.

Peace Palace (The Hague) library online catalog: http://catalogue.ppl.nl/ IMPLAND=Y/SRT=YOP/LNG=EN/. This is a terrific resource for searching (by title, keywords, subject, or author) for materials relevant to international law.

Bibliography and Sources

Books and Book Chapters

Allen, Tim, *Trial Justice: The International Criminal Court and the Lord's Resistance Army* (London: Zed Press, 2006).

Bassiouni, M. Cherif, "Historical Survey 1919–1998," in *ICC Ratification and National Implementing Legislation, Nouvelles Études Pénales* (Saint-Agne, France: Association Internationale de Droit Pénal: 1999), 1–44.

ed., *The Statute of the International Criminal Court: A Documentary History* (Ardsley, NY: Transnational Publishers, 1998).

ed., *Post-Conflict Justice* (Ardsley, NY: Transnational Publishers, 2002).

ed., *The Statute of the International Criminal Court and Related Instruments: Legislative History 1994–2000* (Ardsley, NY: Transnational Publishers, 2002).

Bekou, Olympia, and Robert Cryer, eds., *The International Criminal Court* (Burlington, VT: Ashgate, 2004).

Boot, Machteld, *Genocide, Crimes against Humanity, War Crimes: Nullum Crimen sine Lege and the Subject Matter Jurisdiction of the International Criminal Court* (Antwerp: Intersentia, 2002).

Boraine, Alex, *A Country Unmasked: Inside South Africa's Truth and Reconciliation Commission* (Oxford: Oxford University Press, 2000).

Brague, Rémi, *The Law of God: The Philosophical History of an Idea* (Chicago: University of Chicago Press, 2007).

Broomhall, Bruce, *International Justice and the International Criminal Court: Between Sovereignty and the Rule of Law* (Oxford: Oxford University Press, 2003).

Brownlie, Ian, *Principles of Public International Law*, 4th ed. (Oxford: Oxford University Press, 1991).

Bull, Hedley, *The Anarchical Society*, 3rd ed. (New York: Columbia University Press, 2003).

Carr, Edmund Hallett, *The Twenty Years Crisis 1919–1939* (New York: Harpers, 1964).

Cassese, Antonio, *International Criminal Law* (Oxford: Oxford University Press, 2003).

Cassese, Antonio et al., eds., *The Rome Statute of the International Criminal Court – A Commentary* (Oxford: Oxford University Press, 2002).

Clark, Anthony Arend, "A Methodology for Determining an International Legal Rule," in Charlotte Ku and Paul F. Diehl, eds., *International Law: Classic and Contemporary Readings*, 2nd ed. (Boulder, CO: Lynne Reinner, 2003), chapter 2.

Dallaire, Romeo, *Shake Hands with the Devil: The Failure of Humanity in Rwanda* (London: Arrow Books, 2004).

Daly, Kathleen, "Revisiting the Relationship between Retributive and Restorative Justice," in Heather Strang and John Braithwaite, eds., *Restorative Justice: From Philosophy to Practice* (Burlington, VT: Ashgate, 2000), 33–54.

Donnelly, Jack, *International Human Rights*, 2nd ed. (Boulder, CO: Westview, 1998).

Drakulic, Slavenka, *They Would Never Hurt a Fly: War Criminals on Trial at The Hague* (New York: Viking, 2004).

Falk, Richard, *Human Rights Horizons: The Pursuit of Justice in a Globalizing World* (New York: Routledge, 2000).

Findlay, Mark, and Ralph Henham, *Transforming International Criminal Justice: Retributive and Restorative Justice in the Trial Process* (Portland, OR: Willan Publishing, 2005).

Forsythe, David, *Human Rights in International Relations* (Cambridge: Cambridge University Press, 2000).

Glasius, Marlies, *The International Criminal Court: A Global Civil Society Achievement* (New York: Routledge, 2005).

Gourevitch, Philip, *We Wish to Inform You That Tomorrow We Will Be Killed with Our Families: Stories from Rwanda* (New York: Picador, 1998).

Green, Leslie C., *Essays on the Modern Law of War*, 2nd ed. (Ardsley, NY: Transnational, 1999).

Groenleer, Martijn, "Justice under Construction: The Birth and Early Development of the International Criminal Court," unpublished M.A. thesis, Public Administration, Leiden University, 2003.

Hagan, John, *Justice in the Balkans: Prosecuting War Crimes in the Hague Tribunal* (Chicago: University of Chicago Press, 2003).

Hart, H. L. A., *The Concept of Law* (Oxford: Oxford University Press, 1961).

Hayner, Priscilla, *Unspeakable Truths: Confronting State Terror and Atrocity* (New York: Routledge, 2002).

Hazan, Pierre, *Justice in a Time of War: The True Story behind the International Criminal Tribunal for the Former Yugoslavia* (College Station: Texas A&M University Press, 2004).

Hinsley, F. H., *Power and the Pursuit of Peace: Theory and Practice in the History of Relations between States* (Cambridge: Cambridge University Press, 1963).

Ikenberry, G. John, *After Victory: Institutions, Strategic Restraint, and the Rebuilding of Orders after Major Wars* (Princeton, NJ: Princeton University Press, 2001).

International Justice Tribune, *ICC in 2006: Year One. Legal and Political Issues Surrounding the International Criminal Court* (Paris: Justice Memo, 2007).

Jacobson, Harold, *Networks of Interdependence: International Organizations and the Global Political System* (New York: Knopf, 1979).

Janis, Mark, *An Introduction to International Law*, 2nd ed. (New York: Little, Brown, 1993).

Karns, Margaret, and Karen Mingst, *International Organizations: The Politics and Processes of Global Governance* (Boulder, CO: Lynne Rienner, 2004).

Kerr, Rachel, *The International Criminal Tribunal for the Former Yugoslavia: An Exercise in Law, Politics, and Diplomacy* (Oxford: Oxford University Press, 2004).

Kirsch, Philippe, and John T. Holmes, "The Birth of the International Criminal Court: The 1998 Rome Conference," in Olympia Bekou and Robert Cryer, eds., *The International Criminal Court* (Burlington, VT: Ashgate, 2004), 3–39.

Klotz, Audie, *Norms in International Relations: The Struggle against Apartheid* (Ithaca, NY: Cornell University Press, 1995).

Knoops, Geert-Jan Alexander, *An Introduction to the Law of International Criminal Tribunals: A Comparative Study* (Ardsley, NY: Transnational Publishers, 2003).

Koskenniemi, Martti, *The Gentle Civilizer of Nations: The Rise and Fall of International Law 1870–1960*. Hersch Lauterpacht memorial lectures #14 (Cambridge: Cambridge University Press, 2001).

Krasner, Stephen, *Sovereignty: Organized Hypocrisy* (Princeton, NJ: Princeton University Press, 1999).

Lee, Roy, ed., *The International Criminal Court: The Making of the Rome Statute: Issues, Negotiations and Results* (The Hague: Kluwer Law International, 1999).

States' Responses to Issues Arising from the ICC Statute: Constitutionality, Sovereignty, Judicial Cooperation and Criminal Law (Ardsley, NY: Transnational, 2005).

Lemkin, Raphael, *Axis Rule in Occupied Europe: Laws of Occupation, Analysis of Government, Proposals for Redress* (Washington, DC: Carnegie Endowment for International Peace, 1944).

Leonard, Erik, *The Onset of Global Governance: International Relations Theory and the International Criminal Court* (Burlington, VT: Ashgate, 2005).

Maogoto, Jackson Nyamuya, *War Crimes and Realpolitik: International Justice from World War I to the 21st Century* (Boulder, CO: Lynne Rienner, 2004).

McGoldrick, Dominic, Peter Rowe, and Eric Donnelly, eds., *The Permanent International Criminal Court: Legal and Policy Issues* (Portland, OR: Hart Publishing, 2004).

Melvern, Linda, *Conspiracy to Murder: The Rwandan Genocide* (New York: Verso, 2004).

Mingst, Karen, *Essentials of International Relations*, 3rd ed. (New York: W. W. Norton, 2004).

Morton, Jeffrey, *The International Law Commission of the United Nations* (Columbia: University of South Carolina Press, 2000).

Mladjenovic, Lepa, "The ICTY: The Validation of the Experiences of Survivors in International War Crimes Trials," in Steven R. Ratner and James L. Bischoff, eds., *International War Crimes Trials: Making a Difference?* (Austin: University of Texas Press, 2004), 59–65.

Politi, Mauro, and Giuseppe, Nesi eds., *The Rome Statute of the International Criminal Court: A Challenge to Impunity* (Burlington, VT: Ashgate, 2001).

Power, Samantha, *"A Problem from Hell": America and the Age of Genocide* (New York: Basic Books, 2002).

Prunier, Gérard, *Darfur: The Ambiguous Genocide*, revised and updated edition (Ithaca, NY: Cornell University Press, 2007).

Ratner, Steven, and Jason Abrams, *Accountability for Human Rights Atrocities in International Law: Beyond the Nuremberg Legacy*, 2nd ed. (Oxford: Oxford University Press, 2001).

Ratner, Steven, and James Bischoff, eds., *International War Crimes Trials: Making a Difference?* (Austin: University of Texas Law School, 2004).

Reeves, Eric, *A Long Day's Dying: Critical Moments in the Darfur Genocide* (Toronto: Key Publishing, 2007).

Reus-Smit, Christian, "The Politics of International Law," in Reus-Smit, ed., *The Politics of International Law* (Cambridge: Cambridge University Press, 2004), 14–44.

Risse, Thomas, Stephen C. Ropp, and Kathyryn Sikkink, eds., *The Power of Human Rights: International Norms and Domestic Change* (Cambridge: Cambridge University Press, 1999).

Roach, Steven, *Politicizing the International Criminal Court: The Convergence of Politics, Ethics, and Law* (Lanham, MD: Rowman and Littlefield, 2006).

Robertson, Geoffrey, *Crimes Against Humanity: The Struggle for Global Justice* (New York: New Press, 1999).

Rochester, J. Martin, *Between Peril and Promise: The Politics of International Law* (Washington, DC: CQ Press, 2006).

Rosenberg, Tina, *The Haunted Land: Facing Europe's Ghosts after Communism* (New York: Random House, 1995).

Rotberg, Robert I., and Dennis Thompson, eds., *Truth v. Justice: The Morality of Truth Commissions* (Princeton, NJ: Princeton University Press, 2000).

Ruggie, John, *Constructing the World Polity: Essays on International Institutionalization* (New York: Routledge, 1998).

Sachs, Albie, *The Soft Vengeance of a Freedom Fighter* (Berkeley: University of California Press, 2000).

Sadat, Leila, *The International Criminal Court and the Transformation of International Law* (Ardsley, NY: Transnational, 2002).

Sandholtz, Wane, and Alec Stone Sweet, "Law, Politics, and International Governance," in Christian Reus-Smit, ed., *The Politics of International Law* (Cambridge: Cambridge University Press, 2004), 238–71.

Sands, Philippe, *Lawless World: The Whistle-Blowing Account of How Bush and Blair Are Taking the Law into Their Own Hands* (London: Penguin, 2006).

Schabas, William, *An Introduction to the International Criminal Court*, 2nd ed. (Cambridge: Cambridge University Press, 2004).

Schiff, Benjamin, "Do Truth Commissions Promote Accountability or Impunity? The Case of the South African Truth and Reconciliation Commission," in M. Cherif Bassiouni, ed., *Post Conflict Justice* (Ardsley, NY: Transnational, 2002), 325–44.

Schwarzenberger, Georg, *International Law as Applied by Courts and Tribunals* (London: Stevens & Sons Limited, 1968), 462–6.

Sewall, Sarah B., and Carl Kaysen, eds., *The United States and the International Criminal Court. National Security and International Law* (Lanham, MD: Rowman and Littlefield, 2003).

Shestack, Jerome, "Sisyphus Endures: The International Human Rights NGO," *New York Law School Review*, 24, 89 (1978), cited in M. Dixon and R. McCorquodale, *Case and Materials on International Law*, 4th ed. (Oxford: Oxford University Press, 2003).

Simpson, Gerry, "Politics, Sovereignty, Remembrance," in Dominic McGoldrick, Peter Rowe, and Eric Donnelly, eds., *The Permanent International Criminal Court: Legal and Policy Issues* (Portland, OR: Hart Publishing, 2004), 47–61.

ed., *War Crimes Law*, Vol. 2 (Burlington, VT: Ashgate, 2004).

Steiner, Henry J., and Philip Alston, *International Human Rights in Context: Law, Politics, Morals*, 2nd ed. (Oxford: Oxford University Press, 2000).

Stephen, Chris, *Judgment Day: The Trial of Slobodan Milosevic* (New York: Atlantic Monthly Press, 2005).

Stover, Eric, and Harvey M. Weinstein, eds., *My Neighbor, My Enemy: Justice and Community in the Aftermath of Mass Atrocity* (Cambridge: Cambridge University Press, 2004).

Taylor, Telford, *The Anatomy of the Nuremberg Trials: A Personal Memoir* (New York: Knopf, 1992).

Thakur, Ramesh, and Peter Malcontent, eds., *From Sovereign Impunity to International Accountability: The Search for Justice in a World of States* (New York: United Nations University Press, 2004).

Triffterer, Otto, ed., *Commentary on the Rome Statute of the International Criminal Court: Observers' Notes Article by Article* (Baden-Baden: Nomos, 1999).

Van der Merwe, H. W., *Peacemaking in South Africa: A Life in Conflict Resolution* (Capetown: Tafelberg, 2000).

Vohrah, Lal Chand, ed., *Man's Inhumanity to Man: Essays in Honor of Antonio Cassesse* (The Hague: Kluwer Law International, 2003).

Waltz, Kenneth, *Man, the State, and War: A Theoretical Analysis* (New York: Columbia, 1959).

Theory of International Politics (New York: McGraw Hill, 1979).

Walzer, Michael, *Just and Unjust Wars: A Moral Argument with Historical Illustrations*, 3rd ed. (New York: Basic Books, 2000).

Wendt, Alexander, *Social Theory of International Politics* (Cambridge: Cambridge University Press, 1999).

Williams, Paul, and Michael Scharf, *Peace with Justice? War Crimes and Accountability in the Former Yugoslavia* (Lanham, MD: Rowman and Littlefield, 2002).

Wippman, David, "The International Criminal Court," in Christian Reus-Smit, ed., *The Politics of International Law* (Cambridge: Cambridge University Press, 2004), 151–88.

Woodward, Susan L., *Balkan Tragedy: Chaos and Dissolution after the Cold War* (Washington, DC: Brookings, 1995).

Journal Articles and Academic Papers

Abbott, Kenneth, Robert Keohane, Andrew Moravcsik, Anne-Marie Slaughter, and Duncan Snidal, "The Concept of Legalization," *International Organization*, 54, 3 (2000), 401–19.

Abbott, Kenneth, and Duncan Snidal, "Why States Act through Formal Organizations," *The Journal of Conflict Resolution*, 42, 1 (1998), 3–32.

Akhavan, Payam, "The Lord's Resistance Army Case: Uganda's Submission of the First State Referral to the International Criminal Court," *American Journal of International Law*, 99, 2 (2005), 403–20.

Allain, Jean, and John R. W. D. Jones, "A Patchwork of Norms: A Commentary on the 1996 Draft Code of Crimes against the Peace and Security of Mankind," *European Journal of International Law*, 8, 1 (1997), 100–17.

Ambos, Kai, "The Status, Role and Accountability of the Prosecutor of the ICC: A Comparative Overview on the Basis of 33 National Reports," *European Journal of Crime, Criminal Law and Criminal Justice*, 8, 2 (2000), 89–118.

"International Criminal Procedure: 'Adversarial', 'Inquisitorial' or Mixed?" *International Criminal Law Review*, 3 (2003), 1–37.

Apuuli, Kasaija Phillip, "The ICC Arrest Warrants for the Lord's Resistance Army Leaders and Peace Prospects for Northern Uganda," *Journal of International Criminal Justice*, 4, 1 (2006), 179–87.

Arsanjani, Manoush, and W. Michael Reisman, "The Law-in-Action of the International Criminal Court," *American Journal of International Law*, 99, 2, (2005), 385–403.

Askin, Kelly D., "Legal Precedents in Rwanda Court," Crimes of War Web site, *Magazine: The Tribunals* (May 2001), <http://www.crimesofwar.org/tribun-mag/rwanda_print.html>.

Askin, Kelly D., "Prosecuting Wartime Rape and Other Gender-Related Crimes under International Law: Extraordinary Advances, Enduring Obstacles," Stefan A. Riesenfeld Symposium 2002, *Berkeley Journal of International Law* (2003), 288–349.

Askin, Kelly D., "Reflections on Some of the Most Significant Achievements of the ICTY," *New England Law Review*, 37, 4 (2003), 903–14.

Bassiouni, M. Cherif, "Accountability for Violations of International Humanitarian Law and Other Serious Violations of Human Rights," in M. C. Bassiouni, ed., *Post-Conflict Justice* (Ardsley, NY: Transnational Publishers, 2002), 14–26.

"International Recognition of Victims' Rights," *Human Rights Law Review*, 6, 2 (2006), 203–79.

Bedont, Barbara, and Katherine Hall Martinez, "Ending Impunity for Gender Crimes under the International Criminal Court," *The Brown Journal of World Affairs*, VI, 1 (1999), 65–85.

Benedetti, Fanny, and John L. Washburn, "Drafting the International Criminal Court Treaty: Two Years to Rome and an Afterword on the Rome Diplomatic Conference," *Global Governance*, 5, 1 (Jan.–Mar. 1999), 1–38.

Bolton, John R., "No, No, No to International Criminal Court," *Human Events* (August 21, 1998), <http://www.findarticles.com/p/articles/mi_qa3827/is_199808/ai_n8816982>.

Branch, Adam, "International Justice, Local Injustice," *Dissent Magazine* (Summer 2004), <http://www.dissentmagazine.org/article/?article=336>.

Brennan, Coghlan B., et al., "Mortality in the Democratic Republic of Congo: A Nationwide Survey," *Lancet*, 367 (2006), 44–51.

Burbacher, Matthew R., "Prosecutorial Discretion in the International Criminal Court," *Journal of International Criminal Justice*, 2, 1 (March 2004), 71–95.

Burke-White, William, "Complementarity in Practice: The International Criminal Court as Part of a System of Multi-Level Global Governance in the Democratic Republic of Congo," *Leiden Journal of International Law*, 18 (2005), 557–90.

Burroughs, John, and Jacqueline Cabasso, "Confronting the Nuclear-Armed States in International Negotiating Forums: Lessons for NGOs," *International Negotiation*, 4 (1999), 457–80.

Cassese, Antonio, "Is the ICC Still Having Teething Problems?" *Journal of International Criminal Justice*, 4, 3 (July 2006), 434–41.

Cockayne, James, "The Fraying Shoestring: Rethinking Hybrid War Crimes Tribunals," *Fordham International Law Journal*, 28, 3 (2005), 616–80.

Conso, Giovanni, "The Basic Reasons for US Hostility to the ICC in Light of the Negotiating History of the Rome Statute," *Journal of International Criminal Justice*, 3, 2 (2004), 314–22.

Cook, Julian, "Plea Bargaining at the Hague," *Yale Journal of International Law*, 30, 2 (2005), 473–506.

Copelon, Rhonda, "Gender Crimes as War Crimes: Integrating Crimes Against Women into International Criminal Law," *McGill Law Journal* 46, 1 (November 2000), 217–40.

Cryer, Robert, "Sudan, Resolution 1593, and International Criminal Justice," *Leiden Journal of International Law*, 19, 1 (March 2006), 195–222.

Dembour, Marie-Benedicte, and Emily Haslam, "Silencing Hearings? Victims-Witnesses at War Crimes Trials," *European Journal of International Law*, 15, 1 (2004), 151–77.

El Zeidy, Mohamed, "The Principle of Complementarity: A New Machinery to Implement International Criminal Law," *Michigan Journal of International Law*, 23 (2002), 869–975.

"The Ugandan Government Triggers the First Test of the Complementarity Principle: An Assessment of the First State's Party Referral to the ICC," *International Criminal Law Review*, 5, 1 (January 1, 2005), 83–120.

Fairlie, Megan, "The Marriage of Common and Continental Law at the ICTY and Its Progeny, Due Process Deficit," *International Criminal Law Review*, 4, 3 (2004), 243–319.

Faulhaber, Lilian, "American Servicemembers' Protection Act of 2002," *Harvard Journal on Legislation*, 40, 2 (Summer 2003), 537–57.

Finnemore, Martha, and Kathryn Sikkink, "International Norms and Political Change," *International Organization*, 52, 4 (Autumn 1998), 887–917.

Fletcher, George, and Jens Ohlin, "Reclaiming Fundamental Principles of Criminal Law in the Darfur Case," *Journal of International Criminal Justice*, 3, 3 (July 2005), 539–61.

Forsythe, David, "The United States and International Criminal Justice," *Human Rights Quarterly*, 24, 4 (2002), 974–91.

Franck, Thomas, "Are Human Rights Universal?" *Foreign Affairs*, 80, 1 (January/February 2001), 191–204.

Goldstein, Judith, Miles Kahler, Robert Keohane, and Anne-Marie Slaughter, "Introduction: Legalization and World Politics," *International Organization*, 54, 3 (Summer 2000), 385–99.

Haan, Verena, "The Development of the Joint Criminal Enterprise at the ICTY," *International Criminal Law Review*, 5, 2 (2005), 167–201.

Haas, Peter M. "Introduction: Epistemic Communities and International Policy," *International Organization*, 46, 1 (Winter 1992), 1–36.

Hafner, Gerhard, "An Attempt to Explain the Position of the USA towards the ICC," *Journal of International Criminal Justice*, 3, 2 (2005), 323–32.

Happold, Matthew, "Darfur, the Security Council, and the International Criminal Court," *International and Comparative Law Quarterly*, 55, 1 (January 2006), 226–36.

Hatchell, Michael "Closing the Gaps in United States Law and Implementing the Rome Statute: A Comparative Approach," *International Law Student Association (ILSA) Journal of International and Comparative Law*, 12, 1 (May 2006), <http://www.nsulaw.nova.edu/stuorgs/ILSAJournal/journals/Hatchell_FinalCopy.pdf>.

Hudson, Manley O., "The Proposed International Criminal Court," *The American Journal of International Law*, 32, 3 (July 1938), 550.

Jallow, Hassan B., "Prosecutorial Discretion and International Justice," *Journal of International Criminal Justice*, 3, 1 (2005), 145–61.

Jorda, Claude, "The Major Hurdles and Accomplishments of the ICTY: What the ICC Can Learn from Them," *Journal of International Criminal Justice*, 2, 2 (2004), 572–84.

Jorda, Claude, and Marianne Saracco, "The Raisons d'Etre of the Pre-Trial Chamber of the International Criminal Court," in *Melanges Laity Kama* (2005), typescript.

Kaul, Hans-Peter, "Construction Site for More Justice: The ICC after Two Years," *American Journal of International Law*, 99, 2 (2005), 370–84.

"Special Note: The Struggle for the International Criminal Court's Jurisdiction," *European Journal of Crime, Criminal Law and Criminal Justice*, 6, 4 (1998), 48–60.

Kissinger, Henry, "The Pitfalls of Universal Jurisdiction" *Foreign Affairs*, 80, 4 (July/August 2001), 86–96.

Lado, Cleophas, "The Political Economy of Oil Discovery and Mining in the Sudan: Constraints and Prospects on Development" (undated, accessed June 6, 2006), <http://www.dur.ac.uk/justin.willis/lado.htm>.

Meron, Theodore, "Judicial Independence and Impartiality in International Criminal Tribunals," *American Journal of International Law*, 99, 2 (2005), 359–69.

Miraglia, Michela, "The First Decision of the ICC Pre-Trial Chamber: International Criminal Procedure Under Construction," *Journal of International Criminal Justice* 4, 1 (2006), 188–95.

Mundis, Daryl, "The Judicial Effects of the Completion Strategies on the Ad Hoc International Criminal Tribunals," *American Journal of International Law*, 99, 1 (2005), 142–57.

"Completing the Mandates of the ad Hoc International Criminal Tribunals: Lessons from the Nuremberg Process?" *Fordham International Law Journal*, 28, 3 (2005), 591–615.

New England Law Review, 37, 4 (2003), "Symposium: The International Criminal Tribunal for the Former Yugoslavia at 10: A Critical Assessment," 865–1080.

Nice, Geoffrey, and Philippe Vallieres-Roland, "Procedural Innovations in War Crimes Trials," *Journal of International Criminal Justice*, 3, 2 (May 2005), 354–80.

Nilsson, Cecilia, "Contextualizing the Agreement on the Privileges and Immunities of the International Criminal Court," *Leiden Journal of International Law*, 17, 3 (2004), 559–78.

Nsereko, Daniel D. Ntanda, "The International Criminal Court: Jurisdictional and Related Issues," *Criminal Law Forum*, 10, 1 (1999), 87–120.

"Aggression under the Rome Statute of the International Criminal Court," *Nordic Journal of International Law*, 71, 4 (2002), 497–521.

"Triggering Jurisdiction of the International Criminal Court," *African Human Rights Journal*, 4, 2 (2004), 256–74.

O'Connell, Jamie, "Gambling with the Psyche: Does Prosecuting Human Rights Violators Console Their Victims?" *Harvard International Law Journal*, 46, 2 (2005), 295–345.

Obembo, Jean-Paul, "The ICC: A Work in Progress in the Congo," *Humanitares Volkerrecht*,18, 1 (2005), 11–23.

Olásolo, Héctor, "The Prosecutor of the ICC before the Initiation of Investigations: A Quasi-judicial or a Political Body?" *International Criminal Law Review*, 3, 2 (2003), 87–150.

Otunnu, Olara A., "The Secret Genocide," *Foreign Policy*, 155 (July/August 2006), 45–6.

Peskin, Victor, "Courting Rwanda: The Promises and Pitfalls of the ICTR Outreach Program," *Journal of International Criminal Justice*, 3, 4 (2005), 950–61.

Posner, Eric A., and John C. Yoo, "A Theory of International Adjudication," Law School of the University of Chicago, John M. Olin Law and Economic Research Paper Series, Working Paper No. 206, and University of California, Berkeley Law School Public Law and Legal Theory Research Paper Series, Research Paper No. 146.

Raab, Dominic, "Evaluating the ICTY and Its Completion Strategy: Efforts to Achieve Accountability for War Crimes and Their Tribunals," *Journal of International Criminal Justice*, 3, 1 (2005), 82–102.

Raab, Dominic, and Hans Bevers, "The International Criminal Court and the Separation of Powers" *International Organizations Law Review* 3, 1 (2006), 93–135.

Reeves, Eric, "Why Abuja Won't Save Darfur," *The New Republic* (May 10, 2006), <http://www.sudanreeves.org/index.php?name=News&file=article&sid=103>.

Relva, Hugo, "The Implementation of the Rome Statute in Latin American States," *Leiden Journal of International Law*, 16, 2 (2003), 331–66.

Schabas, William, "Darfur and the 'Odious Scourge': The Commission of Inquiry's Findings on Genocide," *Leiden Journal of International Law*, 18, 4 (2005), 871–85.

Schabas, William, ed., "Truth Commissions and Courts: The Tension Between Criminal Justice and the Search for Truth," *Criminal Law Forum*, 15, 1–2 (2004).

Scharf, Michael,"Legacy of the Milosevic Trial," *New England Law Review*, 37, 4 (2003), 915–32.

"The Politics Behind the U.S. Opposition to the International Criminal Court," *New England International and Comparative Law Annual 1999*, 5, <http://www.nesl.edu/intljournal/vol5/scharf.htm>, accessed 5/18/06.

Scheffer, David, "Article 98(2) of the Rome Statute: America's Original Intent," *Journal of International Criminal Justice*, 3, 2 (May 2005), 333–53.

"Challenges Confronting International Justice Issues," *New England International and Comparative Law Annual*, 4 (1998), <http://www.nesl.edu/intljournal/VOL4/SCHEFFER.PDF>.

"How to Turn the Tide Using the Rome Statute's Temporal Jurisdiction," *Journal of International Criminal Justice*, 2, 1 (2004), 26–34.

"The Future U.S. Relationship with the International Criminal Court," *Pace University School of Law International Law Review*, XVII, II (Fall 2005), 161–78.

Sebenius, James K. "Challenging Conventional Explanations of International Negotiation: Negotiation Analysis and the Case of Epistemic Communities," *International Organization*, 46, 1 (Winter 1992), 323–66.

Sil, Rudra, "Problems Chasing Methods or Methods Chasing Problems? Research Communities, Constrained Pluralism, and the Role of Eclecticism," in Ian Shapiro, Rogers Smith, and Tarek Masoud, eds., *Problems and Methods in the Study of Politics* (Cambridge: Cambridge University Press, 2004), Chapter 14.

"Analytic Eclecticism and Research Traditions in International Relations," paper presented at Oberlin College, Social Sciences Division "Leading Edge" Seminar, April 27, 2007.

Southwick, Katherine, "Investigating War in Northern Uganda: Dilemmas for the International Criminal Court," *Yale Journal of International Affairs* 1, 1 (Summer/Fall 2005), 105–16.

Ssenyojo, Manisuli, "Accountability of Non-State Actors in Uganda for War Crimes and Human Rights Violations: Between Amnesty and the International Criminal Court," *Journal of Conflict and Security Law*, 10, 3 (2005), 405–34.

Struett, Michael J., "The Legitimacy of Prosecutorial Discretion at the International Criminal Court," typescript, paper prepared for UC Irvine Workshop "Judging Transitional Justice," October 30–31, 2004.

Tochilovsky, Vladimir, "Proceedings in the International Criminal Court: Some Lessons to Learn from ICTY Experience," *European Journal of Crime, Criminal Law and Criminal Justice*, 10, 4 (2002), 268–75.

Turner, Jenia Iontcheva, "Nationalizing International Criminal Law" *Stanford Journal of International Law*, 41, 1 (2005), 1–51.

Webb, Philippa, "The ICC Prosecutor's Discretion Not to Proceed in the Interests of Justice," *Criminal Law Quarterly*, 50, 3 (2005), 305–48.

Wendt, Alexander, "Anarchy Is What States Make of It: The Social Construction of Power Politics," *International Organization*, 46, 3 (1992), 391–425.

Zacklin, Ralph, "The Failings of Ad Hoc International Tribunals," *Journal of International Criminal Justice*, 2, 2 (2004), 541–5.

Zoglin, Katie, "Future of War Crimes Prosecutions in the Former Yugoslavia: Accountability or Junk Justice?" *Human Rights Quarterly*, 27, 1 (2005), 41–77.

News Coverage

The Age, "NSW Judge Candidate for International Court," March 12, 2003, <http://www.theage.com.au/articles/2003/03/11/1047144971263.html>.

Agence France-Presse (AFP), "War in Northern Uganda World's Worst Forgotten Crisis: UN," November 11, 2003, posted on Reliefweb, <http://www.reliefweb.int/rw/rwb.nsf/AllDocsByUNID/e1f176894430fdeec1256ddb0056ea4c>.

Aita, Judy, Washington File United Nations Correspondent, U.S. Department of State, USINFO.STATE.GOV, "African Union Tribunal Proposed for War Crimes in Darfur," <http://usinfo.state.gov/af/Archive/2005/Feb/10-767752.html>.

Allio, Emmy, "Sudan Predicts Kony End," *The New Vision* (February 17, 2004), <http://www.newvision.co.ug/D/8/12/340455>.

Allison, Ewen, "News from the International War Crimes Tribunals," *Human Rights Brief* (Center for Human Rights and Humanitarian Law, Washington College of Law, American University), 1997, <http://www.wcl.american.edu/hrbrief/v4i3/tribun43.htm>.

Anderson, Janet, "ICC Enters Uncharted Territory," *Institute for War and Peace Reporting*, TU No. 445, March 24, 2006, <http://iwpr.net/?p=tri&s=f&o=260514&apc_state=henptri>.

"World Court Faces Biggest Challenge," *Institute for War and Peace Reporting*, AR No. 67 June 16, 2006, <http://iwpr.net/?p=acr&s=f&o=321675&apc_state=heniacr2006>.

Associated Press, "International Criminal Court Names Former Sudan Minister in Darfur War Crimes Case," *International Herald Tribune* (February 27, 2007), <http://www.iht.com/articles/ap/2007/02/28/europe/EU-GEN-International-Court-Darfur.php>.

Beaumont, Peter, "Sudan's Gosh Holds Talks in London on Darfur and Terror," *Sudan Tribune*, June 7, 2006, <http://www.sudantribune.com/spip.php?article 14517>.

Bibas, B., E. Chicon, and F. Petit, "Germaine Katanga, Second Congolese Transfer to the ICC," *International Justice Tribune*, No. 76, October 22, 2007.

Boyle, Katherine, "ICC Outreach Budget Gets Big Boost," *Institute for War and Peace Reporting*, TU No. 481 December 15, 2006, <http://iwpr.net/?p=tri&s=f&o=326204&apc_state=henptri>.

BBC, "New Overture to Uganda's Rebels" May 17, 2006, <http://news.bbc.co.uk/go/pr/fr/-/2/hi/africa/4990086.stm>.

BBC, "Powell Declares Genocide in Sudan" September 9, 2004, <http://news.bbc.co.uk/2/hi/africa/3641820.stm>.

BBC, "Sudan 'Will Defy Darfur Warrants,'" May 3, 2007, <http://news.bbc.co.uk/go/pr/fr/-/2/hi/africa/6618527.stm>.

Chicon, Emmanuel, and Benjamin Bibas, "Europe Supports the ICC without Fail and without Zeal," *International Justice Tribune*, No. 68, May 21, 2007.

Clarke, David, "U.S. Wants to Rid Uganda of LRA Rebels this Year," Reuters, Washingtonpost.com, May 16, 2006, <http://www.washingtonpost.com/wp-dyn/content/article/2006/05/16/AR2006051601123.html>.

CNN, "War Tribunal Starts Without US," March 11, 2003, <http://www.cnn.com/2003/WORLD/europe/03/11/world.court/>.

Cruvillier, Thierry, "ICC Joins the Congolese Chess Game," *International Justice Tribune*, No. 8, July 5, 2004.

"International Criminal Court: Prosecution," *International Justice Tribune*, No. 8, July 5, 2004.

"ICTR: A Wind of Change," *International Justice Tribune*, February 2001, <http://www.justicetribune.com/index.php?page=v2_article&id= 2081>.

Darstaedt, Thomas, and Helene Zuber, "The Hague Takes On the Sudanese Blood Bath," *Der Speigel*, August 22, 2005, <http://www.spiegel.de/international/spiegel/0,1518,371348,00.htm>.

Deutsch, Anthony, "Congolese Rebel Leader Extradited to Court," *Washington Post*, March 17, 2006.

Diehl, Jackson, "A Losing Latin Policy: Are We About to Punish Democratic Allies?" *Washington Post*, March 10, 2006, <http://www.washingtonpost.com/wp-dyn/content/article/2006/03/09/AR2006030902194.html>.

Ford, Peter, and Abraham McLaughlin, "Global Law Claims New Turf in Sudan", *Christian Science Monitor*, June 10, 2005, <http://www.csmonitor.com/2005/0610/p01s04-wogi.html>.

Gidley, Ruth, "Oil Discovery Adds New Twist to Darfur Tragedy," Reuters AlertNet, June 15, 2005, <http://www.globalpolicy.org/security/issues/sudan/2005/0615oil.htm>.

Glassborow, Katy, "CAR Case to focus on Sexual Violence", *Institute for War and Peace Reporting*, AR No. 113, May 24, 2007, <http://iwpr.net/?p=acr&s= f&o= 335830&apc_state=henh>.

Global Policy Forum, "Bush Administration Ponders Position Toward International Court," *International Enforcement Law Reporter*, 17, 6 (June 2001), <http://www.globalpolicy.org/intljustice/icc/2001/05icc.htm>.

Mark Leon Goldberg, "Khartoum Characters," *The American Prospect* online edition, July 3, 2005, <http://www.prospect.org/web/page.ww?section=root&name=View Print&articleId=9863>.

Herman, Steve, "Japan's Expected to Support International Criminal Court," Voice of America (December 6, 2006), <http://www.voanews.com/english/2006-12-06-voa14.cfm?renderforprint=1>.

Hoge, Warren, "U.S. Lobbies U.N. on Darfur and International Court," *NY Times Online News Report*, January 29, 2005, <http://www.genocidewatch.org/SudanUSlobbiesUNonDarfurandinternationalcourt1Feb2005.htm>.

IRIN, "IDPs Unlikely to Meet Deadline to Vacate Camps" December 26, 2006, <http://allafrica.com/stories/printable/200612260272.html>.

IRIN, "LRA Leaders not Entitled to Amnesty – Minister" April 21, 2006, <http://www.irinnews.org/report.aspx?reportid=58805>.

IRIN, "Sudan: Darfur War-crime Suspects Won't Go to ICC, Government Says," April 4, 2005, <http://www.irinnews.org/print.asp?ReportID= 46436>.

IRIN, "Sudan: Judiciary Challenges ICC over Darfur Cases," June 24, 2005, <http://www.irinnews.org/report.asp?ReportID=47802&SelectRegion=East_Africa&Select Country=SUDAN>.

IRIN, "Uganda: Too Scared to Return Home," March 21, 2006, <http://www.irinnews.org/report.asp?ReportID=52332&SelectRegion=East_Africa>.

Kajee, Ayesha, "World Court Probes Ex-African Leader," *Institute for War and Peace Reporting* AR No. 66, June 9, 2006, <http://iwpr.net/?p=acr&s=f&o=321552&apc_state=heniacr2006>.

Kessler, Glenn, "Sudanese, Rebels Sign Peace Plan for Darfur," *Washington Post*, May 6, 2006, p. 1, <http://www.washingtonpost.com/wp-dyn/content/article/2006/05/05/AR2006050500305.html>.

Kwera, Francis, "Uganda Violence," Reuters Alertnet, October 9, 2006, <http://www.alertnet.org/thenews/newsdesk/L09279258.htm>.

Leopold, Evelyn, "Japan Expects to Join New Criminal Court in Oct," Reuters News Alert, May 2, 2007, <http://www.alertnet.org/thenews/newsdesk/N02320179.htm>.

Matsiko, Grace, Frank Nyakairu, and Paul Harera, "Kony Charges a Stumbling Block, Says U.N. Chief" *The Monitor* (Kampala), September 13, 2006, <http://allafrica.com/stories/printable/200609130078.htm>.

Mukasa, Henry, "LRA Truce Extended for 2 Months," *New Vision*, December 17, 2006, posted on allAfrica.com, <http://allafrica.com/stories/printable/200612180174.html>.

Muyita, Solomon, Grace Natabaalo, and Emmanuel Gyezaho Munyonyo, "Museveni Insists on Kony ICC Arrests," *The Monitor* (Kampala), October 28, 2006, <http://allafrica.com/stories/printable/200610270919.html>.

The New Vision, "Acholi Leaders to Meet ICC," March 17, 2005, <http://www.newvision.co.ug/D/8/16/423833>.

The New Vision, "Acholi MPs Denounce for Hague Delegation," March 18, 2005, <http://www.newvision.co.ug/D/8/13/424027>.

The New Vision, "Court rules out Kony Immunity," April 18, 2005, <http://www.newvision.co.ug/D/8/12/429736>.

The New Vision, "Drop Kony ICC Case, say NGOs," January 8, 2005, <http://www.newvision.co.ug/D/8/13/410622>.

The New Vision, "ICC Threats Might Mar Peace Talks, Church Says," February 14, 2005, <http://www.newvision.co.ug/D/8/13/418050>.

The New Vision, "Kony Flees into Congo," February 6, 2006, <http://www.newvision.co.ug/D/8/12/480338>.

The New Vision, "LRA Talks Over, Says Bigombe," October 10, 2005, <http://www.lnewvision.co.ug/D/8/12/460057>.

The New Vision, "Museveni Gives Joseph Kony Final Peace Offer," May 16, 2006, <http://www.newvision.co.ug/D/8/12/428862>.

The New Vision, "The New LRA-Uganda Truce," November 2, 2006, <http://www.newvision.co.ug/D/8/459/530045>.

The New Vision, "Probe Army Too, Amnesty Tells ICC," February 5, 2004, <http://www.newvision.co.ug/D/8/338007>.

The New Vision, "ICC May Drop LRA Charges," November 15, 2004, <http://www.newvision.co.ug/D/8/12/400006>.

No Peace Without Justice, "Kremlin Int'l News Broadcast-Press Conference With Kirsch and Kolodkin," February 10, 2004, <http://www.npwj.org/?q=node/1565>.

Nyakairu, Frank, and Agencies, "International Criminal Court Opposes Museveni Peace Offer to Kony," *The Monitor* (Kampala), May 19, 2006, <http://allafrica.com/stories/200605180694.html>.

Okeowo, Alexis, "LRA and Ugandan Government Renew Truce," *Institute for War and Peace Reporting*, AR No. 113, May 24, 2007, <http://iwpr.net/?p=acr&s=f&o=335788&apc_state=henh>.

Oman, Mohamed, "Sudan's Cabinet Rejects U.N. Resolution on ICC Trials," Associated Press, April 3, 2005, No Peace Without Justice Web site, <http://www.npwj.org/?q=node/2105>.

Penketh, Anne, "Extermination of the Pygmies," *The Independent* (London), July 7, 2004, <http://www.globalpolicy.org/intljustice/icc/2004/0707pygmies.htm>.

Petit, Frank, "Interview with Claude Jorda, Judge at the International Criminal Court," *International Justice Tribune*, No. 38, December 19, 2005.

"Minimalist Investigation in Lubanga's Case," *International Justice Tribune*, No. 53, September 25, 2006.

"The Small Steps Strategy of the ICC in Darfur," interview with Antonio Cassese, *International Justice Tribune*, No. 63, March 5, 2007.

Polgreen, Lydia, and Marlise Simons, "Hague Court Investigating Rights Violations in Central African Republic" *International Herald Tribune*, May 22, 2007, <http://www.iht.com/articles/2007/05/22/africa/court.php>.

Price, Stuart, "Kony Probe Begins June," *The New Vision*, January 31, 2004, <http://www.newvision.co.ug/D/8/12/336863>.

Rubin, Elizabeth, "If not Peace, Then Justice," *New York Times Magazine* (April 2, 2006), pp. 42–54, <http://www.nytimes.com/2006/04/02/magazine/02darfur.html>.

Silverstein, Ken, "Official Pariah Sudan Valuable to America's War on Terrorism Despite Once Harboring Bin Laden, Khartoum Regime Has Supplied Key Intelligence, Officials Say," *Los Angeles Times*, April 29, 2005, <http://www.globalpolicy.org/empire/terrorwar/analysis/2005/0429sudan.htm>.

Simons, Marlise, "Argentine Is Expected to Be Prosecutor for War Crime Court" *New York Times*, March 23, 2003, posted on Global Policy Forum Web page, <http://www.globalpolicy.org/intljustice/icc/2003/0323argintine.htm>.

Stuart, Heikelina Verrijn, "Judges and Prosecutor Argue Over Powers," *International Justice Tribune*, No. 22, March 29, 2005.

"Uganda: Reasons for a Bumpy Start," *International Justice Tribune*, No. 37, December 5, 2005.

"Who Will Oversee the Victims at the ICC?" *International Justice Tribune*, No. 41, February 27, 2006.

Sudan Tribune, "Peace and Justice in Darfur: Victims' Rights Hijacked," April 4, 2006, <http://www.sudantribune.com/article.php3?id_article=14871>.

Volqvartz, Josefine, "ICC under Fire over Uganda Probe," *CNN* February 23, 2005, <http://edition.cnn.com/2005/WORLD/africa/02/23/uganda.volqvartz>.

Waddington, Richard, "Arbour Urges ICC to Act on Darfur Crimes," Reuters May 11, 2006, <http://news.scotsman.com/latest.cfm?id=707822006>.

Waugaman, Adele, "London's Confident Realism," *International Justice Tribune*, No. 57 November 20, 2006.

World Leader Magazine, "Biography, Arthur N. R. Robinson," 1994, page available at <http://www.zoominfo.com/directory/Robinson_Arthur_1994384.htm>.

Woudenberg, Anneke Van, Senior Researcher in the DRC for HRW, "Arrest all Ituri Warlords," *Le Potentiel*, March 11, 2005, <http://hrw.org/english/docs/2005/03/11/congo10311_txt.htm>.

Think-Tank/NGO Reports and Web Sites

Allen, Tim, "War and Justice in Northern Uganda: An Assessment of the International Criminal Court's Intervention, an Independent Report," Draft, Crisis States Research Centre, Development Studies Institute, London School of Economics (February 2005), <http://www.crisisstates.com/download/others/AllenICCReport.pdf>.

American Non-Governmental Organizations Coalition for the International Criminal Court Web site, <http://www.amicc.org/usinfo/advocacy_materials.html>.

Amnesty International, "Central African Republic: Five Months of War against Women," AI Index AFR 19/001/2004 (10 November 2004), <http://web.amnesty.org/library/Index/ENGAFR190012004>.

Amnesty International, "International Criminal Court: Implementing the Assembly's Plan of Action for Achieving Universality and Full Implementation of the Rome Statute," IOR 40/009/2007 (May 30, 2007), <http://web.amnesty.org/library/Index/ENGIOR400092007>.

Amnesty International, "Memorandum to the International Law Commission: Establishing a Just, Fair and Effective Permanent International Criminal Tribunal," IOR 40/07/94 (June 12, 1994), <http://web.amnesty.org/library/index/engIOR400071994?open&of=eng-385>.

Amnesty International, "Open letter to the Chief Prosecutor of the International Criminal Court: Comments on the Concept of the Interests of Justice," June 17, 2005, IOR 40/023/2005 (June 17, 2005), <http://web.amnesty.org/library/Index/ENGIOR400232005?open&of=ENG-385>.

Amnesty International, "The Failure of States to Enact Effective Implementing Legislation," IOR 40/019/2004 (2004), <http://web.amnesty.org/library/Index/ENGIOR400192004?open&of=ENG-385>.

Amnesty International, "Uganda: First Steps to Investigate Crimes Must Be Part of Comprehensive Plan to End Impunity," AFR 59/001/2004 (January 30, 2004), <http://www.amnestyusa.org/countries/uganda/document.do?id=80256DD400782B8480256E2B005E9689>.

Civil Society Organizations for Peace in Northern Uganda, "Counting the Cost: Twenty Years of War in Northern Uganda" (March 30, 2006), available on the OXFAM Web site, <http://www.oxfam.org/en/files/report_CSOPNU_ nuganda_060330/download>.

Ferencz, Benjamin B., "International Crimes Against the Peace" (undated), <http://www.benferencz.org/arts/4.html>.

FIDH, Khartoum Centre for Human Rights and Environmental Development, Sudan Organization Against Torture, "International Criminal Court Programme

Sudan: The International Criminal Court and Sudan: Access to Justice and Victims' Rights Roundtable, Khartoum, 2–3 October 2005," available at Relief Web Web site, <http://www.reliefweb.int/library/documents/2006/fidh-sdn-31mar.pdf>.

FIDH, News Release, "War Crimes in the Central African Republic: FIDH Formally Brings Its First Case before the International Criminal Court" (February 13, 2003), <http://www.fidh.org/communiq/2003/cf1302a.htm>.

Human Rights First, "Nominations for ICC Prosecutor Postponed," press release (December 16, 2002), <http://www.humanrightsfirst.org/media/2002_alerts/1216.htm>.

Human Rights Watch, Annual Report, "Summary of Situation in Darfur" (January 2004), <http://hrw.org/english/docs/2004/01/21/sudan6982.htm#3>.

Human Rights Watch, "Benchmarks for Assessing Possible National Alternatives to International Criminal Court Cases Against LRA Leaders" (May 2007), <http://hrw.org/backgrounder/ij/icc0507>.

Human Rights Watch, "Bilateral Immunity Agreements" (June 20, 2003), <http://www.hrw.org/campaigns/icc/docs/bilateralagreements.pdf>.

Human Rights Watch, "Central African Republic: ICC Opens Investigation" (May 22, 2007), <http://www.hrw.org/english/docs/2007/05/22/carepu15980.htm>.

Human Rights Watch, "D.R. Congo: Army Should Not Appoint War Criminals: Congolese Government Must Investigate and Prosecute Warlords, Not Reward Them" (January 2005), <http://hrw.org/english/docs/2005/01/14/congo10014.htm>.

Human Rights Watch, "D.R. Congo: ICC Charges Raise Concern: Joint Letter to the Chief Prosecutor of the International Criminal Court" (July 31, 2006), <http://hrw.org/english/docs/2006/08/01/congo13891_txt.htm>.

Human Rights Watch, "ICC: Investigate All Sides in Uganda – Chance for Impartial ICC Investigation into Serious Crimes a Welcome Step" (February 4, 2004), <http://www.iccnow.org/documents/02.04.2003-HRW-Uganda.pdf>.

Human Rights Watch, "ICC/DRC: Second War Crimes Suspect to Face Justice in The Hague: Investigation Should Expand to Include Senior Officials in the Region" (October 2007), <http://hrw.org/english/docs/2007/10/18/global17125.htm>.

Human Rights Watch, "Lack of Conviction: The Special Criminal Court on the Events in Darfur" (June 2006), <http://hrw.org/backgrounder/ij/sudan0606/sudan0606.pdf>.

Human Rights Watch, "Memorandum on the Strategic Plan of the International Criminal Court" (July 2006), <http://hrw.org/backgrounder/ij/memo00706/1.htm#_Toc139953060>.

Human Rights Watch, "The Meaning of 'The Interests of Justice' in Aricle 53 of the Rome Statute" (June 2005), <http://hrw.org/campaigns/icc/docs/ij070505.pdf>.

Human Rights Watch, "The United States and the International Criminal Court" (2006), <http://www.hrw.org/campaigns/icc/us.htm>.

Human Rights Watch, *War Crimes in Bosnia-Hercegovina*, vol. I (1992), HRW Index No. 0839.

Huß, Sabine, "Human Security Update: Northern Uganda," Liu Institute for Global Issues (March 2004), <http://www.up.ligi.ubc.ca/UpdateNU2004.pdf>.

International Center for Transitional Justice, "New Study Finds Ugandans Favor Peace with Justice" (2005), <http://www.ictj.org/en/news/press/release/262.html>.

International Center for Transitional Justice and Human Rights Center, University of California at Berkeley, "ForgottenVoices: A Population-Based Survey on Attitudes about Peace and Justice in Northern Uganda," by Marieke Weirda (ICTJ) and Eric Stover (UCB/HRC), <http://www.ictj.org/images/content/1/2/127.pdf>.

International Criminal Bar, Web site, <http://www.bpi-icb.org/>.

International Criminal Law Network, "Final Narrative Report, The Regional Workshop on 'The International Criminal Court and the Arab World' Organised by the Regional Human Security Center at the Jordan Institute of Diplomacy and The International Criminal Law Network in cooperation with Columbia Law School" (February 14, 2005), <http://www.icln.net/documents/Narrative%20Report.pdf>.

International Crisis Group, "Northern Uganda: Seizing the Opportunity for Peace," Africa Report No. 124 (April 26, 2007), <http://www.crisisgroup.org/library/documents/africa/central_africa/124_northern_uganda_seizing_the_opportunity_for_peace.pdf>.

Inter-press Service, *Terra Viva*, No. 1 (June 15, 1998), available at <http://www.icc-cpi.int/legaltools/>, ICC preparatory works/4. United Nations Diplomatic Conference/1998, 19980615_NGO_INTERPRESSSERVICEetal(E).

Lawyers Committee for Human Rights, "Effective Public Outreach for the International Criminal Court" (January 2004), <http://www.humanrightsfirst.org/international_justice/icc/outreach_brief_paper011404.pdf>.

NGO Coalition for the International Criminal Court, "Countries Opposed to Signing a U.S. Bilateral Immunity Agreement (BIA): U.S. Aid Lost in FY04 & U.S. Aid Threatened in FY05," <http://www.iccnow.org/documents/CountriesOpposedBIA_AidLoss_16Dec05.pdf>, accessed May 20, 2006.

NGO Coalition for the International Criminal Court, *The Rome Treaty Conference Monitor*, No. 1 (June 15, 1998), available on the ICC Legal Tools Web site, <http://www.icc-cpi.int/legaltools/>, ICC preparatory works/4, United Nations Diplomatic Conference/1998, 19980615_NGO_INTERPRESSSERVICEetal(E).

NGO Coalition for the International Criminal Court, "Are the United States' BIAs on the Way Out? New U.S. Legislation Points to a Possible Change in Direction" (2006), <http://www.iccnow.org/documents/monitor33_eng_web.pdf>.

NGO Coalition for the International Criminal Court, Team on the Crime of Aggression, "Informal Inter-Sessional Meeting of the Special Working Group on the Crime of Aggression, held at the Liechtenstein Institute on Self-Determination, Woodrow Wilson School, at Princeton University, New Jersey, United States, from 13 to 15 June 2005: Report, of the CICC Team on the Crime of Aggression" (2005), <http://www.iccnow.org/documents/CICC_IntersessionalReport_CrimeOf Aggression_June2005.pdf>.

NGO Coalition for the International Criminal Court, CICC Web site, "Building the Court," <http://www.iccnow.org/buildingthecourt.html>.

NGO Coalition for the International Criminal Court, CICC Web site, "Membership Request Form," <http://www.iccnow.org/?mod=membership>.

NGO Coalition for the International Criminal Court, CICC Web site, "States Parties to the Rome Statute of the ICC, According to the U.N. General Assembly Regional Groups," <http://www.iccnow.org/documents/RATIFI-CATIONSbyUNGroups.pdf>.

NGO Coalition for the International Criminal Court, CICC Web site, "Steering Committee," <http://www.iccnow.org/?mod=steering>.

NGO Coalition for the International Criminal Court, CICC Web site, "US and the ICC," <http://www.iccnow.org/?mod=usaicc&PHPSESSID=81959b1e6962f72a72f1c5 0a93125e4b>.

NGO Coalition for the International Criminal Court, "International Criminal Court Must Remain in Final U.N. Reform Document" (September 9, 2005), <http://www.iccnow.org/documents/ICCLang_UNdoc_09Sep05.pdf?PHPSESSID= 4177a7ae548d43468a863eaf1c7883ef>.

NGO Coalition for the International Criminal Court, "The Office of the Prosecutor: Taking Stock Three Years On" (2006), <http://www.iccnow.org/documents/ monitor33_eng_web.pdf>.

NGO Coalition for the International Criminal Court, CICC Web site, "Updates on the United States through December 2005," <http://www.iccnow.org/?mod= newsdetail&news=347>.

NGO Coalition for the International Criminal Court, "Implementation of the Rome Statute" (updated frequently), <http://www.iccnow.org/?mod=rome implementation>.

NGO Coalition for the International Criminal Court, "Summary of Information on Bilateral Immunity Agreements (BIAs) or so-Called 'Article 98' Agreements as of April, 2006" <http://www.iccnow.org/?mod=bia>.

NGO CICC Team on the Crime of Aggression, "Informal inter-sessional meeting ... from 13 to 15 June 2005," <http://www.iccnow.org/documents/CICC_ IntersessionalReport_CrimeOfAggression_June2005.pdf>.

Parliamentarians for Global Action, "Parliamentary Kit on the International Criminal Court (ICC)," New York and Rome (November 2006), <http://www. pga-japan.jp/icckit_e.pdf>.

REDRESS and Forensic Risk Analysis, "The International Criminal Court's Trust Fund for Victims: Analysis and Options for the Development of Further Criteria for the Operation of the Trust Fund for Victims, Discussion Document" (December 2003), <http://www.redress.org/publications/TFVReport. pdf>.

REDRESS, "International Criminal Court: Child Soldiers Prosecution Must Be Seen in Context" (September 26, 2006), <http://www.redress.org/news/englishsummary. pdf>.

REDRESS, "Victims, Perpetrators, or Heroes: Child Soldiers before the International Criminal Court" (September 2006), <http://www.redress.org/publications/ childsoldiers.pdf>.

Stoelting, David, "NGOs and the ICC," *World Order Under Law Reporter* (September 1999), <http://www.morganlewis.com/PDFs/21CC52F7-B792-40C0-813FE3CCBC45F981_PUBLICATION.PDF>.

Wennerstrand, Sofia, "Presidency Promotes 'One Court,'" *Monitor*, 29 (2005), 4 <http://www.iccnow.org/documents/Monitor29_200504English.pdf>.

Wierda, Marieke, and Pablo de Greiff, "Reparations and the International Criminal Court: A Prospective Role for the Trust Fund for Victims," International Center for Transitional Justice, undated (2004), <http://www.vrwg.org/Publications/02/ICTJ%20Trust%20Fund%20Paper.pdf>.

Wilmshurst, Elizabeth, and Francois Buignion, "The Law of Armed Conflict: Problems and Prospects," Chatham House Conference of April 18–19, 2005, Royal Institute of International Affairs, Chatham House, London.

Government Documents and Publications

CIA, The World Fact Book online, Democratic Republic of Congo, <http://www.cia.gov/cia/publications/factbook/geos/cg.html>.

Craddock, General Bantz J., Commander, United States Southern Command, testimony to hearing of the House Armed Services Committee: "Fiscal Year 2006 National Defense Authorization budget request" (March 9, 2005), <http://www.ciponline.org/colombia/050309crad.htm>.

Elsea, Jennifer, "U.S. Policy Regarding the International Criminal Court," Report for Congress, Received through the CRS Web, Congressional Research Service, Order Code RL31495 (September 3, 2002), <http://fpc.state.gov/documents/organization/13389.pdf>.

France, Great Britain, and Russia Joint Declaration (May 24, 1915), available at ANI Web site, <http://www.armenian-genocide.org/Affirmation.160/current_category.7/affirmation_detail.html>.

People's Republic of China, Ministry of Foreign Affairs, "China and the International Criminal Court" (October 28, 2003), <http://www.fmprc.gov.cn/eng/wjb/zzjg/tyfls/tyfl/2626/2627/t15473.htm>.

U.S. Army, "Instructions for the Government of Armies of the United States in the Field" (Lieber Code), 24 April 1863, available at the ICRC Web site, <http://www.icrc.org/ihl.nsf/FULL/110?OpenDocument>.

U.S. Department of Defense, "Quadrennial Defense Review Report" (February 6, 2006), p. 91, <http://www.defenselink.mil/qdr/report/Report20060203.pdf>.

U.S. Department of State, Bureau of Democracy, Human Rights, and Labor and the Bureau of Intelligence and Research, "Documenting Atrocities in Darfur," State Publication 11182 (September 2004), <http://www.state.gov/g/drl/rls/36028.htm>.

U.S. Department of State, "Powell Reports Sudan Responsible for Genocide in Darfur" (September 9, 2004), <http://usinfo.state.gov/xarchives/display.html?p=washfile-english&y=2004&m=September&x=20040909115958JTgnilwoDo.5094873&t=livefeeds/wf-latest.html>.

U.S. Department of State, press statement, Richard Boucher, spokesman, "Letter to U.N. Secretary-General Kofi Annan from Under Secretary of State for Arms Control and International Security John R. Bolton, Washington, DC" (May 6, 2002), <http://www.state.gov/r/pa/prs/ps/2002/9968.htm>.

U.S. Department of State, Trip Briefing, Secretary Condoleezza Rice, En Route to San Juan, Puerto Rico (March 10, 2006), <http://www.state.gov/secretary/rm/2006/63001.htm>.

U.S. House of Representatives, "Amendment to the FY 2005 Consolidated Appropriations Act" (H.R. 4818/P.L. 108–447) (the Nethercutt Amendment).

U.S. House of Representatives, "American Servicemembers' Protection Act of 2000" H.R. 4654 106th Cong. (2000).

U.S. House of Representatives, "American Servicemembers' Protection Act of 2001" H.R. 1794, Senate Bill 857, 107th Cong. (2001).

U.S. House of Representatives, "Foreign Operations Appropriations Act" (HR 3057/P.L. 109=102).

U.S. House of Representatives, "Protection of United States Troops From Foreign Prosecution Act of 1999" (Introduced in House), HR 2381 IH 106th Cong. (1999).

U.S. House of Representatives, Committee on International Relations, Subcommitte on Africa, Global Human Rights and International Organizations, "Sudan: Losing Ground on Peace?" (November 1, 2005), <http://wwwc.house.gov/international_relations/109/24374.pdf>.

U.S. Public Law No. 107-206, Title II, 116 Stat. 820, "2002 Supplemental Appropriations Act for Further Recovery from and Response to Terrorist Attacks on the United States," sections 2001–2005, (22 USC sections 7421–732), American Servicemen's Protection Act of 2002, <http://www.mbe.doe.gov/budget/billrept/fy02/02Supp_PL_107-206.pdf>.

International Organization Documents and Publications

Conference on Security and Cooperation in Europe, "Helsinki Final Act" (August 1, 1975), available from University of Minnesota Human Rights Library, <http://www1.umn.edu/humanrts/osce/basics/finact75.htm>.

Côté, Luc, "International Criminal Justice: Tightening up the Rules of the Game," *International Review of the Red Cross*, 88, 861 (March 2006), 133–44, <http://www.icrc.org/Web/eng/siteeng0.nsf/htmlall/review-861-p133/$File/irrc_861_Cote. pdf>.

ICC, "Chambers," <http://www.icc-cpi.int/organs/chambers.html>.

ICC, "Communications Received," <http://www.icc-cpi.int/organs/otp/otp_com.html>.

ICC, "Communications Received," Annex, Venezuela Response, <http://www.icc-cpi.int/library/organs/otp/OTP_letter_to_senders_re_Venezuela_9_February_2006.pdf>.

ICC, "Communications Received", Annex, Iraq Response, <http://www.icc-cpi.int/library/organs/otp/OTP_letter_to_senders_re_Iraq_9_February_2006.pdf>.

ICC, "Communique from the Chair of the Board of Directors of the Trust Fund for Victims of the International Criminal Court" (November 9, 2006), <http://www.icc-cpi.int/press/pressreleases/200.html>.

ICC, "Facts and Procedure Regarding the Situation in Uganda" (October 14, 2005), <http://www.icc-cpi.int/library/cases/ICC_20051410-056-1_English.pdf>.

ICC, "Joint Statement by ICC Chief Prosecutor and the Visiting Delegation of Lango, Acholi, Iteso and Madi Community Leaders from Northern Uganda," The Hague (April 16, 2005), ICC-OTP-20050416-99-En, <http://www.icc-cpi.int/pressrelease_details&id=102&l=en.html>.

ICC, "List of Names of Suspects in Darfur opened by the ICC OTP," The Hague (April 11, 2005), ICC-OTP-20050411-98-En, <http://www.icc-cpi.int/press-release_ details&id=101&l=en.html>.

ICC, Luis Moreno-Ocampo, "Opening Remarks" to the Fifth Session of the Assembly of States Parties (November 23, 2006), <http://www.icc-cpi.int/library/organs/otp/LMO_20061123_en.pdf>.

ICC, "Report of the Prosecutor of the International Criminal Court, Mr. Luis Moreno Ocampo, to the Security Council Pursuant to UNSCR 1593 (2005)" (June 29, 2005), <http://www.icc-cpi.int/library/cases/ICC_Darfur_UNSC_Report_ 29-06-05_EN.pdf>.

ICC, "Second Report of the Prosecutor, Mr. Luis Moreno Ocampo, to the Security Council Pursuant to UNSC 1593 (2005) (December 13, 2005), <http://www.icc-cpi. int/library/organs/otp/LMO_UNSC_ReportB_En.pdf>.

ICC, "Fourth Report of the Prosecutor of the International Criminal Court to the U.N. Security Council Pursuant to UNSCR 1593(2005)," ICC-02-05-40-Anx A 19–12-06, <http://www.icc-cpi.int/library/organs/otp/OTP_ReportUNSC4-Darfur_English.pdf>.

ICC, "The Management of Preliminary Examination, Article 53(1) Evaluation, and Start of Investigation," *Draft Regulations of the Office of the Prosecutor* (annotated), Part 2, Section 1, Regulation 3.1 (September 2003), <http://www.icc-cpi.int/library/organs/otp/draft_regulations.pdf>.

ICC, "The International Criminal Court to Send its First Official Visit to the Democratic Republic of Congo," The Hague (July 26, 2004), <http://www.icc-cpi.int/pressrelease_details&id=32&l=en.html>.

ICC, "Prosecutor Opens Investigation into the Central African Republic," news release (May 22, 2007), <http://www.icc-cpi.int/press/pressreleases/248.html>.

ICC, "The Prosecutor of the ICC Opens Investigation in Darfur," The Hague (June 6, 2005), ICC-OTP-0606-104-En, <http://www.icc-cpi.int/pressrelease_details&id=107&l=en.html>.

ICC, "Prosecutor of the International Criminal Court Opens an Investigation into Northern Uganda" (July 29, 2004), <http://www.icc-cpi.int/pressrelease_details&id=33&l=en.html>.

ICC, "Prosecutor Receives Referral of the Situation in the Democratic Republic of Congo" (April 19, 2004), <http://www.icc-cpi.int/pressrelease_details &id=19&l=en.html>.

ICC, "Standard Application Form to Participate in Proceedings before the International Criminal Court for Individual Victims and Persons Acting on their Behalf," <http://www.icc-cpi.int/library/victims/Form-Participation-1_en.pdf>.

ICC, "Standard Application Form to Participate in Proceedings before the International Criminal Court for Victims Which Are Organizations or Institutions," <http://www.icc-cpi.int/library/victims/Form-Participation-2_en.pdf>.

ICC, "Statement by the Chief Prosecutor on the Uganda Arrest Warrants" (October 14, 2005), <http://www.icc-cpi.int/library/organs/otp/speeches/LMO_ 20051014_English.pdf>.

ICC, "Statement by Luis Moreno Ocampo to the Press Conference in relation with the surrender to the Court of Mr. Thomas Lubanga Dyilo," The Hague,

(March 18, 2006), <http://www.icc-cpi.int/library/organs/otp/speeches/LMO_20060318_En.pdf>.

ICC, "Statement Made by Mr. Luis Moreno Ocampo at the Ceremony for the Solemn Undertaking of the Chief Prosecutor of the ICC" (June 16, 2003), <http://www.icc-cpi.int/library/organs/otp/030616_moreno_ocampo_english_final.pdf>.

ICC, Assembly of States Parties, First Session Official Records (New York, September 3–10, 2002), ICC-ASP/1/3 United Nations Publication Sales No. E.03.V.2.

ICC, Assembly of States Parties, Fourth Session, "Regulations of the Trust Fund for Victims," ICC-ASP/4/32 (2005), <http://www.icc-cpi.int/library/about/officialjournal/ICC-ASP-4-32-Res.3_English.pdf>.

ICC, Assembly of States Parties, Fourth Session, "Report of the Committee on Budget and Finance on the Work of its Fifth Session," ICC-ASP/4/27 (2005), <http://www.icc-cpi.int/library/asp/ICC-ASP-4-27_English.pdf>

ICC, Assembly of States Parties, Fifth Session, "Report of the Committee on Budget and Finance on the Work of its Seventh Session," ICC-ASP/5/23 (2006), <http://www.icc-cpi.int/library/asp/ICC-ASP-5-23_English.pdf>.

ICC, Assembly of States Parties, Fifth Session, "Court Capacity Model," ICC-ASP/5/10, <http://www.icc-cpi.int/library/asp/ICC-ASP-5-10_English_Reissued.pdf>.

ICC, Assembly of States Parties, Fifth Session, "Strategic Plan for Outreach of the International Criminal Court," ICC-ASP/5/12 (2006), <http://www.icc-cpi.int/library/asp/ICC-ASP-5-12_English.pdf>.

ICC, Assembly of States Parties, Fifth Session,"Strategic Plan of the International Criminal Court," ICC-ASP/5/6 (2006), <http://www.icc-cpi.int/library/asp/ICC-ASP-5-6_English.pdf>.

ICC, Assembly of States Parties, Sixth Session, "Report of the Committee on Budget and Finance on the Work of its Eighth Session," ICC-ASP/6/2 (2007), <http://www.icc-cpi.int/library/asp/ICC-ASP-6-2_English.pdf>.

ICC, Assembly of States Parties, Third Session, "Report of the Committee on Budget and Finance," ICC-ASP/3/18 (August 13, 2004), <http://www.icc-cpi.int/library/asp/ICC-ASP-3-18-_CBF_report_English.pdf>.

ICC, Assembly of States Parties, Third Session, "Report of the Committee on Budget and Finance," ICC-ASP/3/CBF.1/L4 (2004), as cited in Human Rights Watch, "Memorandum to States Members of the Assembly of States Parties" (September 2, 2004), <http://iccnow.org/documents/HRW%20Memorandum%20to%20ASP%20members%20090204.pdf>.

ICC, Office of the Prosecutor, "Communications received by the Prosecutor since July 2002" (July 7, 2003), <http://www.icc-cpi.int/organs/otp/otp_com.html>.

ICC, Office of the Prosecutor, "Paper on Some Policy Issues before the Office of the Prosecutor" (September 2003), <http://www.icc-cpi.int/library/organs/otp/030905_Policy_Paper.pdf>.

ICC, Office of the Prosecutor, "Prosecution's Application to Leave to Appeal Pre-Trial Chamber I's Decision on the Applications for Participation in the Proceedings of VPRS 1, VPRS 2, VPRS 3, VPRS 4, VPRS 5 and VPRS 6" (January 23, 2006), <http://www.icc-cpi.int/library/cases/ICC-01-04-103_English.pdf>.

ICC, Office of the Prosecutor, "Annex to the 'Paper on Some Policy Issues before the Office of the Prosecutor': Referrals and Comunications" (April 21, 2004), <http://www.icc-cpi.int/library/organs/otp/policy_annex_final_210404.pdf>.

ICC, Office of the Prosecutor, "Draft Regulations of the Office of the Prosecutor" (2003), <http://www.icc-cpi.int/library/organs/otp/draft_regulations.pdf>.

ICC, Office of the Prosecutor, "Informal Expert Paper: The Principle of Complementarity in Practice" (2003), <http://www.icc-cpi.int/library/organs/otp/complementarity.pdf>.

ICC, Office of the Prosecutor, Letter from Luis Moreno Ocampo to Judge Claude Jorda, Presiding Judge, Pre-Trial Chamber I, 2005 (June 1, 2005), <http://www.icc-cpi.int/library/cases/ICC-02-05-2_English.pdf>.

ICC, Office of the Prosecutor, Luis Moreno Ocampo, "Statement by the Chief Prosecutor on the Uganda Arrest Warrants" (October 14, 2005), <http://www.icc-cpi.int/library/organs/otp/speeches/LMO_20051014_English.pdf>.

ICC, Office of the Prosecutor, "Report on Prosecutorial Strategy" (September 2006), <http://www.icc-cpi.int/library/organs/otp/OTP_Prosecutorial-Strategy-20060914_English.pdf>.

ICC, Office of the Prosecutor, "Summary of Recommendations Received during the First Public Hearing of the Office of the Prosecutor, Convened from 17–18 June 2003 at the Hague," <http://www.icc-cpi.int/library/organs/otp/ph/ph1_conclusions.pdf>.

ICC, Office of the Prosecutor, "Update on Communications Received by the Office of the Prosecutor of the ICC" (February 10, 2006), <http://www.icc-cpi.int/library/organs/otp/OTP_Update_on_Communications_10_February_2006.pdf>.

ICC, Preparatory Commission for the International Criminal Court, Working Group on the Crime of Aggression, "Discussion Paper Proposed by the Coordinator" (July 11, 2002), PCNICC/2002/WGCA/RT.1/Rev.2, <http://www.icc-cpi.int/legaltools/>, 20020711_PCNICC2002WGCART.1REV.2(E).

ICC, Presidency, Letter from Chief Prosecutor Moreno Ocampo to President Kirsch, ICC-02/04-1 06–07-2004, (June 17, 2004), appendix to July 5, 2004 "Decision Assigning the Situation in Uganda to Pre-Trial Chamber II," <http://www.icc-cpi.int/library/about/officialjournal/basicdocuments/Decision_on_Assignment_Uganda-OTP_Annex.pdf>.

ICC, The Presidency, "Decision Constituting Trial Chamber I and Referring to It the Case of The Prosecutor v Thomas Lubanga Dyilo" (March 6, 2007), <http://www.icc-cpi.int/library/cases/ICC-01-04-01-06-842_English.pdf>.

ICC, Pre-Trial Chamber I, "Decision Concerning Pre-Trial Chamber I's Decision of 10 February 2006 and the Incorporation of Documents into the Record of the Case against Mr. Thomas Lubanga Dyilo," ICC-01/04-01/06-8-Corr (March 17, 2006), <http://www.icc-cpi.int/library/cases/ICC-01-04-01-06-8-US-Corr_English.pdf>.

ICC, Pre-Trial Chamber I, "Decision Concerning Pre-Trial Chamber I's Decision of 10 February 2006 and the Incorporation of Documents into the Record of the Case against Mr. Thomas Lubanga Dyilo, Annex I: Decision on the Prosecutor's Application for a Warrant of Arrest, Article 58" (February 24,

2006),   <http://www.icc-cpi.int/library/cases/ICC-01-04-01-06-8-US-Corr_
    English.pdf>.
ICC, Pre-Trial Chamber I, "Decision on the Prosecution Application under Article
    58(7) of the Statute" (April 27, 2007), <http://www.icc-cpi.int/library/cases/
    ICC-02-05-01-07-1-Corr_English.pdf>.
ICC, Pre-Trial Chamber I, "Decision on the Prosecutor's Position on Pre-Trial
    Chamber I's 17 February 2005 Decision to Convene a Status Conference"
    (2005), <http://www.icc-cpi.int/library/organs/chambers/ICC-01-04-11_English.
    pdf>.
ICC, Pre-Trial Chamber I, "Decision Inviting Observations in Application of Rule
    103 of the Rules of Procedure and Evidence," ICC document ICC-02/05 (July
    24, 2006), <http://www.icc-cpi.int/library/cases/ICC-02-05-10_English.pdf>.
ICC, Pre-Trial Chamber I, "Decision to Convene a Status Conference" (2005),
    <http://www.icc-cpi.int/library/organs/chambers/ICC_01-04-9_English.pdf>.
ICC, Pre-Trial Chamber I, "Decision on the Confirmation of Charges" (January 29,
    2007), <http://www.icc-cpi.int/library/cases/ICC-01-04-01-06-803-tEN_English.
    pdf>.
ICC, Pre-Trial Chamber I, "Decision on the Prosecution and Defence Applications for
    Leave to Appeal the Decision on the Confirmation of Charges" (May 24, 2007),
    <http://www.icc-cpi.int/library/cases/ICC-01-04-01-06-915_English.pdf>.
ICC, Pre-Trial Chamber I, "Decision on the Prosecutor's Application for Leave
    to Appeal," <http://www.icc-cpi.int/library/organs/chambers/ICC_01-04_2005
    March14_e.pdf>.
ICC, Pre-Trial Chamber I, "Observations of the Legal Representative of VPRS 1 to
    VPRS 6 Following the Prosecution's Application for Leave to Appeal Pre-Trial
    Chamber I's Decision on the Applications for Participation in the Proceedings
    of VPRS 1 to VPRS 6" (January 27, 2006), ICC-01-04-103, <http://www.icc-
    cpi.int/library/cases/ICC-01-04-103_English.pdf>.
ICC, Pre-Trial Chamber I, "Observations on Issues Concerning the Protection of
    Victims and the Preservation of Evidence in the Proceedings on Darfur Pending
    Before the ICC," by Antonio Cassese (August 25, 2006), <http://www.icc-cpi.
    int/library/cases/ICC-02-05-14_English.pdf>.
ICC, Pre-Trial Chamber I, "Observations of the United Nations High Commissioner
    for Human Rights Invited in Application of Rule 103 of the Rules of Procedure
    and Evidence" (October 10, 2006), <http://www.icc-cpi.int/library/cases/ICC-
    02-05-19_English.pdf>.
ICC, Pre-Trial Chamber I, Prosecutor's Application under Article 58 (7) (February
    27, 2007), <http://www.icc-cpi.int/library/cases/ICC-02-05-56_English.pdf>.
ICC, Pre-Trial Chamber I, "Prosecutor's Reply to 'Observations of the Legal
    Representative of VPRS 1 to VPRS 6 Following the Prosecution's Application
    for Leave to Appeal Pre-Trial Chamber I's Decision on the Applications for
    Participation in Proceedings of VPRS 1 to VPRS 6,'" ICC-01/04-111 (February
    6, 2006), <http://www.icc-cpi.int/library/cases/ICC-01-04-111_English.pdf>.
ICC, Pre-Trial Chamber I, "Public Redacted Version, Decision on the Applications
    for Participation in the Proceedings of VPRS 1, VPRS2, VPRS3, VPRS4,
    VPRS5, and VPRS6," ICC-01/04 (January 17, 2006), <http://www.icc-cpi.int/
    library/cases/ICC-01-04-101_tEnglish-Corr.pdf>.

ICC, Pre-Trial Chamber I, "Prosecutor's Application to Separate the Senior Legal Adviser to the Pre-Trial Division from Rendering Legal Advice Regarding the Case," ICC-01/04-01/06-373 (2006), <http://www.icc-cpi.int/library/cases/ICC-01-04-06-373_English.pdf>.

ICC, Pre-Trial Chamber I, "Decision on the Prosecutor's Application to Separate the Senior Legal Advisor to the Pre-Trial Division from Rendering Legal Advice Regarding the Case," ICC-01/04-01/06-623 (2006), <http://www.icc-cpi.int/library/cases/ICC-01-04-01-06-623_English.pdf>.

ICC, Pre-Trial Chamber I, "Prosecutor's Position on Pre-Trial Chamber I's 17 February 2005 Decision to Convene a Status Conference," <http://www.icc-cpi.int/library/organs/otp/ICC0104Anx_2005March08-e.pdf>.

ICC, Pre-Trial Chamber I, "Prosecutor's Response to Cassese's Observations on Issues Concerning the Protection of Victims and the Preservation of Evidence in the Proceedings on Darfur Pending before the ICC," ICC-02/05 (September 11, 2006), <http://www.icc-cpi.int/library/cases/ICC-02-05-16_English.pdf>.

ICC, Pre-Trial Chamber I, "Prosecutor's Response to Arbour's Observations of the United Nations High Commissioner for Human Rights Invited in Application of Rule 103 of the Rules of Procedure and Evidence," ICC-02/05 (October 19, 2006), <http://www.icc-cpi.int/library/cases/ICC-02-05-21_English.pdf>.

ICC, Pre-Trial Chamber I, "Redacted Version of the Transcripts of the Hearing Held on 2 February 2006 and Certain Materials Presented during That Hearing" (March 22, 2006), <http://www.icc-cpi.int/library/cases/ICC-01-04-01-06-48_English.pdf>.

ICC, Pre-Trial Chamber I, "Urgent Warrant of Arrest for Germain Katanga," ICC-01/04-01/07-1-US-tENG (September 27, 2007), <http://www.icc-cpi.int/library/cases/ICC-01-04-01-07-1_tEnglish.pdf>.

ICC, Pre-Trial Chamber I, "Warrant of Arrest" (February 10, 2006), <http://www.icc-cpi.int/library/cases/ICC-01-04-01-06-2_tEnglish.pdf>.

ICC, Pretrial Chamber II, "Decision on Prosecutor's Application for Leave to Appeal in Part Pre-Trial Chamber II's Decision on the Prosecutor's Applications for Warrants of Arrest Under Article 58," ICC-02/04-01/05 (August 19, 2005), <http://www.icc-cpi.int/library/cases/ICC-02-04-01-05-20-US-Exp_English.pdf>.

ICC, Pre-Trial Chamber II, "Decision on the Prosecution's Application for Warrants of Arrest Under Article 58," ICC-02/04 (July 8, 2005), <http://www.icc-cpi.int/library/cases/ICC-02-04-01-05-1-US-Exp_English.pdf>.

ICC, Pre-Trial Chamber II, "Decision on the Prosecutor's Request to Separate the Senior Legal Adviser to the Pre-Trial Division from Rendering Legal Advice Regarding the Case," ICC-02/04-01/05-124 (2006), <http://www.icc-cpi.int/library/cases/ICC-02-04-01-05-124_English.pdf>.

ICC, Pre-Trial Chamber II, "Decision on the Prosecutor's Request to Separate the Senior Legal Adviser to the Pre-Trial Division from Rendering Legal Advice Regarding the Case," ICC-02/04-01/05-124 (2006), annexe, "Internal Memorandum from the President to the President of the Pre-Trial Division" (2006), ICC-02/04-01/05-127 Anx1, <http://www.icc-cpi.int/library/cases/ICC-02-04-01-05-124-Anx1_English.pdf>.

ICC, Pre-Trial Chamber II, "Prosecutor's Application to Separate the Senior Legal Advisor to the Pre-Trial Division form Rendering Legal Advice Regarding the

Case," ICC-01/04-01/06 (August 31, 2006), <http://www.icc-cpi.int/library/cases/ICC-02-04-01-05-108_English.pdf>.

ICC, Pre-Trial Chamber III, "Prosecution's Report Pursuant to Pre-Trial Chamber III's November 30, 2006, Decision Requesting Information on the Status of the Preliminary Examination of the Situation in the Central African Republic," ICC-01/05-7 15–12–2006, <http://www.icc-cpi.int/library/cases/ICC-01-05-7_English.pdf>.

International Court of Justice, "Armed Activities on the Territory of the Congo (Democratic Republic of the Congo v. Uganda)" (2005), <http://www.u-paris2.fr/cij/icjwww/ipresscom/ipress2005/ipresscom2005-26_co_20051219.htm>.

ICTR, general information Web site: <http://69.94.11.53/default.htm>.

ICTR, Prosecutor v. Jean Paul Akayesu, Amended Indictment, ICTR Trial Chamber (June 1997), Case No. ICTR-96-4-1, Indictment Counts 1, 2, 13–15 (International Criminal Tribunal for Rwanda, Trial Chamber), available at <http://www.un.org/ictr/actamond.htm>.

ICTY, Prosecutor v. Dusko Tadic, "Decision on the Defense Motion for Interlocutory Appeal on Jurisdiction" (October 2, 1995), para. 55, available at <http://www.un.org/icty/tadic/appeal/decision-e/51002.htm>.

ICTY, Prosecutor v. Gagovic et al., Indictment, Trial Chamber (June 26, 1996), Case No. IT-96-23/2, available at <http://www.un.org/icty/indictment/english/foc-ii960626e.htm>.

ICTY, "Tenth Annual Report to the General Assembly" (2003), available at <http://www.un.org/icty/rappannu-e/2003/index.htm>.

International Law Commission, Statute, ICTY, Rules of Procedure and Evidence, IT/32/Rev. 36 (August 2005), available at <http://untreaty.un.org/ilc/texts/instruments/english/statute/statute_e.pdf>.

International Law Commission, "Yearbook of the International Law Commission 1950," Volume II, available at <http://untreaty.un.org/ilc/publications/yearbooks/1950.htm>.

International Military Tribunal for the Far East, Charter available at Yale University Avalon Project, <http://www.yale.edu/lawweb/avalon/imtfech.htm>.

Kellogg Briand Pact 1928, "Treaty Providing for the Renunciation of War as an Instrument of National Policy," Signed in Paris, August 27, 1928, Entered into force July 24, 1929, available at Yale University Avalon Project, <http://www.yale.edu/lawweb/avalon/imt/kbpact.htm>.

London Agreement (August 8, 1945), available at Yale University Law School Avalon Project <http://www.yale.edu/lawweb/avalon/imt/proc/imtchart.htm>.

Moscow Conference, "Joint Four-Nation Declaration, Statement on Atrocities" (October 1943), available at The Avalon Project at Yale Law School, <http://www.yale.edu/lawweb/avalon/wwii/moscow.htm>.

NATO, press briefing at 15:00 hours, 16 May 1999, Jamie Shea, spokesman, available at <http://www.nato.int/kosovo/press/p990516b.htm>.

Nuremberg Trial Proceedings Vol. 1, London Agreement of August 8, 1945, available at The Avalon Project, Yale University, <http://www.yale.edu/lawweb/avalon/imt/proc/imtchart.htm>.

Regional Human Security Center, Regional Workshop on "The International Criminal Court and the Arab World," organized by The Regional Human Security Center and the Jordan Institute of Diplomacy, and The International Criminal Law Network in cooperation with Columbia Law School, funded by the Foreign Ministries of Canada, Denmark, Switzerland, Ireland, and Germany. Amman (February 14–16, 2005), report available at <http://www.icln.net/documents/Narrative%20Report.pdf>.

United Nations, *Assembly of States Parties to the Rome Statute of the International Criminal Court First Session* (New York, September 3–10, 2002) Official Records, ICC-ASP/1/3, 265–270.

United Nations Diplomatic Conference of Plenipotentiaries on the Establishment of an International Criminal Court, "Final Act" (July 17, 1998), section F (U.N. Doc. A/Conf.183/10), <http://www.un.org/law/icc/statute/final.htm>.

UN General Assembly, "Convention Against Torture and Other Cruel, Inhuman or Degrading Treatment or Punishment" (1984), available at <http://www.unhchr.ch/html/menu3/b/h_cat39.htm>.

UN General Assembly, "Convention on the Non-Applicability of Statutory Limitations to War Crimes and Crimes Against Humanity," Resolution 2391 (XXIII), (1968), available at <http://www.ohchr.org/english/law/warcrimes.htm>.

UN General Assembly, Convention on the Prevention and Punishment of the Crime of Genocide, Adopted by Resolution 260 (III) A (1948), available at <http://www.unhchr.ch/html/menu3/b/p_genoci.htm>.

UN General Assembly, "Declaration of Basic Principles of Justice for Victims of Crime and Abuse of Power," Resolution 40/34 of 29 November 1985, available at <http://www.unhchr.ch/html/menu3/b/h_comp49.htm>.

UN General Assembly, "Definition of Aggression," Resolution 3314 (XXIX) (December 14, 1974), available at <http://domino.un.org/UNISPAL.NSF/a06f2943c226015c85256c40005d359c/023b908017cfb94385256ef4006ebb2a!OpenDocument>.

UN General Assembly, "Establishment of an International Criminal Court," Resolution 49/53, 49 U.N. GAOR Supp. (No. 49) at 293, U.N. Doc. A/49/49 (1994), available at Web site of the University of Minnesota Human Rights Library, <http://www1.umn.edu/humanrts/resolutions/49/53GA1994.html>.

UN General Assembly, "Financing of the International Criminal Tribunal for … Rwanda … Report of Secretary-General on the Activities of the Office of Internal Oversight Services," A/51/789 (1997), Annex.

UN General Assembly, "International Covenant on Civil and Political Rights" (1966), available at <http://www.unhchr.ch/html/menu3/b/a_ccpr.htm>.

UN General Assembly, "International Covenant on Economic, Social, and Cultural Rights" (1966), available at <http://www.unhchr.ch/html/menu3/b/a_cescr.htm>.

UN General Assembly, "International Convention on the Suppression and Punishment of the Crime of Apartheid" (1973), available at <http://www.unhchr.ch/html/menu3/b/11.htm>.

UN General Assembly, "International Criminal Responsibility of Individuals and Entities Engaged in Illicit Trafficking in Narcotic Drugs across National Frontiers and Other Transnational Criminal Activities: Establishment of an International Criminal Court with Jurisdiction over Such Crimes," A/RES/44/39 (December 4, 1989), available at <http://www.un.org/documents/ga/res/44/a44r039.htm>.

UN General Assembly, "Report on the Financing …" of the ICTR and ICTY (December 15, 2005), available at <http://daccessdds.un.org/doc/UNDOC/ GEN/No5/646/08/PDF/No564608.pdf?OpenElement>.

UN General Assembly, "Universal Declaration of Human Rights" (1948), available at <http://www.un.org/Overview/rights.html>.

UN High Commissioner for Human Rights, "Report of the United Nations High Commissioner for Human Rights and Follow-Up to the World Conference on Human Rights: Situation of Human Rights in the Darfur Region of the Sudan" (May 7, 2004), UN Doc. E/CN.4/2005/3, <http://www.unhchr.ch/Huridocda/ Huridoca.nsf/e06a530of90fa023802566870051 8ca4/863d1 4602aa82caec1256 ea80038e268/$FILE/Go414221.pdf>.

UN News Center, "Congolese War Crimes Suspect Turned Over to International Criminal Court" (October 18, 2007), <http://www.un.org/apps/news/story. asp?NewsID=24325&Cr=DRC&Cr1=>.

United Nations Organization, "Charter of the United Nations" (1945), available at <http://www.un.org/aboutun/charter/>.

United Nations Preparatory Commission for the International Criminal Court, "Road Map Leading to the Early Establishment of the International Criminal Court," PCNICC/2001/L.2 (New York, September 26, 2001), available at <http:// www.icc-cpi.int/legaltools/>, Preparatory Works/5, Preparatory Commission/ 2001, 20010926_PCNICC2001L.2(E).

UN Press Release SC/8351, "Security Council Refers Situation in Darfur, Sudan, to Prosecutor of International Criminal Court" (March 31, 2005), <http://www. un.org/News/Press/docs/2005/sc8351.doc.htm>.

UN Secretary-General, "Report of the International Commission of Inquiry on Darfur to the United Nations Secretary-General Pursuant to Security Council Resolution 1564 of 18 September 2004," Geneva (January 2005), <http:// www.un.org/News/dh/sudan/com_inq_darfur.pdf>.

UN Security Council, Press Statement on Darfur, Sudan, by Security Council President (February 4, 2004), SC/8050 AFR 883, <http://www.un.org/News/Press/ docs/2004/sc8050.doc.htm>.

UN Security Council Resolution 1329 (2000), S/RES/1329(2000), <http://daccessdds. un.org/doc/UNDOC/GEN/No0/773/49/PDF/No077349.pdf?OpenElement>.

UN Security Council, "The Rule of Law and Transitional Justice in Conflict and Post-conflict Societies, Report of the Secretary-General," S/2004/616 23 (August 2004).

UN Security Council Report, "Update Report No. 4: Protection of Civilians in Armed Conflict" (January 13, 2006), <http://www.securitycouncilreport.org/site/c. glKWLeMTIsG/b.1357007/k.EA5/UPDATE_REPORT_NO_4brPROTECTION_ OF_CIVILIANS_IN_ARMED_CONFLICTBR13_JANUARY_2006.htm>.

UN Security Council, Resolution 808 (February 22, 1993) (S/RES/808), calling for a report from the Secretary-General on establishment of the International Criminal Tribunal for the Former Yugoslavia, available at <http://daccessdds.un.org/doc/UNDOC/GEN/N93/098/21/IMG/N9309821.pdf? OpenElement>.

UN Security Council, Resolution 827 (May 25, 1993) (S/RES/827) on the establishment of the International Criminal Tribunal for the Former Yugoslavia, available at <http://www.un.org/icty/legaldoc-e/basic/statut/S-RES-827_93.htm>. Legal documents including the Statute (updated) available on the ICTY Web site, <http://www.un.org/icty/legaldoc-e/index.htm>.

UN Security Council, Resolution 955 (November 8, 1994) (S/RES/955) on the establishment of the International Criminal Tribunal for Rwanda, available at <http://www.un.org/ictr/english/Resolutions/955e.htm>. Statute of the ICTR available at <http://www.ohchr.org/english/law/itr.htm>.

UN Security Council, Resolution 1547 (Sudan) (June 11, 2004), UN Doc. S/RES/1547, <http://daccessdds.un.org/doc/UNDOC/GEN/N04/386/26/PDF/N0438626.pdf?OpenElement>.

UN Security Council, Resolution 1556 (July 30, 2004), UN Doc. S/RES/1556 <http://daccessdds.un.org/doc/UNDOC/GEN/N04/446/02/PDF/N0444602.pdf?OpenElement>.

UN Security Council Resolution 1564 (September 18, 2004), UN Doc S/RES/1564 <http://daccessdds.un.org/doc/UNDOC/GEN/N04/515/47/PDF/N0451547.pdf?OpenElement>.

UN Security Council Resolution 1565 (October 1, 2004), UN Doc S/RES/1565(2004), <http://daccessdds.un.org/doc/UNDOC/GEN/N04/531/89/PDF/N0453189.pdf?OpenElement>.

UN Security Council, Resolution 1593 (March 31, 2005), UN Doc S/RES/1593, <http://daccessdds.un.org/doc/UNDOC/GEN/N05/292/73/PDF/N0529273.pdf?OpenElement>.

UN Security Council, Statement of Abdallah Baali, Algeria following the vote on Resolution 1593 (2005) (March 31, 2005), <http://www.un.org/News/Press/docs/2005/sc8351.doc.htm>.

UN Security Council, Statement of Anne Woods Patterson, United States, following the vote on Resolution 1593(2005) (March 31, 2005), <http://www.un.org/News/Press/docs/2005/sc8351.doc.htm>.

Index